Here is a complete and coherent interpretation of the Platonic theory of man, which brings out its relevance to contemporary issues. During the last century, most English and American interpretations of Plato have concerned themselves primarily with the abstract phases of his thought, neglecting his conceptions of man, his ethics, and his social philosophy — which are even more pertinent to the problems of our time. Dr. Wild's view of Plato as an actual, living man with profound moral convictions about individual and social life makes it possible to see Plato's fundamental agreement with Aristotle and to integrate him into the classical tradition as a whole.

This is the only book or work which attempts to explain Plato's theory of human inversions or sophistry in an exhaustive manner, and it contains the only extended treatment of Plato's theory of art. Dr. Wild is Associate Professor of Philosophy in Harvard University.

PLATO'S THEORY OF MAN

LONDON : GEOFFREY CUMBERLEGE

OXFORD UNIVERSITY PRESS

LONDON : GEOFFREY CUMBERLEGE
OXFORD UNIVERSITY PRESS

PLATO'S
THEORY OF MAN

AN INTRODUCTION TO THE REALISTIC PHILOSOPHY OF CULTURE

By

JOHN WILD

Harvard University

Cambridge, Massachusetts
HARVARD UNIVERSITY PRESS
1946

PRINTED IN THE UNITED STATES OF AMERICA

PREFACE

THE predominant interest in problems of epistemology, so characteristic of idealistic modes of thought, has exerted an important influence on modern Platonic studies. It has focused attention
on Plato's "theory of ideas" without fully clarifying or examining
other equally important phases of his thought. Hence there is a widespread tendency at the present time to think of Plato as a soaring
metaphysician or *abstract philosopher* having little to say of direct relevance to the concrete life of living men. More recent historical study,
however, has cast considerable doubt on this general picture. It has
now given us access to another Plato, the youth who survived the great
fifth century of progress so like our own nineteenth century, the man
who lived in a post-war era of disillusionment and decay, the hard-
headed realistic thinker who diagnosed the diseases affecting his culture, and attempted to formulate in the *Republic* and the *Laws* that
natural order which must guide men's endeavors in striving for a
healthy cultural state. The aim of this book is to examine once more
for the possible benefit of the modern reader these reflections of Plato
on the order of human culture, and that realistic view of the nature of
man which lies at their core.

When Plato's theory of man is carefully studied, some light, I
think, is shed upon two further problems, the relation between Plato
and the Aristotelian tradition as a whole, and the classical philosophy
of culture. With reference to the first, the central position assigned
to epistemology in modern interpretations of Plato has also involved
an exaggerated emphasis upon Aristotle's critique of that phase of
his master's philosophy. This has fostered a widespread tendency to
think of the two philosophies as fundamentally opposed. When
Plato's anthropology is more clearly and integrally focused, however,
it is possible to see that many of his practical doctrines supplement
rather than contradict Aristotle's *theoretical* philosophy. I have tried
to call attention to such points of congruence which, in spite of undeniable differences, would seem to accord with the view of the ancient

commentators that Platonism and Aristotelianism are not fundamentally opposed but are rather to be understood as two modes of one and the same realistic philosophy.

If this view is sound we may once again be in a position not only to grasp the great realistic tradition of classical and medieval thought as a coherent body of insight, but also to supply a most serious defect in the predominantly Aristotelian phase of this tradition which is still academically influential. In spite of its great theoretical strength and fertility, this latter phase has been notoriously weak and sterile in the field of practical philosophy, and has never formulated an articulate philosophy of human culture capable of providing modern men with any seemingly relevant guidance in facing social and political issues. Hence communism and national socialism, both derived from German idealistic thought, have won the assent of millions of adherents not even dimly aware of any philosophical alternative. It is true that in this country we are aware of the fact that our democratic way of life is somehow based upon a very different view of the nature of man and the natural order of human culture, but our present understanding of its philosophical principles is not too clear, and is certainly not fostered by sharp and articulate formulations.

I have tried to show in this book that Plato did sharply and articulately formulate such a practical philosophy. In my opinion this philosophy, making no appeal to supernatural authority, sheds light on problems of great contemporary relevance. What, for example, is technical civilization? How are the arts and techniques to be classified? How are they used and misused? How are they related to life and its needs? What is tyranny and how is it to be avoided? What is the relation of the human individual to the human community? What is the basis of individual rights? What is the true order of human life and how is this inverted?

In Chapters II–V I have tried to present Plato's thought on these topics in an orderly manner intelligible to the modern reader. But human culture is simply the perfection of the nature of man, and man is a *rational* animal. Hence in the last three chapters, VI–VIII, I have attempted to present Plato's theory of knowing, that vital and mysterious faculty on which all that is truly human is based, by way of a commentary on the thought of three later dialogues, the *Parmenides*, the *Theaetetus* and the *Sophist*. While I have tried in my text to state the Platonic doctrine in modern terms as clearly as possible, I have sought to provide the more active reader with constant references to the Platonic text, which may aid him in finding out for himself.

Chapter II first appeared as an article entitled "Plato's Theory of TEXNH: A Phenomenological Interpretation" in the *Journal of Philosophy and Phenomenological Research*, vol. I, no. 3 (March 1941). My thanks are due to the editorial board of the *Journal* for permission to reprint this article.

I am deeply in the debt of Professor R. L. Calhoun of Yale University for helpful criticisms and suggestions. To Mr. C. H. Whitman and Mr. Constantine Cavarnos I owe a similar debt of gratitude for their careful reading of the manuscript, and many improvements resulting therefrom. I am also grateful to the Harvard University Press for its editorial assistance.

J. W.

Cambridge, Massachusetts
September 1945

CONTENTS

PLATO'S THEORY OF MAN

CHAPTER I

PLATO AND THE TRADITION OF CLASSICAL PHILOSOPHY

THIS BOOK is not an attempt to expound the whole of Plato's philosophy, nor even of a single part of his philosophy, as "historic" exposition is often understood. Its aim is not so much to reveal the thought of Plato as to reveal the nature of human culture and its inversion, using Plato, the philosopher, as a guide. Though such a purpose may seem strange to a certain version of history as antiquarian research, I am sure that it would not seem strange to Plato. He himself had no interest whatsoever in the thoughts or words of his predecessors, except in so far as they aided him in understanding himself and the world around him, though he often consulted them and wrestled with them at great length when in difficulty.[1] Furthermore, he specifically warns us against taking his own thoughts, least of all his own words, with any seriousness except as possible guides or "reminders" [2] of the real things in us and around us. One of the real things in us and around us, with which we are most vitally concerned, is the intricate maze of human culture. Plato also was concerned with this, and has left us many written "reminders" of what he saw, and of what we also may be able to see, provided we do not become so entranced with the signs and guideposts that we neglect to follow where they point.

They point to a complex maze of agencies, activities, and disciplines, farming, manufacturing, distributing, fighting, governing, teaching, thinking, living, worshipping, which we often summarize by the cryptic word culture. What is human culture? What are its several branches and kinds? What is its healthy or normal state? No one today can doubt that it has diseases. What then are these, and how may they be healed or better still averted? We must keep these ques-

[1] For Parmenides cf. *Parmenides*, 137–142 (*infra*, pp. 205 ff.), and *Sophist*, 244 B–246 (*infra*, pp. 287 ff.). For Heraclitus, *Cratylus*, 439 B ff., and *Theaetetus*, 179 E–183 A (*infra*, pp. 255 ff.). Unless otherwise stated, all references to the works of Plato are to John Burnet, *Platonis Opera*, 5 vols. (Oxford: Clarendon Press, 1901–07).

[2] ὑπομνήματα: *Phaedrus*, 276 D 3.

tions constantly before us if we are to follow Plato in exploring the dark labyrinths of human reality. Let us then plunge in after him. We shall hardly find a better guide.

1. CLASSICAL PHILOSOPHY AND THE MODERN SCENE

Western culture as a whole has been threatened, and in certain countries totally extinguished, by a dreadful disease which has brought the last phase of modern history to a bitter and decisive end. We refer to this disease by many names such as *nationalism, barbarism*, and *tyranny*, and we are generally aware of its major symptoms. Three of these are certainly: first, the absence of any faith in a real order of existence, independent of the opinions and desires of the national group; second, a resulting scorn for reason, except as the contriver of technical instruments, which alone among the human faculties is capable of apprehending such an order as it is; and finally, third, a contempt for the individual person who bears this rational faculty.

To those with even a superficial knowledge of modern philosophy it is apparent that these symptoms have not emerged in a sudden gust of barbaric fury without background or precedent, but that this devastating outburst is the culmination of a long cultural process in which they have been nourished and brought to final fruition. As we now look back on this "new" philosophy from our present-day perspective and compare it *as a whole* with what preceded, we can see that in spite of many internal divergences it was also marked by the three major symptoms of this disease. As against the realism and rationalism of classical philosophy which it attempted to replace, the "modern" philosophy of Descartes, reaching its climax in the German "idealism" of the nineteenth century, was subjectivistic, voluntaristic, or subrational, and consequently anti-personal in its anthropology.

According to this philosophy the function of human understanding was not faithfully to reflect the structure of things as they really are, but rather to impose its own structure and necessities upon things, and thus to subordinate ontology to logic. Reason was thus removed from its ancient position as the guiding, apprehensive faculty of man and enslaved to will, feeling, desire, or some one of the many other subrational candidates competing for the supreme position. The human individual, thus deprived of his immaterial faculties of intellect and will, the twofold source of his natural dignity, had to be viewed rather as an animal compound of sensation and impulse than as a man. There was nothing in human nature so distortedly materialized which could reasonably require that the ephemeral and puny individual should not be subordinated to the far more lasting and stupendous material needs of the state. The recent irruption of barbarism on the European continent must therefore be viewed as a consistent expression of those subjectivistic, irrational, subpersonal trends which have marked the chaotically divergent streams of post-Renaissance thought.

The first effect of this new philosophy at the beginning of the modern period was a release of disintegrating forces which weakened the bonds hitherto linking all the elements of Western culture into a more or less integral and intelligible structure. Religion was decimated into an increasing number of diverging sects. Philosophy was separated from religion and similarly broken into diverging streams of thought. The sciences separated themselves in turn from philosophy and then from one another, rejecting any unifying principle save those spuriously provided by a coördinate discipline like mathematics or psychology, supposed by successive waves of fashion to be the master science. Without clear and integrated guidance from the pure sciences and philosophy, educative agencies such as schools, literature, and the fine arts lost their sense of responsibility to truth, conceiving of their function rather as that of pleasing those under their charge than as that of instructing them. With no clear view of the nature of human life as a whole or of its end, politics also lost its sense of direction and fell increasingly under the sway of subordinate economic agencies of distribution and production. Finally chaos spread into these agencies, and in spite of great advances in industrial organization and efficiency they increasingly failed to provide the disordered community with even the bare, material necessities of human life.

The new philosophy, during this period of cultural inversion, having severed all vital connections with classical and medieval thought, was unable to establish any overarching metaphysical insights in the light of which the whole vast complex of human culture could be integrated or understood. The fundamental ontological discoveries of the Greeks, together with the labors of the greatest minds of fifteen centuries by which these discoveries had been further extended and refined, were consigned to a dusty ignominy on the library shelves on the ground that they had been completely superseded by the destructive criticism of the German philosopher, Kant. So, except for some bizarre idealistic system celebrating the God-like function of the human mind, or some indigestible encyclopedic accumulation of scientific data, metaphysics was abandoned for the subordinate disciplines of epistemology and logic.

Plato was turned over to antiquarian grammarians and specialists, with little concern for the possible truth or contemporary relevance of what he said. An almost exclusive emphasis was laid upon his epistemology, but his thoroughgoing and elaborate attempt to lay bare the hierarchical structure of human culture, including art, life, and thought, and his impassioned attack upon that primary cultural disease of *sophistry*, by which this hierarchy is inverted, to which so many dialogues are primarily devoted,[3] were either disregarded or dismissed as the petulant defense of an archaic class society. No one dreamed that the progress-phenomenon of the nineteenth century, vast proliferation of the subordinate techniques together with sophistic decay of the higher arts, had an analogue in the great fifth century of ancient Greece, and that Plato's pointed and profound diagnosis of this as the primary cause of barbarism and tyranny might have a modern as well as an ancient factual verification.

Those of us who are still alive at the present time, however, have lived to see this factual verification. We have seen the great bubble of universal, automatic progress, so similar to its sophistic analogue, burst suddenly into nothingness: Like our cultural ancestors of fifth-century Greece, we have seen a great era of commercial expansion, technical proliferation, and supposed enlightenment terminate in an orgy of barbarism and the most destructive war of all times. We have seen the great systems of liberal idealism constructed in the nineteenth century, via skepticism and pragmatism, pass into open irrationalism and the worship of force, just as *they* saw the great liberal humanism of Protagoras and the early sophists, via intermediate skeptical stages, pass into the brutal *Machtpolitik* of men like Thrasymachus and the Callicles of Plato's *Gorgias*. It is not surprising, therefore, that in the ever more restricted areas where knowledge can still be pursued for its own sake rather than as an implement for action, the twentieth-century mind, now coming to birth, is already showing symptoms of a growing disillusionment with the subjectivist assump-

[3] These certainly include the *Hippias Minor*, *Hippias Major* (if genuine), *Protagoras*, *Gorgias*, *Euthydemus*, *Cratylus*, *Theaetetus*, and *Sophist*, though the critique of sophistry is by no means restricted to these dialogues. There is hardly a work of Plato in which it does not play at least a minor role. Cf. *Republic*, Book VI, and *Laws*, 716.

tions of modern thought, and a reawakening of interest in the great tradition of philosophy as it was before modern idealism broke all genuine continuity with the contributions made during the first fifteen centuries of its history.

This contemporary revival of classical realism and rationalism is most clearly apparent in the so-called Neo-Thomist movements of our time, which have now escaped from the rigid confines of ecclesiastical authority in which they were hitherto imprisoned. This purely secular interest in Aristotelian philosophy was foreshadowed by certain rebellious developments in the late intellectual history of the dying era. Perhaps the most influential of these was Bergson's critique of a certain inability of post-Cartesian thought (which he confused with an inability of human reason itself) to deal adequately with the primordial philosophic fact of change. This inevitably led to an anti-idealistic preoccupation with the natural phenomena of change and evolution, expressed in various preliminary philosophies of evolution, emergent evolution, etc. This could not fail to establish the possibility of a closer rapport with classical philosophy, which in Aristotle and Aquinas, and, indeed, universally before the decay of modern scholasticism, was indubitably and incurably in its treatment of *nature* an evolutionary philosophy.[4]

The second manifestation of a spontaneous Aristotelian trend in modern thought was Kierkegaard's critique of a certain inability of Hegel and the post-Cartesian tradition (which he also confused with an inability of human reason itself) to deal adequately with the phenomena of individual existence. This led to the elaboration of that *Existenzphilosophie* which was certainly the most striking manifestation of intellectual life on the European continent before it was plunged into the blackness of the Nazi revolution. As over against the intellectualism of post-Cartesian philosophy, this philosophy called attention to the individuality of concrete existence, and to the contrast between the practical concern of such an individual with his own existence and the universalized detachment of theoretical contemplation. Like Bergsonian philosophy, therefore, it could not help but bring the wandering modern mind closer to a recognition and reapprehension of that primordial natural principle of *matter*, which, more than any other classical concept, is so strikingly absent from all the

---

[4] Cf. an unpublished Harvard doctor's thesis by Albert Hamel on "The Hylomorphic Structure of Evolution."

modern schools of thought, "materialistic" as well as "idealistic," but which, as Aristotle pointed out, is not only the source of natural dynamism and evolution but also the source of individuality as well (*principium individuationis*).

This widespread release of natural philosophy from the chains of an idealistic logic and epistemology which had so long imprisoned it was inevitably leading many thinkers to wonder whether, after all, Kant had really destroyed metaphysics, the foundation of the rational sciences; and even before the advent of the war, this science was once again stirring from her centuries of slumber. There is only one realistic *metaphysics* which can be genuinely opposed to the fantastic systems of German idealism, and that is the *metaphysics* partly formulated by Aristotle. But while the scholarly study, reassimilation, and revitalization of this metaphysics is well under way both in England and in America, there is one phase of classical thought as a whole that is as yet strangely undeveloped. This is what we must call, for want of a better term, *the philosophy of culture*.

Such a philosophy, if it existed, would be a branch of political philosophy, a division of ethics ultimately subsumed under the philosophy of nature, which deals theoretically with a *practical* object, the proper order of human life as a whole. It would provide us with sound knowledge concerning the nature of human perfection or happiness and the hierarchical order of necessary means to this end. It would enlighten us as to the chief causes responsible for the maintenance of this order, the chief causes responsible for its inversion, the major stages of this inversion as it becomes progressively worse, and finally the ideal structure of a perfectly inverted society or barbarism. These are questions which we may legitimately expect any adequately realistic philosophy to consider and at least begin to answer. The Neo-scholastic philosophy of the present day, which emodies fragments of the only realistic philosophy ever formulated in the West, does not clearly answer these questions so crucially important for us.

While Aristotle clearly formulated the theoretical foundations for such an answer, and even began to answer them in his *Politics* and *Ethics*, he did not *fully* answer them, nor even thoroughly consider them in any of the works which have come down to us. In his case, there are good reasons for this omission. For one thing, these questions were very thoroughly discussed in the exoteric works of Plato, which Aristotle was no doubt attempting to refine and supplement.

Another reason, as we shall see later, was the formal method which Aristotle followed in his philosophizing, and which was indeed necessary in order to avoid some of the dangers and obscurities into which Plato's concrete and practical method of thought was leading some of his less critical followers. But these reasons cannot explain the neglect of these practical questions by later representatives of the Aristotelian tradition.

It has been pointed out that "St. Thomas Aquinas wrote no special treatise on the subject of culture," and that "he does not use the word at all in its modern connotation." [5] He attempts neither to work out any exact classification of the arts and crafts, nor to go beyond Aristotle's vague statement at the beginning of the *Nicomachean Ethics* [6] that there is a hierarchy of the arts, an unmistakable reference to Plato's many discussions of this topic. Late scholastic discussions of the practical order *at the natural level* are extremely vague and general. Art is correctly distinguished from moral virtue, the end of such virtue (*beatitudo*) is defined, and intermediate necessary ends are vaguely referred to. [7] But nothing is said of these intermediate necessary ends in any detail, nor of their natural, hierarchical order. One is almost left with the impression that this *natural order* of necessary cultural means to the common good is a contingent matter which must be left purely to prudential calculation, though the necessary hierarchical structure of the *supernatural practical order* is emphasized and described in great detail.

To this lack of any practical synthesis *at the natural level* we must trace many of the inadequacies and failures of late scholasticism. There is, for example, the deadness and woodenness of exhaustive formal analysis, unrelieved by any practical synthesis. In particular, there is the well-authenticated reactionary drift of historic Aristotelianism, and its notorious failure to inspire practical programs of cultural guidance or reform. This has been one of the great tragedies of Western history. It has left the modern secular world without any programs for cultural guidance save those, like modern communism and Fascism, which have been derived from the distorted foundations of German idealism.

[5] R. E. Brennan, "The Thomistic Concept of Culture," in *The Maritain Volume of the Thomist* (New York: Sheed and Ward, 1943), p. 111.

[6] *Nic. Eth.*, 1094 A 1 ff.

[7] Cf. Joseph Gredt, *Elementa Philosophiae Aristotelico-Thomisticae* (Friburgi Brisgoviae: Herder and Co., 1926), I, 480–485, especially sections 594 and 596.

Modern scholastic textbooks and manuals provide us with the only means of access to a living Aristotelian or realistic philosophy, which are widely available at the present time. In spite of their lack of any Platonic protreptic (introduction to philosophy) and their failure to make any vital contact with the modern reader and his actual intellectual situation, these works provide the carefully trained, advanced student with precise and accurate summaries of the results of philosophic science in the fields of general metaphysics, the philosophy of nature, theoretical psychology, and logic. These theoretical subjects are *formally* developed by the normal manual, and left lying side by side with little or no attempt to connect them with opposed methods and opposite results, or with any practical or material synthesis including other phases of human culture. There is little or no attempt to deal with broad practical questions or the moral order itself.

Many of the available books on ethics, such as Rickaby's *Aquinas Ethicus*, consist either of translated excerpts from the "Prima Secundae" of the *Summa Theologica* or of discourses concerning individual ethical problems. Social, political, and cultural problems have been either evaded or treated in an archaic and reactionary manner which is out of touch with the living aspirations of our time, and unworthy of the tradition established by Plato and Aristotle. In recent years, there has been a recognition of the need for such discussions and a consequent outburst of treatises dealing with social and political questions from contemporary representatives of the scholastic tradition. But they have certainly revealed a widespread disagreement and confusion. Mr. M. J. Adler has devoted the last chapter of a recent book (*A Dialectic of Morals*) to a consideration of such questions, but the results are not reassuring. Mr. Adler, on the one hand, defends the thesis, hitherto peculiar to representatives of totalitarianism, that "the state is identical with the common good,"[8] but, on the other, attempts to remove its Fascist implications by the even more paradoxical thesis that "normally the good of the individual is paramount" over the common good.[9] Neither of these doctrines has any ground either in the genuine Aristotelian tradition nor certainly in the facts.[10]

The ablest, and certainly the most influential, books along this line

[8] M. J. Adler, *A Dialectic of Morals* (The Review of Politics, Univ. of Notre Dame, Ind., 1941), p. 113.

[9] Adler, p. 115, note.

[10] Cf. pp. 133–136.

are those of M. Maritain, but in spite of his sensitiveness to the claims of natural reason in other fields such as metaphysics and epistemology, his social and political thought is supercharged with a theologism which entangles him in the thesis that only religion can save man from totalitarianism.[11] This theory simply does not accord with the facts. In the first place, it is certainly incorrect to describe the political theories of Plato and Aristotle as either supernatural or totalitarian. If it is replied that these are only *theories*, and that we must turn to the actual data of history, the thesis of practical theologism is in no better case. Religion in its modern, concrete manifestations has often allied itself with totalitarianism instead of opposing it. Furthermore the democratic institutions of England and the United States are primarily founded on principles of natural reason and natural law.

Much of the argument by which Maritain and other Neo-Thomists attempt to justify this exaggerated disparagement of the order of natural practice, so similar in this respect to the corresponding Lutheran view of human politics, is radically out of accord with Thomistic and Aristotelian principles. This is especially true of Maritain's unfortunate distinction between man as *individual*, as such subordinate to the claims of the state, and man as a *person*, as such transcending the claims of the state. This runs a radical Cartesian cleft through the unity of man, and is inconsistent with the scholastic doctrine of the person as the *ultimate* substratum (*id quod*) or *hypostasis*, underlying not only all human acts but all the acts of man as well.[12]

As Professor Gilson has pointed out,[13] theologism, the attempt to replace philosophy by theology, is a ubiquitous intellectual tendency, found wherever religion exists. When reason fails at any given time to provide a clear and adequate solution to some problem capable of a rational solution, such as the problem of causation or the problem of knowledge, it is most tempting to brand the problem as naturally insoluble and to seek refuge in theology, before reason has actually been allowed to exercise itself properly within its proper limits. This tendency, so characteristic of the *liberal* attitude towards philosophy

[11] Jacques Maritain, *Freedom in the Modern World* (New York: Charles Scribner's Sons, 1936), pp. 49–53. Cf. Adler, p. 115, note.

[12] Cf. L. de Raeymaeker, *Metaphysica Generalis* (Lovanii: E. Warny, 1935), pp. 209–219. For an exhaustive criticism of this distinction, see J. A. Creavery in *New Scholasticism*, XVIII, no. 3 (July 1943), 231.

[13] Etienne Gilson, *The Unity of the Philosophical Experience* (New York: Charles Scribner's Sons, 1937), chap. ii.

in general, is also visible in the contemporary Thomist disparagement and neglect of the natural philosophy of culture.

Modern idealistic thought has signally failed to provide an adequate cultural synthesis capable of guiding the practical endeavors of modern man. The individualistic synthesis of utilitarianism and the social contract theorists has now utterly broken down. Only two modern alternatives so far have arisen — totalitarianism and communism. The former is a brutal type of anti-rationalism and anti-humanism which threatens to plunge the world into lasting barbarism. The latter, because of its incoherent philosophical basis, is able to justify neither the cultural aspirations of Western man, nor even the sacrificial zeal of its adherents for social justice.

It is not surprising, therefore, that, in the manifold confusion engendered by this impasse, a theological mode of escape should be suggested by representatives of the medieval and classical tradition. Why not use reason against reason in behalf of religion? This is a constant temptation facing the religious apologist. It was followed by the Mohammedan theologian Gazali [14] in his *Destruction of the Philosophers*, written in the year 1090. But this mode of apologetic is very apt to become a boomerang, as Gilson points out. Even theology must be rationally assimilated and applied. The skeptical pathway to religion is just as likely in the end to lead to the opposite. Thus Gazali's *Destruction of the Philosophers* was soon answered by Averroes' *Destruction of the Destruction*, a book with a distinctly anti-theological tinge. To hamstring reason is never to perform a genuine service to faith. Nor is the denial of a rational philosophy of culture a genuine benefit to religious culture.

Such skepticism, besides its own inherent falsity, tends to produce two further serious consequences. First of all, it tends to paralyze the exercise of reason with respect to matters of primary practical importance, and thus spreads social and cultural irrationalism. Secondly, it makes us blind to the cultural philosophy which is actually inherent in classical philosophy, most evidently and explicitly in Plato, less evidently and more implicitly in Aristotle. These two errors, and the practical cultural skepticism on which they are based, can be remedied in two ways, first, by a serious effort to show that there are certain practical principles actually accessible to the natural reason of man, and second, by a demonstration that many of these are clearly formulated

[14] Gilson, pp. 33–34.

in the great tradition of classical philosophy, particularly in the cultural philosophy of Plato. Such is the dual aim of this book.

Plato's exoteric dialogues are written from a practical point of view concerning primarily the moral order of means and ends. He is not only interested in unveiling the truth but also in showing men how to attain the truth, and in stirring, arousing, awakening them to the requisite effort of will. This *itinerarium mentis naturalis in Deum* is Plato's unique contribution to the living tradition of classical thought, a contribution of which it is at the present time sadly in need. We shall, therefore, achieve both aims if we can lucidly and cogently interpret the essential outlines of this *itinerarium*, together with the essential outlines of that inverted *itinerarium*, called sophistry by Plato, to which it is at every level essentially opposed.

But at the same time we shall try not to forget that the practical order is subordinated to the formal or theoretical order, as Plato himself taught.[15] We cannot decide to go somewhere unless we have some conception of *where* we are going and of the nature of *what* we are going through. But the end of man lies beyond the material environment, and his itinerary to this end involves every phase of this environment, including the nature of man himself. The reliable mapping of a trustworthy route, therefore, presupposes a general knowledge of these things, which can be achieved only by pure formal analysis. Hence the practical, as we understand it, presupposes and includes the theoretical. In many precise respects, Plato's *formal* analyses (which he called dialectic) are insufficient and inaccurate. Many of these have been further corrected and refined by Aristotle and his followers. But in spite of these theoretical defects, we need not discard Plato's general itinerary or oppose his philosophy to that of Aristotle.

Each is writing from a different point of view, and using a different methodology. Aristotle is a speculative theorist, Plato a practical philosopher. One is like a map-maker with a purely topographical interest, interested only in the formal correctness of his map in every detail. The other is like the roadbuilder who, it is true, has to have *some* knowledge of the topography, but whose primary aim is rather to build a satisfactory road to a given destination. Even though his topographic knowledge may be seriously lacking in detail, if he knows the general lay of the land, he may map an adequate road. Thus, in spite of the grave theoretical ignorance of many of the early road-

[15] Cf. *Rep.*, 473, 500–501, *et passim*.

builders of this continent, our modern railways and highways still pass over the ancient routes.

Plato's theory of culture is like the rough sketch of such a pathway, long neglected because of the crudeness of its topographic technique. Our theoretic knowledge is now much more advanced. But in general Plato's itinerary is sound. It shows us how to get where we still want to go, and how to avoid cliffs and swamps. Our job is to dig this pathway out of the dialogues, and secondarily to relate it to the more accurate structures disclosed by the later tradition of classical thought. But before we embark on our task it will be well for us to consider the general question of Plato as *opposed* to Aristotle, and in more detail, the nature of that means of reconciliation we have just suggested. Is there any precedent for such an attempt? What is the theoretical order; what is the practical order; and how are they related?

2. The Opposition of Plato to Aristotle, and How It Is to Be Understood

Until the period of the Renaissance, Western philosophy was based upon certain metaphysical truths first expressed in the writings of Plato and Aristotle. During this period, in which realistic metaphysics was really alive, these two classic authors were not fundamentally opposed to each other. The prevailing view, which arose in the early Neo-Platonic schools, was rather that the two philosophies could be ultimately harmonized, and that the two philosophers were each of them exploring the same hierarchical order of being, Plato in a less exact and more practical manner, Aristotle in a more exact and theoretical manner. In the great idealistic revolution of the Renaissance, however, the break with the whole Aristotelian tradition could not be concealed.

Descartes, Locke, Spinoza, Berkeley, Hume, and Kant all waged an openly hostile polemic against various phases of Aristotelian philosophy, and there is hardly a modern thinker of this tradition who has not explicitly or implicitly expressed his scorn for the barbaric dogmatism of the schools and his joy in the modern release from the empty word-juggling of the schoolmen. In seeking for a historic anchorage, therefore, modern thinkers have shown a marked tendency to turn to Plato in support of their idealistic doctrines. Descartes began this with his attack on the reliability of the senses, and his doctrine of innate ideas, each of which bears a certain superficial similarity with corresponding Platonic theories. Kant specifically refers to Plato in introducing his transcendental ideas.[16] Idealistic philosophy as a whole has tried to embellish itself in a Platonic dress, which has exerted a two-fold influence on the modern tradition of Platonic studies.

In the first place, it has encouraged a tendency to produce such misinterpretations of Plato along the lines of speculative German idealism as Jowett's famous English translation,[17] Bosanquet's commentary on the *Republic*, and Natorp's Kantian reformulation of the *Ideenlehre*. Plato was looked upon primarily as the author of an "idealistic" epistemology, or "theory of ideas." His realistic metaphysics was disregarded, his hard-headed theory of human culture was merged with myth or overshadowed by epistemology,[18] and the letters in which he gives a realistic account of his vain attempts to *apply* philosophy in practice branded as forgeries. This is that ethereal, soaring Plato of the Jowett translation by whom the more casual reader on the one hand is still emotionally inspired, and the more serious reader on the other hand is introduced to the creative mechanisms of mind.

The necessary corollary of this ghostlike rendition was a marked development of a tendency to oppose Plato to Aristotle, whose lucid description of individual substances as they really are laid the theoretical foundations for the only realistic metaphysics that has ever been fully developed in the West, and which required the dialectical genius of a Hegel to distort into a preamble to idealism. But for the most part, idealistic scholarship has followed the less daring course of rejecting Aristotle as an antiquated dogmatist with outmoded biological prejudices and of assimilating Plato via "the theory of ideas" to the idealistic tradition.

Recently, however, this idealistic picture of Plato has received many rude shocks. Epistles VI, VII, and VIII are now universally accepted as genuine. Professor A. E. Taylor has revealed the glaring inadequacy

---

[16] *Kritik der reinen Vernunft*. Des Ersten Buchs der transszendentalen Dialektik Erster Abschnitt. Von den Ideen überhaupt (Berlin: Cassirer, 1922), pp. 256–257.
[17] Benjamin Jowett, *The Dialogues of Plato*, 5 vols. (3rd ed.; Oxford, 1892).
[18] Thus in Constantin Ritter's famous book *Platon* (München: Beck, 1910–23), the Platonic *Metaphysik* is merged with *Erkenntnislehre* (vol. II, Erstes Abschnitt), and, if we judge by the number of pages devoted to each topic, epistemology is almost as important as Cosmology, Philosophy of Nature, and Anthropology *combined*.

14 PLATO'S THEORY OF MAN

of Hegel's reformulation of the *Parmenides*,[19] as well as the systematic cogency of many aspects of Plato's anti-idealistic anthropology and moral philosophy.[20] Professor F. M. Cornford's careful and exact commentaries on the later dialogues have rescued many sound and illuminating technical passages from the literary twilight of the Jowett approach.[21] The inspiring but artless Plato of the nineteenth century has now receded into the limbo of romantic delusions, and in his place we are beginning to see the philosopher Plato, fully equipped to defend his realistic, rationalistic vision of the world, not only by his mastery of literary imagery and style but by a technical mastery of descriptive insight and logical analysis as well.

This independent movement of critical scholarship has inevitably led to a revolutionary reëxamination of the fixed modern tendency to oppose Plato to Aristotle. Professor Cornford's studies, for example, have shown in detail the way in which Aristotle's later formulations grew out of structural insights and subtle distinctions already present in the later dialogues of Plato.[22] But perhaps the most serious blow yet delivered at the nineteenth-century dogma is the monumental work of Professor Jaeger in tracing Aristotle's gradual development to a final stage during which, in spite of his critique of subsistent essences, he never ceased to regard himself as an academic philosopher, refining, deepening, and extending the insights of his master.[23]

But it is not to be expected that a fixed mode of thought so deeply rooted in the post-Renaissance tradition of scholarship and so congenial to its world-view can be uprooted without a struggle. Thus Professor J. Burnet in 1924 answers Jaeger by a short essay in which he still speaks defensively of Aristotle's "breach with Platonism," [24]

[19] *Mind*, N. S., No. 19, pp. 325–326. Cf. F. M. Cornford, *Plato and Parmenides* (New York: Harcourt Brace, 1939), pp. 202–203.

[20] Cf. A. E. Taylor, *The Faith of a Moralist* (London: Macmillan, 1930), especially Series I, pp. 68 ff., 101–102, 229 ff., 324–327; Series II, pp. 8, 233–234, 389–391.

[21] Cf. especially *Plato and Parmenides*, pp. 194–204, where he presents an intelligible rendition of a passage left almost wholly opaque by the Jowett translation; also *The Republic of Plato* (London: Oxford University Press, 1941), pp. 127–135; and many other technical passages similarly rescued from mellow obscurity in Cornford's translation of the *Timaeus* (*Plato's Cosmology*, New York: Harcourt Brace, 1937), and in his translations of the *Theaetetus* and the *Sophist* (*Plato's Theory of Knowledge*, New York: Harcourt Brace, 1935).

[22] Cf. particularly *Plato and Parmenides*, pp. 89–90, 110–111, 142, 148, 160–161, and 201–202.

[23] Cf. W. Jaeger, *Aristoteles* (Berlin, 1923), pp. 190–199 and pp. 393 ff.

[24] Burnet, *Essays and Addresses* (Macmillan, 1924), p. 291.

of "the divergence between Plato and Aristotle," [25] and finally of "the radical differences between the two men." [26] Aside from Aristotle's critique of the doctrine of separated ideas, also criticized by Plato in the first part of the *Parmenides*,[27] Burnet rests his case that "Aristotle had a philosophy of his own to teach" [28] on only two points. The first is "Aristotle's return to his Ionian predecessors," which "had a wholly unfortunate effect on his general view of the world," [29] and which prevented him from following the Academy in developing a heliocentric astronomy,[30] though it now seems more than dubious that Plato himself in the *Timaeus* held any view that could properly be called heliocentric,[31] and in any case a difference of opinion concerning astronomy, even if it were granted, would in itself hardly indicate a fundamental philosophical "divergence." The second point is the more important. This is "the apparent degradation of our psychical faculties which impresses us in the first two books of the *De Anima*" and the "degradation of *phronesis* in the sixth book of the *Ethics*," both of which are "intended to prepare the way for the exaltation of theoretical wisdom." [32]

Most of the contemporary attempts to oppose Plato to Aristotle are based upon this notion that "Platonism is moralistic." [33] whereas Aristotle is a purely theoretical or contemplative philosopher. Thus Professor Erich Frank has summarized what is perhaps the strongest and most adequate contemporary statement of this position in the following words:

For a philosopher like Plato for whom the realization of his own *arete* is the necessary presupposition for the knowledge of true being, of the *agathon*, this being can remain only transcendent idea, because it is recognized by the philosopher as just that which he himself is not and which he, being conscious of his own limitations, of his own non-being and ignorance, is able, therefore, to conceive. That implies, however, Plato's irreconcilable opposition to the Aristotelian concept of philosophy as a merely theoretical science of being which is able to know the world and the objects in it, even those of ethics, through the logical analysis

[25] Burnet, p. 292.   [26] Burnet, p. 292.
[27] Cf. pp. 212–217.   [28] Burnet, p. 291.
[29] Burnet, p. 292.   [30] Burnet, p. 293.
[31] Cf. Cornford, *Plato's Cosmology*, pp. 120–137.
[32] Burnet, p. 296.
[33] George Santayana, *Platonism and the Spiritual Life* (New York: Charles Scribner's Sons, 1927), p. 92.

of their phenomenal appearance, and to comprehend and teach them through general concepts which are equally true for everybody.[34]

The essential contrast is that "between theoretical objectivity and ethico-religious existence philosophy." [35]

That a general contrast of this sort is evident in the writings of Plato and Aristotle when compared *en masse*, it would be fruitless to deny. While there are many purely theoretical and descriptive passages in Plato's writings, he is always tending to regard things from the *practical* or *moral* point of view, seeing them all together as means to the ultimate end, and constantly employing the direct technique of protreptic imagery and questioning to awaken and arouse the individual reader to act in the light of the truth already discovered. Aristotle, on the other hand, while he was aware of the practical order of concrete means and end, and certainly wrote on ethics and politics, is always tending to regard things from the detached theoretical point of view, formally distinguishing each from the rest, and dealing with them one by one, attempting even in his practical writings not so much to produce proper action in the light of theory as to produce the proper theory about action so far as possible. No doubt this sense of contrast would be mitigated if we knew more about Plato's later esoteric teaching, and if we had a more complete knowledge of Aristotle's early exoteric writings.[36] But even as things are, we may well ask the question whether this contrast represents a "fundamental opposition" between two "divergent" philosophies, or rather two distinct though inseparable phases of one and the same philosophy.[37]

First of all, as we shall point out later in detail,[38] Plato's basic division of all science (*episteme*) is into the theoretical which only knows and the practical which also acts or makes.[39] But the theoretical sciences are then subdivided into two divisions: first, those which seek knowledge for its own sake alone; and second, those which seek knowledge for the sake of action, like that of the architect who does nothing with his hands, but knows how to direct all the practical artisans and crafts-

[34] "The Fundamental Opposition of Plato and Aristotle," *American Journal of Philology*, LXI, no. 2 (April 1940), 182.
[35] Frank, "The Fundamental Opposition of Plato and Aristotle," p. 183.
[36] Cf. Jaeger, *Aristoteles*, pp. 23–25.
[37] Jaeger has judiciously recognized this contrast without turning it into an opposition. Cf. *Aristoteles*, pp. 394–399 and 416–423.
[38] Cf. p. 60.
[39] *Statesman*, 258 E 4–5: τὴν μὲν πρακτικὴν προσειπών, τὴν δὲ μόνον γνωστικήν.

men to the end of the finished building.[40] The first kind of science is pure theory, the second pure theory concerning practice. Likewise Aristotle divides all science (*episteme*) into the theoretical which seeks knowledge for its own sake, and the practical or *poietic*, which concerns the general principles of practical life and art.[41] Like Plato also, he subordinates the practical sciences to the theoretical,[42] since before we can devise adequate means to achieve the end, this end must be known.[43]

Philosophy in each view must be *both* theoretical and practical. In his published writings Plato directs himself rather to the synthetic practical portion of this task. In his lecture notes, as might be expected, Aristotle directs himself rather to the abstract theoretical portion. Man must try to gain an accurate understanding of all being, including his own nature and the nature of his end. He must also try to gain an understanding of the necessary and contingent means to this end, and incite both himself and others to the common task of achieving it more effectively. Aristotle devotes himself primarily to the former part of the task, Plato primarily to the latter. Neither can exist without the other. Is it not evident that far from constituting a "fundamental opposition" between Plato and Aristotle, the distinction between the theoretical and the practical orders, when correctly understood, provides us with the essential means of harmonizing them, by enabling us to discern the dual function of all philosophy?

As a matter of fact, this was discerned by the post-Aristotelian tradition of classical philosophy. One essential part of philosophy is to discover the theoretical truth concerning being. If you need this, turn to Aristotle! The other essential part of philosophy is to arouse yourself and others to act in the light of this truth, choosing the particular means which will lead to the end revealed only by such theoretical light. If you need this, turn to the dialogues of Plato for protreptic inspiration and practical guidance in the confused flux of concrete history! Every man really needs both. So here are the writings

[40] *Statesman*, 260 B 3–5.

[41] *Topics*, 145 A 13–16. Cf. *Meta.*, 1064 A 17, and *Meta.*, VI, 1025 B 25, where διάνοια is used instead of ἐπιστήμη as the inclusive term.

[42] *Nic. Eth.*, 1145 A 7 ff.

[43] Plato is primarily interested in this synthetic practical-theoretical knowledge, sometimes calling it wisdom (*sophia*) and sometimes moral insight (*phronesis*). Aristotle, on the other hand, restricts *sophia* to the theoretical and *phronesis* to the practical. But he admits that the latter must be subordinated to the former in an overarching synthetic knowledge. Hence the basic conception is the same.

of Plato and Aristotle, which are not fundamentally opposed, but which marvellously supplement each other, and which have, therefore, been held together and treasured throughout our cultural history! Such is the judgment of the classical tradition of philosophy, before the Renaissance. It was maintained only in the light of the Aristotelian distinction between the theoretical and the practical. When this distinction was ignored or exaggerated into an opposition, as in the thought of Kant, the union could no longer be maintained, and Plato was opposed to Aristotle. If, as in modern times, theory is opposed to practice, then Aristotle is opposed to Plato. If, as in the classical tradition, theoretical philosophy and practical philosophy are viewed as subordinate divisions of philosophy, then the two may be harmonized.

In the so-called middle-Platonism of the first and second centuries A.D. we find, among both Platonists and Peripatetics, a revival of the authentic division of philosophy into a theoretical and a practical part,[44] and, at the same time, the beginning of those harmonizing tendencies which were fully developed in later Neo-Platonism. Thus Albinus distinguishes theoretical from practical philosophy, and incorporates many Aristotelian doctrines in the former. But when it comes to practical philosophy, including Ethics, Economics, and Politics, he follows Plato, seeing in "the imitation of God" [45] described in the *Theaetetus* [46] and so many other similar passages [47] the end of human aspiration.

The harmonizing of Plato and Aristotle was an essential phase of Neo-Platonic doctrine. This was in fact said to have been the great contribution of Ammonius Saccas, the teacher of Plotinus. Porphyry (born in 232–3 A.D.), the first of the great Neo-Platonic commentators, wrote a treatise *On the Disagreement of Plato with Aristotle*, in which he defended their essential agreement, and, so far as we can judge from his recorded commentaries, devoted hardly less attention to the latter than to the former. In logic certainly, and in such theoretical matters as the division of the faculties of the soul, he followed Aristotle, but in his practical philosophy, he followed the familiar hierarchical pattern of Plato, and adopted the Platonic formula of "like-

[44] Friedrich Ueberweg, *Grundriss der Geschichte der Philosophie*, 5 vols. (12th ed.; Berlin, 1924–28), *Das Altertum*, I, 375–376.
[45] ὁμοίωσις θεῷ κατὰ τὸ δυνατόν. Cf. Ueberweg, *Das Altertum*, p. 543.
[46] *Theaetetus*, 176 B 1–2.
[47] Cf. *Rep.*, 501 A–C, and *Laws*, 716 C.

ness towards God "[48] in defining the aim of aspiration. The same structure of thought can be observed in his successors Syrianus and Proclus. Simplicius held that Plato and Aristotle were in essential agreement. If he pays attention only to the *words*, the superficial reader will be confronted by innumerable, apparent contradictions, which tend to vanish when, through careful study, he begins to understand *that which is signified*. His commentaries on the *Categories*, *Physics*, *De Caelo*, and *De Anima* still survive as one of the most valuable and enduring contributions of the Neo-Platonic schools.

Boethius, the last great Neo-Platonist of the Latin West, agreed with his predecessors in holding that Plato and Aristotle were in harmony on all *essential* points. Like his predecessors also, he looked to Aristotle for the formal, theoretical basis of his philosophy, to Plato for its practical, material content. He planned to translate and annotate all the writings of both Plato and Aristotle, but succeeded only in partially fulfilling the last part of this task. These works constitute what was perhaps the most essential link between the ancient and the medieval worlds.

St. Augustine classified Aristotle as a Platonist,[49] and it is certainly incorrect to think of early medieval philosophy up to the twelfth century as *Platonic*, in the modern exclusive sense. The *Timaeus* was the only dialogue known in its entirety, through the translation of Cicero, and the so-called commentary of Chalcidius, which certainly drew heavily from Aristotelian sources.[50] As for Aristotle, only two treatises were known, the *Categories* and the *De Interpretatione*, through the translations of Boethius the Neo-Platonist. So any *opposition* of Plato to Aristotle in the modern sense was altogether out of the question. The intellect is the highest human faculty, and it brings us closer to the nature of ordinary objects than the will. But in the case of an object which transcends our understanding it is more important for us to love than to try to understand it. Hence it is not difficult to see why Plato's *practical* mode of reflection, in which *both* intellect and will are brought into play, provided the gateway through which Greek philosophy as a whole was first assimilated to theology, itself a practical as well as a theoretical science.[51]

---

[48] πρὸς θεὸν ὁμοίωσις: Ueberweg, *Das Altertum*, p. 611.
[49] *De Civitate Dei*, VIII, 12.
[50] Ueberweg, *Grundriss, Die Patristische und Scholastische Zeit*, II, 148.
[51] Cf. Aquinas, *Summa Theologica*, Part I, qu. 1, art. 4.

But the preëminence of Plato over Aristotle in the early middle ages cannot be attributed to any voluntaristic disparagement of reason and pure theory. There was an intense eagerness for light wherever light was to be found. This was clearly indicated during the early eleventh century by the attitude of the School of Chartres, where contact was first made with the *Analytics, Topics,* and *Physics* of Aristotle. Like their predecessor, Adelard of Bath,[52] the members of this school welcomed the new learning, seeing no essential opposition between Plato and Aristotle, and, as we are informed by John of Salisbury, taking great pains to mediate between the two.

It is even incorrect to think of "the Augustinians" of the thirteenth century as Platonists in any sense which would *oppose* them to Aristotle. For Bonaventura, Aristotle is subordinate only to Augustine in authority. In spite of certain criticisms of Aristotle, at least one of which rests on misinterpretation,[53] he uses the Aristotelian definition of the soul, follows the Aristotelian division of the psychic faculties, attempts to combine his Augustinian apriorism with Aristotelian empiricism in the theory of knowledge, and speaks in Aristotelian terms of the *intellectus speculativus* and the *intellectus practicus.* As he shows so clearly in his *Itinerarium mentis in Deum,* he is primarily a practical philosopher in the Platonic manner, seeking to describe the hierarchical means and stages through which the individual soul may aspire to its ultimate end. *Intellectus* and *intelligentia* are thus viewed practically as stages on this way, not as in any sense inimical to the final ecstatic stage of *ignorantia docta.*

Intellectual vagueness and confusion do not foster moral aspiration. The struggle between "the Augustinians" and "the Aristotelians" of the later Middle Ages was not a conflict between the theoretical and the practical orders, but rather a conflict *within* the theoretical order, between partially assimilated and confused Aristotelian insights, and an implacable advance towards the completion and final clarification of these insights. When this was achieved in the philosophy of Aquinas, there was no absorption of the practical by the theoretical, but rather a deeper appreciation of the true nature of the practical order. Although he was more interested in developing the full detail of the supernatural phases of this order, Aquinas nevertheless recognized the existence of natural phases, and in laying the foundations for a

---

[52] Ueberweg, *Grundriss,* II, 231.
[53] Ueberweg, *Grundriss,* II, 387.

natural philosophy of the practical order he drew very heavily on Plato. For example, like his teacher Albert the Great,[54] he accepted the divine ideas as exemplary causes, and the idea of beauty as a transcendental term, coördinate with truth and goodness. In ethics he adopted the four Platonic cardinal virtues, and the Platonic distinction between appetitive desire and arduous striving. Like Plato, in political theory he asserted the primacy of the common good, virtue as the necessary means to happiness, and law as the necessary predisposing means to virtue.[55]

As long as this tradition was in the ascendancy, there could be no question of any opposition between the theoretical and the practical. By speculative insight, each being was formally analyzed and distinguished, including the voluntary action of men. Illumined by such insight and intensified by such vision, aspiration could then guide practical reason in determining the hierarchical means leading from contingent individual circumstances and choices to the ultimate end. Indeed, realistic metaphysics, whether it be regarded from the Platonic or from the Aristotelian standpoint, is incapable of producing an opposition of the practical to the theoretical, for if man is to achieve any actual goal in a world of real, independent entities, he must be guided in his practical aspirations by a pure theoretical knowledge of these entities. After all, it is the very same things which are known as the objects of contemplation, and striven for, or avoided, as the objects of aspiration. It is the stable nature of things as they really are in themselves which alone is capable of uniting our disparate faculties.

But in the modern period, when metaphysical knowledge became vague and confused, when the unalterable thing in itself was allowed to disappear beyond the horizon of verifiable insight, and realism was overcome by idealism, only the disparate faculties remained, with nothing to unify them. Subjectively the two supreme human faculties of intellect and will are quite distinct. Unless their objects are clearly and rightly grasped, the faculties by themselves easily drift apart and fall into opposition with each other. This process, already incipient in the late scholasticism of Scotus and Suarez, is clearly marked in Descartes, who begins his philosophical reflections by stipulating

---

[54] On the general question of harmonizing Plato with Aristotle Albert wrote: "et scias quod non perficitur homo in philosophia nisi ex scientia duarum philosophiarum Aristotelis et Platonis." Lib. I, *Meta.*, Tract. V, Caput 15, Borgnet ed. (Paris, 1890–99), vol. 6, p. 112.

[55] Plato, *Laws*, 630 E ff. Cf. *Summa Theol.*, Prima Secundae, qu. 92, art. 1.

that his radical theoretical doubts are to have no effect whatsoever upon practice.[56] In the Cartesian deity, the will is finally so completely independent of reason that should it so desire, it could will the interior angles of a triangle to be unequal to 180 degrees.

Once the faculties were subjectively opposed in this way, only three positions with respect to them were possible. Either they may be left in this giddy and unstable state of opposition as in Descartes, Hume, and our present-day common sense, which tends to oppose theory to practice, and the thinker to the so-called man of action, or the attempt may be made to reduce the one to the other. Thus in thinkers like Spinoza and Hegel, we find the practical categories of indeterminacy, deliberation, choice, volition, and freedom either eliminated or merged with the theoretical categories of determinism, intellection, and necessity. In Kant, on the other hand, we find a moralistic protest against this intellectualism, which has tried to base theories and arguments on arbitrary postulates and decrees, and which has led to the many schools of voluntarism and irrationalism so prevalent in our own day. Where, in fact, can the scorn of the man of practice for the man of theory be equalled except in the scorn of the man of theory for the man of practice?

But are the two essentially opposed? If so, there can be no hope of reconciling Plato and Aristotle, nor of ever regaining an understanding of pre-Cartesian philosophy. What is the relation of the theoretical to the practical order? Without some initial light on this problem, gained from pre-Cartesian sources, we can hope to understand neither Plato's practical philosophy of human culture, nor its relation to the great stream of classical and medieval realistic thought.

3. The Practical and the Theoretical Orders

When I ask *what is x*, I am asking a theoretical question. The answer tells me simply the universal and necessary nature of *x*, what any *x* must be, if it is to be *x*. If I could answer all such questions, I would find myself confronting the theoretical order, that is, an order of entities arranged according to their ontological dignity or causal dependence upon one another. On the other hand, when I ask *what is the good of x for man*, I am asking a practical question, which involves something more.[57] The answer to such a question must tell me not only the nature of *x* but also its relation to human aims and aspirations. Will it frustrate man, or further his perfection? Is it something which can be used, or something which can be enjoyed? If I could answer all such questions, I would find myself confronting the practical order of human action, that is, an order of concrete entities arranged as means and ends for human aspiration.

Which order is the more inclusive? Certainly there is a sense in which the practical is included under the theoretical, for I may learn the truth about my aspiration, about any one of its objects, and even about the whole practical order. But two things are left out. The desire which I *actually have* is not necessary. I may desire either *x* or *not -x*. But the truth about my desire omits this element of contingency. It tells me only what my desire must be, *if* I am to have it. In the second place, the desire which I *actually have* is a particular desire for some concrete, existing object. But the truth about my desire omits this element of particularity. Thus the practical order is a *material* order of concrete entities existing in the world. But the theoretical order disregards the material phases of this order, abstracting only its intelligible phases which can be assimilated by the mind. As Aristotle pointed out, good and bad are actually in existing things, truth and falsity in the mind.[58] Hence we must conclude that while the theoretical *formally* includes the practical it does not altogether or *materially* include it.

But does the practical include the theoretical? We may answer *yes* without any restriction. The habits and acts of understanding, the objects of these acts, and the relation of truth between objects and understanding are all good things which are *totally* included *without abstraction* in the material, practical order. When I seek after these things, or try to avoid them, I do not relate myself to some partial aspect of them, but to their *whole* being, with no essential or even accidental aspect excluded. Thus we have gained an answer to our

---

[57] The transcendental term good is *not* the same as good-for-man. All things are good, but all things are not good-for-man. Since man possesses reason, however, all being is brought into relation with his aspiration as either good or bad; and falls into what we shall hereafter call the practical or moral order of means and end, together with its inverted form. As Aristotle points out (*Nic. Eth.*, VI, ch. 7), there is another practical order for fishes, etc. We must guard against the fallacy, therefore, that the *human* practical order is *the* one practical order, as *the* theoretical order is one and the same for all.   [58] *Metaphysics*, 1027 B 25.

question. The practical order is *more* inclusive than the theoretical order, in spite of the fact that each, in a sense, includes the other.[59] But the theoretical includes the practical only partially or formally, while the practical includes the theoretical completely and materially.

Now let us turn to another question. Will is the faculty which pursues the practical order, reason that which apprehends the theoretical order. Which of these faculties moves the other? Here we must answer that each moves the other, but in a different sense.[60] Will moves understanding as an *extrinsic*, efficient cause. It can prevent the understanding from being exercised, or it can decide that it be exercised. Once having so decided, however, the understanding must exercise itself as its own *intrinsic*, efficient cause. Should the act of understanding be influenced by the will, or any other factor in this intrinsic exercise, it will then be prejudiced and corrupted except in the special case of *faith*.

On the other hand, intellect "moves" will as a specifying formal cause of its intrinsic proper perfections.[61] In order to will, the will must will something rather than something else. This "something" which the will wills must be presented to it by the intellect if it is to will properly. Hence we may say that the will moves the understanding as an *extrinsic, efficient* cause, while the understanding moves the will as an *intrinsic, specifying* cause. Thus each faculty governs the other. The will *moves* the understanding. The understanding specifies the will. Granting this, we may still ask which faculty is rather determined by the other? This may enable us to answer which of the two orders is really prior to the other, the theoretical or the practical? In fact we can already see the answer.

An unspecified efficient action is impossible. Every real act must be for *something*. Hence the will cannot act without first being specified

---

[59] "Et *simili ratione* bonum continetur sub vero, inquantum est quoddam verum intellectum; et verum continetur sub bono, inquantum est quoddam bonum desideratum." *Summa Theol.*, Part I, qu. 82, art. 4, ad. 1. Aquinas here does *not* call attention to the *difference* between the two modes of inclusion.

[60] Cf. *Summa Theol.*, Part I, qu. 82, art. 4.

[61] Intellect, of course, does not specify the formal cause of will *as such*, for will is not intellect. Hence the will in first act may tend to the good in general, and in second act to an apparent good without intellect. But it cannot *properly* perfect itself in second act unless the good in general is properly specified, and unless specific action in accordance with this end is elicited from the will by the intellect as an extrinsic formal cause. By this eliciting action, the cognized pattern enters into *the form* of voluntary action, and intellect has an intrinsic formal effect upon will, which, unlike the former, once in act, cannot perfect itself.

by some apprehensive faculty, either sense, imagination, or reason. It cannot act perfectly without first being specified by the most perfect apprehensive faculty, reason. The same priority may be also seen in the *objects* of the two faculties. That which is (the simple object of the knowing faculty) is prior to that which is good and perfects aspiration (the complex object of the willing faculty).[62] A thing must first *be* before it can perfect any aspiration, even its own. Thus from the standpoint of both faculty and object the theoretical order of truth (the relation of being to the knowing faculty) is absolutely prior to the practical order of goodness (the relation of being to our striving faculty).

This is strictly true in the case of all those material entities whose natures we may immaterially assimilate. It is better to understand material things than to love them, and the pure sciences of nature deserve to be more highly prized than the crafts and techniques which place such objects at our disposal. But here a most important qualification must be introduced. What about objects *higher* than our understanding, which, therefore, cannot be properly assimilated? In this case, we must say that *by accident*, not strictly speaking, the love of such an object, if we do really love it, is higher than an imperfect understanding of it,[63] though the understanding of this (as of any other being), so far as we can actually understand it, is absolutely higher than aspiring to it.

Thus the relation between the moral order and the theoretical order is a composite one. The moral order includes the theoretical, though in a limited sense it is included by the latter. But the theoretical order is naturally prior to the practical and intrinsically determines it, though in a limited sense it is efficiently and extrinsically moved by the latter. We may put the matter even more summarily by saying that the practical is the richer and more inclusive order, whereas the theoretical is the higher and more determining order. Each order so to speak has a certain advantage over the other. When we tend to forget one of these advantages, or merge it with the other on the analogy of material things in which the whole determines the part, we fall into a one-sided intellectualism or a one-sided voluntarism. If we think of the intellectual not only as the determining order but the more

---

[62] Cf. *Summa Theol.*, Part I, qu. 82, art. 2.
[63] Cf. *Summa Theol.*, Part I, qu. 82, art. 3, resp.: "melior est amor Dei quam cognitio."

inclusive order as well, we fall into intellectualism. On the other hand, if we think of the practical not only as including the intellectual but also determining it as well, we fall into voluntarism. *These* are irreconcilable opposites, for when the two orders are separated without a proper understanding of their inter-relationship, the differences which really distinguish them are accentuated into a contrariety. There are five such primary points of difference which easily lead us to misapprehend the theoretical as opposed to the practical order. Let us now examine them one by one.

1. As we have already pointed out, our desires are directed towards individual things existing independently of us, while we understand only the intelligible structure of such entities, so far as this can be assimilated by concepts in the mind. We *understand* what is universal and necessary in the world, while we *seek* what is particular and contingent. The former is really distinct from the latter but inseparably embodied in it. It is a great temptation, however, to *separate* the two, and thus to oppose the one to the other as though they existed apart.

2. As we have also seen, theory completely abstracts from all normative reference to desire or aspiration. The aim of theory is simply to conform to the thing as it is. Conformity with aspiration is entirely irrelevant. But the aim of practical reflection is not only truth but also conformity with right desire. Such conformity inseparably includes conformity with the truth. Otherwise the desire would not be right, but it introduces an extraneous "subjective" factor (aspiration to a practical end) which often leads to a shift in the position of terms in the theoretical order. Thus, considered theoretically, an animal is higher than a mass of gold. But in the moral order of means and end the gold may be worth more than the animal.[64] Thus when we become aware of such striking differences between the two orders, it is easy for us to ignore their interdependence, and to oppose the one as *objective* to the other as *subjective*.

3. The practical order, as we have shown, existentially includes the theoretical order without in any way distorting or mutilating it. Every actual entity or actual order of entities lies integrally within this order. Indeed, the right, practical order includes the true, theoretical order but the former is determined by the latter. The theoretical order does not include *the whole* of the practical order, but only its formal aspects, so far as they are formally distinct. Its greatest obstacle is the con-

[64] Cf. Aristotle, *Politics*, 1257 B 10 ff.

fusion of one thing with another. Hence, for it, distinctions are more important than synthesis. It is *meroscopic*, examining one thing at a time, and forming rather the whole out of the parts than the parts out of the whole. The greatest *practical* obstacle, on the other hand, is partiality, the confusion of means with end, part with whole. Hence, for it, connections are more important than distinctions. Practical reflection is always synthetic or holoscopic,[65] keeping the whole structure, from ultimate concrete means to ultimate end, clearly in view, and forming the parts out of this whole, rather than the whole out of the parts. Hence it is very easy to oppose the two orders on this basis — the *holoscopic* order of practice *vs.* the *meroscopic* order of theory, in which certain disjointed parts lie over against each other side by side.

4. Any order involves something that is first, something intermediate, and something that is last. Thus theoretical reflection passes from necessary first principles, through intermediate middle terms, to a universal conclusion, and practical reflection passes from an ultimate end, through intermediate means, to an ultimate contingent means. But if we compare the two, we can see that the hierarchical subordination of the practical order to its end is more intense than the causal subordination of the theoretical order to its first principle. This is because the first cause can only be inadequately and analogously apprehended through its effects, as something transcending our rational power. As the ultimate end, however, it can be loved in a manner less inappropriate to its proper transcendence, since will is always an inclination to something external, not a process of assimilation. The first principle, therefore, dominates the practical order more transcendently than it dominates the terms of the theoretical order.

This difference in the mode of domination may be traced down through the subordinate terms of the two orders. Certain universal intermediates, for example, such as the structure of human culture, may be theoretically apprehended as necessarily subordinate to this

---

[65] Plato's *holoscopic* method has been opposed to Aristotle's *meroscopic* method by Professor R. McKeon. But he does not seem to have taken the further step of relating this to the distinction between the theoretical and the practical orders, which might lead to a genuine reconciliation of the two opposed methods. Cf. W. A. Wick, *Metaphysics and the New Logic* (University of Chicago Press, 1942), pp. x and 89. Furthermore, *his* distinction would seem to involve the intrusion of a purely "semiotical" factor wholly foreign to Plato, Aristotle, or any classical, realistic philosopher. Cf. Wick, pp. 47–48.

transcendent end, should this end be desired. But when they are actually desired as necessary means to this ultimate end, another mode of hierarchical subordination is *added* to the first and the domination thus intensified. Finally, the last theoretical term, or conclusion, is still universal and necessary, for reason simply abstracts from the particular and contingent as such. But practical reason cannot be so abstract. Its last term is an individual operation.[66] Hence practical reason must achieve the final absolute subordination of the contingent and material to the necessary and immaterial, which is never found in the theoretical order. Hence it is easy to contrast the accentuated hierarchical subordination of means to end in the practical order, with the less accentuated subordination of universal, theoretical terms which are all more or less on the same level.

5. The last difference was clearly noted, though not fully exploited, by Aristotle. Science (*episteme*) has a privation but no contrary.[67] Hence the theoretical order, though full of lacunae, cannot become entirely inverted. If reason apprehends anything at all, it apprehends its first principles. But an active tendency or habit (*hexis*), such as virtue, does have a contrary — vice.[68] *Its* first principle (the supreme good-for-man) is not a theoretical first principle but a conclusion resting on complex premises and argument. Hence the first moral principle may be misapprehended, and the whole moral order inverted. Furthermore even though the ultimate end is theoretically understood as it is in itself, this does *not* compel practical reason to pursue it as the ultimate end. *Practical* necessity is always hypothetical. *If* I choose to seek it as the ultimate end, then I must also seek the necessary means. But I may not so choose. Hence it is possible for the whole moral order to become *inverted* with ultimate end subordinated to means. Practical aspiration can move either up or down with respect to what is *really* the practical order. Hence it is easy to *oppose* this contrariety and tension, characteristic of the moral order, to the determinacy and immobility which is characteristic of the theoretical order. Plato's approach to philosophy is primarily practical, Aristotle's primarily theoretical. Hence it is easy to discern all of these five differences in their respective writings. These *differences* are in fact

[66] Cf. Aristotle, *Nic. Eth.*, Book III, ch. 3.

[67] *Nic. Eth.*, V, 1129 A 11 ff.

[68] This is even true of science subjectively regarded as a habit. Thus we speak of an unscientific mode of procedure, and *oppose* foolishness to wisdom as well as imprudence to prudence.

the foundation upon which the modern tendency to *oppose* Plato to Aristotle is based.

1. According to Aristotle, the intelligible structure of the world is to be found *in* the individual things of the world, and no philosopher has ever devoted himself more assiduously to the task of examining these individual facts in their detail. But his aim is not merely to gather such facts but to abstract from them their intelligible structure. Hence he is rightly regarded as primarily a theoretical philosopher.

Plato also saw clearly that theoretical truth was an intermediate end in itself, and devoted himself to this end. But this philosophy led him beyond this to the further reaches of the concrete practical order. Socrates expresses this typical Platonic yearning for a reunion of theory with the living, individual processes of history near the beginning of the *Timaeus*, after a theoretical discussion in which the nature of the city has been considered theoretically as it is *in general*. "I feel now about this order," Socrates says, "as if someone had beheld certain, fine, living creatures either only painted or perhaps alive but utterly at rest, and had come to desire to behold them moving and exercising. . . ." [69] After making the arduous ascent to the realm of truth, the Platonic guardians must then redescend to struggle with their companions in the darkness of material change and flux. Plato is *primarily* a moral philosopher.

2. In accordance with this overarching, practical interest in concrete history, and a practical program for both individual and social salvation, the Platonic philosopher is not only a lover of truth for its own sake, but also a lover of the good. Thus in the *Symposium*, [70] Socrates is portrayed *primarily* as the representative of love or aspiration towards the beautiful, though this requires that he be also a lover of wisdom. From the writings of Aristotle we learn the unadulterated universal truth. From the dialogues of Plato, we receive a living impression of the man Socrates, and our wills are stirred to that aspiration without which such knowledge would never be achieved in the first place, nor ever applied to the actual lives of living men. These two tendencies are distinct but inseparable. Each naturally reinforces the other. They are not *opposed*, but it is easy to oppose them.

3. As has recently been pointed out, [71] Aristotle's method is meroscopic, as all purely theoretical insight must be. He examines one

---

[69] *Timaeus*, 19 B 4 ff.   [70] *Symposium*, 204.
[71] By McKeon as reported by Wick, pp. 48 ff.

thing at a time, without attempting a grand practical synthesis on a vast scale. The theoretical understanding is by its nature abstract, and incapable of the *broadest* synthetic sweep. Contrary to a widespread misconception, it is only with a view to practice that theory achieves its most inclusive integration, *only in the light of the good* that all things can be seen in their proper station.[72] Hence Plato, the practical philosopher, in a single dialogue, the *Republic*, achieves a synthesis of the philosophical sciences within the integrating compass of the ideal state. In the last great cycle of dialogues (the *Timaeus*, *Critias*, *Hermocrates*,[73] and *Laws*) he planned to include the most sweeping cosmological speculations within a practical framework, as the necessary prelude to the political program of the *Laws*.[74] Theory directs all proper practice, but it is proper practice alone which can give theory its final integration.

4. Aristotle regards God *in relation to his effects* as the unmoved mover and the first cause, as he must be theoretically regarded. Hence his transcendence is only dimly discerned, the hierarchy of being is less accentuated, and interpreters are even led with some plausibility to the view that the Aristotelian God is merely "the divine core of nature," its "true entelechy and energy." [75] Plato adds to this the practical apprehension of God as the final cause of actual human aspiration, the idea of the good *beyond* all theoretically knowable being.[76] The transcendence of the first principle is more sharply discerned, and the upper human levels of the ontological hierarchy are more sharply accentuated as steps or levels in that "practical ascent of being" which Plato called "true philosophy." [77] Hence the hierarchy of the arts, the hierarchical structure of social life, the order

---

[72] The Platonic philosopher embraces "all things human and divine" within the sweep of his practical vision (*Rep.*, 486 A 5–6), and sees "all time as well as all existence" (A 8–9). He achieves this insight only in the light of the good. *Rep.*, 508 E ff.

[73] Cf. *Critias*, 108 B and Cornford, *Plato's Cosmology*, 1–2.

[74] Cf. Cornford, *Plato's Cosmology*, pp. 7–8.

[75] See Frank, "The Fundamental Opposition of Plato and Aristotle," p. 180.

[76] οὐσία, *Rep.*, 509 B 9–10. To translate this word as *being*, following Frank (p. 179), makes an empty tautology out of the whole phrase τὸ εἶναί τε καὶ τὴν οὐσίαν, B 7–8. Cf. οὐκ οὐσίας ὄντος τοῦ ἀγαθοῦ; B 8–9.

Aristotle clearly recognized the transcendence of God in his early practical writings. Cf. Jaeger, *Aristoteles*, pp. 162 ff.

For a general critique of the "mystical" interpretations of *Rep.*, 509 B, cf. Cornford, *Plato and Parmenides*, 131–132.

[77] *Rep.*, 521 C 7–8.

of the human soul, and the different levels of knowledge. Aristotle's *ALL* philosophy is a set of exact theoretical analyses capable of being hierarchically synthesized when apprehended by right desire. Plato's practical philosophy is the attempt to perform this synthesis in beckoning man to the upward way leading to human perfection and blessedness, the ladder of the *Symposium*, the human ascent out of the Cave.

5. Aristotle's reflections are resolved at the level of pure contemplation, which is beyond all opposition and contrariety. Reason here is simply determined, by a determinate object, to distinguish that which is essentially distinct, and to register things as they really are. Thus he notes the general nature of the theoretical, and *separates* it from the practical,[78] which is necessarily subject to a contrariety. But he does not attempt to clarify this contrariety from a more synthetic practical point of view. He neither traces out in detail the necessary cultural steps leading to the ultimate end nor those of the opposed ascent, really a descent, which arises from a practical confusion of ultimate end with means.

Plato's practical concepts, on the other hand, are all divided into contraries. There is true art and false art, the rationally governed republic and its inverse, tyranny, the philosophical soul and the inverted soul, the upward path from opinion to knowledge, and the downward path from knowledge to opinion. The basic opposition underlying all these, between *being* and *seeming to be*, is not a purely theoretical opposition but a *practical* opposition (not excluding theory) between the philosopher with the philosophic culture of philosophy, and the sophist with the sophistic culture of inverted philosophy. In his inimitable exposition of the *itinerarium hominis naturalis in Deum* we are provided with an inclusive description of the necessary natural or cultural means to the human good, which was hardly attempted by Aristotle, but which constitutes an essential link in the structure of sound philosophy. This is not another theoretical philosophy which contradicts that of Aristotle, but a practical *mode* of the very same philosophy which it completes and supplements.[79]

The most peculiarly Platonic phases of Platonic philosophy, the Socratic doubt, the protreptic turning of the soul to contemplation,

---

[78] *Nic. Eth.*, 1178 A 21. Cf. *De An.*, 430 A 18.

[79] Albertus Magnus suggests this very terminology in commenting on the diverse treatment of universals in Plato and Aristotle. "Nec est differentia inter Platonem et Aristotelem in re aliqua, sed tantum in modo." *De Natura et Origine Animae*, Tract I, Cap. II, Borgnet ed., vol. 9, p. 378.

ALL

the use of analogy and myth, which have no place in the enterprise of pure understanding, and finally the upward and downward path of the Platonic dialectic, are all directed to the essentially practical goal of achieving this reconciliation. The final synthesis of the theoretical and the practical lies, of course, in actual history itself. But practical philosophy can prepare the way, and these peculiar tools of Platonic discourse are devised to carry us as far as reason can go in this direction.

The individual will is the governing faculty of man. It is originally directed to the good *in general*, not to any specific good. Unless this good is properly specified the *whole* order of human practice will be inverted. It can be properly specified or determined only by something else, the faculty of reason. But it will not choose to exercise reason unless it is first stung by humility and roused from its lethargy. This is the function of Socratic doubt which is no purely theoretical hesitation. It is rather a practical doubt concerning the end of action, which acts on the sluggish will, "in need of awakening." [80] This is utterly out of place in a purely theoretical investigation which presupposes a decision to think as already having been made. But Plato's dialogues presuppose nothing. They confront the individual will in its wild and untamed state, "arousing it and persuading it" to reflection by the gadfly of Socratic skepticism.[81]

Once roused from complacency, the will must be gently led away from those immediate contingent matters concerning which reason as such has nothing of a moral nature to say, towards its ultimate end, concerning which reason has something of a moral nature to say. This function is performed by the Platonic protreptic or introduction to philosophy, which introduces men to the specific nature of the ultimate goal they are seeking (happiness), and the means by which it may be achieved, and thus fills them with longing for "that knowledge which will make us happy." [82] This is not yet a purely theoretical aspiration for the truth, but rather a prior practical aspiration to theory in general. Then and only then is the soul free to rise on the wings of contemplation, and to behold the essential nature of things as they really are in themselves. This is *dialectic*, which, proceeding "without the aid of any sensible object, from ideas, through ideas, also ends in ideas." [83]

80 *Apology*, 30 E 5.   81 *Apology*, 30 E 7.
82 *Euthyd.*, 292 E.   83 *Rep.*, 511.

But of what use, we may ask, is such an abstract science to the will, which must act individually on individual contingent objects of sense? Here we must make a distinction, and give a divided answer. So far as these objects are individual and contingent, it will be of no use. But we must remember that the will deals *prudentially* with these things for the sake of an end. Theoretical reason alone determines the essential nature of man, and the nature of that end which can perfect him. Only in so far as the human will chooses to be so specified can it be sure of pursuing what is *really* its end. Only by devoting itself without restraint to this end can it disentangle itself from lesser goals, and thus become free to choose its own course amidst the network of contingent circumstances encompassing it. This is the major practical function of reason.

But theory, concerning itself theoretically with practice as an object, can do even more than this. Having once determined the nature of the final end, "the unhypothetical first principle of the whole," [84] and the nature of that imperfect being, man, who seeks to attain this end, it may then attempt to formulate a theoretical philosophy of culture which will determine the necessary, not the contingent, hierarchy of means by which this end *must be* achieved by man.[85] We cannot know the nature of man without also knowing the general nature of that whole physical realm of change to which he belongs, and of which he is the climax. We cannot know the end of man without also knowing the general nature of that being which is the cause and source of nature. No philosophy of culture can be formulated *without* including a philosophy of nature and a metaphysics. But, in addition to these theoretical sciences, so far most fully developed in the writings of Aristotle and his followers, the philosophy of culture must attempt to bring their results into vital relationship with the practical aspirations of man, laying down the necessary course which he must follow in spite of accidental deviations, from wherever he may be located in the contingent ocean of historic circumstance.

[84] *Rep.*, 511 B 6–7.

[85] This distinction between necessary means and contingent means to the human good is clearly recognized by Aquinas in *Summa Theol.*, Part I, qu. 82, art. 2, resp.: "Sunt autem quaedam habentia necessariam connexionem ad beatitudinem"; though the context shows that he is thinking primarily of the supernatural order. Cf. Part I, qu. 19, art. 3, resp.: "ea autem quae sunt ad finem, non ex necessitate volumus volentes finem, nisi sint talia sine quibus finis esse non potest; sicut volumus cibum, volentes conservationem vitae; et navem, volentes transfretare."

This is the final and most synthetic phase of the philosophic task, which has, in fact, been followed by Aquinas, who not only synthesized the theoretical philosophy of Aristotle with parts of the practical philosophy of Plato, but both of these with the content of Christian revelation. The *Summa Theologica* is basically a *practical* order, including, as it must, a complete theoretical order. Beginning with God, the final end, it then examines the nature of the creature, finally that of man. Then it carefully describes the twofold pathway, first, in outline, the natural, then in more detail the supernatural, by which man may move back *practically* to his source and end. The decadent scholastics of the late Middle Ages failed to recapture the primary insights of Plato and Aristotle. They repeated the phrases of the great Thomistic synthesis without fully understanding them, or relating them to the actual, cultural matrix which is their essential starting point. Hence this synthesis, and philosophy itself, fell into neglect and disrepute.

Recent Aristotelian studies have revived the theoretical portions of this synthesis. The theological portions of the synthesis persist behind rigid ecclesiastical barriers. But before the synthesis as a whole can be revived, and philosophy can once again be made to live in our schools, and most of all in our minds and hearts, we must revive the explicit and implicit cultural philosophy of this synthesis and recognize the guidance it offers for the practical natural aspirations of man. This phase of our western philosophy has its roots in Plato.

Let us then turn to the cultural philosophy of Plato and those practical elements in it which are so conspicuously absent from the "classical" philosophy of our time. We shall have to pass over the Platonic protreptic, still the most adequate introduction to philosophy which has been written, in order to concentrate our attention on Plato's philosophy of culture, the necessary means to the good, the upward and the downward path, and especially on that practical *contrariety* between the *true* mode of following this composite path and its *false* or *inverted* form which we shall follow Plato in calling *anatropé*.

4. PLATO'S CONCEPTION OF ANATROPÉ

As Aristotle points out, "the very same rational account explains a thing and its privation . . .," though "it applies rather to the positive fact." [86] We do not require one science for health and another for

---

[86] *Meta.*, 1046 B 8–10: ὁ δὲ λόγος ὁ αὐτὸς δηλοῖ τὸ πρᾶγμα καὶ τὴν στέρησιν, . . . ἔστι δ' ὡς τοῦ ὑπάρχοντος μᾶλλον.

disease, but the very same medical science is sufficient for both. Theoretical knowledge as such is above all contrariety, and "medical art can produce both disease and health." [87] The very same theory thus determines action which is towards or away from the natural end. "There must then be something else that decides; I mean by this tendency or will." [88] Action, therefore, always faces two opposed contraries, genuine art or quackery, virtue or vice, the actual exercise of reason or sophistry. Wherever we confront such a contrariety, we are confronting the sphere of the practical. Aristotle clearly indicates the possibility of such a practical contrariety, but his theoretical method leads him to abstract from it. Plato's dialogues, on the other hand, are constantly presenting us with just such a contrariety. Hence we must regard him as primarily a practical rather than as a theoretical philosopher, and if we are to understand him properly, we must devote ourselves to the task of tracing this practical contrariety through the dialogues.

As Plato himself carefully explains in the *Phaedo*,[89] "opposite things come to be out of opposites," and "in all cases, between the two opposites there are two opposed processes, — from the positive down to the negative, and from the negative up again to the positive." [90] In Greek the prefix *ana* commonly indicates this return to the natural state. Thus in opposition to the process of going to sleep there is that of waking up again (ἀνεγείρεσθαι), to the process of forgetting, that of returning again to memory (ἀναμνησθῆναι), and as Plato argues,[91] to the process of dying (ἀποθνήσκειν), that of returning again to life (ἀναβιώσκεσθαι). So Plato gave the terms down (κάτω) and up (ἄνω) a practical meaning, and in his language the term κάτω generally means the downward path towards the privative state, while the term ἄνω is used for the opposed upward path which returns to the natural end.

But here we must remember a most important point. No man would choose to go down simply for the sake of going down.[92] In general all men by nature seek the good. But good and evil are closely linked to one another as opposites, and, therefore, readily confused by prac-

[87] *Meta.*, 1046 B 7: ἡ δὲ ἰατρικὴ νόσου καὶ ὑγιείας.
[88] *Meta.*, 1048 A 10–11: ἀνάγκη ἄρα ἕτερόν τι εἶναι τὸ κύριον. λέγω δὲ τοῦτο ὄρεξιν ἢ προαίρεσιν.
[89] *Phaedo*, 71 A 10.
[90] μεταξὺ ἀμφοτέρων πάντων τῶν ἐναντίων δυοῖν ὄντοιν δύο γενέσεις, ἀπὸ μὲν τοῦ ἑτέρου ἐπὶ τὸ ἕτερον, ἀπὸ δ' αὖ τοῦ ἑτέρου πάλιν ἐπὶ τὸ ἕτερον: *Phaedo*, 71 A 13–B 2.
[91] *Phaedo*, 71 B–73. [92] *Prot.*, 358 B 7.

tical reflection. This confusion in the eye of the soul is like the inversion of a mirror image in which the lengthwise curvature of the lens makes "everything appear upside down," down looking like up, and up like down.[93] Thus our warped "imaginative power"[94] leads us astray "and often makes us interchange up with down."[95] In this case, a man may *seem* to himself to be proceeding towards a greater good or a lesser evil, whereas, in fact, he is proceeding towards a lesser good or a greater evil.

Plato uses the expressive noun ἀνατροπή (inversion) or the corresponding verb ἀνατρέπω (to invert) for this complex, *dynamic* confusion which lies at the root of moral evil and sin. The verb means literally to turn upside down, or to turn over, and is often used of ships capsizing.[96] But even when Plato is using the word in its original sense of "upsetting," he is also thinking of the rational confusion which is its cause.[97] In the *Laws* [98] he explains the general sense in which he uses this ubiquitous word by asking the following question: "do you not know that when the pilot becomes stupefied, every ruler of whatever enterprise overturns (ἀνατρέπει) whatever is piloted by him whether it be ship or chariot or army?" According to Plato, therefore, anatropé, or inversion, is defined as the miscarriage of human action involving misapprehension of the hierarchical structure of means and ends. It can be exclusively identified neither with theoretical falsity divorced from all practice,[99] nor with practical deviation from the right rule, divorced from all theory,[100] but involves both theoretical misapprehension and malpractice as they are combined in the actual inversion of moral order.

93 *Tim.*, 46 C 3.

94 ἡ τοῦ φαινομένου δύναμις: *Prot.*, 356 D 4.

95 *Prot.*, 356 D: καὶ ἐποίει ἄνω τε καὶ κάτω πολλάκις μεταλαμβάνειν. . . .

96 Cf. Aristotle, *Meta.*, 1013 B 14; Plato, *Rep.*, 389 D, and *Laws*, 906 E.

97 Thus in the *Euthydemus*, 278 B–C, he speaks of the Sophist as "upsetting and overturning others by the ambiguity of names," διὰ τὴν τῶν ὀνομάτων διαφορὰν ὑποσκελίζων καὶ ἀνατρέπων, "like those who pull stools out from under those who are about to sit down, and then make merry and laugh when they see someone turned over upside down on his back," ὥσπερ οἱ τὰ σκολύθρια τῶν μελλόντων καθιζήσεσθαι ὑποσπῶντες χαίρουσι καὶ γελῶσιν, ἐπειδὰν ἴδωσιν ὕπτιον ἀνατετραμμένον. The joke is not so much the catastrophe itself as its contrast with an obvious expectation. Cf. *Phil.*, 48 C 4–49 C 5, where Plato analyzes the funny (τὸ γελοῖον) as a harmless ἄγνοια or practical misapprehension.

98 *Laws*, 640 E.

99 Aristotle's ψεῦδος.

100 Aristotle's παρέκβασις, which is ἀνατροπή *in abstraction from its theoretical roots.* Cf. *Nic. Eth.*, VIII, ch. 10, and *Pol.*, III, ch. 7.

Plato carefully analyzes the structure of this practical anatropism throughout his dialogues pointing out its disastrous consequences at every level of human action, at the level of art, in which we act on something besides ourselves, and at that of understanding, in which we attempt to exercise our guiding faculties in uncovering the truth. By revealing examples and painstaking analysis he shows that at each of these levels there is a natural hierarchy of means and ends, which may be inverted by practical misapprehensions. Plato has a special term for the anatropic art we now call *quackery*, which puts on the appearance of true art, "pretends to be that which it puts on," [101] and which, in the case of medicine for example, beguiles the patient by the administration of soothing syrups and palliative anodynes into think-ing that he is being medically treated. Here the patient confuses pleas-ure, which attends the true end, health, with health itself, and, there-fore, the false means of pseudo-technical manipulation with genuine medical treatment. Plato calls this "fawning art" or "flattery," [102] and extends it to all the arts [103] without falling into our unfortunate tendency to restrict the phenomenon of *quackery* to medicine.

He even applies it to the more basic modes of human action, in which we do not so much act on something else as on the human soul itself in moving it towards or away from its ultimate goal. There is an art of managing the soul as well as an art of managing the body, and an art of healing the soul analogous to that of healing the body.[104] Nevertheless they differ from one another,[105] for the soul aspires to an ultimate end which is good in itself, whereas art aims only at some intermediate end such as wealth, physical safety, or health.[106] Hence the quack forms of soul management are fraught with far more serious consequences than the quack forms of medicine. There is an upward way leading towards this ultimate good.[107]

When our practical judgment goes astray, however, and we confuse some means with the *ultimate end*, then not some minor portion but the whole of human life is thrown into confusion, up itself being taken for down, and down for up. The sensitive part of the soul, which

---

[101] *Gorg.*, 464 C 7.
[102] κολακεία; *Gorg.*, 464 E 2, 465 A and B 1.
[103] *Gorg.*, 464 C 5, 466 A 4–6.
[104] *Gorg.*, 464 B 3 ff.
[105] *Gorg.*, 464 C 3.   [106] *Euthyd.*, 288 D 5–293.
[107] Cf. the last sentence of the *Republic*, which urges us "always to hold the upward way": τῆς ἄνω ὁδοῦ ἀεὶ ἑξόμεθα . . . (517 A 3, *et passim*).

includes the appetites, is peculiarly likely "to be misled and to inter-change up with down." [108] Thus confused as to moral direction, the soul, believing itself to be alive and in motion towards its true good, in reality will be dying and burying itself in a corporeal tomb.[109] Plato generally uses the verb *invert* (ἀνατρέπω) of this living death.

In its most sensational and final manifestations also noted by Aristotle,[110] it spreads into contracts, laws, and constitutions "until finally it turns upside down all things both private and public."[111] In this way whole communities may suffer the cultural death of anatro-pism.[112] But the disease has its root in that demonic, practical ignorance (ἀμαθία) of the individual mind and will, "from which all evil takes root and yields bitter fruit," and which, in the case of Dion's plans for Sicily, "for the second time both overturned and destroyed everything." [113]

If the individual does not rule rationally over his passions and appetites, he must be ruled over by them, and achieve evil (ἀδικία) rather than good.[114] As "irrational force" gets into the saddle it *inverts* many things one by one,[115] but finally, as its authority is extended, "it will *invert* the whole life of everybody." [116] This verb (ἀνατρέπω) is thus Plato's way of expressing the violent opposition between the true, upward way of life, and the downward way which *thinks* it is going up. Of course every man pursues the *apparent* good, and thus, if we trust to appearances, it is easy to confuse the two. But if we really make the effort of prying below the surface, we shall see that the one appearance is correct, and the other only a sham imitation. Hence the two lives are in the most complete and perfect opposition to one another. Callicles is an inverted Socrates, and Socrates an inverted Callicles. This is clearly stated in so many words by Callicles himself, who, after listening to Socrates' views of the true

---

[108] *Gorg.*, 493 A 3: τῆς δὲ ψυχῆς τοῦτο ἐν ᾧ ἐπιθυμίαι εἰσί, τυγχάνει ὂν οἷον ἀναπείθεσθαι καὶ μεταπίπτειν ἄνω κάτω.

[109] Cf. *Gorg.*, 493 A 2. Thus the imprisonment of the soul in the body for Plato is not an original, natural state, but a subsequent, unnatural state, brought about by a vital anatropism. Cf. *Phaedo*, 82 D 9–83.

[110] *Pol.*, III, ch. 7, and *Nic. Eth.*, VIII, ch. 10, where the term παρέκβασις conveys the same general sense as Plato's ἀνατροπή.

[111] *Rep.*, 424 E 2: ἕως ἂν τελευτῶσα πάντα ἰδίᾳ καὶ δημοσίᾳ ἀνατρέψῃ.

[112] Cf. *Polit.*, 302 A, and *Rep.*, VIII.

[113] *Epistle*, VII, 336 B: αὕτη πάντα τὸ δεύτερον ἀνέτρεψέν τε καὶ ἀπώλεσεν.

[114] *Tim.*, 42 A 5 ff.

[115] *Laws*, 863 B 4: πολλὰ ἀνατρέπει.

[116] *Rep.*, 442 B 3: ξύμπαντα τὸν βίον πάντων ἀνατρέψῃ.

use of rhetoric, asks in bewilderment if he is serious, and if he realizes that according to his teaching "the life of us men is turned upside down, and we now do in every way the very opposite, it would seem, of what we ought to do." [117]

How can this anatropism of individual life be avoided? There is only one means according to Plato — education. By this, he means not only the attainment of pure theoretical insight but also, first of all, the essential aspiration of the soul to such insight, and finally the actual direction of human life by such insight. Understood *practically* in this way education (παιδεία) also has an inverted opposite (ἀπαιδευσία).[118] Hence, after a study of the contrast between true art and its inverted form (Chapter II), the order of social life and its inversion (Chapter III), individual life and its inversion (Chapter IV), we shall study the contrast between Platonic and sophistic education as it is vividly portrayed by the great myth of the Cave in what we may now clearly recognize as Plato's *anatropic* or practical language. Here also we have a contrasting up and down, light and dark, ascent and descent.[119] The anatropic social environment, into which the infant soul is "normally" born, leads it to become devoted to sensible pleasures, and "they turn the eye of the soul downwards." [120] Nothing is wrong with the theoretical faculty as such. "Have you ever noticed," Plato asks, "in those who are said to be evil but clever men, how sharply the little soul sees, and how clearly it beholds those things to which it is turned, having no mean faculty of sight. But, forced to serve an evil end, the clearer it sees, the worse are the things which it achieves." [121]

Nothing could reveal more clearly the practical, synthetic orientation of Plato's whole philosophy. Theoretical insight is not sufficient. A great revolution or turning around must be performed, not with the theoretical faculty only, but "with the whole soul" (will as well as intellect).[122] Hence education is practically defined by Plato as "the practical science" (τέχνη) of this revolution, which arranges

---

[117] *Gorg.*, 481 C 3: ἡμῶν ὁ βίος ἀνατετραμμένος ἂν εἴ η τῶν ἀνθρώπων καὶ πάντα τὰ ἐναντία πράττομεν, ὡς ἔοικεν, ἢ ἃ δεῖ.

[118] *Rep.*, 514 A 2.

[119] James Adam, *The Republic of Plato* (Cambridge University Press, 1929), 515 E 32, 516 E 30, 517 A 3, A 7 ff., *et passim*.

[120] *Rep.* (Adam), 519 B.

[121] *Rep.* (Adam), 519 A 1.

[122] *Rep.* (Adam), 518 C: ξὺν ὅλῃ τῇ ψυχῇ ἐκ τοῦ γιγνομένου περιακτέον εἶναι.

the manner in which this *turning around* may be achieved most rapidly and most effectually.[123] Unless the soul is properly turned around and led to look in the right direction, men must remain in the dusky cavern "unable to *turn* their heads around." [124] Even if such a prisoner should suddenly be forced from the outside "to gaze on the light itself, his eyes would be pained and he would flee away, *turning around* towards the thing he was able to see, and he would suppose these things in reality to be clearer than what was shown to him." [125] The determinate objects of theoretical contemplation do not *turn* or *revolve* in this way, but the practical order is subject to an anatropic contrariety. Plato even notes that "there are two forms of visual confusion produced by two opposite causes, the change from light into shadow (which is less serious and more easily corrected) and the change from shadow into light (which is more serious and less easily corrected)." [126]

Human education, when synthetically conceived, is a practical transformation, involving will as well as intellect, subject to an opposite or anatropic form. Hence in the *Protagoras*, as, indeed, throughout the Platonic dialogues, we find the Socratic, arousing, awakening protreptic constantly opposed to the sophistic education which, instead of turning the soul towards real light and the ultimate end of human aspiration, under this pretext, really leads it into the haze of sensationalistic subjectivism, and chains it to its lower material appetites.

But the whole order of practice is subordinated to the theoretical order. Hence, after examining Plato's practical program of education, we shall turn to certain later dialogues (the *Parmenides* and the *Theaetetus*) which are more purely theoretical in character. But even here Plato's interest extends beyond the range of the purely theoretical. He is concerned not only with the naked truth itself but also with the ascending process by which the *seeking* mind achieves this truth, in Aristotelian language with the order of knowing as well as the order of being. When thus regarded from a concrete or material point of view, the life of mind reveals the bipolar anatropic structure which attaches to all human action. Here also there is an upward way to causes and first principles, and a downward way to those changing,

---

[123] *Rep.* (Adam), 518 D 2: Τούτου τοίνυν, ἦν δ'ἐγώ, αὐτοῦ τέχνη ἂν εἴη τῆς περιαγωγῆς, τίνα τρόπον ὡς ῥᾷστά τε καὶ ἀνυσιμώτατα μεταστραφήσεται.

[124] *Rep.* (Adam), 514 B 1–2: τὰς κεφαλὰς ὑπὸ τοῦ δεσμοῦ ἀδυνάτους περιάγειν. Cf. *Rep.* (Adam), 515 C 18.

[125] *Rep.* (Adam), 515 E 28.

[126] *Rep.* (Adam), 518 A 1.

THE TRADITION OF CLASSICAL PHILOSOPHY 41

sensible things which are only secondary effects. What we now call *mathematics* first "leads the soul up and forces it to think about the pure quantitative structures" which cause "the numbers having visible and tangible bodies" to be as they are.[127] Here and there, what we call *science* makes its way to pure, formal structure, but it "never goes to the first cause." Hence science as such is unable to climb up beyond bare assumptions and clings to sensible data (really derived) as though they were archetypal causes.[128]

It is the power of dialectic alone which "draws and lifts the eye of the soul upwards" beyond all assumptions "into the very first cause." [129] Unless this supreme moving power of thought keeps "lifting the soul" towards that which is the immaterial, intelligible source of all being, which needs no further source, the mind will tend downwards in the opposite way, *from* the intelligible *to* the sensible, trying to explain what is prior by what is really derived, and following the common tendency to treat secondary causes (συναίτια) as though they were primary causes (αἴτια).[130] Thus the actual causal order of reality is inverted in the anatropic understanding, which is intellectually ordered in a manner precisely opposite to what is really the case. Plato also uses the verb *anatrepo* of this mental confusion, in which "all the things appearing in rational discourse are in every way turned upside down," [131] and for which "neither any thing nor any argument is sound or trustworthy, but everything in a marvellous manner as in the River Euripus is turned upside down." [132]

Thus even in his later, abstract and speculative dialogues, Plato's interest never terminates in the theoretical determination of the truth, but extends beyond this to the practical process of thought by which this truth is either apprehended or misapprehended. Once this is understood, we may be in a position to see that many of the peculiar features of Plato's doctrine are not so much opposed as supplementary to Aristotle's philosophy. The object of truth does not change or move, but the human mind does move in what Plato called the dia-

127 *Rep.*, 525 D.
128 Shorey translates correctly. Paul Shorey, *The Republic*, 2 vols. (Loeb Classical Library), 511 A 3–9, vol. II, p. 113.
129 *Rep.* (Adam), 533 C 20: οὐκοῦν, ἦν δ' ἐγώ, ἡ διαλεκτικὴ μέθοδος μόνη, ταύτῃ, πορεύεται, τὰς ὑποθέσεις ἀναιροῦσα, ἐπ' αὐτὴν τὴν ἀρχήν, ἵνα βεβαιώσηται καὶ . . . . τὸ τῆς ψυχῆς ὄμμα κατορωρυγμένον ἠρέμα ἕλκει καὶ ἀνάγει ἄνω. Cf. *Rep.* (Adam), 534 E 2.
130 Cf. *Tim.*, 46 C 7 ff.
131 *Soph.*, 234 D: καὶ πάντα πάντῃ ἀνατετράφθαι ἐν τοῖς λόγοις φαντάσματα.
132 *Phaedo*, 90 B 9. Cf. *Gorg.*, 511 A, and *Euthyd.*, 276 D.

lectical process of its discovery. In the concrete thing form is not separated from matter, but the process of understanding does involve, just such a separation of the pure form in itself as Plato describes, in his account of the more inclusive material order of practice. In this the pure order of being is synthetically combined with practical "subjective" factors which are *formally* irrelevant to them. Much of what is now generally interpreted as "Aristotle's attack on Plato" is not an "attack" at all, since it proceeds from a purely theoretical point of view, quite distinct from the synthetic approach of Plato. It is rather an attempt to translate Plato's vaguer and more inclusive formulations into the more determinate and abstract language of the purely theoretical order. Aristotle's account of this order is more exact but less inclusive. Plato's account of the material order of execution is less exact but more inclusive. It gives us light on the order of being as we experience it practically, mixed with various "subjective" factors arising from our own purposes and aims. In this account many things are left indeterminate and even confused from the purely theoretical point of view.

For further light on the order of being as it is in itself, we must turn to Aristotle and the Aristotelian tradition. But though we must think of Aristotle as primarily a theoretical philosopher, we must not take this to mean that he denied the existence of practice, or that he left no place for practical philosophy. A glance at the *Nicomachean Ethics* would soon dispel such a delusion. But though his *object* is practical, Aristotle's procedure in this case is theoretical and meroscopic as always. His aim is to distinguish the practical from the theoretical, and then to dwell upon those peculiar contingent features which are most characteristic of it. It does not extend to the further, essential task of formulating a complete practical philosophy or theory of culture, in which the peculiar, subordinate features of practice are integrated in their entirety with the theoretical order, to which the order of practice is as a whole subordinated.

Though they never achieved such a practical synthesis of the two orders, at least at the natural level, both Aristotle and Aquinas showed that such a synthesis was possible. The ultimate end of practice can be correctly determined only by pure theoretical insight.[133] Furthermore, in addition to the contingent means to this end, the choice of which must be left to prudence, there are certain necessary means

[133] Cf. *Summa Theol.*, Prima Secundae, qu. 58, art. 4.

which may be determined by the theory of culture as *objectively* necessary, though they need not be necessarily *chosen*. Aristotle took only
the initial steps in the formulation of such an integral philosophy of
culture. Aquinas went much further, but his emphasis on the supernatural levels of the practical hierarchy led him to pass more lightly
over the natural levels of this hierarchy, and to dismiss many necessary
natural means as mere matters of prudence,[134] thus leaving unanswered
many burning modern questions concerning the natural practical
order. This deep contemporary need can only be filled by an integral
philosophy of culture, ordered to the theoretical content of the tested
tradition of classical philosophy. The exoteric writings of Plato
which have survived contain the outlines of just such a practical
philosophy of human culture.

Our task in this work, therefore, will be to follow Plato in his
account of all the *necessary* levels of the practical hierarchy, beginning
with the classification and ordering of the various arts (a question
not considered in any detail by either Aristotle or Aquinas), then
the structure of social life, on which the arts are causally dependent,
the structure of individual life on which social life is dependent, and
finally the structure of theoretical apprehension on which the whole
practical order is dependent. This hierarchy, however, is only *objectively* necessary, not *practically* so. One need not choose what is
objectively a necessary means to the end. We shall, therefore, also
adopt Plato's fruitful notion of inversion (*anatropé*), and follow
him in attempting to show *at every level* the possibility of an inverted
or anatropic art, an anatropic society, an anatropic individual practice,
an anatropic understanding of the world, and an anatropic use of the
apprehensive faculties. Our task will be concluded by an examination
of Plato's dialogue the *Sophist*, in which he attempts to define and
describe the anatropic man (the sophist), who bears within himself
the seeds of cultural inversion and decay.

From a not too unsuccessful achievement of this none too easy task,
we might expect two things: (1) much needed light for the formulation

[134] For St. Thomas the word *prudentia* includes the determination and choice of
both the necessary and the contingent means to the end, though he carefully distinguishes these two. Following this terminology, it would contribute to clarity if
we distinguished *objective* prudence concerning the right end and the necessary means
which can be determined by theoretical reason, and *subjective* prudence concerning
the contingent means which cannot be so determined. St. Thomas' failure to make
this distinction explicit has led to misunderstanding.

of a sound and integral philosophy of human culture; (2) far-reaching suggestions for the harmonizing of Plato's practical philosophy with the Aristotelian tradition, which, if history be a reliable guide, is a necessary precondition for the revival of living philosophy in our midst. Let us then now turn to the first step of our task, an examination of Plato's theory of the necessary human arts and crafts.

CHAPTER II

THE HUMAN ARTS AND THEIR INVERSION

THE SYNTHETIC, practical nature of Plato's approach to philosophy is made evident by his employment of the term *techne*
in a peculiarly wide sense to cover both what we call *pure science* or
theory and what we call *art, craft*, or practice. We not only follow
Aristotle today in distinguishing these, but we also tend to separate
them so sharply that no synthesis is possible except by way of reducing one to the other. Thus action is supposed to generate its own
norms, as in Kant, as though it could proceed effectively without
theoretical guidance, and theory is isolated in a special realm of *mind*,
as though it sprang up *in vacuo* without the voluntary effort and cultivation of living men. As we have seen, this isolation of the two
orders into separate compartments is as foreign to the intention of
Aristotle as it is to that of Plato, though Aristotle never devoted himself to the task of exploring the concrete practical order as a major
aim. This *was* a major aim of Plato. Hence he is constantly forced
to *stretch* the meaning of ordinary *abstract* words to give them a wider
practical meaning.

Since he is interested not only in the *formal* nature of science but
also in its concrete occurrence in the life of men, he *stretches* the word
techne to cover not only the pursuit of lesser ends, but also the pursuit
of knowledge for its own sake. Thus for him the word *techne* sometimes covers the *whole* practical order of art, life, and understanding
in the concrete order of execution where they merge and interpenetrate
either properly or in an upside down, inverted order. Hence he often
approaches ethical or epistemological problems by means of examples
chosen from the humbler arts such as carpentry and shoemaking.
The whole of human life is like a vast and complex art in which we
are attempting to reach an end by the rational control of action.

In spite of this synthetic interest in the practical order, however,
Plato, as we shall see, was aware of the distinctions between art and
life and abstract understanding.[1] In this abstract sense, art (τέχνη)

[1] Cf. *infra*, pp. 88–92.

is the rational control over some special phase of human life or the environment. It is by *art* that man subordinates external nature and his own nature so as to achieve his rational aims. Without the arts in this restricted sense, man is naked and defenseless, the most helpless of all the animals. Without these arts *man* cannot exist. Hence Prometheus had to bring them down from Heaven at the very beginning of human history. What is art in this sense; and what is its anatropic form? Are the different kinds of art true and false; finally, what is the true order of the various arts, and how does this order become inverted? Let us now turn to these questions which concern the technical basis of that great practical order which we call human culture, and which was a primary object of Plato's philosophical concern.

1. The General Nature of Art and Its Characteristic Deformation

No modern word embraces the whole complex structure indicated by the word τέχνη. The word "art" now tends to be restricted to the production of *beautiful* objects, while the word "craft," perhaps the nearest equivalent, tends to be restricted to the production of what is only useful. Thus we do not speak of a bricklayer as an "artist," or of a musician as pursuing a trade or "craft." This distinction, as we shall see, is wholly foreign to Plato, for whom "the useful is beautiful or fine, and the hurtful ugly or base." [2] The word thus includes both *art* and *craft* of present-day usage. Words like "skill," "cunning," "ingenuity," etc., are inadequate, since they refer only to individual proficiency in the whole endeavor. "Technique" is also an inadequate translation, since it refers to the subsidiary rules and procedures of an art, rather than to the art itself. Hence in the "fine" arts, we distinguish between the "technician," who only follows such rules, and the artist, who really masters them, or uses them for a particular purpose. As Plato points out, true art or craft is always susceptible to such a degeneration into "technique" (τριβή). This "bad" sense, which now attaches to the modern derivatives of the Greek word, is particularly apparent in the words "technical" and "technicality." The original word, as so often happens, has now come to stand for the characteristic debasement of the original meaning. The word *techne* thus has no exact modern equivalent, and we must

[2] *Rep.*, 457 B.

be content with approximate makeshifts, turning to Plato himself
for light on its wider, authentic meaning.

In the *Cratylus*,[3] the word is derived from ἕξιν νοῦ, or "active disposition of insight." Human reason is not viewed as a substantial
"mind" locked up in itself, but rather as flowing out of itself into
other forms of activity, "holding" them or directing them in certain
ways.[4] Results that simply happen by chance do not happen by *techne*.
But any act which can give a rational account of itself, explaining *why*
it does what it is doing,[5] is *technical* in the proper sense. The true
craftsman does nothing at random, but imposes upon his behavior a
"certain orderly arrangement," [6] which he "has in view" from the very
beginning. This constitutes the standard or measure (τὸ μέτριον),[7]
by reference to which he measures his work at every stage. In the
lower arts which deal with physical things, this measurement takes a
quantitative form, as in building and stonecutting, where the work
is done according to specifications of size, weight, length, etc. In
the higher arts, which deal with non-physical structures (as education
for example), measurement is qualitative, and the work is measured
by the "mean," the "fit," the "seasonable," and "what is required." [8]
It is a great mistake to suppose that these latter arts are therefore less
"exact" than those subject to quantitative measurement.[9] The form
of the state, with reference to which the statesman measures his procedure, is no less "exact" than the blueprint of the architect, though
the former exacts a qualitative order of temporal acts rather than a
quantitative order of spatial materials.

These are two types of formal structure, and "very different from each
other." But whatever the type of form, some known standard there
must be, with reference to which the technician may *measure* what he
is doing. "Where there is such a standard, there is art τέχνη; where
there is no standard, there is none." [10] Thus, first of all, the true
technician must know the nature of what he is about.[11] If he is
tending some type of living body, he must know, for example, that
it is the body of *man*, and how this differs from the body of other

---

[3] *Cratylus*, 414 B. As Hermogenes' answer shows, this is *not* to be taken seriously
as etymology.
[4] Hence τέχνη is a kind of power or δύναμις. Cf. *Soph.*, 219 A 6.
[5] Cf. *Gorgias*, 501 A.
[6] *Gorgias*, 503 E 4.   [7] *Statesman*, 284.
[8] *Statesman*, 284 E.   [9] *Statesman*, 285.
[10] *Statesman*, 284 D 6.   [11] *Phaedrus*, 271 A.

living beings. He must also be able to distinguish the various kinds of human body, and the structural parts of each kind. If he is *making* some implement, as, for example, a shuttle, he must know what a shuttle is, the various kinds of shuttle, and the component parts of each. Without such pure structural (dialectical) knowledge, he will be at best only a "copyist," performing blind acts without knowing why.

But such pure knowledge of genus and species, although essential, is insufficient. The technician is himself an active agent. He must also know, therefore, how this structure *acts* or manifests itself,[12] what it "does" to other things, and how it responds to this or that treatment. Only so may he guide his own active *procedure* to its proper end. Should he know *only* such rules of procedure, being able to produce this or that "result," but without an adequate synoptic knowledge of the whole structure, he has not as yet mastered the art, but only certain conditions of its exercise.[13] Should he continue to produce such effects, no matter how sensational they may be, he is not exercising an art, but merely repeating a routine.[14] Nevertheless art is rational *action*. Hence, in addition to pure knowledge of form, the technician must possess, in the second place, rules of procedure governing *action*.

But there can be no action without something which is acted upon.[15] The carpenter, if he is to make a shuttle, must put that formal order or arrangement which enables a thing to function as a shuttle, by some rationally guided procedure, *into* this wood. The smith, if he is to make an awl, must put another, formal order or arrangement *into* the iron — not such an order as he may fancy or desire, but such as the nature of the instrument requires.[16] The particular matter, as Plato says, "into which" the form is placed, may vary.[17] Any number of individual wooden blocks may be formed into shuttles. But the form itself, which the carpenter "has in view," does not vary. Thus, should a shuttle be broken in the making process, he will throw it aside, beginning once more, not needing to copy the broken one if he has any skill, but referring rather to the same general form or

---

[12] Cf. *Phaedrus*, 271 A–B.
[13] τὰ πρὸ τῆς τέχνης ἀναγκαῖα: *Phaedrus*, 269 B.
[14] τριβή; cf. *Phaedrus*, 268 A–270 C.
[15] *Gorgias*, 476 B, 4–5.
[16] *Cratylus*, 389 C–D.
[17] *Cratylus*, 389 E.

arrangement he had in his mind before.[18] All *techne* is rationally guided
action *on* some individual stuff to "transform" it into a certain order
or structure, apprehended by reason. According to the formula of
the *Republic*,[19] each art gives something (form) *to* something (matter).
Accordingly, in the third place, the genuine technician must not only
know general rules of procedure but also how to apply them to the
varying individual matter *on* which he works. Such *skill* can be gained
only from actual practice,[20] since the accidental variations of material
things are too manifold to be encompassed in any "theory" of essential
structure.

The completed action, the material arranged in its proper form, is
the work (ἔργον) or specific achievement of the art. Thus "to make
a rudder" is the work of the carpenter.[21] To steer the ship is the work
of the navigator. Each art has its own specific work to do. The
finished temple is the work of the building art — restoration of health
the achievement of the physician. Some arts like mining and hunting
and fishing are not so much engaged in arranging and ordering a given
matter as providing the matter for other arts. But even *procuring* and
providing are modes of rearranging or reordering certain things, and
hence come under the general formula. The various procedures of
the mining art, which makes certain metals *accessible*, act on matter to
give it this different arrangement with respect to further use. Even
the arts of discovery, such as prospecting, which seem to do nothing
more than "locate" the matter, to this extent order it in the structure
of knowledge, and hence prepare the way for further rational arrang-
ment. The various arts of transportation and navigation make
"located" places and materials continuously accessible, and thus *place*
them in a certain order — *at the disposal of* further arts. Many of these
are not so much engaged in forming a matter which is previously
unformed as preserving the structure of what is already formed. Thus
animal husbandry, hygiene, preventive medicine, and the legislative
art, which preserves the essential structure of the state, are not so
much formative, or constructive, as therapeutic in character. But the
work or function of any art is the ordering of its appropriate matter,
according to rational plan or form, with a view to some *further* end.

The work of each art is accomplished for the sake of something.[22]

[18] *Cratylus*, 389 B. [19] *Rep.*, 332 C ff.
[20] Cf. *Phaedrus*, 271 D–E. [21] *Cratylus*, 390 D.
[22] οὗ ἕνεκα: cf. *Gorgias*, 467 C 6, *et passim*.

Arrangement and order are useful; lack of order is worthless.[23] The mineral is located in *order* that it may be made accessible, in *order* that it may be purified, in *order* that it may be transported to shop or factory, in *order* that it may be formed into instruments which are useful for this and for that, and so on. Not only do the different arts exist *for the sake of* one another, but this aspect of "forness" penetrates into the minutest details of each particular art.[24] Each minor act has its *appropriate* time and season. A man may know all the rules of a certain art, but if he does not know where and when to apply them, the "effects" will be of no real use. He will then be a technician rather than a true artist, for he knows only the conditions required by the art, not the art itself.[25] The specific end of the art is its *work*, and this is always something good or useful for some further end.[26]

We have thus enumerated five essential factors belonging to the structure of *techne* as such: (1) the useful end, *on account of which* the art exists; (2) the work or concrete achievement of the art, which can serve this purpose; (3) the general form or structure which every such work must exemplify if it is to meet the end; (4) the technical procedure *by which* this form is imposed on the matter; and finally, (5) the concrete matter, *on which* the form is imposed. We have named these factors in the order of their importance for the art, as will be explained. No art can altogether lack any of these factors. Nevertheless factors 1, 2, and 3 are subject to a loss of controlling power which leads to the characteristic deformation of *techne* into mere technique (4 and 5 alone).

In the most highly perfected forms of *techne*, all of these five structural aspects are exactly known beforehand. Thus in medicine we find treatises on sociological medicine, that relate health as a whole to the larger purposes of life (1); on hygiene, that give an account of the normal functioning of the organism as a whole, the maintenance or restoration of which is the work of the science (2); on anatomy, physiology, and other attendant subjects, that describe the various structures necessary for such healthy functioning (3); on medicine, surgery, etc., that deal with various active procedures or modes of

---

[23] *Gorgias*, 504 A.
[24] Cf. Martin Heidegger, *Sein und Zeit* (Halle a.d.S.-M. Niemeyer, 1929), for a penetrating contemporary description, especially "Zeug" and "Zuhandensein."
[25] *Phaedrus*, 268 E ff.   [26] *Gorgias*, 467 E ff.

treatment *by which* such structures are maintained or restored (4); and finally on pathology, diagnosis, etc., that classify the abnormalities or diseases of the organism *to* which treatment is applied (5). The larger purposes of life (1) require health in general (2), which requires further detailed conditions in the various parts of the body (3), which require certain modes of treatment (4), in case of certain diseases or maladjustments (5). Such is the general structure of the science.

It is important to note that the student does not begin by the study of surgery (4) and pathology (5). He must first *know* something of hygiene, anatomy, and physiology (1, 2, and 3). But in the *actual practice* of medicine. this noetic order, from form to matter, is reversed. The doctor is confronted first of all with the sick or diseased body (5). Using his knowledge as a guide, he *then* applies some mode of treatment (4), thus restoring some particular part to its normal state (3), bringing about health in general (2), and thus serving the larger purposes of life (1). *Knowledge* proceeds *from* end, *through* formal structure, *to* matter. Practice proceeds *from* matter, *through* form and structure, *to* the end.[27] Practice is technically correct or adequate so far as it is *dominated* by knowledge, that is, so far as the order 5-4-3-2-1 is controlled by the *prior* order 1-2-3-4-5. If the doctor is to achieve the order 5-4-3-2-1 in a concrete case, his action must at every step be controlled by the order 1-2-3-4-5, which alone is capable of providing *guidance* and understanding of the *cause*. If, at any stage of the process 5-4-3-2-1, he is not thus *guided* by knowledge (1-2-3-4-5), his success, even though it be "achieved," will not have been achieved by art. It will have been "achieved" through luck, or "nature," or some factor other than art, which, as Plato says, is simply knowledge (1-2-3-4-5) flowing out into action (5-4-3-2-1).

In any art 1 and 5, the end and the material starting point, are presupposed. They are constant peripheral factors, which do not, strictly speaking, fall *within* the particular range of the art itself. A student who is about to learn to play the piano must already recognize in some form the utility or value (1) of this achievement, and must be confronted with a material piano (5). What he has to learn falls into two groups: the nature of a musical composition, and its various structural features such as time, melody, harmony, etc. (3); and the various technical procedures required (4). Should he learn primarily

[27] Cf. Aristotle, *Meta.*, 1032 B 6 ff.

rhe former (3), he will become primarily a theorist. Should he learn primarily the latter (4), he will become a technician. But he can become a true artist only so far as he succeeds in mastering both theory and practice. These divisions may be discerned in any art,[28] which invariably embodies certain intelligible forms or structures materialized through the agency of certain techniques.

Both these factors (3 and 4) are essential to the existence of any genuine *techne*, and it is impossible to learn either of them *entirely* alone in isolation from the other. Nevertheless, as we have pointed out, there is an unmistakable priority of the formal factor over the technical factor. The order 1-2-3-4-5 is the "real" or primal order, dominating all the various materializations which have to occur in the reversed order of generation (5-4-3-2-1). Music is judged or criticized by the theorist or expert, who understands the form or nature of musical composition, and in the building arts the architect, who understands the whole structure of what is being built (2), and what this structure requires at each step (3), dominates the laborers or technicians who, as we say, "do" the work (4).[29] The form can exist even though not materialized, but an activity or technique that achieves no order at all is impossible. Hence form must preëxist, and determine the application of technique in any truly technical enterprise. At each step of the technical *process* 5-4-3-2-1, the action must be directed "from before" by technical knowledge in the order 1-2-3-4-5. We cannot proceed, for example, from 4 to 3 unless 3 is already clearly visualized. All art is a kind of foresight. Hence the arts in general are the gift of Prometheus (Fore-thought), who enables man to think ahead. His twin-brother, Epimetheus (After-thought), who adjusts himself to each circumstance after it has occurred, brings only trouble and finally punishment.[30] This is apparent even in those games such as chess which require a certain technical proficiency. The able player is not he who merely adapts to each situation as it arises, but rather he who, from his general knowledge of the structures involved, can see several moves *ahead*.

The *way* to such guiding knowledge is through practice or direct experience with the matter itself (ἐμπειρία).[31] First of all we must

---

[28] Cf. *Philebus*, 55 D.
[29] *Statesman*, 259 E.
[30] *Prot.*, 320 D–322.
[31] This word indicates an initial, incipient, or experimental skill, which *may* develop either into true art (τέχνη), or lapse into meaningless repetition (τριβή). Hence

become acquainted with edible stuff, for example, testing its various effects (purgative, fattening, thinning, etc.) by actual experiment, and so far as possible distinguishing types or kinds (εἴδη). As long as such a classification yields us only a superficial knowledge of the *appearance* of different foods (such as green, red, sweet, sour, etc.), technical use is impossible. But as soon as certain types can be correlated with certain active effects, some use may be made of this knowledge. We may discover, for example, that certain animal foods such as butter and cream are fattening. Such isolated bits of information may be used to produce "results," but they do not constitute a *techne*. As long as we are forced to "feel" our way pragmatically, we can never be sure that we are really achieving the end. We may succeed in "fattening" the thin patient only to discover that we have undermined his constitution in other ways. Genuine technical control arises only when a *causal* classification, embracing *all* types of food in relation to the needs of the organism, is arrived at. When we apprehend this food structure as a whole, and discover, for example, that foods are either fats, proteins, carbohydrates, or certain vitamins, we have passed beyond the level of crude trial and error.[32] We can now *take account* of the whole food situation, and plan diets *ahead*, leaving little to luck or to chance. The apprehension of such structures or patterns, which often with apparent suddenness fit vast ranges of hitherto isolated bits of knowledge into a single coherent pattern, is the *goal* of all experimentation. When this occurs, it is no longer necessary to "wait and see" what will happen. The nature of a given process may be classified and causally understood *in advance*. Then an all-embracing plan of action may be formulated.

the word is used in both a good and a bad sense as the source of true art, or its characteristic perversion.

In connection with the former, we must note that the word is derived from πειράω — to attempt or to *try*. Hence ἐμπειρία, the skill or experience which arises from having actually "tried" a thing, is opposed to ἀπειρία — the absence of any direct experience. Art comes into being *through* such direct experimentation. (Cf. *Ep.*, VI, 323 A: τέχνη δι' ἐμπειρίας.) In the following passages, for example, ἐμπειρία is used in this "good" sense, as incipient τέχνη: *Rep.*, 582 B–C–D, where the philosopher is said to judge best of pleasures because of his testing (ἐμπειρία) of their chief kinds; and *Laws*, 720 B, where it is asserted that certain doctors, not possessing the art in themselves in the highest sense, nevertheless "possess the art in an experiential sense" (κατ' ἐμπειρίαν τὴν τέχνην κτῶνται). Cf. *Laws*, 957 B 2, 968 B 8, *Rep.* 422 C, where it is used in association with ἐπιστήμη, and *Rep.* 467 A.

The adjective ἔμπειρος — skilled or acquainted with a thing — always has a "good" sense connected with τέχνη. Cf. *Laws*, 632 D; *Statesman*, 529 E, *et passim*.

[32] ἐμπειρία: cf. *Gorgias*, 463 B.

Chance, however, can never be entirely eliminated. The goal of *techne* is the *control* or *domination* of matter, not its annihilation. Matter, as such, involves an indeterminate or unpredictable factor. It would thus be a great mistake to identify *techne* with the ability to predict in every *detail*. A sea captain may be a very able navigator, and yet not able to predict the weather, or precisely when he will arrive in port. A general may be a very able strategist, and yet not know when the enemy is about to strike. The true technician may be largely ignorant of the individual matter confronting him, and its infinite idiosyncrasies. What constitutes the foundation of his art is not the knowledge of its individual traits but of its universal structure, *how* it must act, *not* when and where. By this formal, structural knowledge he can *take account* of the various possible variations, and meet them as they come. Thus the captain stays on his course *in spite of* storms. The general carries out his plan *in spite of* unforeseen exigencies. The true technician commands his subject matter. He does not eliminate it or create it. He achieves his work. He performs no miracles. The test of his skill is the extent to which he can *govern* his matter by an inclusive plan, which in some way takes account of *all* the factors involved.

Thus the skilled animal trainer is ready for the lion *whatever* he may do. He has taken account of the complete repertoire of acts of which the brute is capable. He knows each *kind* of act, *what* it may lead to, and *how* it may be influenced. Hence he is able to conceive a coherent plan, and carry it out to the end. The aim of *techne* is the *complete* permeation of action by plan. Where events are within our power, *nothing* must be left to chance; where they are not, we must work out the various possibilities, and *take account* of them. The whole complex sequence in all its relations must first be grasped as a whole. Then, in the light of this, a course of technical action must be charted out which will really bring us to the end. When the whole of life, in each of its distinct aspects, has thus been taken account of, each act rendering what is *due* [33] to each situation, the aim of *techne* will have been achieved. Of course knowledge is extremely difficult, and many arts, especially those dealing with the human environment, are still in a rudimentary stage. *One* obstacle in the path of technical progress is the hiddenness of truth.[34] As Heraclitus said, "nature

[33] ὀφειλόμενον: *Rep.*, 332 C.
[34] As is indicated by the Greek word ἀλήθεια — the revealing of what is first *hidden*. Cf. N. Hartmann, *Platos Logik des Seins* (Giessen: A. Töpelmann, 1909), p. 239, and Heidegger, *Sein und Zeit*, pp. 219 ff.

loves to hide." But perhaps this is not the *most* serious obstacle. Even where art exists, it is apt to be corrupted and misused by those who practice it. These enemies work from within the very citadel of *techne* herself, and thus constitute an ever-present and most formidable menace. Two such *internal* corruptions of *techne*, both of which were clearly described by Plato, are of peculiar interest.

Of the five factors belonging to *techne*, the first three are of supreme importance. The matter to be acted upon is simply given to each art. Nothing can be done about this. The technical procedure is guided by 1, 2, and 3. Of course, failures in technical proficiency (4) are serious, but they may be remedied by skill and ingenuity, provided that there is sufficient knowledge of the end, and of those subordinate, formal structures on which its realization depends. The chief dangers confronting *techne* lie in this area (1, 2, and 3). First of all, there may be a failure of the second guiding factor, insight into the complete causal structure of the matter being dealt with (3). In this case, even though the proper end be kept in view, the correct technical procedure rigidly adhered to, and the "result" achieved, we do not have art in the proper sense of the word but, as Plato points out, mere routine (τριβή),[35] a *blind* procedure or "technique." To know that such and such a procedure produces such and such a result is not to know why.[36] The process is now guided not from ahead but from behind. Such routine procedure may often be *successful*, and indistinguishable from true *techne* so far as its "results" are concerned. But the time is

---

[35] This word is never used by Plato in a "good" sense. It is derived from τρίβω, to rub, wear away, or use constantly. It suggests monotonous repetition for a long period of time (cf. τρίβος, a worn or beaten path), with a consequent wearing or wasting effect.

Plato uses τριβή to indicate that meaningless repetition of practices into which skilled experiment (ἐμπειρία), or fully developed art (τέχνη), may degenerate. Such practices are no longer guided from ahead by any insight, but are simply remembered and repeated: hence μνήμῃ καὶ τριβῇ, *Epin.*, 976 B 3. Thus by constant association (ξυνουσία), and the routinizing of time (χρόνου τριβῇ, cf. *Ep.*, VII, 344 B), the "sophist" becomes familiar with the various moods and reactions of "the great beast." (*Rep.*, 493 B; cf. *Soph.*, 254 A.) It is the *privation* of true art: ἄτεχνος τριβή, *Phaedrus*, 260 E.

The experimental skill (ἐμπειρία), out of which true art may develop, is peculiarly apt to decline into mere τριβή, if it rests satisfied with pragmatic "results," and ignores the general, guiding structures of pure theory. Hence the common reference to the two together — intelligent experiment, which may develop into true art, falling into the mere routine production of results: ἐμπειρία καὶ τριβῇ in this order (*Phil.*, 55 E; *Laws*, 938 A; *Gorgias*, 463 B; and elsewhere).

[36] Cf. *Gorgias*, 501 A.

apt to come, in an unforeseen emergency, when it will no longer *work*. Thus the navigator who has learned to go through certain processes by rote in order to determine his position, without knowing the reasons for his acts, is apt to be lost when something happens to one of his instruments, or some other contingency arises. The trouble with a routine that is only "pragmatically" justified is that it does not really *work*.

Furthermore this corruption leads into another which is even more serious. The end (1) is closely involved with the intermediate structure (3), which it demands, and which conditions its realization. When insight into structure (3) is overshadowed by technical power (4), and the art sinks into a mere "production" of routine results (τριβή), the conception of the integral end to be achieved by the art (1 and 2) is apt to become vague and confused. In this case, no matter how adequate the structural knowledge (3) and technical proficiency (4) may be, the whole procedure will be relatively aimless, and thus degenerate once more into guesswork (ἐμπειρία).[37] This guesswork may not be a genuine work (ἔργον) at all, but a mere "result," perhaps superfluous or by the way (πάρεργον). Some achievements are genuine, and demanded by the very structure of things as, for example, human health. Other "ends" are merely accidental concomitants of the real end as, for example, the appearance of health, a rosy complexion, etc. When the broad structure of the end (1), together with all its various subordinate phases and sub-structures (3), is no longer clearly held in view, some such minor phase is apt to be confused with the real end, and the whole art subordinated to the production of some such "result" (πάρεργον) rather than to its proper work (ἔργον). For example, a complex knowledge of chemical and organic structure and a vast manufacturing technique may be employed for purely cosmetic purposes to give pleasure rather than health. We then have the final degeneration of true *techne* into a false or "fawning" art.[38] The true end (1) is not only obscure, as in the case of pure guesswork (ἡ στοχαστικὴ τέχνη), but a false end has been substituted.

---

[37] Actual experimentation, or "trying," is the *source* of all art. Hence, as we have pointed out (note 35, above), this word is often used in a "good" sense by Plato. If experimentation, however, rests satisfied with mere "results," neglecting understanding, it becomes, with the passage of time, mere routine (τριβή). Hence ἐμπειρία also has a "bad" sense, as passing into τριβή. Cf. ἐμπειρία καὶ τριβή as noted above (n. 35), *Phil.*, 55 E; *Gorgias*, 463 B; *Laws*, 938 A; and elsewhere.

[38] ἡ κολακευτικὴ τέχνη: *Gorgias*, 464 C 5.

This is a disease which affects *techne* at its basic source, and corrupts it as a whole.

Plato identified many such wholly corrupt or "fawning" arts, detached from their true ends, and devoted to the production of mere "results" (πάρεργα). Thus cookery, in detachment from hygiene, of which it is properly a subordinate part, may devote all of its resources to the achievement of a mere pleasing effect,[39] without reference to health. Rhetoric may use cultural knowledge and command of language not for its proper end, the instruction of an audience, but rather for mere pleasure.[40] Finally sophistry may devote considerable logical skill and information to produce the pleasing appearance of knowledge, a mere by-product (πάρεργον), rather than knowledge itself, the real *product* (ἔργον). Such distortions find an apology in the doctrine of "the relativity of ends." But if the fundamental aim of an art is only arbitrary and indefensible, the whole art is arbitrary and indefensible from beginning to end, and becomes what we now name "quackery." Those who assert a "relativity" of ends, therefore, are asserting a relativity of science, and attacking the whole technical enterprise. If one end is as good as another, one form of action is as good as another, and one science is as good as another. Hence what is the use of technical investigation, which always aims at the *true* structure, and the *correct* procedure demanded by this structure? The science of the doctor is really more useful than the pretended, "fawning" science of the quack. Hence certain ends are more useful and legitimate than others, and the doctrine of the relativity of ends is false.

Men will not always admit this necessary conclusion, however. This is because it is exceedingly difficult to grasp the *broad* causal structure involved in any science or art (1-3). This is even more true of the practical structure of the world as a whole, which we regard as though it consisted of a set of isolated chunks or *ends*, just as an incipient science has only a vague understanding of the nature of its field as a whole, and is forced to separate it into *this* comparatively luminous area, and *that*. We are commonly forced to look upon the world in the same disjointed way. There is *this* end with its appropriate structure of means, say health, and *that* end, say effective government, with its appropriate means. So vast is the *whole* field in its totality, that it is most difficult to gain any conception of

---

[39] *Gorgias*, 464 D.   [40] *Gorgias*, 463 A–B.

the true relation between these various ends. Hence the conception of a relativity of ends, each independent of the rest, or, as we say, "just as good as another." The very employment of the word "end" for each of these subordinate goals fosters this delusion. As a matter of fact, each separate technical "end" is not truly the "end" at all, but the *beginning* of a further endeavor. Even health is of no use to a man whose whole life has become meaningless.

What we call ends are really *intermediate* ends, within which unities of structure have been discerned, and some measure of technical control achieved, but over and above which the structural unities are as yet unclear. There is no more reason for doubting the existence of such more inclusive structures than of those less inclusive patterns which already constitute the object of scientific knowledge. But they are harder to grasp. Hence there is a tendency to suppose some arbitrary world-structure in accordance with subjective desire, just as the quack, in a more limited field, supposes some structure which will enable him to realize his wishes, rather than the proper end and means demanded by the nature of things. The isolation of one technicalized area from another, and the consequent neglect of broad structure, prepare the way for subjective synthesis and speculation. As a result of this, the technical conquest of great areas, resting upon carefully sifted understanding of structure and tested procedure, is often corrupted or misused for what is not a legitimate achievement (ἔργον) at all, but a mere superfluity (πάρεργον). Such undominated efficiency, working *from behind*, and guided by no plan, is the peculiar corruption of art. If allowed to progress without reference to any more embracing structural scheme, it will fall under the sway of spurious ends, and lead whole cultures to destruction.

We may thus conclude our account of the characteristic deformation of *techne*. Art begins with a given matter (5), and a vague sense of what it is seeking to do (1 and 2). It then proceeds by trial and error (ἐμπειρία) to establish the exact nature of its end in all its subordinate detail (1 and 3). When this goal is approximated, it is no longer a mere "knack," but an art (τέχνη) in the proper sense, capable of guiding its various acts (4) by an exhaustive knowledge of each step (3), and why it is taken (1-2-3). When "correct" procedures are merely "followed" without actual understanding, the art has already begun to degenerate into "routine" (τριβή). If this goes far enough, even though considerable technical proficiency (4) is retained, this procedure will not really be guided from ahead (1-2-3), but from behind (5-4). Hence it sinks back to the level of blind experimentation (ἐμπειρία), which merely guesses at the end to be achieved, and thus may succeed in producing only an apparent effect (πάρεργον). If genuine knowledge of the true end is not restored, some such false end will be substituted for the true, and the whole art distorted into a form of flattery or quackery (κολακεία). As we shall now see, these various distortions may be observed, in different degrees and combinations, in the various arts and crafts.

2. THE CLASSIFICATION OF THE TRUE AND SPURIOUS ARTS

We often think of our present culture as preëminently technical, and this word plays an extremely prominent role in all discussions of the contemporary world and its problems. But there is very little consideration of the nature of *techne* itself, and its various kinds. So bewildering is the array of arts and techniques which have been accumulated in the history of western civilization, and so complex are the interrelationships between them, that the task of distinguishing one from another seems hopeless. This task must be undertaken, however, if we are ever to understand our world and master it. Yet it is a subject strangely ignored by philosophers. Since the time of Descartes, a vast number of treatises have been written on the philosophy of nature and the philosophy of mind, but the philosophy of *techne* (mind flowing out into nature) has been strangely neglected. Contemporary positivism, for example, has devoted its attention to the methods of science. But the nature and methods of *techne* have largely escaped its notice.

To this feature of the modern tradition Plato offers a most striking contrast. Although most of the arts and crafts of his day were far less developed than those of our own, he regarded them as essential to man, and hence as a primary object of philosophic attention. In fact so much does he have to say about *techne*, and its various true and spurious kinds, that it is extremely difficult to gather together the many references scattered through different dialogues into a single synoptic theory. Without attempting to give an exhaustive account, we shall content ourselves with showing that such a theory, which is not without relevance to the problem of classifying the welter of arts in existence today, does exist in Plato. The very simplicity of the situation in the ancient world made it possible for him to discern

certain broad connections, now perhaps more easily lost sight of.
It is to these broad types, existing among the various arts, and their
general relations to which we must now turn our attention, taking
our point of departure from the beginning of the *Statesman*, where
all the forms of knowledge (πάσας τὰς ἐπιστήμας) [41] are basically distinguished.

A modern writer would probably begin by following the example
of Kant in separating the "theoretical" from the "practical," and
bringing the arts and crafts under the latter. Plato, however, begins
with science (ἐπιστήμη), reliable insight which is not subject to
change. This science falls into two major kinds: (1) that which
provides insight alone; [42] and (2) the various arts and crafts (χειρουργία), which involve technical *action*, but *also* possess scientific
insight as part of their inherent structure (ἐνοῦσαν σύμφυτον τὴν
ἐπιστήμην κέκτηνται).[43] Thus art is neither "applied science" nor
a blind "practice," but the concrete science of practice which grows
by various degrees into activity. Genuine insight into the nature of
things is the source of *techne*. These two forms of science are now
further divided. Of the knowing arts (τῶν γνωστικῶν τεχνῶν), there
is one part which simply distinguishes or classifies things as they are
(τὸ δὲ κριτικὸν μέρος), and another which arranges or disposes of
things (τὸ μὲν ἐπιτακτικὸν μέρος).[44] Thus there are sciences, like
arithmetic and geometry, which simply determine the exact nature
of certain things (numbers and figures), and other sciences, like
architecture, which organize and arrange various enterprises such as
that of building. These are both referred to as arts (τέχναι), since
even the "pure" sciences involve a technique of pursuit and discovery.
Nevertheless they may be distinguished from the directing arts,
where the end to be achieved is other than that of insight alone.

The other portion of the sciences, where the noetic factor "grows
into" the technique itself (σύμφυτον), is constituted by all the special
arts and handicrafts (χειρουργία). In the *Sophist*,[45] they are referred
to simply as the arts (τέχναι), and divided into two major groups:
those which make or bring into existence something not in existence

[41] *Statesman*, 258 C 6.   [42] *Statesman*, 258 D 5.   [43] *Statesman*, 258 D 9.
[44] *Statesman*, 260 B. Plato thus *stretches* the word ἐπιστήμη to include both Aristotle's *theoretical* and his *practical* knowledge. Speaking from the *practical* point of
view, he sees the former as a phase of the latter, but does not deny the distinction
between the two.
[45] *Sophist*, 219 A.

before, or preserve it in being (αἱ ποιητικαὶ τέχναι); and those which (like hunting, and the art of war) simply bring into our possession what is already in existence (αἱ κτητικαὶ τέχναι). Thus of the arts providing insight alone, we have two major divisions: (1) those that provide insight alone for its own sake; (2) those that provide insight alone for the sake of something else. Also, of the sciences providing not only insight but something else as well, we have two divisions: (1) those providing power over things; and (2) those providing being to things not first in existence, either producing them in the first place, or preserving them. We must now turn primarily to the *Sophist*, in order to discover something about the highly complex manner in which each of these four chief groups is further divided.

We shall start first of all with the arts of possession or conquest, since these include what are perhaps the first and most necessary arts in the order of generation. Man is an embodied being. Hence he cannot exist without at least a degree of power over the natural environment. First of all, he must have some skill in moving about from place to place. Later on, this develops into the highly complex arts of transportation, navigation, and other subsidiaries, which make places accessible.[46] Furthermore man cannot exist without the power of acquiring certain inorganic substances such as water and rock. This is provided by rudimentary craft in digging, quarrying, damming, and diving (specifically mentioned by Plato in *Sophist*),[47] which develop into the arts of mining, excavation, irrigation, deep-sea diving, etc. Even more essential for human existence is the acquisition of living substance both for shelter and for food; hence the primitive arts of woodcutting, fishing, and hunting, with their modern technical offspring. Irrational beings cannot be brought under technical control without the employment of force. These arts, therefore, achieve their ends in ways which are required by the very nature of their matter, and are genuine.

When we approach those arts which provide men with power over other men, however, we find a multitude of spurious forms. There

[46] This art underlies all the other branches of acquisitive art, though it is not specifically mentioned in the *Sophist*. Plato often speaks of navigation, but he nowhere places it in any system of classification. Like so many other important details, this is left to the reader. Clearly the arts of transportation do not make anything not in existence before. They bring something already in existence (place) into our possession. Hence, according to the distinction of *Sophist*, 219, we must include them under the possessive or acquisitive arts.   [47] *Sophist*, 220 A 2.

are two chief ways of acquiring such power. One is by force or conquest, which may be either open, as in the case of the military commander, or secret, as in that of the popular demogogue who sways
the multitude by the appearance of rational argument. It is also
employed in private by the erotic art, which achieves its end by the
skillful offering of gifts, and by the sycophant and sophist, who use
different forms of flattery to gain money from others. Since man is
a rational being, his nature does not demand the employment of such
force, which acts without conscious consent (ἄκων). These "arts,"
therefore, are either altogether degenerate froms of flattery (κολακεία),
or makeshifts (ἐμπειρία), which are required only through lack of
the true art of human management, "the voluntarily accepted control
over voluntary bipeds" (τὴν δὲ ἑκούσιον καὶ ἑκουσίων διπόδων ἀγελαιοκομικὴν
ζῴων).[48] The use of military force or secret power over men is a
sign not of art, but of the failure of art. As true technical control is
gained over the human environment, these forcible makeshifts will
wither away.

The other way of exercising or acquiring power over men is by
voluntary exchange, or business, whose various subdivisions into
wholesale and retail, etc., we need not follow through in detail.[49]
These "arts" also, so far as they rest upon only *formal* consent, are
not legitimate. Economic *conquest* over other men is not in itself an
authentic work demanded by the nature of man, even if carried on
with the uninformed, and hence not really voluntary assent of him
who is conquered. At best, therefore, these arts of exchange can be
regarded only as incipient arts (ἐμπειρία), proceeding blindly, in
ignorance of their proper work and what it really demands. They
are, in fact, subsidiary techniques, distributing goods for body and
soul as required by the higher arts of public health, or hygiene, and
education under the direct supervision of statecraft. Accordingly both
in the *Republic* and in the *Laws*, Plato insists upon the most rigid
control of exchange by the state. So far as the arts of exchange have
detached themselves from all higher control and subordinated themselves to private gain, they have degenerated into a "fawning" art
(κολακεία), which achieves a mere accidental result (πάρεργον),
individual wealth, rather than the real work (ἔργον) — wealth for
the whole community.[50] As such they threaten the very life of the
whole technical enterprise. So much for the acquisitive arts.

[48] *Statesman*, 276 E.   [49] Cf. *Sophist*, 223 C 5 ff.   [50] Cf. *Rep.*, IV, 420 B ff.

We are now ready to turn to the *second* grand division, comprising the making or producing arts. These are of two sorts: (1) those which bring something into existence not previously existing before at all; and (2) those which exercise care over something already existent, which would otherwise pass away, and thus bring *further* existence into being. The former has divisions different from those of the possessing arts, for man cannot manufacture true *natural* things, such as rocks, or rivers, or oceans, though he may gain power over them. What he can make or produce falls into only two chief classes: (1) synthetic articles put together or formed from natural things, which are either instruments for the achieving of some positive aim, for "doing something" (ἔνεκα τοῦ ποιεῖν τι), as tools and implements of all sorts,[51] or for guarding against something (τοῦ μὴ πάσχειν ἀμυντήρια), as clothing, dwellings, and arms; and (2) the copies or idols (εἴδωλα) of these as well as of natural things. Accordingly there are two main branches of the making art, that which makes real synthetic things (αὐτουργική), and that which makes only idols (εἰδωλοποιική).[52]

The latter art, which plays a most significant role in human existence, is carefully analyzed in the *Sophist*,[53] since it comprises the art of thinking. First of all, "copies" may be of two kinds, one which is faithfully copied after the original (ἡ εἰκών), or one which is rather copied after the way this original thing appears to our faculties (τό εἴδωλον). This is a most essential distinction, though most apt to be overlooked. According to Plato, the whole difference between a good "artist" and a bad one lies in this distinction. If he succeeds in constructing only an "idol," which *seems* to be like the real thing he is imitating, the "artist" has no place in a well-governed city. If, on the other hand, he constructs a genuine image (εἰκών), which reveals the true nature of the thing, he is performing the useful educational function of eliciting insight into reality, or even the purely noetic function of discovery. Sculpture which employs the medium of stone, painting which employs the medium of color, music which employs the medium of sound, and drama which employs the motions

---

[51] *Statesman*, 279 C 8. These are later classified into implement proper (ὄργανον), vessel or container (ἀγγεῖον), and vehicle (ὄχημα) — 287–289. Coins, seals, and stamps may be viewed as implements of a certain sort, or as ornament (εἰς κόσμον, 289 B 6), in which case they cannot be ranked as truly technical works — cf. *Gorgias*, 464.

[52] *Sophist*, 266 D.   [53] *Sophist*, 233–237, and 266 D–end.

and acts of living men, may all achieve true images of reality, though mere subjective phantasms are by far more common. But the most important medium for the making of copies is that of verbal arguments and thoughts (λόγοι). If they are combined in such a way as to embody the real structure of reality, they constitute the true images of science and philosophy. If, on the other hand, they are "made up" so as to resemble appearances only, they constitute that false opinion on which rest sophistry (false philosophy) and rhetoric (false education), two of the most basic forms of "flattery" or quackery.[54] So much for the idol-making arts.

The arts which bring *new* artefacts into being comprise weaving, shoemaking, architecture, shipbuilding, carpentry, forging, etc. The guiding factor in all of them is the art of quantitative mensuration (μετρητική, *Phil.*, 55 E), and they become more exact, or more truly technical, in so far as they proceed by an exact canon of measurement rather than by mere rule of thumb.[55] They easily sink to the level of routine practice (τριβή), and, if not properly guided, may fall prey to distorted types of distribution.[56]

We may now turn to the therapeutic arts which do not so much bring a new thing *into* being as preserve the being of something already there. Such therapy is involved in all the making arts, for no one ever really brings an artefact into being, if he has made no provision for its continued duration. Thus today, for example, the pressing and cleaning of clothes is a part of the art of tailoring, and shipbuilding includes the painting and overhauling of ships. To each manufacturing art belongs a subsidiary art, devoted to the care and preservation of the finished product. Even certain inorganic things, such as the soil used by agriculture, now have special arts devoted to their therapy, such as agricultural chemistry which seeks to maintain the fertility of the land. But the most important therapeutic arts are devoted to the preservation of living things. First of all, there are forestry and agriculture which look after the welfare of trees and plants, then the various kinds of animal husbandry, cattle raising, shepherding, poultry farming, etc., with all their subsidiary

---

[54] Cf. *Sophist*, 233 ff.; *Gorgias*, 465 B–C. Thus there are two forms of copymaking, εἰκαστικὴν καὶ φανταστικήν, philosophy and its false imitation, sophistry, *Soph.*, 236 C. For the true art of rhetoric, τὴν τοῦ τῷ ὄντι ῥητορικοῦ τε καὶ πιθανοῦ τέχνην, cf. *Phaedrus*, 269 C 6 ff., and *Gorgias*, 480 ff.

[55] *Phil.*, 55 E ff.

[56] Cf. *infra*, pp. 86–87 and 309 ff.

crafts, such as veterinary surgery, etc., which look after the welfare of animals. Finally, as the most essential of such arts, there is medicine which tends the human body.

In this, as in all therapeutic art, we may distinguish two portions,[57] one which corrects diseases and malformations once they have attacked the organism, the art of healing (ἡ ἰατρικὴ τέχνη), and another which prevents disease by a maintenance of the normal state, hygiene in the broad sense (γυμναστική). In the latter we may distinguish two further varieties, one which corrects malformations at an early stage before they become serious enough to require surgery or medicine,[58] and another, hygiene proper, which is purely preventive, reinforcing that proper regimen which constitutes health, and thus avoiding the tiniest root of disease. These distinctions bear an important analogy, as we shall see later, to those separating the different branches of statesmanship and education, the arts which tend the rational soul. In the case of all such therapeutic arts, the corrective portion is more apparent but less important, while the regulative portion is largely hidden but far more essential. Hence there is grave danger lest "prevention" and "maintenance," the real work (ἔργον) of the art, be overlooked, and attention exclusively devoted to the correction of diseases already there, a mere by-product of the art (πάρεργον). In this way, medicine comes to be looked upon as essentially consisting of surgery and the giving of drugs, while social hygiene and public health administration are overlooked. It may thus lose all guiding or planning power, and sink to the level of a mere routine correction of cases (τριβή), as is also true of the art of justice or maintaining the law.

We have now completed our survey of the various handicrafts (χειροτεχνίαι), which either gain possession over something, bring something into being, or care for the welfare of something. We must now turn to the third major division of the arts, that which commands or directs (ἐπιτακτική), providing not so much skill or technique as knowledge for the *direction* of those manifold activities and techniques comprised under any developed art. Thus, in the naval art, there is the guiding knowledge of the commander, who does not so much sail any particular ship as direct the operations as a whole, determining the appropriate time (καιρός) for each maneuver. In the building art,

---

[57] Cf. *Gorgias*, 464 B 6.
[58] Cf. *Sophist*, 229 A 1: περὶ μὲν αἴσχος (slight deformity).

there is the architect, who is neither excavator, mason, nor carpenter, but who directs these subordinate activities in accordance with the blueprint or plan. In addition to the groom, the trainer, and the coachman, who look after each horse individually, there is the horse-keeper (ἱπποφορβός), who looks after the common needs of the whole stable.[59] In accordance with the general principle that the higher natures are subject to the more serious corruptions,[60] it is precisely these controlling arts which are the most difficult to carry out, and hence the most easily distorted into subjection to spurious ends (κολακεία). It is always possible for the practitioner of a directing art to substitute his own interest for the proper work of the art. This confusion concerning the end then penetrates into the whole formal structure of the art. *Apparent* results will often fit in better with the subjective interest of the person in command than genuine achievements, since they usually require less effort. If such misuse is allowed to persist, the genuine knowledge which guides the art will gradually give way to a set of technical prescriptions for producing this or that desired "result." In this way, the art will be paralyzed at the very head, its moves being dictated by a combination of blind desire plus detailed technique, hidden beneath a deceptive cloak of advertising propaganda, devised to flatter its victims. An elaborate technical terminology is often employed to convey a false sense of difficulty and deep accomplishment. As Plato indicates in the *Phaedrus*,[61] this use of an unnecessarily "technical" vocabulary, which cannot be coherently explained, is one of the sure indications of a decadent art. The two most important directing arts, that of statesmanship and that of education, are peculiarly susceptible to such corruptions.

The relation between these two supreme arts, both of which are therapeutically directed towards improving the life of men, is a most complicated one. So intricately are they interwoven with one another that Plato himself, in his involved and lengthy considerations of them, seems hardly to have made up his mind as to which really directs the other. At first, proceeding according to the analogy of the other tending arts, it would seem as though the statesman, like the horse-raiser, should dictate to "the trainer" how the citizens are to be educated. The state embraces all the various activities of man. Hence the art of statesmanship is all-inclusive. Even education must be carried on under the guidance of the statesman for the service of the state. Such, in fact, is the view of Callicles in the *Gorgias*.[62]

But it rests upon the confusion of two arts which are distinct though not separate. The political art (ἡ πολιτικὴ τέχνη) attends to all those needs of the citizens which may be contrived or arranged by art. Hence its function is directive or legislative (ἐπιτακτική). This function is divided into two portions, analogous to the corrective (ἰατρική) and preservative (γυμναστική) portions of medicine.[63] Thus it belongs to the art of government to apply corrective justice (δίκη) through the courts for the healing of disorders once they have developed. But its primary task is purely therapeutic or preventive. This is achieved by "the art of setting laws" (ἡ νομοθετικὴ τέχνη), which establishes the correct order of subordination in the lesser arts, and governs the proper distribution of their products to the citizens, thus providing them with "wealth, freedom, and immunity from faction" [64] in the proper proportions.

But these things will not improve the citizens unless they understand what is being done, and hence themselves participate in the whole process. To provide this understanding is the special task of the educative art (ἡ διδασκαλικὴ τέχνη), which devotes itself to the nurture of the rational part of the soul, and directs the teaching of all special disciplines to this end. Hence it belongs to the directing arts, like politics, with which it was confused by the Sophists, who conceived of education as the imposition of a certain external pattern on the thought of a child.[65] But, as Plato was careful to point out,[66] and as the English word still implies, education is not so much the imposition of an externally contrived order as a "drawing out and leading up to the correct order" already in existence.[67] It is the apprehension of this order by the soul itself which education must arrange. Hence it stands midway between statesmanship, which directs all that can be contrived, and philosophy which seeks only to reveal what is true. The task of education is, so far as possible, to arrange for this in the young. By its various contrivances it "leads" them to an insight which in itself is uncontrived, since it apprehends what is real and independent of all human contrivance. Education is, there-

[62] *Gorgias*, 484–485.   [63] *Gorgias*, 464 B and C.   [64] *Euthydemus*, 292 B.
[65] Cf. *Prot.*, 325 D–327 B, and *infra*, p. 275.
[66] *Rep.*, 518 C–D.
[67] *Laws*, 659 D.

fore, distinct from statecraft, which supervises all the lesser arts of contrivance. The end of education, however, is the truth, which is uncontrived. Hence it follows methods peculiar to itself, and stands over statecraft as the primary art.

The statesman himself, being no god, must be educated, like all the rest, in his art, and the space of a single lifetime is insufficient for perfect mastery. Even under the ideal conditions visualized in the *Republic*, the guardians spend the last years of their lives in attempting to complete their education.[68] The dying soul leaves everything else behind but takes its education to the other world with it for further improvement and completion.[69] Life under earthly conditions is insufficient for the education of a human being. Hence the true statesman will not interfere with the peculiar processes essential to rational nurture, but will rather order all the other agencies and activities of the state *to* this end, guarding it in its full integrity and preserving it from all external distortion.[70] His own acts, of course, will be determined by the true principles which education has "led" him to understand. When a government refuses to be so determined, and "takes the law into its own hands," distortions occur, no matter how effectively it may achieve lesser goals. Thus monarchy passes into tyranny, aristocracy into oligarchy, and democracy into the rule of a mob.[71]

Statesmanship attends rationally to all the nonrational needs of the human flock. Education attends rationally to the specifically rational needs of the rational animal. Hence it is also defined as therapy of the soul (παιδεία δύναμις θεραπευτικὴ ψυχῆς),[72] keeping its governing portion, reason, in a sound condition, just as statecraft maintains the general welfare of the citizens, and hygiene maintains the health of the body. Thus, as in the case of these therapeutic arts, education also consists of a corrective and a regulative portion.[73] The first, which includes the elementary education of the child, sets the child right (νουθετητική), checking bad tendencies by punishment and fostering good ones by praise. It produces a formal correctness but leaves the root of the matter untouched, just as medical "treatment" may only conceal a disease by constantly eliminating minor symptoms. Admonition from external sources may similarly

---

[68] *Rep.*, 540 A–B.
[70] *Rep.* 424 B–427.
[72] [Plato], *Definitiones*, 416.

[69] *Phaedo*, 107 D.
[71] *Statesman*, 291 C–292.
[73] *Sophist*, 229 E–230 D.

produce a child who will do nothing wrong while under supervision, but who, since his faculties are untrained, will at once do wrong as soon as he is left to himself, as he must be sooner or later. The purely *regulative* branch of education, which is much more difficult and rare, helps the child by helping him to help himself. It attacks the *basic source* of all intellectual disease, *involuntary* ignorance.[74] Hence it does not so much admonish the child or pupil as show him the reasons for things, and does not so much *impose* the real reason on the child as enable him to distrust his own opinions, and hence to discover this reason for himself. Its procedure is thus indirect and ironical. This lengthy and arduous procedure is the most effective mode of teaching, though admonition, especially in dealing with children, is indispensable. Even the Socratic dialogues are full of *direct* warning and advice. Because the goal of education is to teach the pupil to apprehend the truth himself, does not mean that he is simply to be left alone. Direct admonition is the cruder, but nonetheless indispensable, corrective tool of education, the suggestions of free education (παιδεία) its more delicate, consummatory instrument.

This art must always guard itself against political interference. The statesman, of course, has an interest in the education of the citizens. Indeed, as we have seen, this is the proper end of all true statesmanship. But politics is subject to constant strains both internal and external, and decisions must constantly be made. In difficult situations it is very easy for statesmen to forget the true aim of their art, and to conceive of their function as merely to preserve things as they are, or to keep a certain party in power. Such a lawless government, whether it takes the form of tyranny, oligarchy, or mass rule, will then try to dominate education and reverse the proper relation between the two. The cry is raised that education must be "useful" or "practical" — that is, useful for the interests of those in control, as Callicles frankly argues in the *Gorgias*.

Education is then regarded as the art of indoctrinating children with a particular "point of view." The higher and more essential part of education (παιδεία) is entirely sacrificed, and only the lower admonitory part (νουθετητική) remains. The teacher no longer considers himself as a guide or servant, leading the pupil toward a reality independent of all human caprice, but, like Protagoras, regards himself as a master, indoctrinating the pupil with customs, habits,

[74] ἀμαθία: *Sophist*, 230 A–B.

and theories which men have contrived.[75] Any particular law or custom which happens to prevail is its own justification.[76] There is no *ultimate* justification lying in the nature of things. Hence education loses all stable guidance, falls under the domination of the *status-quo*, and sinks to the level of quackery (κολακεία). The so-called educator is then "free" to devote himself to different, complicated, admonitory techniques, all of which are more or less capable of producing that general command of language and culture (ἡ ῥητορική), or that mastery of particular crafts (χειρουργία), which are pleasing to the state, and, therefore, lead to social success, a mere accidental concomitant of the real work (ἔργον) of the educator. There is no external or forcible remedy for this disease once it has arisen. The only remedy is to undertake the task of reviving in both teacher and pupil that hunger for the truth without which a free or rational education [77] is impossible.

By the criticism of mere opinion, which is artificial or contrived, it is possible to lead men to those stable and permanent truths embodied in the sciences and philosophy. These alone are capable of illumining education, together with statecraft and all the other subordinate arts, with a clear and trustworthy guiding light. Hence we now turn to the last of the four major divisions of *techne*, that which provides knowledge for its own sake alone, and upon which all the others depend.[78] Thus there is no art or craft which does not involve arithmetical counting and reckoning. Navigation depends upon the pure science of astronomy, which seeks only to discover the structure of the earth and the heavenly bodies with no ulterior purpose at all. Medicine depends upon the pure sciences of anatomy and physiology, which simply describe living structure as it is — and similarly with the rest of the arts. If the guiding knowledge, which lies at the core of each, is not based on things as they really are, apart from all contrivance and construction, their own technical constructions cannot be distinguished from magical charms, and the doctor, for example, from a successful quack.

The pure sciences, therefore, are acquisitive rather than productive in character. Scientists are really "hunters." [79] They seek to penetrate

[75] *Prot.*, 325 D–327 B.   [76] *Theaet.*, 172 A.
[77] Cf. *Ep.*, VII, 334 B, and *Prot.*, 312 B.
[78] Which Aristotle called theoretical science, dividing it against *techne*. But the basic conception is the same.
[79] θηρευτικοί: *Euthyd.*, 290 C 1.

through every disguise of appearance and opinion in order to discover the nature of each thing as it is. This discovery is their work (ἔργον). Before the basic acquisitive arts can make the physical, biological, and social environments accessible for further technical control, something must be already known of their nature. The sciences, physical, biological, and social, seek to advance this basic knowledge further, and thus to make the world intellectually accessible to man. Each different phase of the environment requires a different technique of investigation, and in the more advanced sciences this technical side has been developed to enormous proportions, but the true aim of all scientific instruments, operations, and experimental procedures is to discover the nature of things. When this aim is lost sight of, and no further *insight* into reality is achieved, science ceases, and its various operations and procedures fall prey to an illicit domination by the various arts and crafts. Physics tends to serve engineering, physiology to serve medicine, and sociology to serve the needs of some particular form of statecraft. But neither the craft nor the science is really served by this inversion of order. The crafts continue to "go on," or "progress," with new technical elaborations, but *essentially* as they were before. Without more light on the nature of the various structures which determine their procedures they cannot really advance from the level of ἐμπειρία in a truly technical direction. The sciences, on the other hand, lose their intelligibility, and disintegrate into more and more atomistic specialities without relation to one another. Unless some remedy is found, the whole culture will fall under the sway of some plausible sophistry, which is contrived or invented by the rulers of the state to further their interests, and bears no real relation to things as they really are.

Science can be protected from this catastrophe only by the cultivation of philosophy, which examines the basic hypotheses,[80] such as "number," "matter," "motion," "living creature," "animal," and "man," which the various sciences simply accept without careful criticism, in the attempt to discover their true nature, and the broader structures into which they fall as parts of the world as a whole. Such discovery is its work (ἔργον). The whole technical enterprise depends upon the success or failure of this crucial endeavor. So far as it succeeds, the vast array of arts, and crafts, and sciences is provided with a legitimate, final end, and a reliable, guiding light. So far as it fails,

[80] ὑποθέσεις : *Rep.*, 510 C.

no matter how clearly minor areas are understood, and how successfully minor ends are achieved, the rationality and legitimacy of the
whole enterprise is jeopardized. In the last analysis, no one of the
myriad craftsmen and technicians will be able to give an account
(λόγον διδόναι) of what he is doing, or why he is doing it. They
will be like sailors on a great ship, without any pilot, sailing off on
a voyage, perhaps full of revelry and mutual congratulation, but without any well-conceived plan.[81] As Plato says, the final end of such
a voyage may be easily predicted.[82] Indeed, he himself witnessed the
catastrophic end of just such a voyage, undertaken by his own city of
Athens, in the stormy days of his youth.

The most essential portion of the philosophic art is dialectic, which
combines and separates the major, formal structures of being, such
as motion, rest, identity, and difference, as they actually are. Every
definition is a combining of distinct things together into a genus,
and a separating out of the specific differences. Hence dialectic lies
at the root of any science, which must possess at least a vague conception of what it is (τὸ τί ἐστι) it is studying. As the science
becomes more exact, its definitions become clearer and more independent of factual observation. Thus geometry advances to a position where it no longer has to measure the sides and angles of this or
that particular triangle, but where it penetrates to the formal structure
of *the* triangle, which explains the various relations of sides and angles
approximately exemplified in any particular. But even mathematics,
the purest of the sciences, never reaches the point where it can altogether dispense with examples, constructions, and empirical general-
izations. This is because its "hypotheses" (number, space, figure,
etc.) are simply assumed on the basis of concrete observation or
imagination. Dialectic takes these basic structures, "placed under"
(ὑποθέσεις) the sciences, and attempts to determine how they are
combined and separated with one another to constitute the formal
pattern of the world. But this means, it may be shown that there is
one supreme principle (ἀρχή) in which they all "blend," and which,
though distinct from all the subordinate forms, nevertheless enables
them to be ordered into a single, universal pattern. To reveal this
pattern as clearly as possible, and to achieve some knowledge of its
unifying principle and source, is the peculiar task of dialectic.

This goal may be achieved, however, only to a limited degree. The

---

[81] *Rep.*, 488.   [82] *Rep.*, 488 C 21.

supreme principle lies beyond any intelligible object of our apprehension.[83] Hence, instead of starting with this and proceeding downward [84] through the lesser forms, explaining them with reference to their "source" (ἀρχή), we are forced to take "the second best course." [85] Starting from less important forms, which are, however, better known to us, we "place under" them (ὑποθέμενος) [86] those higher forms which are judged the strongest. Thus by proceeding up *toward* the source rather than down, we may gain a hazy knowledge of its nature. Here and there, dialectic succeeds in laying bare certain formal structures so that we may go in *both* directions, up (ἐπὶ τὴν ἀρχήν) [87] and down ([ἀπὸ τῆς ἀρχῆς] ἐπὶ τελευτήν).[88] But when it comes to the *ultimate* principle we can move only hesitantly upward.[89] This leaves many questions of supreme importance to every human soul unanswered. In these matters we must take what reliable knowledge we can gain, and then proceed to formulate the *best opinion*. The *final* portion of philosophy is the construction of such grounded opinions, which Plato called speculation (μυθολογία), and generally placed at the end of a dialogue or dialectical discussion, in order to guide it by as firm a rational, or dialectical foundation as possible.

One of the gravest dangers confronting the whole philosophical enterprise is the tendency to indulge in myth *too quickly*, before the resources of dialectic have been fully exploited. This leads to scepticism, and a general discrediting of philosophy. One opinion is regarded as no more well grounded than another, and the whole of philosophy is thought to consist in the formulation of such opinions, and their argumentative defense by one individual against another, both being mere concomitants (πάρεργα). One essential duty of philosophy is to guard the enterprise against such speculative sophistry, and the further distortions it brings with it, and to recall men to those basic dialectical truths which are within their reach. Hence

[83] ἐπέκεινα τῆς οὐσίας: *Rep.*, 509 B.
[84] Cf. καταβαίνῃ: *Rep.* (Adam), 511 B 13.
[85] *Phaedo*, 99 C 9.
[86] *Phaedo*, 100 A 3.
[87] *Rep.* (Adam), 511 B 12.
[88] *Phaedo*, 510 B 11; cf. Aristotle, *Eth. Nic.*, 1095 A 32. In general it may be said that, in the earlier dialogues, the movement is upward or hypothetical, from the instances to the genus, while, in the later dialogues, the movement is downward, from the genus to the species and subspecies.
[89] Cf. *Ep.*, VII, especially 341 C–D.

philosophy has four distinct functions, each of which can be identified in almost any dialogue of Plato: (1) protreptic, introducing the student to philosophy by showing him its supreme importance as underlying the whole technical enterprise, and awakening him to its possibility; (2) the criticism of sophistry and ungrounded speculative opinion; (3) dialectic, the process of arriving at exact definitions which lay bare the formal structure of things, particularly the basic structure of the world as a whole; and (4) mythical speculation, with some ground in 3, concerning the nature of the supreme principle, and the ultimate destiny of the soul.

The last division brings us to what is now termed *religion*, defined in the *Euthyphro* as "devotion to the divine" (τὴν τῶν θεῶν θεραπείαν),[90] or, more exactly, "the art of carrying on transactions between Gods and men." [91] Hence the art has two aspects: first, that of prayer (εὔχεσθαι), in which we ask something of the Gods, and second, sacrifice (θύειν), in which we render to them what is their due. Such activities must, so far as possible, be guided by knowledge.[92] All men have a sense of reverence (αἰδώs),[93] even though it never be fully awakened, for that which is holy (τὸ ὅσιον), and thus demands worship. But since worship is directed to what lies beyond our perfect apprehension, it is peculiarly susceptible to mixture with all sorts of false opinion, when it sinks to the level of superstition. Instead of being the supreme art, to which all the other arts are ordered, religion is then apt to shrink to a few special theories and magical practices divorced from the rest of life.[94] The second and more important sacrificial phase of religion then sinks into oblivion, and only the asking or seeking function remains. Once again πάρεργον is substituted for ἔργον. We turn to religion for the sake of comfort or relief, or something else we can obtain, and thus "get the better of the bargain, gaining good things from the divine but giving nothing in return." [95]

Religion can be protected against these distortions only by the philosophic understanding, which purifies the sacred myths and practices of tradition, restoring them to that supreme and culminating position from which human ignorance (ἀμαθία) and pride (ὕβρις)

---

[90] *Euth.*, 12 E 6.
[91] Ἐμπορικὴ ἄρα τις ἂν εἴη, ᾧ Εὐθύφρων, τέχνη ἡ ὁσιότης θεοῖς καὶ ἀνθρώποις παρ' ἀλλήλων. *Euth.*, 14 E 6.
[92] *Euth.*, 14 C 5.
[93] Cf. *Euth.*, 12.
[94] Cf. *Euth.*, 5 and 6.   [95] *Euth.*, 15 A 2–4.

are constantly seeking to remove them for their own ends, and thus to reduce them to forms of quackery (κολακεία). Hence in the *Euthyphro*, Socrates attempts to reason with a "religious" fanatic who has uncritically accepted many of the current myths and magical formulae, and in the *Republic* [96] he has only scorn for "those mendicant priests and seers" who peddle protective charms and incantations. The upshot of such criticism is not so much to substitute other opinions and theories, "to make up new Gods," [97] as to make men aware of their own ignorance in such matters, and to bring them face to face with the truly mysterious but undeniable fact of "the holy" (τὸ ὅσιον).

3. The Technical Hierarchy and Its Inversion

It is impossible to study any careful classification of the arts and crafts, such as that of Plato, without discerning the hierarchical order into which they fall. Thus the acquisitive arts provide those geographic, mineral, plant, and animal materials which are utilized by the productive arts for further purposes. After catching his prey, the hunter hands it over to the cook.[98] After capturing the city, the general hands it over to the statesman, who alone knows how to govern it.[99] Conquest is never an end in itself. The raw materials, provided by the basic acquisitive arts of exploration, mining, woodcutting, and hunting, are utilized by the productive arts, which form these materials into implements, houses, ships, and food. These products then serve as materials for still higher arts which use them for their purposes. The house is managed by the household manager, the ship is sailed by the navigator, the food administered by the doctor and the dietician. It is the art of statesmanship in some form which must direct these subordinate arts, distributing their various products, and regulating them for the best interests of the community, in accordance with the knowledge preserved by tradition (νόμος), and rationally purified by higher education (παιδεία). This knowledge is further clarified and amplified by the pure sciences, and philosophy, which, in union with theology, brings it into relation with that for the sake of which (τὸ οὗ ἕνεκα) all things exist, and thus embraces all technical agencies and activities within the scope of a single plan. Only so may the technical enterprise be maintained in its full integrity.

[96] *Rep.*, 364 B 12 ff.
[98] *Euthyd.*, 290 B.
[97] *Euth.*, 5 A 7.
[99] *Euthyd.*, 290 E-D.

At this point, we may well raise the question as to what is the function (ἔργον) of this enterprise as a whole. What is the purpose of all this planning and contriving? Plato's answer is unambiguous. Art (τέχνη) is always *for* the sake of something. The whole enterprise exists for the sake of practice (πρᾶξις). This takes us at last beyond the range of art, which is rational action flowing out into the external world, and hence distinct from the reason which flows into our own acts. Such reason is not art but rather virtue (ἀρετή), which is not concerned "with things outside a man but with his own action." [100] The *primary* task of virtue is to achieve actual insight (σοφία) so far as possible. On this all other virtue depends: (1) justice (δικαιοσύνη), or rational action in general, which demands (2) courage (ἀνδρεία), or persistence through time, and (3) temperance (σωφροσύνη), submissiveness of instinct, desire, and passion, the "raw material" of life. The work (ἔργον) of virtue is "life itself" (τὸ ζῆν),[101] "according to its real nature" (κατὰ φύσιν).[102]

Thus the whole technical hierarchy provides conditions materially necessary for the exercise of virtue, as the shipbuilder provides a condition materially necessary for the exercise of navigation. Virtue without art is like a navigator with no ship. But art without virtue is like a fleet with no navigator. Hence virtue is superior to art, and can "make up" for technical deficiencies, just as a skillful commander can often "do well" with a very deficient navy. It is *possible* for individuals here and there to live virtuous lives in communities where art is undeveloped, or even where the whole technical order has been inverted and corrupted.[103] Anyone who succeeds in doing this "will have achieved a great work, . . ." but not the greatest, unless he finds a technically well-ordered community (πολιτεία).[104] Without this he will be hampered and thwarted, like an able captain in a rotten ship. The understanding of *techne*, therefore, while not the most important part of wisdom, is a branch of wisdom or philosophy, subsidiary to virtue. Disorganization and disorder in the arts constitute grave, though not the gravest, obstacles lying in the way of human life. To these we must now turn.

---

[100] οὐ περὶ τὴν ἔξω πρᾶξιν τῶν αὑτοῦ ἀλλὰ περὶ τὴν ἐντός. *Rep.*, 443 C 20. Cf. *infra*, pp. 90 ff.
[101] *Rep.*, 353 D 27.
[102] *Rep.*, 444 D.
[103] Cf. *Rep.*, VI, 496 B ff.
[104] *Rep.*, 496 E.

Wherever things merely happen without plan (ἀλόγως) there is no art. Even though he shows great technical proficiency in minor respects, the shipbuilder is not really practicing his art unless he produces something which meets the requirements of the navigator. Shipbuilding exists for the sake of the ship. The ship does not exist for the sake of shipbuilding.[105] It is the "using" art,[106] in this case navigation, which plans what the "lower" art, in this case shipbuilding, is then "free" to carry out in the most effective manner possible. The work (ἔργον) of the lower art is a condition materially necessary for the higher. In this case, the lower art is an accessory to the cause (συναίτιον). But the higher art (navigation) is the cause (τὸ αἴτιον), since it apprehends the complete structure which is dictated by the end, and thus achieves the real goal.[107] Of course, each "requires" the other. But the higher "requires" the lower only equivocally, as a *condition* for its actualization in this or that situation. Such conditions may vary over a wide range. Thus the navigator needs *some* sort of a ship, it is true. But if he knows his art, he can "get along with" a small yacht or even a skiff. The improvement of such conditions must not be confused with the improvement of the art itself. Of what "use" is a technically perfect navy, if no one knows how to navigate it? The lower arts, on the other hand, "require" the higher unequivocally, as what is always essential (αἴτιον) under *any* condition (συναίτιον). This hierarchical order is sometimes difficult to determine, especially in the case of the higher arts. But we have never really understood an art until we know which arts minister to it as accessory agencies, and which art makes use of its final achievement. Each "work" serves as a condition for some further goal.

This is true throughout the hierarchy. The "ends" of the arts and sciences are not separate or "relative." Each is subordinate to another. Theology lays down certain specifications which determine the general form of philosophy, which in turn defines or determines the basic structures, such as matter, motion, life, and man, governing the procedures of the sciences. This knowledge, embodied in the sciences and philosophy, guides the various activities and agencies of education in forming the young. The nature of these processes prescribes the duties of the statesman, who, "above all," [108] must strive to estab-

---

[105] *Phil.*, 54 B.
[106] ἡ χρωμένη τέχνη: *Euthyd.*, 289 C 3; cf. 280 C–281 C and *Rep.*, 601 D.
[107] *Statesman*, 281 D 11 ff.   [108] *Rep.*, 424 A–B.

lish and maintain a proper system of education. Only with this end in view can he proceed to regulate the various arts of therapy and production, weaving them all together into a truly harmonious pattern.

This domination by the using or directing art (ἐπιτακτική) over its subordinate arts is in no sense an arbitrary dictation, but arises out of the very nature of art, the rational control of a certain changing matter for a specific end. Each art, therefore, dominates its matter, but is in turn dominated by the form or structure determined by its end. When an art "frees" itself from its determining form, giving way rather to the matter which it should dominate, the natural order is reversed, and the various distortions we have noted in the case of specific arts at once arise. But each art is not an isolated phenomenon. It is structurally united with other arts in a hierarchy. Hence no single art can sink to the level of a technique without at the same time distorting other arts which lie below it. Distortions of this sort in the higher arts, which are more comprehensive and difficult to maintain, are therefore peculiarly dangerous, since lack of plan here affects the whole subordinate hierarchy. Each art, as its guiding light becomes dim or confused, loses its control over those lying beneath it, and instead of dominating them and directing them to a clearly envisaged goal, gives way to their blind, material demands. In this way the whole technical process is pushed *from behind* by material pressure, rather than being guided *from ahead* according to plan, and becomes a gigantic system of routine, subject to various types of illicit control (κολακεία). This *materializing* of the arts is not peculiar to any particular branch, such as the arts of production, but is discernible at every level of the hierarchy. It is to this *general* inversion of the whole hierarchical order and its principal causes that we must now turn.

Each art deals with a certain matter of its own, organizing or forming it according to plan. Hence any art, no matter how relatively "immaterial" its matter may be, is subject to materialization. Indeed, it is precisely the "higher," or "most immaterial" arts, which are peculiarly prone to imperceptible domination by their matter. Thus philosophy, becoming isolated from theology, and losing its organizing principle, gives way to science,[109] either passively receiving its "results" without serious criticism, and incorporating them in great, synthetic systems, or else obeying the pressure of some particularly vigorous science,

---

[109] Cf. *Rep.*, 495 C ff.

such as mathematics or sociology, and looking at everything else from this point of view. Both of these represent a passive submission to matter which really requires *philosophical* ordering. But even when such ordering is attempted, the theories so formulated may only express the absence of any purely philosophical formalizing structure, as is true of scepticism in its various forms. This privative mode of philosophizing is most clearly manifest, and, therefore, least dangerous in theories of materialism, which more or less explicitly deny the reality of all form, frankly abdicating in favor of matter, and thus providing an *apologia* for the philosophical failures of philosophy. It is less apparent, but even more dangerous, in the contrary theories of idealism, which deny the reality of any matter requiring organization, and thus leave the way clear for irresponsible, sophistic speculation. These two opposite types of theory are closely related,[110] as are all opposites.[111] When one appears on the philosophic horizon, the other is close at hand. Each is a danger signal, betraying the fact that the vast array of facts and structures, revealed by common sense and the sciences, is not being properly comprehended and ordered. By denying, on the one hand, that they can be comprehended, or on the other hand, that there is really anything to comprehend, these opposite doctrines [112] only prepare the way for complete capitulation to one or more of the sciences.

The sciences themselves are then distorted in the direction of one or the other of two opposite extremes. They either disintegrate into a set of disconnected specialties in which no mutual order is discerned, or they are arbitrarily subjected to the tyrannical control of some particular method or "point of view" appropriate to certain ones but not to others. Thus, without that philosophic guidance which is capable of seeing the peculiar nature of each one without ignoring its relations to the rest, the sciences are either artificially separated or artificially confused. Oscillation from one extreme to the other only betrays more clearly a fundamental lack of guiding insight. This cannot be supplied by any search for "*the* nature of scientific method as such," or any "unity of science" imposed from the standpoint of science alone. Each science has its own peculiar subject matter, and

110 *Theaet.*, 180 D–181 B; cf. *Sophist*, 246 A–C.

111 τὸ γὰρ ἐναντιώτατον τῷ ἐναντιωτάτῳ εἶναι μάλιστα φίλον: *Lysis*, 215 E 3; cf. *Phaedo*, 70 D 7 ff.

112 τἀναντία: *Theaet.*, 180 D 9.

its own peculiar methods of discovery. The true "unity of science," which will apprehend the nature of each in relation to the rest without any distortion, is not to be found in science but in philosophy, as the true rationale of *what* the shipbuilder is doing is not to be found in any of the subordinate aspects of this craft, but rather in the "higher" art of navigation.

When philosophy loses control of its matter, and the various sciences decompose into the anarchy of special techniques, education is also affected through this confusion of its only true, *measuring* principle. It may be most capable of producing this result or that, but loses its guiding sense of which result is the more correct. The result of this uncertainty is that, instead of imposing a certain rational pattern on its matter, the instinctive tendencies and desires of the child, it loses its control and gives way to the desires and interests of the child. Thus enfeebled, it falls an easy prey to statecraft, which, instead of guarding it and maintaining it, takes it under its own wing and uses it for its own ends. The concrete flow of events must be guided in one way or another, and when philosophy and education fail to offer proper guidance, the statesman must take things into his own hands, weaving the vast complex of lesser acquisitive powers and productive agencies into some sort of unity. Thus both philosophy and education, finally even religion, fall under the dominance of the state. This reversal of the natural order (philosophy — education —politics) was as familiar to Plato as it now is to us. He describes it at length in the *Gorgias*, and attributes to it the collapse of his own city, Athens.[113]

Without adequate guidance, supplied by education and philosophy, the statesman is at sea. He does not dare impose any rational pattern on the whole community. Indeed he is not cognizant of any such pattern. He must yield to the pressure of this subordinate interest or that, and thus materialize his statesmanship. At best he will be a compromiser, balancing one interest against another, so that no one tendency gets completely out of hand. But since such a balance is dictated not so much by the real nature of things as by an accidental, temporary state of affairs, it cannot endure. Certain subordinate agencies or interests *will* get out of hand. State policy will thus be "economically determined," or "controlled by party interest," or simply shifted from day to day to meet the caprices of popular desire.

[113] *Gorgias*, 517–520.

Such anarchy soon brings forth its opposite,[114] the imposition of an arbitrary authority or tyranny, both opposites being symptoms of the same disease, lack of rational guidance due to the materialization of higher arts.

It would be most tempting to follow this hierarchical inversion down through the lower arts, all of which are affected by failure at the top. We have time to pause briefly only for a short discussion of the malformation so far as it affects the productive arts in their two branches, copy-making (εἰδωλοποιική), and the production of independent things (αὐτουργική). Both of these technical malformations were clearly described by Plato, and both are peculiarly characteristic of our own supertechnicalized society.

We shall begin with the copy-making arts, since when properly carried out they perform the higher functions, though as is always the case, when imperfectly performed, they are fraught with the more serious consequences. Every man possesses the faculty of phantasy (φαντασία), and is, therefore, a maker of sensuous images or as we should say, an "artist." There is a "painter" in each one of us, who paints copies of those things, which have deeply impressed him, in his soul.[115] When this painter makes images in accordance with the nature of things, they are true (εἰκόνες ἀληθεῖς), but when he represents only some opinion, they may be false idols (εἴδωλα). The kind of picture to which a man most constantly clings in his phantasy is a good index of his character.[116] Since the community is "the individual soul writ large," [117] the analogous function is performed for society at large by the "artist" proper, who contrives images not merely out of the private stuff of imagination, but out of marble, color, sound, and spoken words, which can be perceived by all in common.

Since all men are first of all guided by what they perceive through the senses, this function of contriving sensuous copies of things plays a most important role in all the major directing arts. Thus divine frenzy may inspire the creation of hymns, and other types of image (εἰκών), which really convey religious truth, and thus "teach later generations." [118] The highest truths of philosophy and science are often arrived at through phantasy, and they must first be embodied in a sensuous or mythical form, if they are ever to be more adequately

114 *Rep.*, 565 ff.   115 *Phil.*, 39 B.   116 *Phil.*, 39 C–D–E.
117 *Rep.*, 368 D–E.   118 Cf. *Phaedrus*, 245 A.

understood by the child, who is incapable of pure reasoning. Hence image-making plays a dominant role in all elementary education. The creation of flags, emblems, memorials, and particularly persuasive images of speech, is essential to the art of statesmanship, which must constantly explain its purposes to the free citizen in terms which he can readily understand. Such images (εἰκόνες) provide both children and adults with an opportunity to exercise all of their faculties, without being *fully* exercised, as they must be in face of the dangers and stresses of actual life. Thus in plays and games the child imitates the trials and conflicts of maturity. All learning is a rehearsal, or half-serious imitation, of things which must be later performed with serious intent (reading, writing, reckoning, etc.). The wise educator, however, will keep this serious intent so far as possible in the background. All education is a kind of play.[119]

Play itself is one of the major arts, which continues to be practiced all through adult life, for a man never outgrows his phantasies. The images produced by the religious artist enable him to imitate, in an imaginary form, certain religious truths which he might not otherwise understand at all. The sculptor, the painter, the musician, the dramatist, and the planner of festivals surround him with a whole world of images, in terms of which he may imitate the real world, and all the various phases of real life, in the form of semi-thoughts and semi-acts, never *completely* carried out, but initiated under the guidance of phantasy. This *techne* of play (τὸ παίγνιον) [120] performs an essential function in practicing and maintaining faculties that might otherwise atrophy, and when guided properly by philosophical statesmanship is indispensable to healthy community life. When misused, however, it constitutes one of the most serious perversions of the whole technical enterprise, of which Plato was most keenly aware, and to the description of which he devoted many pages of his dialogues.[121]

It all depends on what the copy-maker succeeds in copying. If he is guided by science and philosophy to concentrate his attention on something as it really is in its own peculiar nature, he may, through perfect command over his material, succeed in making an image (εἰκών) which is more capable of suggesting the truth about that

---

[119] *Rep.*, 537 A.
[120] *Statesman*, 288 C.
[121] Cf. especially *Rep.*, Books II, III, and X (595 ff.); *Gorgias*, 501–503; *Laws*, 668 ff. and 796 ff.

thing than the common examples we see about us. Thus a skillful dramatist may succeed in suggesting more about the true nature of some passion, such as patriotism, for example, than is ordinarily suggested by the so-called "real" examples of this passion with which we are familiar. So far as the "artist's" images thus succeed in revealing reality as it is, they may be safely used in education and statesmanship. Such images, because of their revealing power, are more useful than all other technical products, since they aid no mere subordinate power, but the power of reason itself. Thus the maker of such images ranks higher than the mere artisan.[122]

But the attainment of genuine insight, which penetrates beyond the average, is a most difficult task, requiring prolonged effort and discipline (ἡ εἰκαστικὴ τέχνη). It is always a temptation for the artist "to free himself" from the shackles of all such guiding restraint, and to rest content with sheer technical control over his matter. This enables him to construct all sorts of copies in a certain material medium, without bothering about *what it is* they represent (ἡ φανταστικὴ τέχνη).[123] The first step in the degeneration of the image-making arts arises with the cry of "art for art's sake," and the attempt to isolate art from all subservience to religion, philosophy, and the higher guiding arts. While such a point of view is often defended as "idealistic" or "formalistic," its upshot is to concentrate attention on the material copy or "idol" (εἴδωλον) by itself, and thus to materialize the art. The copies come to occupy a special realm of their own in galleries and museums, apart from any social, educational, or philosophical context. This uselessness is regarded as the definitive value of art, and those arts to which this privilege of utter uselessness is granted, are termed "fine arts," in distinction to those which are "merely" useful.

The artist comes to regard himself as the maker not only of a "copy," but of an independent thing, having no further utility for the technical enterprise, but being an end in itself, which no shoemaker or potter, of course, would be arrogant enough to claim for his "useful" artefacts. By thus confusing himself with the artisan, as the maker of a *finer* sort of independent thing, the artist really becomes not superior but inferior to the artisan. Every maker must have something in mind when moulding his material. This is even more true of the copy-

---

[122] *Phaedrus*, 248 E.
[123] *Soph.*, 266 D 2 and 235 ff. Cf. *infra*, pp. 276–284.

maker than the ordinary artisan. What he has in mind is so important that he seeks to make no independent thing, but something reflecting what he sees with the eye of his mind. If his copy really radiates the essential nature of this thing, it is a truly fine image (εἰκών) of the original, and of great use to the higher art whose duty it is to understand this thing. But if the "artist" refuses to imitate such real structures, in order to free himself from all domination by higher arts, he does not thereby become a *finer* artist, as he pretends, but in reality much less "fine." He must have *something* in mind when he makes his image. Otherwise it is not an image at all, but an inferior artefact — this piece of colored canvas, or a lump of clay. Clearly he must form them after *some* model or archetype. If he refuses to take those real structures, which are the objects of philosophic and scientific study, for his models, he must simply descend to the level of imitating concrete things *as they appear*. Since these things are only imperfect examples, mixed with all sorts of alien, accidental matter, he will then be imitating an imitation, like an inferior carpenter, taking some individual, cast-off shuttle for his model, and simply copying this without having any understanding of the real nature of *what* he is about.[124] The product of such copy-work (τὸ φάντασμα) will be an inferior artefact, one remove further from reality than that of the ordinary craftsman, who holds before himself some essential structure, not a mere particular example. Some unity of form or structure doubtless radiates even from such imitations of imitations. But they have less true utility, and thus less true beauty, than a real pot or pan. As a matter of fact, they are a most formidable danger to any community in which they are cultivated.

Once the fine arts have "freed" themselves from all higher supervision, they become susceptible to the control of those impulses and desires of the "audience" which it is their true function to guide. The "free" artist cannot long resist the temptation of constructing that sort of image which will not so much instruct his audience as please it.[125] In this way, the true order of art is reversed, and the artist, whose function it is to work on the onlookers, is really worked on by them. Hence temples and places of worship are filled with objects which do not so much direct phantasy into truly religious channels as distort religion in such a way as to correspond to the unguided phantasies of the worshippers. Newspapers, theatres, and

---

[124] Cf. *Cratylus*, 389 B.   [125] Cf. *Gorgias*, 501 ff.

amusement palaces do not so much use easily comprehended figures and phantasies to convey essential truth as use essential truth to pander to the imagination of the multitude. The statesman does not so much use rhetoric to guide men into statesmanlike acts as merely to say to them most eloquently what they want to have said. In this way, a false and artificial world of phantasms (φαντάσματα) is created, which does not so much reflect the stable character of what is really so, as the fleeting opinions of the masses. The effect of such distortion on those youthful imitators who are given nothing better to imitate is disastrous in the extreme.

Instead of being led to exercise his faculties in ways which will prepare him for the real struggles of mature existence, the child, growing up in such a fantastic environment, will be taught to imitate whatever happens to accord with momentary desire. In this way, his reason, capable of apprehending the true structure of reality, is lamed and misused for the purpose of fitting all the particular facts making up his meagre experience into a distorted dream world, whose general outlines have been determined not so much by genuine insight as by the "interest" of those who control the state, and those "educators" and image-makers who have now become their tools. When this flimsy structure comes tumbling down, as sooner or later it must, with increasing age and the nearer approach of reality,[126] the youth is left confused and bewildered. He busies himself with argumentation (ἀντιλογικοὺς λόγους), and fancies himself "most wise" in holding that "no thing nor argument is really sound or trustworthy, but that everything is whirling up and down, topsy-turvy, as in the river Euripus, and never standing still." [127] Identifying this subjective confusion with the real state of things, he then becomes an irrationalist or misologist, distrusting all reason and argument, than which there is no greater evil.[128] But this is itself only pretense, for he cannot proceed to live the life of a man without some conception of himself and his world.

Instead of applying his skepticism to the delusive phantasms and opinions which have led him astray, he applies it indiscriminately to truth as well as to fiction. As a result he is no longer able to distinguish the two, and falls even more easily a victim to the "pleasing" phantasms provided by the rulers of this dream state, though he may scornfully refer to them as only "useful fictions or illusions." Nevertheless,

[126] *Sophist*, 234 D.   [127] *Phaedo*, 90 C.   [128] *Phaedo*, 89 D 2.

together with his fellow imitators, he is guided by them. Since they are far more "pleasing" and comfortable than the stark realities which cannot be altogether escaped, he turns to them more and more, living his life for the sake of play and amusement, sacrificing his real concerns to what is, properly speaking, only practice and preparation. As he turns more and more from reality for "relaxation" and escape, the gulf between illusion and reality is constantly widened, until the whole fantastic structure collapses in some great communal disaster, and the cycle begins once more.

The general materialization of *techne* so far as it affects the productive type of art ($\alpha\dot{v}\tau o\pi o\iota\kappa\dot{\eta}$), as also described by Plato,[129] is no less characteristic of modern society. When the guiding arts of philosophy and statesmanship become weakened and confused, the productive arts chafe at the leash, and set up the cry for autonomy and *laissez faire*. When this is achieved, the sheer production of various goods and articles no longer submits to the control of a distribution, *planned* by the statesmen to meet the *real* needs of the whole community, but is regarded as an end in itself. Hence essential needs are overlooked, and vast energy is consumed in the manufacture of articles which meet only accidental or apparent needs. This distortion was serious enough under the restricted, technical conditions of the ancient world, but as more and more raw materials have become available, and technical proficiency has progressed, it has now assumed gigantic proportions, and, in the modern world, constitutes perhaps the most obvious example of the degeneration of true art into technique.

Art is regarded as the mere ability to *produce* articles. Distribution and use, the true guiding factor or "cause" of the art, is viewed as a mere automatic consequence of production, and contemptuously dismissed as "consumption." Hence a situation arises analogous to that which would arise, for example, in a ship with powerful engines, if the engine-room crew should take the position that the navigation of the ship was a mere "result" of their productive activity in making it go, and should refuse to take any orders from the captain, insisting that he must simply take what *they* give him. The world is flooded with useless goods poured forth by unplanned productive activity. This leads at home to the vast waste involved in the huge industry of competitive advertising, which seeks to dispose of unnecessary goods, and, abroad, to the competitive struggle for markets which

---

[129] Cf. especially *Gorgias*, 517 D ff.

leads to imperialism and war. Unguided production thus causes "almost all the evil in states, private as well as public." [130]

It would be illuminating at this point to turn to the final distortions arising from the detechnicalizing of the acquisitive arts, when they also seek to establish their autonomy, subordinating not only the productive arts, which they naturally serve, but even statesmanship, education, and religion to the end of unlimited advance or expansion (πλεονεξία). This phenomenon, appearing in the ruinous policy of the Athenian state, was also described by Plato, and carefully examined in his criticism of the views of Callicles and Thrasymachus in the *Gorgias*, and Book I of the *Republic*, where its implications for the whole technical enterprise are thoroughly analyzed. But we must now turn to the *end* of technique which certainly lies beyond *techne* itself. What is the nature of this end? What is the nature of that activity which may not only *possess* all the arts, but which, in academic language, may also *use* them properly? Is this activity also subject to inversion and misuse?

[130] *Rep.*, 373 E.

CHAPTER III

SOCIAL LIFE AND ITS DEFORMATION

WITH THE AID of Plato, we have now perhaps gained some genuine insight into the complex structure of human culture or *techne* — the care or cultivation of something, rationally guided for the sake of achieving some legitimate end. As we have seen, each *art* simply accepts the matter on which it works from some alien source. Guided by a certain range of structural insight, which is peculiarly its own, it then acts on this alien matter to mould it into that form which is essential for the attainment of some further end or form. This further attainment, however, falls within the province of a higher art. Thus each art is *conditioned* by the lower arts which provide it with matter, and *determined* by the higher arts which provide it with an end. Within these limits, however, each art is a distinct province within itself, proceeding in its own way to achieve the right effect.

This independence of the various arts and crafts enables a higher art to proceed effectively in spite of handicaps arising from the defective functioning of lower arts. Furthermore, as we have seen, no matter how adequately the lower arts perform their work, this work may be misused and ruined through the corruption of a higher art. This is true even of the highest arts, for philosophical and theological insight may certainly be misused and misapplied. As we have already had occasion to remark, the whole technical hierarchy, which achieves rational control, so far as this is possible, over each phase of human and subhuman nature, must serve the ends of life. It is time, therefore, to turn now to the structure of "life," first of all attempting to examine the distinction between *techne* and life.

1. The Distinction between Life and "Techne"

That life is one thing and *techne* or profession another we all agree. Nevertheless it is not difficult to discern certain widespread confusions concerning the relation between these two distinct modes of *action* in the broad sense of this word. Thus the distinction is often made in terms of the non-human world versus man himself. By science and technique we may hope to gain control only of "the external environment"; man himself is subject only to a moral or "spiritual" control. But as we have seen, such a dichotomy is not sustained by any careful examination of the technical hierarchy as a whole. Certain well-recognized arts, such as agriculture and food production, depend upon such humane arts as hygiene and medicine for direction and control. Indeed, each phase of man's nature, his body as well as each vital faculty, is tended by an art caring for its peculiar needs, and while their function is doubtless a most difficult one to achieve, there seems to be no legitimate reason for denying to them their truly technical character. In fact, the art of medicine would seem to be more highly developed and genuinely technical than many of the arts tending other animals — sheep raising for example. Such reflections as these lead others to the converse fallacy of rejecting the distinction between art and life. They anticipate a time when the arts and sciences of man will make possible a thoroughly technical control of life. Art will then replace life, and technical efficiency will take the place of what we now call virtue. Such a day, however, will never come. Life, while it is not without structure, has a structure quite distinct from that of art.

Life, like art, is rationally directed procedure. Like art, it involves an end which dictates a certain formal structure, which in turn dictates the active disposition of a certain matter — verbally distinguished from technical procedure as *action* or *behavior*. The essential difference lies in the fact that all these elements are bound together in one and the same substantial structure, whereas the arts are only loosely joined together in a hierarchy.[1] Each art is responsible only for a certain function, not for others, but a man is responsible for all his acts. One technical procedure provides the matter for another which forms it, but no act is the matter for another act. The technical deficiency of a lower art can be made up for by greater directing skill in a higher art, but a vicious act is irrevocably vicious.[2] Similarly, there is no technical

---

[1] Thus Aristotle begins his account of φρόνησις (*Nicomachean Ethics*, 1140 A 25) by pointing out that it involves the ability to plan well concerning what is good and advantageous, οὐ κατὰ μέρος, οἶον ποῖα πρὸς ὑγίειαν, ἢ ἰσχύν, ἀλλὰ ποῖα πρὸς τὸ εὖ ζῆν ὅλως.

[2] Hence, as both Plato (in the *Hipp. Major*) and Aristotle (in *Nic. Eth.*, 1140 B 22) point out, in art the ἑκὼν ἁμαρτάνων is to be preferred to him who errs involuntarily, since he has the *power* to make it up. But in action this is not the case. The more

proficiency which is unqualified in the sense that it may not be put to an evil use. But there are no circumstances in which the virtue of action can turn out to be evil. As Plato says in the *Charmides:*

I do not hold that he who technically produces (ποιοῦντα) not goods but evils is virtuous in act (σωφρονεῖν) but only he who achieves goods but not evils. I clearly define moral sanity or virtue (σωφροσύνη) as the acting out (πρᾶξις) of good things.[3]

In every act, as well as in life as a whole, end, structure, procedure, and matter are all included. Each technical procedure, indeed the technical hierarchy as a whole, provides only the means for some higher end, and is therefore in itself neither good nor bad, but potentially one or the other, depending on its *use*, while each act is actually directed to the final end, and therefore must be judged as in itself actually good or bad.[4] Each technical step needs to take only certain relevant matters into account. Each plan of action needs to take everything into account.[5] Thus, action is directly and immediately philosophical, while *techne* is only indirectly and derivatively so. Technical procedure, which is action of a certain sort to do a certain work (ἔργον), has its origin (ἀρχή) in that action which is its own work (ἔργον).[6] Hence, as Plato says in the *Apology:*

Virtue does not have its origin in things and possessions, but rather things, possessions, and all the other human goods whether public or private, have their origin in virtue (ἀρετή).[7]

Finally, technique always acts on a matter which is not naturally or intrinsically subject to it, and which must therefore be controlled or guided from the outside. Life, on the other hand, acts on a matter (the living body) which is intrinsically subject to it,[8] and incapable

intentional the vice the worse it is (for example, first degree murder is worse than accidental murder), for a vicious act is final and cannot be made up for. Hence, no one really intends such an act. When *intentionally* committed, therefore, it reveals an almost complete *loss* (not presence) of the power of moral insight.

[3] Plato, *Charmides*, 163 E 8.

[4] Cf. *Nic. Eth.*, 1140 B 6: τῆς μὲν γὰρ ποιήσεως ἕτερον τὸ τέλος, τῆς δὲ πράξεως οὐκ ἂν εἴη.

[5] Cf. *Nic. Eth.*, 1140 B 7 ff. Not *all* judgment (that of science and art) is distorted by vice. The vicious man may remain technically proficient and scientifically precise here and there, but the whole structure of his judgment is distorted since: ἔστι γὰρ ἡ κακία φθαρτικὴ ἀρχῆς. Cf. Plato, *Republic*, VII, 519 A.

[6] Aristotle, *Nic. Eth.*, 1140 B 7: ἔστι γὰρ αὐτὴ ἡ εὐπραξία τέλος.

[7] Plato, *Apol.*, 30 B 2.

[8] *Nic. Eth.*, 1140 B 5: Moral insight concerns *man* himself: περὶ τὰ ἀνθρώπῳ ἀγαθὰ καὶ κακά.

of resisting either its domination or its failure to dominate. Hence the virtue of art is only "a shadow of active virtue." [9] Justice is some such thing as this — not the external practice of what belongs to him,[10] but rather the internal practice of it,[11] as truly concerned with himself and what belongs to himself.[12]

While, therefore, there is a clear analogy between the structure of art and that of life, the two must not be confused. An art which could supply itself *at every point* with its own matter and its own apprehension of the final aim, would then become truly self-activating. An art which could do this, however, would no longer be art but life. A scientist might combine matter in such a way that it could become a physical basis for life. But this would be far from the technical activation of life. Such a thing would really be a contradiction in terms, because life is by nature precisely that which is not externally activated, but which brings itself into being, having all the conditions and causes required for action in itself. Art is action on a foreign matter for a foreign end. Life is action on one's self for one's own proper end.[13]

Though not sufficiently emphasized by modern interpreters, this distinction was clearly apprehended by Plato,[14] who never leaves the slightest doubt in the mind of the thoughtful reader as to the hierarchical supremacy of life over *techne*. It might seem, indeed, as though the vast and all-inclusive structure of the sciences and arts must in the end somehow "include" the whole of life within its scope. Such a natural expectation, though lying at the root of certain modern varieties of "determinism," rests upon a gross confusion of structure. The arts advance only by first dividing and then conquering, one step at a time, but a man lives and acts as a whole all at once. Hence, no matter how vast and inclusive the arts may become, they can do no more than provide the potential conditions for life, not life itself, which must rather "include" art, as one of its concerns. The whole

[9] εἰδωλόν τι τῆς δικαιοσύνης: *Rep.* (Adam), 443 C 3.

[10] οὐ περὶ τὴν ἔξω πρᾶξιν τῶν αὑτοῦ: *Rep.* (Adam), 443 D 1.

[11] ἀλλὰ περὶ τὴν ἐντός.

[12] ὡς ἀληθῶς περὶ ἑαυτὸν καὶ τὰ ἑαυτοῦ: *Rep.* (Adam), 443 D 1 and 2.

[13] τὰ αὑτοῦ πράττειν: *Charm.*, 162 A 7.

[14] As is clearly borne out by Aristotle who takes the distinction between ποίησις and πρᾶξις from the ἐξωτερικοὶ λόγοι, p. 1140 A 2, i.e., Aristotle's early literary works. Jaeger does not consider the distinction here involved, but he has shown that Aristotle's early ethics on the whole was developed along thoroughly Platonic lines. Cf. *Aristoteles*, 86 ff.

is greater than the parts, life itself more than one of its aspects. Hence a man's profession is always something less than the man, and all the various professions, occupations, and vocations something less than the state. To confuse the two only prepares the way for that final subordination of the higher to the lower, in this case of life to technique, that slavery of man to his own artifacts, against which Socrates, as we are informed in the *Apology*, attempted to warn his fellow citizens,

seeking to persuade each of you not to devote yourself more to one of your belongings than to your very self, as to how it may be in the best and wisest state, nor to devote yourself more to the belongings of the state, than to the very state itself.[15]

As we have seen, the vast array of generated, changing, altering things we commonly refer to as nature does not exhaust the real nature of the world which we inhabit. This real nature also includes the various arts and crafts which realize further potentialities only implicit in an artless nature. As susceptible to the action of such agencies, or as actually ordered by them, brute nature becomes the world of man. Stars and seasons become the cosmic order, concealing a rich store of hidden truth. Land and sea become a territory to be explored and conquered; their inorganic elements materials to be possessed and reformed into artifacts. The plants and animals which inhabit this original wilderness become prey for capture, domestication, therapeutic care, and use. This reformation of brute nature is accomplished as we have seen by the arts and crafts.

But these arts in their entirety (τέχνη) are a phase of human action or life (πρᾶξις). They are all accomplished through the agency of human bodies governed by their moving principle the *psyche*. No matter how many instruments an art may employ, the *first* indispensable instrument is the living body or one of its living organs. Life itself (ψυχή) from which the arts take their origin, and of which they are only phases, is this motion of the body and the order according to which it moves, a higher and more integrated order, to which the hierarchy of the arts is subordinate. This order of life has two phases, a social order, governing the motions of many living bodies, and an individual order of which the former is an analogous copy or replica. We must accordingly begin with the more subordinate order, that of social life or the community. What is its essential structure?

15 *Apol.*, 36 C 5 ff.

2. Materialism and Society

The general order of human life as over against that of inhuman nature was recognized in ancient times through the distinction between νόμος, including the norms of true art, and what we now term custom as well as law, and φύσις or nature on the other. This distinction has been given what is perhaps its most classic modern formulation in T. H. Huxley's two essays on *Evolution and Ethics*. But it is universally recognized. Who is not aware of the difference between the law of the garden and the law of the jungle, the artificial selection of the one and the *natural* selection of the other? What is not so commonly recognized, however, is the nature of the hierarchical relation between them. Like Huxley and the ancient sophists, we are content to separate the two, without noting the generic structure which holds them together.

To place them in this way statically side by side, however, as two isolated *territories*, the garden and the jungle, is to submit to a fatal misunderstanding which must lead eventually to materialism, a complete inversion of the true and actual order. After all, the jungle was there first. It now completely surrounds the garden, and without the natural air, the natural rain, and the natural sun which shines on jungle and garden alike, the garden would be impossible. Hence we are led to the inverted conclusion that the jungle is not only the *condition* but also the *cause* of the garden, and that the *different* regimen of the latter is somehow temporary and "artificial." But the presence of the wood *before* the fire does not mean that the wood is the *cause* of the fire, nor that the wood is natural and the fire artificial. The natural tendency to argue in this fashion, noted by both Plato[16] and Aristotle,[17] is reinforced by a certain mode of apprehension arising from our own material existence as men.

No intelligible structure is ever perfectly exemplified.[18] No natural body, for example, ever falls exactly according to *the* laws of falling bodies. No concrete stomach perfectly exemplifies *the* digestive system. Neither is any historical society a perfect example of *the* social order. Since we are actual members of such an order, we are always more painfully aware of the deviations and distortions which prevent a given order from being truly correct or just than of those

16 Plato, *Phaedo*, 98 C–99 C.
17 Aristotle, *Meta.*, 983 B 7 ff.
18 Plato, *Rep.*, 472 E 34 ff.

deviations and distortions which prevent a given stomach from adequately functioning, or which prevent a given triangle from being truly triangular. This awareness, which we call *conscience*, is constantly informing us of the gap between the order we are aiming at and the relative disorder we achieve. Hence Socrates and many other primarily *moral* theorists have emphasized the gulf or χωρισμός between the moral form (the ought) and its concrete exemplification (the is).

This is morally wholesome and stimulates aspiration *unless* the χωρισμός is exaggerated to such a degree that the "norm" or "ideal," as it is then called, is interpreted as an artificial or subjective construction of man rather than as a genuine phase of his real nature. Aspiration (i.e. human life) is then viewed as something peculiar or extraordinary, and artificially divorced from other *natural* kinds of change, where we are not too vividly aware of the difference between the thing as it really ought to be, and the thing as it only is. When the moralist, however, who is convinced of the moral gulf, does become aware of this, he is apt to fall into the even greater error of regarding *all* structure as artificial, and of separating the whole realm of form from the whole realm of material exemplification by an insurmountable χωρισμός.

Such mistakes can only be corrected by a broad examination of ontology, which reveals that no concrete entity, whether it be a stomach, a triangular piece of steel, or a social system, can be at all, without its formal structure, no matter how imperfect this may be. Moral and social norms are no exception to this rule. They must be exemplified, at least *to a degree*, in any society whatsoever, though not necessarily in a very adequate or unconfused manner. We may come to see this if we attempt to follow the argument of Books II–IV of Plato's *Republic*,[19] where the broad structure of social life is clearly outlined and guarded against the commoner forms of inverted misunderstanding.

Human life is a certain pattern which dominates the vital motions of individual living bodies, enabling them to act together in realizing life. Since the individual motions, out of which life emerges, genetically precede life itself, which is often on the verge of collapsing into such disorganized expression through social disorder, there is a widespread tendency, analogous to that which we have observed in the case of art, to identify life itself with its indispensable condition (individual instinct and desire), and to think of its form or pattern

---

[19] A *natural* division of the *Republic*, as Professor Cornford has now made clear. Cf. F. M. Cornford, *The Republic of Plato* (Oxford University Press, 1941), p. v.

as only temporary or artificially imposed. The expression of any desire or instinct is thus conceived as good, while all suppression or restraint is evil.[20]

The natural state of life is thus conceived *materialistically* as a war of each against all in which every tendency fights a losing battle against the rest. Of course *if* this were the natural state of life, it should persist, and should be found wherever life is found. As a matter of fact, it never is found except in the imagination of social *materialists* who, like Callicles, and Glaucon in Book II of the *Republic*, attempt to defend the social-contract theory of society. Such theorists explain this remarkable lack of precisely what their theory calls for by making a most significant concession. The original *good* state of nature is not really good at all, for there is in it a natural excess of suffering and repression over action and expression.[21] This is why it cannot endure. But then it is not the good or *natural* state, for life cannot endure it.

This difficulty is easily ignored by asserting that the natural state while not good and hence unable to endure, is nevertheless not evil. Much good may be realized in it.[22] Here and there a superman may express more units of natural instinct than anyone living under the restraints of the social contract. *If* all men could do this, and simply express their instincts without restraint, this would be the best state. But, as it is admitted, *all* men *cannot* do this, since natural good, doing injustice, necessarily involves natural evil, suffering injustice. Hence the best state is a sheer impossibility. We are confronted with the following dilemma. Either the Callicles-Hobbesian state of nature is not a description in accordance with the actual, enduring facts, or it is an impossible "ideal." It is either false or impossible. In neither case can it appropriately be called natural.

Of course it may be held that the goal of the materialist natural state may be *approximated* though never realized. This is doubtless true. Societies do disintegrate into a state of anarchy that sometimes approaches that of the state of nature. But such tendencies are not towards the better and more enduring natural state. They lead towards its complete destruction. This is admitted by the social-contract

---

[20] Plato, *Rep.*, 359 B 14 ff. Cf. *Gorg.*, 494 C 2.

[21] Plato, *Rep.*, 358 E 4, where the contradiction in asserting that acting unjustly (ἀδικεῖν) is good, while being acted on unjustly (ἀδικεῖσθαι) is evil, is clearly suggested. Cf. *Gorg.*, 476–477.

[22] Cf. *Rep.*, 358 E 5: the evil merely *exceeds* the good.

theorists themselves when they concede, as they must, that the neutral structure of justice is at least not so evil as the state of nature.[23] This judgment clearly indicates that the ideal or natural form of society, without which life cannot endure, is the structure of perfect justice, rather than the extreme limit of its deprivation, injustice, or anarchy. Actual given states lie somewhere between the two. None is perfectly just; none is perfectly unjust. Some are moving in the one direction; some in the other. But it is very easy theoretically to confuse the two opposite limits, and the two opposite directions, one towards a greater degree of form and order, the other towards a less. The social materialism of the famous social-contract theory, which has played such an important role in modern political thought, really rests on such a confusion. The natural ideal it momentarily flourishes before our eyes is really formless matter, the entire lack of ideality or structure, the extreme unnatural state. Opposites in truth are closely akin to one another.

Socrates' account of the origin of the state [24] is, indeed, precisely opposite. The so-called independent, "feral" man, wandering about by himself in the jungle and preying on others without restraint, is not only nonhistorical but contrary to the clearly discernible structure of human life itself. We need only reflect for a moment on the protracted helplessness of the stage of infancy to apprehend this fact. The bloodthirsty men of nature who throng the jungles of the naturalistic imagination cannot even there unfortunately spring at once full grown from their mothers' wombs. As Socrates painstakingly points out, the expression of the most rudimentary instincts requires coöperation and division of labor in carrying on at least those arts which supply food, clothing, and shelter. Such orderly coöperation, arising not from any arbitrary contract but from necessity, constitutes a reflection of true social order which has appealed to the imagination of primitivists in all ages. Thus the first idyllic state portrayed by Socrates [25] provides the bare necessities of life to its rude but friendly inhabitants. The restraint imposed by such an order is in no sense artificial but arises from our natural need.[26] Since, however, no provision is made for anything but the minimal desires, it cannot endure. As Glaucon remarks, it is "a city of pigs," taking no account of other more important aspects of human nature.

[23] *Rep.*, 359 B 2.   [24] *Rep.*, 369 ff.   [25] Plato, *Rep.* (Adam), 369 B–372 D.
[26] ἡ ἡμετέρα χρεία. *Rep.* (Adam), 369 C 20.

In addition to animal desire (ἐπιθυμία), man also possesses imaginative aspiration (θυμός) which directs itself to more than momentary satisfactions.[27] He will seek luxuries which can only be provided by further mimetic arts, appealing to his imagination.[28] These objects will stimulate further desires beyond necessity. If unchecked by any rational control, this imaginative expansion will be realized by productive art, and enforced by warlike military action which will then lead the city to war and eventually to ruin.[29] The warlike, protective spirit of man (θυμός), if guided only by imagination, will be stimulated in turn by desire, and must eventually lead the city not only to war but to "those evils which especially afflict states both in private and in public."[30]

The spirited or warlike element belongs to the very nature of man. Without it not even an animal could long endure, for it imaginatively arouses him and leads him to take precautions against those *future* perils which cannot be perceived. But without guidance this must lead, in the case of man, to aggression rather than to protection. Hence the remainder of Book II and the whole of Book III are devoted to the necessary education of this guarding or conserving factor, and the consequent purification [31] of the imperialistic state to which its unbridled expression must lead. Education is the only possible check upon unnecessary luxury and imperialism. Nothing but reason is even capable of controlling an army. If the soldiers are not trained like a good watch dog when to fight and when not to fight, they will either withstand nothing, and hence become a weak and useless appendage, or will rise up against everything, even those whom it is their duty to protect, as in the later days of the Roman Empire. They must therefore be trained militarily or gymnastically to prevent the extreme of effeminacy, as well as imaginatively to prevent the extreme of harshness and brutality. If imagination is not thus led to paint in the soul true pictures of what is dangerous and what is not, it will confuse aggression with legitimate defense, and the whole state will be led either into unbridled aggression or spineless indifference.

[27] The omission of this complex element of human nature from Marxian anthropology is responsible for some of its more serious oversimplifications of human history and behavior. Cf. the dogma that all war is of economic origin.

[28] *Rep.* (Adam), 373 A 4 ff.

[29] As Adam points out, it is important to realize that the unchecked expansion of the πρώτη πόλις into a τρυφῶσα π. is suggested by Glaucon "who is nothing if not θυμοειδής." Note on 372 D 26.

[30] *Rep.* (Adam), 373 E 31–32.

[31] Cf. *Rep.* (Adam), 399 E.

98   PLATO'S THEORY OF MAN

Such training belongs to the essential structure of human life though easily ignored. In early communities it is provided by the heroic myths and tales of custom and tradition, later on by the vast array of images constructed by the various mimetic arts of literature, drama, music, sculpture, painting, and the dance. They impress upon the collective imagination of the purified community a certain structure of order or νόμος, capable of guiding it through the confused turmoil of life.

No human community can possibly abandon the order of the *nomos*, which is embodied in its myths and traditions, without falling into chaos and confusion. Even the simplest communities, which achieve little more than the necessities of life, are guided by some conception of the good, pictorially expressed in stories and ceremonies. Hence "wearing garlands they celebrate the Gods." [32] In this light the *nomos* reveals the nature of each external thing, and the appointed task of each member of the society. Particular decisions, of course, must be made to meet peculiar exigencies. But these must be made with reference to the *nomos* itself which is not "restricted to any special interval of time." [33]

Nevertheless it is ever subject to such accidental admixture. The mythical matter in which it is clothed may be confused with its substance, and hence certain restricted applications of *nomos* with the *nomos* itself. Traditions and customs of different peoples thus develop vital differences and become a far less trustworthy guide. Unless this ruling decision is purified of all accidental accretion, it may be easily overthrown by sophists and rhetoricians who may then substitute their even less trustworthy opinions, with disastrous results. This is why the second city (Books II–IV), purified by education in music and gymnastic based upon a sound tradition, must be subjected to a further purification, giving rise to the third city of Books V–VII,[34] the city of purified law or philosophy.

The ruling tradition of the human community always involves something besides imaginative hope and fear for the future and the protective action determined by them (θυμός). These hopes and fears are always in turn to some degree determined by rational insight into the timeless nature of things (νόησις) and the corresponding aspira-

[32] *Rep.* (Adam), 372 C 15.
[33] *Def.*, 415 B 8: οὐκ εἰς τινα χρόνον ἀφωρισμένον.
[34] Cf. *Rep.* (Adam), note on 372 D, and the *Rep.*, 543 D.   •

tion arising from this ($\xi\rho\omega s$). In any community, therefore, there is always at least a legislative tendency ($\nu o\mu o\theta\epsilon\sigma i\alpha$) which aims at purifying tradition from all accidental accretions and at establishing a purely rational plan for social action. It is not to be identified, therefore, with the blind traditionalism of men like Glaucon and Anytus nor with the blind anti-traditionalism of the sophists for whom all *nomos* was arbitrary or conventional, though it shares with the former a realization of the supremacy of law as essential to human life, and shares with the latter an intense pursuit of the natural or rational.

This true legislative spirit is poignantly revealed in the life and death of Socrates the Athenian as well as the philosopher. Devoting himself passionately to the pure pursuit of truth, still he never forgot that he was an Athenian, and consequently never ignored the concrete temporal actualities surrounding him. A ceaseless critic of accidents, distortions, and misapplications, he nevertheless remained true to the laws ($o i$ $\nu o\mu o i$), and their heavenly brothers,[35] refusing to disobey them in the end.[36]

Many sophists of a later day have seen in this final loyalty a betrayal of the philosophic quest for super-national truth. Plato saw in it the highest tribute to such truth, the actual fulfillment of the quest, the unyielding legislative attempt to bring it into the actual houses and market places of men where it must function as the only truly reliable guide. Hence, as he says in the *Gorgias*,[37] Socrates, the philosopher, is the "only true politician of his time." The so-called politicians, blind to the laws, sought only to meet each situation as it came by pleasing the people. The so-called philosophers sought only to achieve the truth without applying it to themselves and the common life of the people, thus mistaking the very nature of what they sought — that to which it belongs to rule.[38]

Unless this effort is ceaselessly made by legislators to bring life under the control of reason and law, the state must fall under the control of blind adherence to custom, or else it must collapse into a chaos and tyranny which is far worse.

Until philosophers are kings, or the kings and princes of this world have the spirit and power of philosophy, and political greatness and

---

[35] $o i$ $\dot\eta\mu\dot\epsilon\tau\epsilon\rho o i$ $\dot\alpha\delta\epsilon\lambda\phi o i$ $o i$ $\dot\epsilon\nu$ *Aιδου* $\nu o\mu o i$.
[37] Plato, *Gorgias*, 521 D 6.

[36] Plato, *Crito*, 53 to end.
[38] Plato, *Rep.*, 489 B 11.

wisdom meet in one, and those commoner natures who pursue either to the exclusion of the other are compelled to stand aside, cities will never have rest from their evils.[39]

The supremacy of the legislative branch over the executive in those modern states which have succeeded in avoiding slavery still bears witness to the truth of this basic Socratic insight.

We are now ready to examine the broad or essential structure of the state.

3. THE STRUCTURE OF THE STATE

We have now been introduced to the two ruling elements in the structure of human life, the legislative and the conservative or executive, as it is now named, as well as the unfortunate consequences arising from legislative or executive failure to guide the third element, that tumultuous array of limitless demands which constitute the most obvious and ever-present material component of social existence. But we still need to examine this structure in its entirety as each element functions together with the others all at once. The whole hierarchy of the arts is involved, for legislation is the use of philosophy and the pure sciences in actual social life, conservation is the use of educational, administrative, and military technique, and the satisfaction of material demands is the use of productive and possessive arts under the control of hygiene in the living social process itself. Indeed it is only with reference to this process and its integrated structure that the various arts and techniques may be seen to lose their autonomy and to fall into a hierarchy.

This completely integrated structure, including its three distinct but never separate phases, legislation, conservatism or administration, and the satisfaction of limitless vital demands, is indicated by such modern terms as the state or the social order which correspond to the ancient πολιτεία. The degree to which any given community succeeds in realizing this legislatively dominated structure is the degree of its social rightness or justice.[40] While the just social order must exist as a whole, since life, unlike the various arts, cannot be accomplished piecemeal, it nevertheless possesses distinguishable aspects. These aspects must first be considered in the order of their importance.

---

[39] *Rep.*, 473 D (Jowett translation).
[40] Δικαιοσύνη . . . ἕξις ὑπηρετικὴ νόμων: *Def.*, 411 E 4.

First of all, the state must be wisely planned. Such a plan can be formulated only in the light of what is finally valuable and a correct determination of the general aim of life. This involves an understanding of man and the nature of the world in which he lives (philosophy and the sciences), together with a grasp of the peculiar nature and history of the particular people for whom the plan is being devised. Such a plan cannot be formulated without intense aspiration for truth (ἔρως) and that respect for truth, once it is achieved, which always attends it. Αἰδώς, "susceptibility to legitimate criticism," [41] is the essential condition of social wisdom. As is pointed out in the myth of the *Protagoras*, men cannot live together, and therefore cannot live at all, without *aidos*, respect and shame before the wisdom of the law.

But this law must constantly undergo the difficult purification of philosophy, or it will become confused with accident, and lose its guiding power. This necessity is indicated by the gradual transformation of custom and tradition, as well as by the more conscious revisions of the modern legislative process. This process lays down the general plan of community life, and initiates the task of its accomplishment. Even the most despotic tyranny must proceed according to some plan, distorted as it may be by the subjective opinions of the tyrant. No plan is adequate unless it takes into account the interests of every member, and is therefore intelligible to him, for no member of a human society is totally incapable of apprehending what his interests really are. Such a plan must accord with the truths of philosophy and the pure sciences. Nevertheless social planning, as an aspect of life, is more than any art or group of arts, such as the social sciences, the art of regional planning, city planning, etc., each of which may exist more or less in isolation from the others. Social planning on the other hand cannot come into actual existence without the active protection of the plan.

It is not enough simply to apprehend the truth and to construct the plan (νομοθεσία). The living plan must be guarded even in the making — for life is always going on. The legislative process cannot endure in a community threatened by general illiteracy, internal revolution, or external invasion. Hence the nature of society demands first of all, the conserving agencies of tradition and education to maintain the plan. These have a preventive and a corrective aspect. The schools

[41] εὐλάβεια ὀρθοῦ ψόγου: *Def.*, 412 C 9.

and the mimetic arts, by means of admonition and images, protect the law against the inborn confusion and ignorance of succeeding generations, while the judges and the courts protect it against violations which arise in spite of such precautions. If possible they correct the malformation of soul in the offender. If this is not possible, they seclude him from the rest of society, and thus attempt to avoid contagion. In the second place, the law must be preserved not only in the minds and souls of the community, but also in all the subordinate "active" phases of their lives. The distribution of the products of the arts, for example, must be administered so as to preserve the law. Executive officers and agencies must guard the social plan against violation and corruption in daily life.

Finally, in the third place, the law must be preserved against external imperialism and forceful invasion, leading to a state of slavery (δουλεία) which may make the free or rational conduct of life impossible. Man is a rational animal. Hence the irrational or unexamined life is unlivable by man.[42] A herd of animals can pursue an animal life in a state of servitude. A group of men cannot. Hence men "who ought to be free fear slavery more than death."[43] Exigencies will therefore arise when war is necessary for free men, and when the state must be defended against aggression. So it must have an army. But the decision *when* it is proper to fight, and when not, cannot be left to soldiers who are only masters of the military art. It can only be adequately made by those whose imaginations have been trained by education to recognize in general what things in the future are truly terrible and what things are not.[44]

These are especially the auxiliaries, or true politicians, who carry the law imprinted upon them like a well-dyed cloth,[45] though all the members of a free community must be well-dyed to a degree. There is no free member of any state who, by the very act of submission to prevailing law, does not acquiesce in its general structure, and guard it in every uncriminal act of his daily life. As is pointed out in the *Protagoras*, every living member of a living community, by his daily thoughts, is a practitioner of the art of philosophy, by his daily intercourse with his children and friends, a practitioner of the art of educa-

---

[42] Plato, *Apol.*, 38 A 11.
[43] Plato, *Rep.*, 387 B 5–6: οὓς δεῖ ἐλευθέρους εἶναι, δουλείαν θανάτου μᾶλλον πεφοβημένους.
[44] *Rep.*, 429 C.
[45] *Rep.*, IV, 429 D.

tion, and by his daily decisions and course of action, a practitioner of the art of politics. All men to some degree understand and practice these arts. But the *practice* of the arts all together must be distinguished from the arts themselves, taken one by one. *The* art may be pursued by itself as a specialty. But the *living* art may be *practiced* only all at once together with the rest. The plan of a living community cannot be guarded and maintained by the practice of education and politics without social stability.

In contrast with social wisdom (σοφία), which belongs to one distinguishable part, the legislative process, and social stability (ἀνδρεία), which belongs to another, the administrative agencies (schools, courts, and executive offices), a third quality of harmony (σωφροσύνη) clearly belongs to all the distinguishable parts.[46] It lies in a readiness of each subordinate part to be ruled by that which is really capable of ruling it — "a concord of life with respect to ruling and being ruled."[47] It is "that tendency by which whoever has it is ready to choose and to receive whatever is rightly demanded of it."[48] Its presence or absence is especially evident in the appetitive demands of society and those possessive and productive arts which supply them with the necessities of life. Even the simplest type of society must make some provision for the exchange and distribution of such goods.[49]

Unless such exchange is carefully and hygienically regulated, however, one of two forms of social insubordination must ensue. Either certain demands will be excessively satisfied at the expense of others, which will lead to strife between those who have and those who have not,[50] or all the desires will be satisfied to excess,[51] which will bring about a state of "luxury and indolence,"[52] making any persistent action impossible. Both interfere with the realization of that constitutional plan which constitutes the essence of a state. In the former case statesmanship is first disrupted by internal strife and revolution. In the latter, with the progress of the disease, it is entirely dominated and forced to fawn on those material demands which, for their own good, require rather to be regulated and controlled.[53]

[46] *Rep.*, IV, 432 A.   [47] *Def.*, 412 A 1.
[48] *Def.*, 412 A 1: ἕξις καθ' ἣν ὁ ἔχων αἱρετικός ἐστι καὶ εὐλαβητικὸς ὧν χρή.
[49] Plato, *Rep.*, 371 ff.   [50] *Rep.*, 422 E–423 B.
[51] *Rep.*, IV, 422 A.
[52] *Rep.*, IV, 422 A.
[53] Plato, *Gorgias*, 517 B–519.

Social soundness or order requires not only the ready submission of material demands, but also the ready submission of the so-called executive agencies, to rational control. This is why Plato named the active agents of government auxiliary guardians,[54] and classified them, in contrast to modern political theory, with judges and educators whose function is clearly to guard or preserve the law through the flux of time. The very words "sovereign," "leader," and even "executive," which are so characteristic of modern usage, carry with them a false indication of blind action for its own sake, the root conception of fascist political thought. Power is always the power *for* something; execution requires *something* to execute.[55] *Pure* sovereign power, or executive leadership, far from constituting the normal state, is really a characteristic form of social insubordination or intemperance. It arises from an initial failure of the legislative process with a consequent attempt of the conserving forces of administration to usurp legislative authority.

As the schools lose the sense of *what* they are teaching, and the courts lose the sense of *what* they are enforcing, both finally fall into the hands of administrators who have lost the sense of *what* they are administering. This confusion of plan means either that the state relapses into a rule of uncriticized tradition, or that it embarks on a career of imperialistic expansion under pressure from material demands no longer held in check, or that it combines the two, attempting, like modern fascism, to escape from all rational responsibility by the excitement of continuous expansion, as well as by the authoritative relapse into tradition. Plato recognized this as one of the major types of social disease.[56]

It has its roots, however, in a less apparent but even more fundamental insubordination, the sophistic rebellion against law and reason which attacks the legislative process itself. This is the ultimate root of social revolution. The rational plan does not spring ready made from the mind of a supreme legislator. Even when once formulated, and embodied in a written constitution or in the habits and dispositions of a parliamentary body, it must constantly be maintained by philosophic reflection and reformulated and reapplied to meet new situations and exigencies. The law must be continuously guarded

---

[54] ἐπίκουροι, as distinct from ἄρχοντες. Both are guardians: φύλακες.
[55] Plato, *Gorgias*, 468–469.
[56] Plato, *Rep.*, VIII, 546 D–548 D.

by the legislative guardians (φύλακες). But the law, before it may be discovered and maintained, must first be cherished.

The guardians must have *aidos*, respect and shame before the law. They must be ready to pursue it with passion and devotion, even when it is obscured by the accidents of tradition and private opinion. They must be ready to follow it through, even when it is accessible only in the form of pitiable approximations. Social stability can be achieved only by *aidos*, "the conscious effort to withdraw from all self-assertiveness over against even the apparent good." [57] Without this, the state is already prepared for the tyrant who rules "according to his own opinion." [58] For the motto of the true guardian, "*moi, je suis l'état*," [59] he substitutes the inverted motto, so easily confused with the true, "*l'état, c'est moi.*"

We are now in a position to apprehend the nature of a just social order. It is simply that which gives to each social phase and function its due.[60]

As indicated in the accompanying diagram, justice is the hierarchical order of the functioning state *viewed from the higher down to the lower*,

Social
Justice

Wisdom — the rational purification of the plan, aided by religion, philosophy, and the pure sciences of man.

Guarding the plan through time, aided by the educational arts.

Social stability — guarding the plan by political choice and action, aided by rhetoric, law, military defence, and the special arts of government.

Coöperative satisfaction of all the needs of life, in accordance with the plan, aided by the arts of hygiene, distribution, production, and acquisition.

Social
Order or
Harmony

each part properly performing its function, and thus actually controlling the lower functions. Social temperance or harmony, which also permeates the whole, is the very same order, but *viewed from the lower*

[57] *Def.*, 412 C 8.
[58] *Def.*, 415 C 8: ἄρχων πόλεως κατὰ τὴν ἑαυτοῦ διάνοιαν.
[59] Plato, *Rep.*, IV, 420 B ff.   [60] ὀφειλόμενον: *Rep.*, 332 C 3.

up to the higher. Wisdom resides especially in the legislative part, but it cannot be actualized without producing order and harmony of all the parts. Stability resides especially in the administrative part, but it cannot be actualized without wisdom and harmony.

No state can actually exist in the world without some sort of intelligible plan, which is persistently adhered to throughout a period of time, without interruption by insurrection and revolution. The degree to which it actualizes the plan (justice) will be the degree to which the plan is actually formulated (wisdom), actually pursued (courage or coherence), and actually obeyed (temperance). These are four universally inseparable but distinguishable aspects of social structure. This structure includes the hierarchy of the arts, but while the virtue of art may be achieved piecemeal in this or that area one by one, the four "virtues" of social life must be achieved all together at once. A state cannot achieve stability without also achieving adherence to a plan, and it cannot achieve such adherence unless a wise plan is wisely formulated. It cannot achieve stability, adherence, and legislative wisdom without also achieving justice. No single virtue may be achieved by a society without at the same time achieving the other three virtues, together with the whole hierarchy of the arts, at least to some degree.

This hierarchy by itself is only the potential condition for life, "that without which the real cause cannot be the cause." [61] Life, on the other hand, is the cause ($\alpha\ddot{\iota}\tau\iota o\nu$) of art, that which first brings it into being, and maintains it in its true order towards its proper end. Hence the arts may degenerate considerably without seriously affecting the virtues of life. Life, on the other hand, cannot degenerate without seriously affecting the order of the arts. In fact, the inversion of the technical hierarchy we have studied in Chapter II is due to a prior inversion of life. We must now turn to a closer study of the basic vital cause which is responsible for such inversion.

4. THE INVERSION OF SOCIETY

Plato's account of the decline or inversion of the state, in Book VIII of the *Republic*, has often been commended for its scattered insights but seldom presented in a manner capable of making its vital meaning accessible to the modern reader. To do this we must try to translate

---

[61] Plato, *Phaedo*, 99 B 3: ἐκεῖνο ἄνευ οὗ τὸ αἴτιον οὐκ ἄν ποτ' εἴη αἴτιον.

Plato's social vocabulary into living terms, and exemplify his discussion by familiar modern examples, subordinating literal, "historical" accuracy to philosophical exactitude. In order to do this we must, above all, pay attention to the general, structural patterns involved, without getting lost in a maze of detail. Only so can we make adequate allowances for these incidental cultural changes which now make the illustrative detail of Plato's discussion definitely cumbersome and archaic.

The literal or rather thoughtless translation of ἀριστοκρατία by *aristocracy* has led to what is perhaps the most widespread, fundamental misunderstanding of Plato's so-called "ideal" state. This state does not involve the rule of any elite class of superior culture or attainments (timocracy or oligarchy). It does not involve the rule of any class at all, for, as Plato specifically points out, the development of different classes with "opposed" interests is precisely the first apparent sign of social disease.[62] Plato's *Republic* is a "classless society" supported not by slaves [63] but by workers possessed of legal rights and protected by governmental authority. No "class" exploits any other "class." All phases or parts of the state are ruled by wisdom which belongs to no special individual or group.[64] As in the case of true technical procedure, such wisdom *dictates* a rigid hierarchical structure of subordinate functions.

The captain, who charts the course, *dictates* to the navigating officer, who in turn *dictates* to the engineers, but this is only a manner of speech.

---

[62] Plato, *Rep.*, 547 C 1–4.

[63] Cf. *Rep.* (Adam), 469 C n.; Ritter, *Platon* (München: Beck, 1910–23), II, 604 ff.; and Ernest Barker, *Greek Political Theory* (London: Methuen & Co., 1918), p. 267 n. Glenn R. Morrow, *Plato's Law of Slavery* (Urbana: University of Illinois Press, 1939), denies "that slavery is absent in the 'first-best' state described in the *Republic*" (p. 130). But in favor of this view he adduces only three casual references, 495 and 549 which refer to individual men, and 563 which refers to slavery in a *democratic state*. Thus as Morrow himself admits (p. 130), "there is no mention of a slave class" in the *Republic*. In view of his historic situation it is not surprising that Plato did not object in principle to the subjection of the barbarian (469 C). If invaded, the Republic as a Greek city might be forced to enslave barbarian enemies. But this would be incidental and contingent. The *Republic* in its essential internal structure does *not* involve any slavery whatsoever. It is in this respect, perhaps, more than any other, that Plato's political conception most remarkably frees itself from contemporary accidents. Slavery is, of course, present in the *Laws*, where concessions are made to immediate practicability.

[64] Thus the *number* of guardians is a matter of indifference. They may be "one or many" so long as the laws of social structure are maintained. *Rep.*, 445 D–E, cf. 540 D 4–5.

It is not the captain, but rather the structure of ocean, wind, and tide, as truly apprehended by him so far as he really performs his function, that *dictates*. *Dictation* in the proper sense arises only when such structure is not truly apprehended, and guidance relapses into a merely arbitrary adherence to subjective caprice. This leads to loss of morale, and ultimately into rebellion and strife. The class differentiation of existing states is a symptom of disease. Hence no ancient or modern "aristocracy" provides us with an example capable of even suggesting the classless structure of the true *Republic*. Plato did not know of any such example, though abundant instances of what is commonly called "aristocracy" were at his disposal.[65] Had he lived at a later date he might have found this example in the early Apostolic Church.

There are, of course, certain differences, but the general parallelism is so striking that it should not be passed over in attempting to illustrate Plato's meaning. Let the reader think of the early Catholic Church and he will be provided with a key to Plato's general conception. Like the *Republic*, it was a society of friends and equals, living together as members of a single body. Nevertheless, within this single body, there is the most rigid differentiation of function. "For the body is not one member but many." [66] Certain functions are more important than others. "Are all apostles? are all prophets? are all teachers?" [67] Yet all are brothers in the common life. One and the same wisdom, which is accessible to all, demands not only the complete subordination of one technique to another (the hierarchy of the arts) but also the subordination of all the vital activities of the general body to the general doctrinal plan, formulated and guarded by the great councils, maintained and enforced by the schools and administrative offices of the Church.

In great saints and doctors like Athanasius and Augustine, who carried out the arduous task of formulating the logos of the Church and of guarding it against distortion, we find a really suggestive example of what Plato meant by his φύλακες, or "guardians." The teachers, administrative bishops, and members of militant and protective orders carried out the doctrine, protecting it against internal and external violation, and applied it to the ever-shifting flux of cir-

---

[65] Still he argues that such an example might even then exist "in some far distant foreign region" or might "hereafter come to be." *Rep.*, 499 C 18 ff.
[66] I Corinthians, 12, 14.
[67] I Corinthians, 12, 29.

cumstance. These are precisely the functions of Plato's ἐπίκουροι or auxiliary guardians. The great "body of the faithful," to which also the guardians belong, and for whom they exercise their onerous functions, correspond to the friendly brotherhood of the *Republic*, each of whom must be educated to the limit of his capacity and given all that he requires for the proper performance of his function, whatever it may be.

Not only is the *Republic* illumined by the ideal structure of the Church, but its primary distortions are also more clearly grasped if we bear in mind those parallel distortions of ecclesiastical structure with which centuries of Church history have now so mournfully familiarized the modern reader. This history points unmistakably at precisely those dangers against which Plato warns in his account of the course which must be followed in the decline of any historically existent ἀριστοκρατία or theocracy.

This decline has its origin in a failure to realize that wisdom on which the whole structure of art and life depends. Human life in its vast complexity becomes opaque to insight, which then rests content with the mere reiteration of a past wisdom that it never quite recaptures. Pressing problems are not so much answered as "met" by *ad hoc* opinion and rule of thumb. True philosophy (which for Plato embraced what we now call theology) is more and more removed to a position of ineffective isolation, divorced from the rest of life. The inability of the guardians to give any adequate reason for what they direct is accompanied by a corresponding inability of the rest to understand what and therefore *why* they must obey. As auxiliary or administrative guardians come to replace the guardians who really understand, arbitrary "hierarchical" authority, commanding a blind respect, comes to replace the natural authority of wisdom, naturally commanding faith and trust. Antagonism and instability are the inevitable result.

Such "rule of the spirit" (timocracy) takes two discernible forms, corresponding to the twofold structure of the auxiliary administrative function, imaginative opinion, and the power directed by this. First of all, there is a traditional rule guided by those traces of insight still held intact by the communal imagination. But as this wears away, the principle of "authority" takes its place, and the mere command becomes its own justification. Education, at first sinking to a respectful repetition of the past and a skeleton of general principles, is finally transformed into an equipment with the external paraphernalia of command. One learns what a ruler ought to know, how to look, act, and speak in a commanding way. Genuine understanding either is relegated to a few, who pursue it as a specialty "off in some corner," [68] or is neglected altogether. The executive function becomes an end in itself, and the human hierarchy, with its opinions and dogmas, takes the place of the logos.

Such a decline is perfectly consistent, as in the post-Constantinean Church, with growth of "power" and accumulation of wealth. The lesser arts may go on of themselves without adequate direction. But the whole order of life is weakened and distorted. Without decisive guidance from above, administration here and there gives way to those material demands which expand in company with the successful application of the lesser arts. The hierarchy grows rich, and actually confuses the welfare of the whole body with its material stability. Power is used for security and for accumulation rather than for the Kingdom of God. Concordats or compromises with worldly forces are justified so far as they further the universal material advantage of the Church.

The changes in the structure and policy of the Church which attended the Edict of Constantine illustrate very precisely what Plato meant by the oligarchic drift of a higher form of society. The teaching of the Church was crystallized into a fixed tradition. Administrators noted for their organizing ability rather than their wisdom and learning came into power. The worldly position and wealth of the Church became decisive in determining the formulation of all policy. There is a growing chasm between the administrative hierarchy and the body of the Church which is now rather commanded than represented. This timocratic hierarchy yields more and more to the demands of security and prestige, and sinks through traditionalism and hierarchical regimentation at last into oligarchy, the rule of wealth. Nor has modern history verified the proposal so passionately defended by Dante to escape oligarchy by delimiting a special sphere of influence for the Church and separating the spiritual from the natural sphere. This Cartesian isolation of "the soul" of social life from its "body" has only accentuated the original disease. Reason and insight, once deprived of their universal authority, have been shoved ever further to one side, in a perpetual and ever more one-sided "concordat,"

[68] Cf. Plato, *Gorgias*, 485 E 1.

leaving the whole structure of modern society to drift into a more and more accentuated oligarchy.

The only remedy is to follow Plato in seeking to purify reason from its corruptions, at the same time asserting its inalienable right to rule, no matter how fantastic this claim may sound to those who see only the failures of those who have pretended to possess it.[69] Rule is indivisible. There are many intermediate stages between the indivisible rule of reason and the indivisible rule of tyranny. But we cannot move in the two opposite directions at once. What we mean by "democracy" today is movement in the direction *away from* tyranny and private opinion *towards* the classless theocracy of the *Republic*, or at least *towards* some society actually integrated, as our present-day "democracy" only pretends to be, by a common reference to the stable, and therefore superhuman, source of all genuine science and wisdom.

If such a society is impossible, then what we mean by "democracy," that is, the escape from tyranny, is also impossible. If that which is really good does not rule, then man must be subjugated by a class or a mob or an individual. From the tyranny of human opinion and force in its myriad manifestations there is one and only one alternative — theocracy. Plato's *Republic*, as a whole, describes its general structure. The first part of Book VIII describes the primary dangers, first of timocracy, embracing both traditionalism and blind authority, and second of oligarchy, which, as we may see from the history of the Church, are ever sapping its rational foundations.

The perpetual concordat by which a "convenient" Cartesian dualism has been established between the rational soul and the animal soul of society, the so-called Church and the so-called State, has given the whole of modern life an oligarchic tinge. Once allotted a territory of their own, and appeased by gradual concessions and concordats, the organized animal demands with the productive organization required for their satisfaction have been able to dominate the whole social structure, bringing politics, education, philosophy, even religion itself, within the orbit of their sway. So characteristic has this oligarchic taint become that the keenest social theorists of the modern world, the Marxians, have come to regard this diseased state of class warfare as normal, defining man himself as a mere productive-consumptive animal, thus closing their eyes almost completely to the rational

[69] Cf. Plato, *Republic*, VI, 484 ff.

element of social life and the traditional-protective core by which it is guarded. This has led them to confuse traditional loyalty itself, the ancient *pietas*, with its corrupt subservience to oligarchic domination and thus to dream of eliminating it altogether. The identification of life itself with those symptoms of oligarchic disease, broadly outlined by Plato,[70] has led to many further distortions in Marxian theory, most of which are discernible in its picture of the ideal state.

Socialism, the great moving ideal of modern times, is simply an idealization of what Plato called the oligarchic principle. Man is conceived invertedly as a producing and consuming animal. He is a bundle of needs requiring material goods to be satisfied. But the two principles of production and consumption, unless subsumed under some higher principle, cannot be reconciled with each other. On the one hand production, like any other technical activity, requires coöperation and rigid obedience to control. It is hierarchical in structure. Consumption, on the other hand, is something which each individual must do for himself. It is atomistic and divisive in structure. But any oligarchic state must consist both of producers or workers on the one hand, and consumers or "drones" [71] on the other.

The inevitable tension between these two uncontrolled and hence opposed principles of productive organization and consumptive anarchy must lead to one of three alternatives: socialism proper, the conquest of productive order over the so-called democratic anarchy of consumption; oligarchy proper, an unstable equilibrium between the two, in which rich and poor struggle for consumptive control of the productive apparatus; and anarchic democracy, the conquest of individualistic consumption over productive order. No one of these three alternatives is capable of constituting a stable social structure, as is quite apparent not only from Plato's penetrating analysis of the "class-war," but also from the concrete history of post-renaissance society, which has continued to move restlessly from the one oligarchic extreme of efficient and hence "undemocratic" productivity to the other extreme of widespread, "democratic" consumption and hence inefficient production. Since these interdependent principles are mutually antagonistic, the modern state has found a relative degree of stability only by abandoning the oligarchic principle altogether. Indeed this must be the case, for the oligarchic order is necessarily divided against itself. "It is not one city but two, the city of the rich and the city of

---

[70] Plato, *Rep.*, 551–562.   [71] *Rep.*, 552–553.

the poor." [72] It cannot avoid the disease of class warfare. The workers make drones and the drones require workers, but the workers cannot avoid hating the drones.

The socialist "solution" is to make every man a drone. However, as Plato pointed out, there is no limit to the insatiable, "bourgeois" desires. [73] Hence the continuous expansion of consumption must interfere with the rigid discipline which alone makes efficient production possible. Each man must be trained and disciplined to perform his productive function. This rigid technical subordination, however, is incompatible with the anarchy of expanding consumption. Hence, as we now know, the only way in which socialism can be actualized is by abandoning the oligarchic principle, and subordinating *both* production and consumption to some actually or supposedly higher end. The consuming instincts are by nature incapable of rule. Hence socialism in actual practice must be transformed into some form of authoritarianism, *Christian* socialism or *State* socialism, or into some form of tyranny such as so-called *national* socialism. If such a transformation does not occur, we are left with the unstable equilibrium of the class war between workers and drones which Plato correctly identified with oligarchy proper.

From the socialistic or materialistic viewpoint, the ultimate aim is the mere satisfaction of interest or consumption of goods. Those who control the productive organization — and it must be controlled somehow — must inevitably have an advantage in the satisfaction of their particular interests. In an oligarchic society there can be no higher check on such functionless private satisfaction. Hence an oligarchic society must produce a class of parasites or "drones," who realize the only aim of unguided production — unguided consumption. Most of them live on the honey provided by the workers. Those spendthrifts who use up all their advantage in idle luxury and sink into pauperism soon develop a sting. Unable to perform any useful function and moved by the universal oligarchic urge, they must seek

[72] *Rep.*, 422 E–423 A.

[73] These parasitic demands for more and more goods and luxuries must ruin both oligarchy and democracy, leading in the end inevitably to tyranny. Social parasitism which must result from lack of social planning, is the efficient cause of social inversion. Cf. Plato, *Rep.*, 564 B–D. This crucial role played by the parasites or drones in the inversion of society has often been missed by commentators on the Eighth Book of the *Republic*. Cf., for example, Bernard Bosanquet, *A Companion to Plato's Republic* (New York: Macmillan, 1895), whose commentary, pp. 320–334, loses the structure in a maze of detail.

by crime and insurrection to regain their lost advantages.[74] But they can do this only by stirring up the workers to democratic license. This interferes with the essential hierarchy of production, and kills the goose which lays the golden egg. Should the workers, on the other hand, attempt to do away with all functionless consumption and parasitism, they would begin to interfere with that "satisfaction of desire" which is the only oligarchic motive for production, and soon find themselves, as modern "socialists" have found themselves, in some form of authoritarian or tyrannical state.

So the disease pursues its relentless course. Neither production nor consumption can get along without the other, and yet each must work against the other. The workers only produce drones whom they hate, while the drones depend upon workers whom they despise. Such is life in the modern, oligarchic state. Plato has summed up its four necessary and major defects with incomparable penetration in the eighth book of the *Republic*.[75] First of all, it is guided, so far as it is guided at all, not by wisdom but by the rich, or those who know only how to produce, and are therefore blind to every other consideration. This is its first and fundamental defect. Secondly, it is at war with itself, and thus weakened against both external and internal dangers. Thirdly, those who rule the state may be good productive executives, but they must also, in one way or another, manage education and external defense, arts for which they may be utterly unqualified, and which must be distorted and corrupted under their control. Finally, the state will be full of parasites performing no legitimate function in the state.

If such a state does not fall prey to external conquest, it must at least fall prey to internal consumptive disorder. This must at last break down productive discipline which requires subordination of one function to another, and lead to "democratic" anarchy. This can, of course, be achieved only to a certain degree, as the basic acquisitive and productive arts must be carried on somehow. Nevertheless "liberty," as we still misname it, can flourish in all portions of the state for a long time before destroying it, as a dread disease may only slowly make its way throughout the living body before death finally ensues. This democratic drift towards *laissez faire*, or the "don't care" attitude, as Plato refers to it,[76] is an easily identifiable aspect of modern "democratic" life. It can never be more than a downward, destructive tend-

---

[74] Plato, *Rep*., 552 C–E.   [75] *Rep*., 551 C–553.   [76] *Rep*., 558 B 1.

ency, for its actualization would constitute an anarchy unable to endure. As we now know, from observation of the climax of Renaissance history, before this limit is reached it must be replaced by its opposite and inevitable consequence, tyranny.

Before we can understand the transition from democracy into tyranny we must first understand the composite elements of a "democratic" society.[77] First of all, there are many more drones than in the oligarchic order where they originate, for no check is now placed on their multiplication. A "democratic" order must be full of non-functioning persons who merely waste the energy of the state, consumers who produce nothing at all, as well as unconsuming consumers ("stinging drones"), the most dangerous of all, consumed wholly by the passion to recover their lost consuming power whether by crime or insurrection. With the general decay of law and order, these individuals, the "stinging drones" or gangs of parasites, being the most daring and unscrupulous, usurp the position of the political guardians and gain more and more power in the state, which they use to squeeze honey from those higher up in the productive hierarchy who have the greatest opportunity to enrich themselves.

Such traces of law and order as still remain belong to this "orderly class" (which has usurped the position of the true guardians). They keep the productive organization working by means of such rational humility and sheer respect for authority as is left by oligarchy. The oppressed masses or economic slaves who do the work "have little to live upon." [78] They constantly grow poorer as the rich grow richer. Since unbridled consumption is the only recognized aim supported by education, and the very structure of the state, it is easy for parasitic "political bosses" [79] to "deprive the rich of their estates for distribution among the people, at the same time taking care to reserve the larger part for themselves." [80] Hence the orderly rich are forced to band together for defense against the encroachments of "democracy." If they succeed, they will set up a Fascist regime of law and order, accentuating the traditional hierarchies of the state, and ruthlessly suppressing all "democracy." The only other possibility is that a political genius or stinging drone may "protect" the people from such a class revolution and become an absolute dictator.

In either case, the great bulk of the people must be ruthlessly held

---

[77] Cf. *Rep.*, 564 C–565 D.   [78] *Rep.*, 565 A 2.
[79] οἱ προεστῶτες.   [80] *Rep.*, 565 A 5.

down by a regime having no really rational justification, but subordinating all demands of tradition and reason to private consumptive considerations. The only way such a tyrant can endure is by "constantly stirring up wars in order that the people may always need his leadership," [81] and under one pretext or another getting rid of every truly just or orderly element in the state. This may result in a complete inversion of the social order, when, as we are now so well aware, instead of the lower being ruled by the higher, the higher may be ruled by the lower. Education, the authority of tradition, political organization, and productive capacity, instead of preserving their proper rational order, are turned upside down. All the factors are present, but in the wrong pattern. Uncriticized tradition controls education; education is manipulated for political ends; politics is determined by productive efficiency; and production is subordinated to blind conquest and acquisition. Thus the arts are turned upside down.

This we can now see is due to an inversion of life itself, in which reason and law first yield to tradition and authority, which then give way to the mechanism of blind production-consumption, which is sapped by the insatiable demands of blind consumption, until the whole of life is governed by an ungovernable and really ungoverning passion for pure power. The rigid subordination of one part to another which it introduces by force bears a close resemblance to the rigid subordination of a truly rational order. It is easy for tyranny to masquerade as a rational or Platonic state and for "scholars" to interpret the *Republic* as an "aristocracy" or tyranny.[82] As a matter of fact the two are at opposite poles. Even the anarchy of pure "democracy" is preferable to this enforced rigidity of irrational social death.

What we mean by "democracy" today is the movement *away from* that Fascism and tyranny, towards which our nineteenth-century "democracy" has carried us. Liberty alone, therefore, will not really carry us from tyranny. It will plunge us into it. Democracy can only be permanently achieved by leading it first of all in a socialistic *direction*, controlling the productive hierarchy in "the interest of all." The interest of all, however, does not mean the interests of each private

[81] *Rep.*, 566 E 35.
[82] This favorite fallacy of German nineteenth-century scholarship has now become fashionable in America. Cf. a recent presidential address before the Pacific Division of the American Philosophical Association by E. O. Sisson, who calls Plato's *Republic*

citizen, the blind consumption of as much as possible by everyone.[83]

The only escape from such tyranny, which will really escape, is a domination of the whole productive-consumptive order by some rational authoritarianism, either Christian socialism or Nazi socialism, either control by rational authority or control by irrational authority. These are the two exclusive alternatives now facing the dying oligarchic or bourgeois anarchies of our era. Anarchy (democracy) can proceed no farther. It must pass either into Fascism or tyranny, the natural and easy course, or it must be slowly transformed into a true order, guarded by a tradition and an education, which has its roots in a source transcending the private individual who, as such, is the source only of shifting opinion and private interest. Our great "democracies" must go one way or the other. Order must be achieved. This order will be either a *true* order dictated by science, philosophy, and religion, the order of the Platonic-Christian state, or an *inverted* order, dictated by the mystical opinions and interests of the tyrant.[84] There is no longer any way of postponing the choice.

5. SOPHISTRY AND SOCIAL INVERSION

The confusion of these two opposed directions, up and down,[85] is the basic curse of social existence. A state may be thoroughly convinced that it is being guided by capable leaders towards unity and justice, when, as a matter of fact, it is being misguided by incapable bunglers towards disunity and tyranny. The persuasion of truth bears a fatal resemblance to the persuasion of untruth, the authority of justice to the force of tyranny. The tyrannical state itself, the lowest depth to which human life can sink, contains within itself a pretense of wisdom, which is really sophistry; a pretense of authority and defensive spirit, which is really force; a pretense of education, which is really propaganda; a pretense of productive organization, which is really regimentation from below; and a pretense of youthful vitality and dynamism, which is really the expansive burning of political

"that original philosophical charter of Fascism." *Proc. and Addr. of the Amer. Phil. Ass'n.* XIII (1939), 143.

[83] The true aim of Socialism, to make every man a worker, will never be achieved by trying at the same time to make every man a drone. Some higher principle must be supplied either by authority or reason or the two in combination. Otherwise unnecessary consumption (parasitism) must lead to tyranny.

[84] Cf. Wild, "The Inversion of Culture, and the World Revolution," *Sewanee Review*, 1943.   [85] Cf. *Rep.*, 529 C 1.

disease. The worst possible state is, in fact, a bad imitation of the best possible state.

It possesses rulers with a sort of plan, auxiliaries guarding and enforcing the plan, and a highly efficient productive capacity to satisfy all material demands — the essential structure of social life. It is easy to make it look like the rational state. The most opposite things are very closely related, and easily mistaken for one another. They have the very same material elements, differing only in the order or pattern *according to which* these elements are arranged. Both the true state and its inversion, tyranny, are materially based on the same vital demands and the same acquisitive and productive arts. It is only *the order* of organization that is different. The former is organized by reason and rational authority. The latter is organized by irrational opinion and private interest imposed by brute force.

Only insight into structural form can reveal this crucial difference, and the direct opposition between movement towards the one and movement towards the other. But such philosophic insight into the pure structural pattern (ἰδέα) also bears a fatal resemblance to sophistic opinion. One may easily come to suppose that he has genuine insight into the nature or structure of some thing, when, as a matter of fact, he possesses only an imaginative picture, incapable of providing directional guidance. Such confusion lies at the root of social disease and tyranny. Sophistry is the original curse of society. Before we may understand the nature of social inversion, we must gain some understanding of this source of disease as it actually works in all living societies. We may hardly hope to find a better guide to such understanding than the sixth book of Plato's *Republic*.

The essential structure of the state can be revealed only by rational insight which must penetrate beneath the accidents of historic states and institutions, and once inaugurated must attempt to complete itself without the aid of any particular material exemplification. But the corruption of this structure may occur in an infinite variety of possible deviations from the norm.[86] Here the selection of examples must follow the direct experience of the philosopher, who can do no better than choose that instance of social degeneration with which he has become familiar by direct contact. Hence, in his account of social sophistry and its effects in the sixth book of the *Republic*, Plato obviously speaks of his own experiences in his own city state of Athens.

[86] *Rep.*, 445 C 18.

SOCIAL LIFE AND ITS DEFORMATION 119

The text is full of thinly veiled allusions to such historic figures as Alcibiades [87] and Isocrates,[88] and often betrays the personal pathos of Plato's own historic destiny in his declining fatherland. The whole discussion is not a scientific or technical one, where forms may be abstractly considered one by one. It is a necessarily pictorial account of historic life which can only be lived actually with reference to all the forms in concrete embodiment. This life is no longer a matter of some isolated work (ἔργον), to be achieved by technical procedure (τέχνη), but of actual living or practice itself (ζωή).[89]

The form which dominates the material procedure of an art must exist in separation from this procedure.[90] Hence the formal structure of *techne* may be adequately laid bare without material exemplification and the actual application of the art. The form which dominates life, however, must not only be separated from practice but also united with it in the same substantial being. Hence the nature of life cannot be adequately laid bare without exemplification and actual living. One who is not himself a doctor may understand the nature of medicine. One who is not alive cannot hope to understand life — an art that cannot escape being practiced. Hence images are always necessary to reveal the ever-proceeding motion of life, and the corruption of philosophy, which is constantly taking place in all social life, can only be presented by an image which "unites many things into one,"[91] and is, therefore, capable of suggesting not only the motionless pattern of the motion but the motion itself. Plato's account of social sophistry is introduced by the famous image of the ship of state.[92]

[87] *Rep.*, 494 B–495.   [88] *Rep.*, 495 E–496 B.
[89] It is life itself, in the living of it, which dominates the whole discussion. The book begins with a description of the philosophic nature which alone may "truly live " ἀληθῶς ζῴη (*Rep.* (Adam), 490 B 12); considers the corrupted natures, like Alcibiades, who because of lesser gifts, "deem themselves sufficient to carry out the most far-flung schemes in actual practice," καὶ τὰ τῶν Ἑλλήνων καὶ τὰ τῶν βαρβάρων ἱκανὸν ἔσεσθαι πράττειν (494 C 19), but who themselves live neither a suitable nor true life, αὐτοί τε βίον οὐ προσήκοντα οὐδ᾽ ἀληθῆ ζῶσιν (495 C 15); describes the life of the individual philosopher, who may succeed for himself in avoiding these social evils, thereby "accomplishing what is not least important in actual life," οὐ τὰ ἐλάχιστα ἂν διαπραξάμενος (497 A 1); and ends with a mythical account of "that which all life pursues, and on account of which it does all the things that it does," Ὃ δὴ διώκει μὲν ἅπασα ψυχὴ καὶ τούτου ἕνεκα πάντα πράττει (505 E 1).
[90] Cf. pp. 52 ff.   [91] ἐκ πολλῶν αὐτὸ ξυναγαγεῖν: *Rep.* (Adam), 488 A 4.
[92] This single image portrays the four interdependent factors discussed in the book: (1) the true philosophic nature, (*Rep.* (Adam), 484–488 and 502 C–end); (2) the uselessness of philosophers in existing states (488–489 D 26); (3) "the corruption of the many" (489 D 28–495 A 7); and (4) the private sophists (495 A 7–502 C 20).

The following points are worth noting in interpreting the myth. The ship is a moving thing, responding and reacting to the surrounding forces of the winds and waves as well as to the helmsman. However, it is directed or misdirected it must move in some way either towards or away from its goal towards shipwreck and disaster. The pilot (κυβερνήτης), who apprehends something of the structure of the heavens, the earth, the wind, and the tides together with the structure of the ship itself and her destination, is the natural commander. It is his *duty*, not his desire, to direct the subordinate officers and sailors in accordance with genuine knowledge of the proper course: It is the duty of these auxiliary guardians to keep the ship on this course, thus realizing the interests of the shipowner or commander (ναύκληρος).[93]

The early history of the voyage may be readily supplied from Book VIII. The sailors, or auxiliary guardians, are at first obedient to the commands of the pilot. As he has to spend much time in the study of the moon and stars and currents, however, they become restive under his intermittent control, the reasons for which they only imperfectly understand. Finally they take the helm into their own hands. Unable to give any rational account of their actions, they fall into disagreement with themselves as well as with the owner who, though more powerful than the rest, is "hard of hearing, hardly able to see, and ignorant of nautical matters."[94] Not even possessing the habitual grasp of navigation which belongs to the sailors, he is soon at a loss. This is the point where the myth takes up the tale.

What it represents is the confusion of oligarchic democracy, standing, in Plato's day as in our own, at the turning of the ways — either towards authority and reason, traces of which still remain in the state, or towards further confusion and tyranny. The ship is still able to sail. The pilot, with his trustworthy knowledge of heaven and sea, is still present, though now shoved off to one side by himself. The sailors are still equipped, though now in open rebellion. The owner is still anxious to reach the harbor and to have his interests satisfied.

---

[93] The ναύκληρος, as Adam remarks in the note on p. 488 A 7 of the *Republic*, *owned* his own ship. Hence he represents the material interests of all those on board. In a democratic state this is the Demos.

[94] He "does understand about other matters" (*Rep.*, (Adam), 488 B 9); that is, there may be a high degree of cultural and technical proficiency in the inverted state. Cf. Plato, *Apol.*, 22 C 1 ff.

All the ingredients of a successful voyage are at hand, knowledge, power, and scope for action. But the harbor is never reached. The pilot continues his observations, as long as the ship remains afloat, in isolation. His place is usurped by others who befuddle the owner "by drink or some narcotic drug," [95] and thus enable the mutinous crew to grab the helm. Finally, by force as well as by persuasion, the most unscrupulous members of the crew take over the ship, and, making free with the stores, "proceed on their voyage in such manner as might be expected of them." [96] The disaster is traceable to three causes: first, the pilot's isolation and loss of authority; second, the mistaken confidence of the owner and the crew, which leads them to confuse their power over one another with genuine power over the ship and the elements; [97] and third, the soporific effect of those who drug and befuddle the captain. As Plato proceeds to point out, the isolation of philosophy, the mistaken confidence of the many, and the bewitchment of professional sophists are the three major aspects of sophistry in social life, and he proceeds to take them up in the order of their importance, beginning with the isolation or uselessness of philosophy.[98]

As we shall see, all sophistry involves an artificial separation of what is really joined together in those broad, generic structures which are hidden to "the narrow intelligence flashing from the keen eye" of the clever sophist.[99] A serious example of such artificial separation is the isolation of knowledge itself into a special province divorced from the various arts and from the "rest" of life, when as a matter of fact it is united with both of them as their common guiding source. To a large degree this isolation is due to the nature of philosophic insight which requires rare concentration and detachment to be very fully achieved. To achieve philosophy requires detachment. But it does not follow that what is thereby achieved is detached from practical relevance. The pilot cannot study the heavens without temporarily abandoning the steering. But this does not prove that the structure of the stars has nothing to do with the nature of steering. The true philosopher who gains a slightly more than ordinary insight

---

[95] *Rep.* (Adam), 488 C 18. Not merely "pleasure," as Adam suggests, but the magic constructions of sophistic opinion. Cf. *Soph.*, 235 ff. These yield a certain false pleasure.
[96] *Rep.* (Adam), 488 C 20.
[97] *Rep.* (Adam), 488 C 21 ff.
[98] *Rep.* (Adam), 489 A 2–489 D 26.   [99] *Rep.* (Adam), 519 A.

will not forget that he is a man on a dangerous voyage. The true
pilot will not become so entranced with the stars that he will forget
his own location on the ship. If he does so, his insight is certainly
subject to question. On the other hand, while he must be expected
to assume the responsibility bestowed by his knowledge, *he* cannot
be expected to struggle for power like the rest. The patient must come
to the doctor, and not the reverse. Should genuine knowledge merely
assume the role of one "point of view" among other equal claimants,
the whole situation would simply be plunged into greater confusion.

The chief blame for the isolation of philosophy rests with those
who refuse to use it,[100] who insist either that no broad knowledge of
the nature of things is possible or that, if so, it has no application to
practical affairs. Thus each of the sailors insists that he has a right
to steer "though he has never learned the art of navigation and cannot
tell who taught him or when he learned, and they will all further assert
that it cannot be taught, and are ready to cut in pieces anyone who
says the contrary." [101] This mysterious mistrust of universal knowledge is identified by Plato as the source of social corruption. It is a
peculiarly widespread phenomenon which may be found in connection
with every important social endeavor. It is visible now in the sharp
separation of "the theoretical" from "the practical" which stems from
Kant, and which has exerted such an universal influence upon our
modern "common sense."

As we have already pointed out, it is clearly involved in the modern
separation of "church" and "state." Within the church it has led
to the artificial isolation of theology from worship, and the consequent
rise of infallible, oracular "authority." In secular societies it has led
to an equally artificial isolation of the schools and universities apart
from public affairs and their consequent, destructive transformation
into trade schools and bureaus of propaganda. In political theory
it has led to the principle of "sovereignty" and the rise of so-called
executive government, which now threatens to dwarf legislation into
complete subordination. In psychology it has led to the conception
of unelicited "free will" and the rise of modern voluntarism and
irrationalism.

Why should men come to distrust the guidance of reason, the only
reliable guidance accessible to them? Why should human history
reveal this universal tendency, as evident in our own as it was in

[100] *Rep.* (Adam), 489 B 10.   [101] *Rep.* (Adam), 488 B 11 ff.

Plato's day, to follow reason so wholeheartedly in the arts and crafts taken one by one, but to deprive her of all actual authority in the broad direction of life itself? Why should philosophic insight into the wide structure of things, the hierarchy of the arts, the nature of human life and justice, and the broad pattern of change, which is accessible to all men, why should the attempt to further elaborate and clarify this basic structure of the world be first regarded from afar with a stupid admiration, then openly hated, and finally denied?

Is it that the attainment of such knowledge is too difficult? But the very existence of the arts and sciences shows that it cannot be impossible. We cannot know the aspect without knowing something of the whole. Is it that the conclusions suggested by the insights of philosophy are displeasing and disquieting to men? How could this be, unless men had already fallen away from their guidance? Why does man first fall away from what he already implicitly and secretly *to a degree* must know to be so? Why has man fallen and failed to become what he really is? These questions cannot be fully answered, at least by philosophy, except in a vague and mythical form.[102] Such light as can be shed upon them must come from a deeper understanding of the general phenomenon of sophistry, the self-perversion of philosophy, of which the separation of philosophy from other phases of social life is a major feature. But the broad phenomenon has a further structural phase to which we must now turn. This concerns "the corruption of the many," [103] left abandoned by philosophy.

The result of the sterilization of true philosophy is not the abandonment of all rational guidance, for this cannot be abandoned by any living human group. The result is the substituted supremacy of what we rightly call "public opinion," which invariably comes to rule the course of events in the place of reason and tradition. The apprehension of pattern or structure can be achieved first of all only by the individual intellect. The pilot is an individual. "It is impossible for a collection of men to achieve philosophy." [104] The recognition of this basic fact by Plato and by classical philosophy in general has been responsible for that respect which has been commonly accorded to the human individual throughout the course of Western culture,

---

[102] Cf. Plato, *Phaedrus*, 248 ff., where "the fall" is ultimately attributed to τινι συντυχίᾳ, involving both λήθη and κακία.
[103] τῆς δὲ τῶν πολλῶν πονηρίας: *Rep.* (Adam), 489 D 28.
[104] φιλόσοφον μὲν ἄρα, ἦν δ' ἐγώ, πλῆθος ἀδύνατον εἶναι. *Rep.* (Adam), 494 A 2.

at least until modern times. If it is denied, as in Hegel's theory of objective spirit (der objective Geist) and other social or sociological theories of knowledge,[105] the theory of the totalitarian state [106] must be accepted as a consequence.

In every other respect the state is supreme over the individual. It preëxists him historically or genetically. It outlasts him. It is far more powerful, and embraces within it a far wider array of partially realized values. But one thing it clearly cannot do is to grasp the universal undiluted truth. The state cannot understand itself as it is as a whole. Physically, temporally, even psychologically, the individual is "included" by the state. But structurally, rationally, the whole of the state is "included" by the reason of the evanescent individual. For the achievement of reliable guiding insight the state must call upon the individual intellect for guidance or perish. If this unique prerogative of the individual is denied, if the state be supposed to reason and plan for itself effectively, there is no recourse from totalitarianism. The individual must then sacrifice not only his property, his body, and his life, but also himself and his intellect to the state. The premise, however, is false. The state cannot reason and plan for itself effectively unless there is present in it some single individual who has achieved some stable understanding of the permanent idea of the pattern of the state as a whole.[107]

But while it is impossible for a collection of men really to think, they can, unfortunately, together perform something that may be easily mistaken for genuine thought. They may be subjected to the same external influences which impress the same symbols or images on their imaginations, and suggest the same opinions or prejudices to their dimly awakened noetic faculties. These "public opinions," of course, must be distinguished, as they are commonly distinguished, from the common insights, shared by those who maintain a growing science, or by a company of scholars who maintain a philosophic tradition. Public opinion is susceptible to control by individually achieved

[105] Many of which have a Hegelian origin like that of Dewey, who holds that "philosophy originated not out of intellectual but out of social and emotional material" (Reconstruction in Philosophy, New York: H. Holt and Co., 1920, p. 25), and that of Marxism, which confuses philosophical truth with the social dialectic.

[106] Where, to quote Hegel," Staatsmacht, Religion und die Principien der Philosophie in Eins zusammenfallen." System der Philosophie, vol. 10, p. 444, in Sämtliche Werke, vols. 1–26, Glockner, ed. (Stuttgart: F. Frommann, 1927–40).

[107] Rep. (Adam), 497 D 1.

science and tradition.[108] Without such control it merely masquerades as philosophy, providing a wholly inadequate and unreliable substitute, the second important social manifestation of sophistry, the corruption of "the many" by public opinion. This section of the *Republic* [109] is an introduction to the phenomenology of public opinion. Since no one has really developed this basic phenomenology, we cannot do better than to follow Plato, attempting as best we can to illustrate and elaborate his suggestive insights.

No pure idea can be transmitted from one man to another. This is the basic fact. A form or pattern embodied in color, or stone, or, more commonly, in human speech may be so transmitted, and impressed by rhetorical propaganda on a whole group of men all at once. In this way, they may be made to share some sensuous image or pattern capable of influencing conduct. These pictorial patterns or opinions are mixed with a particular matter. They are *many* rather than one.[110] The element of pattern which is identical in all is mixed with a material element private to each. Hence a group, bound together by the very same *opinion*, will suddenly discover that its guiding images are not really the same, and split into various subgroups, or even into private units. Furthermore the nature of the problem or situation, so far as it is apprehended by public opinion, is never more than a certain phase or aspect of the situation, never the situation itself,[111] free from all illustrative admixture. Hence the view taken by public opinion must be always an incomplete or partial view. It is the situation seen from only one "point of view," with other aspects of the complex structure omitted because of imaginal limitations. Public opinion is always partial and biased. It is incapable of grasping the *broad* structure itself as a whole, and therefore views the ordered phases of a hierarchy as though they were a set of units lying side by side.

This may be seen in the unsuccessful attempts of public opinion to apprehend the invariably complex structure of a concrete, changing situation. If the state, for example, is threatened by war, being neither yet actually at war, nor yet at peace, but on the way from one to the

---

[108] Philosophy and science *may* control tradition (πίστις), which *may* in turn control public opinion (εἰκασία). Such δόξαι ἀληθεῖς are the hope of the state, for men cannot be deprived of imagination.
[109] *Rep.* (Adam), 489 D 28–495 A 7.
[110] τὰ πολλὰ καλά: *Rep.* (Adam), 493 E 3.
[111] αὐτὸ τὸ καλόν: *Rep.* (Adam), 493 E 3.

other, in response to many external and internal causal factors, public opinion tends to distort the situation. The incipient, transitional movement will be misapprehended by the one side as already an actual state of war; by another as no war at all. From the former point of view, legitimate caution will be regarded as cowardice, while from the latter, legitimate measures of defense will be regarded as warlike aggression. The hierarchy of causal structure is always over-simplified and disfigured, conditions, for example, being invariably confused with causes. Thus, for example, in the situation at hand, the actual cause of war, a movement of aggression, is actually confused by the peace-party with a mere condition, defensive measures taken for protection.

It might be thought, as in the optimistic Hegelian view, that while each position is partial and biased, taken together, in their union and synthesis, they make up for each other's defects. Unfortunately, this is never true. Each view, it is true, misapprehends some partial aspect of the situation. But two misapprehensions taken together do not equal a true apprehension. As we may learn from actual observation, the two opposed views, far from leading each other to sane moderation, really egg each other on to more and more exaggerated extremes, until at last what each one says of the other becomes true, and the cautious party comes to advocate cowardly appeasement, while the defensive party becomes more and more militant until it finally does advocate aggression. Nor is a better solution to be found in the inevitable compromise or "synthesis," which combines elements of stupid appeasement with elements of stupid militancy, and is, there-fore, apt to incorporate the worst elements from both plans. Such a complex changing situation can be adequately met only by an under-standing of its broad hierarchical structure which encompasses both actuality and opposite potentiality all in one.

All the important situations confronting social life are changing, and hence involve opposite potentialities both embraced in a single generic structure. Such a structure cannot be adequately conveyed by any image or figure of speech. It is too long a process to distinguish the essential thing from the accidental states it is already leaving behind and the accidental states already emerging. Hence public opinion is marked by an opposition between "conservatives" who cling to the past no matter how accidental it may be and radicals who cling to something in the future which is apt to be even more accidental, since it has not as yet been temporarily realized at all. Both are apt to miss the essential thing itself whose realization through the change is the real purpose of both. The future ever facing us, being only potential, is always opposite. One opinion grasps one opposite. Another grasps another. Neither grasps the genus.

Hence opinions themselves are always "opposite" to each other, very closely related, and therefore easily interchangeable. Public opinion will quickly shift from a pacifist extreme to a militant extreme in response to wholly accidental circumstance, and the young radical will become a conservative simply "because" he is growing older. This inability to grasp the genus, and to identify it rather with one or the other "opposite," leads it to deny any composite structure as an inconsistent contradiction, and thus to dismiss the species as an impossibility. The genus, defense, for example, is identified either with pusillanimity or militancy, and the species, *legitimate* defense, dismissed as an impossible attempt to combine the opposite extremes. Hence what is really one and the same is viewed as though it were opposite. On the other hand, public opinion is constantly attempting to bring the opposites themselves together in some compromise policy which may be satisfactory to both parties. In this way, two tendencies or directions which are really opposite are viewed as though they were one and the same.

The result of this artificial shifting from one partial and opposed view to another leads to a confusion and instability of public opinion which can only be eliminated by the forceful domination of one point of view over all the rest by controlled rhetoric or propaganda. When this happens, the natural shift from opposite to opposite, and from opposition to compromise, is blocked. No shift is possible, not even for the better, and the whole of public life, like an insane man, is guided by a set of distorted opinions which may have a certain artificial consistency with one another, but which unfortunately have no consistency with the actual structural facts. As in certain types of individual insanity, the state will become wholly absorbed in one of its own subjective phantasies, unable even to listen to any alternative view. Such social subjectivism is the second manifestation of social sophistry. Capable of corrupting even the most naturally gifted intellects and bringing them under its sway, it governs, or rather misgoverns, the ordinary course of social life that has been "freed" from "the bondage" of custom and tradition.

128 PLATO'S THEORY OF MAN

The bondage of such an "advanced" state, under the ever-shifting but ever-tightening yoke of public opinion, however, is even more disastrous. Enchaining both rich and poor, both oligarch and democrat alike, it must in the end lead to complete slavery. The mass of mankind, including politicians and educators, who complain of the shallow opinions of professional teachers and intellectuals (σοφιστῶν) are themselves the greatest sophists of all,[112] for they have no other guide than the shifting flux of opposite opinions and points of view. They are the great educators of mankind against whose arguments, enforced by ridicule, threat, and finally by brute force no single individual or private group can hope to prevail.[113] Such private teachers and teaching institutions if they are to endure must fall into line with the ruling outline of public opinion. The technical philosophers, however, for the most part aid and abet this system of opinion by the technical means at their disposal. They constitute the third important manifestation of sophistry in society.

In the next portion of the sixth book where they are considered [114] there can be no doubt that Plato is commenting upon the recognized teachers of philosophy in Periclean Athens as well as in his own day. The first deformative tendency which Plato notes in the socially recognized philosophy of his own time is that of confusing philosophy with other sciences and arts which are restricted to certain theoretical provinces and technical procedures. When those of a naturally broader vision are drawn into political and business careers by mass sophistry [115] the field of philosophy is left vacant, forlorn, and desolate. But this field is soon invaded by narrow-minded, little technicians, trained only in the special arts and sciences.[116]

These men have been warped in mind by the special techniques with which they have learned to produce successful results in certain special fields of endeavor.[117] Their method is that of the special arts — to divide and conquer. They split that wide, hierarchical structure which is the true object of philosophical apprehension into a host of special autonomous problems and disciplines, such as ethics, aesthetics, logic, and epistemology, where each sets himself up as an au-

---

[112] *Rep.* (Adam), 492 B 1.
[113] *Rep.* (Adam), 492 A 5–493 E.
[114] *Rep.* (Adam), 495 A 7–502 C 20.
[115] *Rep.* (Adam), 495 A–B.
[116] οἳ ἂν κομψότατοι ὄντες τυγχάνωσι περὶ τὸ αὑτῶν τεχνίον. *Rep.* (Adam), 495 D 3–4.
[117] *Rep.* (Adam), 495 D 27 ff.

thorized dealer in certain manufactured wares, which he advertises before a rapidly sophisticated audience by elaborate demonstrations in a supertechnical vocabulary. Thus philosophy is broken to pieces and carried on, after the model of subordinate disciplines, as a special sort of mathematics, a peculiar branch of rhetoric, or possibly as psychology.

When the broad structure, binding together these various distinct though not separate areas, is lost sight of, there is nothing to prevent each special point of view from attempting to generalize itself. Mathematics, for example, becomes the *clavis universalis*, or psychology is put forth as the most basic of the sciences. As one thus encroaches upon the territory of another, disputes arise as to which is really the more fundamental "science," and problems of a more truly philosophical character loom upon the horizon. But such problems obviously lie beyond the province of any particular discipline. The relation between mathematics and psychology, for instance, belongs neither to mathematics nor to psychology. But, lacking the broad, descriptive disciplines of philosophy, speculation is necessarily resorted to.

As Plato noted, the sophistic tendency towards division and "technical" atomization of structure is always attended by a tendency to unbridled speculation. The little men (ἀνθρωπίσκοι) rush out into the great spaces of philosophy as from prison into a temple.[118] Seeing at last that none of their special techniques is adequate, they jump to the conclusion that *no* technique is adequate, and that they are free to proceed adventurously as they will. The result is the construction of illegitimate and vulgar (νόθα καὶ φαῦλα)[119] speculative systemre in which certain insights having a restricted range of application as, falsely generalized until they verge upon the fantastic or even surpass it.

Thus some arrive at great systems of motion, in which it is maintained that since some things move, which is certainly true, therefore everything whatsoever must be moving in every mode and manner,[120] and that nothing ever stands still. It is not difficult to elaborate such a point of view into various varieties of materialistic philosophy. On the other hand, since some things stand still, like the truths of mathematics, which are certainly true, others deduce great systems of rest

---

[118] ὥσπερ οἱ ἐκ τῶν εἰργμῶν εἰς τὰ ἱερὰ ἀποδιδράσκοντες. *Rep.* (Adam), 495 D 1–2.
[119] *Rep.* (Adam), 496 A 36.
[120] Cf. *Theaetetus*, 179 E–180 B.

in which it is maintained that all motion and change is contradictory, and that consequently the whole universe is a motionless absolute.[121] Some point to the indubitable existence of mind, and hence infer that everything must be mind, developing great systems of panpsychism. Others point to the equally indubitable existence of the non-mental and the non-vital, and hence infer that everything both mental and vital must be reduced to this. As we shall see, these tendencies towards overgeneralization have their roots in a deontological logic which disregards potentiality, and hence regards all qualification as a contradiction. Thus the pushing of some partial insight to a fantastic extreme is regarded, in the so-called history of philosophy, as praiseworthy "logical consistency," and the result, if it is sufficiently elaborate, widely heralded as a triumph of "the philosophic genius."

The only real result of this combination of an overtechnical atomization of structure with "free" speculation is increasing scepticism and confusion among those to whom the crucially important task of deepening and clarifying the basic insights underlying the arts and the common life has been allotted. Instead of performing this essential function, the professional philosophers, in their schools and classrooms, peacefully secluded from the actual flow of life, tend rather to doubt whether there are any such insights at all. Finding certain things subject to doubt, which is certainly true, they begin to doubt everything whatsoever. They doubt the so-called existence of other minds, the existence of the society which has nurtured them and entrusted to them an important task, and even their own existence, including the existence of the task on which they are supposedly engaged.

The profession is then filled with those who uselessly consume the precious time and energies of the community in consciously trying to demonstrate that this task, committed to their charge, is non-existent or impossible, as though architects should feverishly spend their days and nights in the construction of long monographs to show that there is no such thing as architecture, and that the edifice they are supposed to construct is all a naïve mistake, or as though doctors should erect an elaborate "science," demonstrating the non-existence of medicine, and the genuine hopelessness of trying to heal any actual patient committed to their charge. In other walks of life, such self-confessed quacks would soon be denounced as saboteurs, re-

[121] *Theaetetus*, 180 E–181 B.

moved from their stations, and put to some more humble but useful work. But as philosophers, if they argue cleverly enough, and write enough technical books, they are regarded as men of penetrating intellect, who make others see the difficulties of the task, though the obvious upshot of their philosophic scepticism is that there is no task at all, and hence no difficulties.

No matter how far this debased procedure may isolate itself from the main-stream of social existence, its general effect, as Plato remarked, is never a wholly negligible one. Even the slightest weakening of common insight, or even of the common faith in the possibility of such guiding insight ($\pi\iota\sigma\tau\iota\varsigma$), gives freer play to the ever-present material impulses, which are always on the verge of leading the community along the road to anarchy and tyranny.

Plato compares the effect of professional sophistry on the community at large to that of strong drink or a soporific drug on the individual.[122] In truth, the bedlam of opposite sects, and schools, and warring systems which constitute what is commonly taught as "the history of philosophy," cannot fail to have a confusing and befuddling effect on the common insight of the community. Reason is undermined. Even the dogged clinging to rational principles, not fully understood but only imaginatively pictured and trusted, is undermined. Their place is inevitably taken by fleeting whims and fancies like those of the drunkard, which play across the confused surface of his consciousness as he gradually falls under the sway of ever-present vegetative instincts. Such is the effect of professional sophistry. Instead of purifying men of opinion, and leading them towards the stable truth, the true function of philosophy, it rather purifies men of all traces of truth, leading them towards the flux of opinion.[123] In this way, the control of reason and its guardian, tradition, is relaxed. The community is left to its increasingly subjective and unfounded delusions, until, blindly led by an imperialistic surge, it drifts into the delirium of tyranny.

[122] *Republic* (Adam), 488 C 19.
[123] Cf. *Sophist*, 231 A ff. Both philosophy and sophistry are purifying ($\kappa\alpha\theta\alpha\rho\tau\iota\kappa\dot{\eta}$). Like all opposites they are "alike" (*Sophist*, 231 A 4), as the wolf which is the fiercest of animals is like the dog, the tamest of animals. Hence "we must ever be on our guard" about "likenesses" ($\pi\epsilon\rho\grave{\iota}$ $\tau\grave{\alpha}\varsigma$ $\dot{o}\mu o\iota\dot{o}\tau\eta\tau\alpha\varsigma$). They are a genus which is "the hardest of all to catch and keep hold of without slipping" ($\dot{o}\lambda\iota\sigma\theta\eta\rho\dot{o}\tau\alpha\tau o\nu$). Two things may appear to be the most alike and yet be moving in the very opposite directions.

CHAPTER IV

INDIVIDUAL LIFE AND ITS DEFORMATION

W E HAVE SEEN that the arts and crafts do not bring themselves into existence. They are not self-actualizing or alive, though they do constitute an indispensable condition without which social life is impossible. This life of the living community is a kind of action or motion. As such, it must involve something that is acted upon and something that acts. The living bodies of the members together with their environment are acted upon. The executive agencies of the state act on them. This action cannot proceed without some pattern or plan, unified with respect to some end. Since the community contains within itself these four factors, patient, agent, plan, and end, it must be called a self-moving or living being. With the aid of Plato we have now tried to give an account of the real nature of this living being and that inversion which is its peculiar evil.

As we have also seen, however, the community as such does not bring itself into existence without the aid of something else which is contained within it, to be sure, but nevertheless distinguishable from it. This is individual life, from which the form of community life is derived.[1] Neither community nor individual can exist actually without the other. Nevertheless the relation between them is not a "symmetrical" one. The state supplies the material and certain of the efficient conditions without which individual life is impossible. But the individual supplies knowledge of the formal and final causes of the state. Hence the state is even more dependent upon the individual than the individual upon the state. The misunderstanding of this intricate hierarchical relationship has led not only to disastrous misconceptions of Plato's philosophy, but also to disastrous misconceptions of the nature of man himself. Let us, therefore, attempt to follow Plato's guidance in clarifying certain important phases of the crucial difference between social life and individual life.

[1] Plato, *Rep.* (Adam), VIII, 544 D 27.

1. The Distinction between Individual and Social Life

The most evident and most important feature of this intricate relationship is the primary fact that the community is "larger" ($\mu\epsilon\hat{\iota}\zeta o\nu$) than the individual,[2] or, as Aristotle states, is related to the human individual as a whole (though *not* a substantial whole) to its parts.[3] There is no conflict between Plato and Aristotle on this fundamental point. The community is not a substantial entity as modern idealistic social theorists like Hegel have supposed. Only the individual man is a substance, existing in his own right. Society is a composite, being made up of many individual men living together at one time, and succeeding one another in different times. The state is a compound whole, made up out of ($\dot{\epsilon}\kappa$) the characters of individual men.[4] This is true of each of the four structural factors of social life. The body of the state is made up out of the bodies of the citizens, together with the whole array of physical substances which these bodies technically control. But so is the individual living body a composite made up out of physical organs and the whole array of physical substances they control. Why, then, may we not look upon the state as a single life, animating its vast composite body, as the life of an individual animates his small composite body?

This is a tempting hypothesis which has unfortunately been embraced by certain modern social theorists. Nevertheless, it is not sustained by the actual facts. As Plato noted, it is not merely the body of the state that is made up of individual bodies, but the whole order of social life itself, the *politeia*, including all four structural aspects, body, agent, form, and end, which is made up out of individual lives.[5] Not only is the social body a compound — as all bodies indeed are compounds — but social action also is compounded out of many individual acts. The state has no hands to do its work except human hands. When I meet the state in action I meet a human individual, the senator, the judge, the sheriff, and the executioner. The action of the state is composed out of the acts of these men. But such composite action is again paralleled by that of the human body as a whole which is similarly made up of the acts of the head, the heart, the mouth, the stomach, etc., united into a single pattern of life by

---

[2] *Rep.*, 368 E 4.
[3] Aristotle, *Politics*, Bk. I, ch. 2, 1253 A 25; cf. *Nic. Eth.*, Bk. I, ch. 2.
[4] $\dot{\epsilon}\kappa$ $\tau\hat{\omega}\nu$ $\dot{\eta}\theta\hat{\omega}\nu$ $\tau\hat{\omega}\nu$ $\dot{\epsilon}\nu$ $\tau\alpha\hat{\iota}\varsigma$ $\pi\dot{o}\lambda\epsilon\sigma\iota\nu$: *Rep.* (Adam), 544 D 28.
[5] *Rep.* (Adam), 544 D 28.

the intelligence. Hence this constitutes no insuperable obstacle to the organic theory of the state. Why may not the various acts of different individuals be similarly guided into a single pattern of life by the intellect of the state? This is the crucial point of difference. There is no such intellect of the state! Nevertheless there is something *like* an intellect, derived from genuine intellect in the state.

If the facts showed that the state itself possessed an intellect in which individual opinion could only participate, the organic theory of the state might be defensible. The facts, however, show quite the reverse. Not only is social action compounded out of many individual acts, but social thought is also compounded out of many varying individual thoughts. A group ($\pi\lambda\hat{\eta}\theta$os) will apprehend "the many particulars" ($\tau\grave{a}$ πo$\lambda\lambda\grave{a}$ $\check{\epsilon}\kappa a\sigma\tau a$), not "the single nature of the particular" ($a\mathring{v}\tau\acute{o}$ $\tau\iota$ $\check{\epsilon}\kappa a\sigma\tau o\nu$).[6] It is only the puny, evanescent individual who possesses the single intellectual capacity to grasp the single truth, in which the ever-varying flux of public opinion can only participate. Contrary to first appearance, it is the state which is a whole of many substances, and the individual who is substantially one. It is the state which is ever tending to fall apart and to drift into opposite traditions and opinions, leading to opposite states and social forms, while it is only the individuals in them who are always *able* to understand each other. It is the great individual philosophers who come closest to real agreement in approximately apprehending the intricate structure of things, while it is their followers who, grasping different aspects of the same truth, fall into opposite points of view, and divide into warring schools and sects. The group is always divided or ever dividing in understanding. This is because "the group mind" as such cannot rise above the level of opinion expressed in varying private images. Even though these images suggest correct opinions and are effectively disseminated by traditional authority through the external agencies of rhetoric and other forms of propaganda, they must always differ from individual to individual and from group to group. At best they only resemble one another and hence the truth. Unless this resemblance is constantly recaptured and restored by a propaganda which has its source in real understanding, it must disintegrate into difference, and finally into opposition. Only the individual intellect has access to the pure form ($a\mathring{v}\tau\grave{o}$ $\tau\grave{o}$ $\epsilon\mathring{\iota}\delta os$) which is unmixed with any material embodiment, and hence ever the same.

6 Plato, *Rep.*, 493 E 3 ff.

Such derived unity of plan and purpose as a community possesses must, therefore, emanate from this source. At best, however, this unity must be imperfect and transient.

The essential difference between social life and individual life, therefore, does not lie in the more composite character of the body and action of the state. It is not wholly true to say that the individual is simply a simplified state, or that the state is a vast and more complex whole made up of individuals. *Intellectually* the individual is more complex than the state, since he is capable of knowledge as well as opinion. By means of his insight (νόησις), which is always realized at least to a degree, the living individual may understand the whole structure of the state including its oscillating opinions. It is only materially and efficiently that the individual is dwarfed by the state. *Intellectually*, the state is dwarfed by the individual, and causally dependent upon his understanding for the formulation of that complete, structural plan without which it ceases to be a state and collapses into anarchy and destruction. The individual, however, is not dependent upon any such external source for the intellectual realization of such a plan. Indeed the pure form must be grasped by the unaided, individual intellect alone without distortion by any external influence whatsoever. The minute such an influence intrudes, insight (νόησις) degenerates into opinion (δόξα).

Social life is formally and finally dependent on something external to itself, and hence heteronomous. Thus in considering the compound life of society we have been considering what is nôt life in its truest and purest form, but only a larger composite effect of such life, bearing a close resemblance to its model.[7]   Only individual life, given its various *conditions*, is able to realize itself freely without external, *causal* support. Only the individual is autonomous in the sense of thinking and willing for himself. Thus, as Plato points out,[8] exceptional individuals here and there, through certain fortuitous coincidences or possibly through supernatural aid (*theia moira*), may come to live the true life, even in a corrupt society. Just as life, which provides art with its efficient, formal, and final cause, may exist in spite of an inadequate and even decadent culture, so individual life, which provides the state with its formal and final causes through insight, and with its primary, efficient cause through will, may exist in spite of an inadequate and decadent society.

[7] *Rep*. (Adam), 368 C 19 ff.   [8] *Rep*. (Adam), 496 A 8 ff.

This does not mean, of course, that the individual can exist *without* society. As Aristotle says, "the individual, when isolated, is not self-sufficient." [9] Organized social life arises out of essential *needs* of human nature.[10] Thus while sociability is an accident of man, and "the state is nothing but an accidental being," [11] it is a *necessary* or *proper* accident of man, whose development into rational modes of organized action *cannot* conflict with rational individual development, unless one or the other of these is misconceived. Neither Plato nor Aristotle held that there could be any natural opposition between the individual good and the common good. This was *not* because they thought of individual men as "substantial parts of a substantial whole," [12] or because they had little appreciation for "freedom," as is often supposed. It was because sociability is a *proper* accident of man, rooted in his essential nature and flowing from it necessarily. It is as absurd to think of the state (as such) as opposed to individual happiness as to think of conscience (as such) as opposed to individual happiness.

The individual person cannot exist without society. Individual life in its purest form is *conditioned* by food, clothing, shelter, and other products of the arts, which can be provided only by the technical hierarchy of a coöperative society. It is conditioned further by the continued protection of this society against internal and external dangers. Even the exercise of his intellect is *conditioned* by a proper training of the lower faculties of opinion, imagination, and perception by external agencies. But the actual achievement of insight is by the individual intellect alone. "Things in themselves must be beheld by the soul in herself." [13] Such pure understanding of the pure nature of each thing considered [14] must be sharply distinguished from the fleeting and shadowy apprehensions of opinion, which at best can only temporarily reflect its vague outlines. It makes possible a mode of life more unified, more clear, more stable, and more sharply articulated than that of its reflected social counterpart.

[9] Aristotle, *Politics*, 1253 A 27.   [10] Plato, *Rep.*, 369 B ff.

[11] Cf. M. J. Adler, *A Dialectic of Morals* (The Review of Politics, Univ. of Notre Dame, Indiana, 1941), p. 115 n. Mr. Adler is apparently unaware of the ambiguities of this statement. For him "accident" means only "contingent accident"; cf. p. 112. Hence he completely misunderstands the classic meaning of sociability as a *proper* accident of man.

[12] Adler, p. 115 n.

[13] αὐτῇ τῇ ψυχῇ θεατέον αὐτὰ τὰ πράγματα: *Phaedo*, 66 E 1.

[14] αὐτὸ ἕκαστον διανοηθῆναι περὶ οὗ σκοπεῖ: *Phaedo*, 65 E 3.

We must now turn to examine the general structure of this archetypal life, which is always accessible to the living individual, in the hope of coming to understand more clearly its rational source and its complete structure, both of which are only dimly reflected in the derivative life of society.

2. MATERIALISM AND LIFE

We have already observed in the case of the arts a tendency to separate the passive, material element (*physis*) from the active formal element (*nomos*), and the disastrous inverted effects of this separation. We have also observed a similar tendency in the case of life, clearly manifested by the so-called social-contract theory. This view also separates the instincts and demands which constitute the matter of life and artificially reifies them into an imaginary state of nature (*physis*), divorced from their social form or pattern (*nomos*). As we have seen, it leads to an inversion or materialization of social life. Before we turn to the phenomena of inversion as they appear in individual life, we must first consider the same artificial separation of matter and form from which they likewise take their origin — the so-called materialistic view of life. Since it represents a permanent possibility of human misunderstanding, it was already ancient at the time of Plato, and we find it clearly represented in different degrees by Simmias and Cebes in the *Phaedo*.[15] Both the "epiphenomenalism" of Simmias [16] and the interactionism of Cebes [17] are widely current in our own day. Since Plato's examination of these materialistic views points clearly to those phenomena of vital unity which alone are capable of refuting them, we shall save ourselves much time and trouble by using Plato again as our guide.

The indispensable matter of individual life is the individual living body with its basic urges and drives. Wherever we find human life, such a body is obviously present. Hence we are easily led, like Simmias, to suppose that life is "mixed" with the motions of this body.

[15] *Phaedo*, 84 C ff.

[16] Simmias holds that life is a mere "mixture" or by-product of physical elements or changes in the body. Hence Professor Taylor (*Plato*, London: A. Constable & Co., 1908, p. 196) has appropriately applied this modern epithet to his view.

[17] Cebes holds that the soul is independent of the body, both preëxisting it and possibly outlasting it. He holds that it not only affects the body but is itself affected by it as well, being worn down by this interaction. Soul and body are two substances interacting on one another. Since Descartes, this type of "dualism" has been appropriately termed "interactionism."

Certain modern materialists have actually held this without qualification. Life *is* simply matter in motion. Since this would seem to make the whole of nature alive, and lead to the absurd consequences of panpsychism, it was never seriously considered by Plato. Simmias' view is more refined. Life is not merely the motion of matter. This would mean that even a corpse is alive. It is a certain pattern or harmony of material motion. As long as this material order or harmony remains, the body is alive. As soon as it no longer moves according to this harmony, it is dead.

So far, no objection could possibly be raised against the view as an adequate description of the phenomena of life, which certainly must be described as a certain order or pattern *of* physical motion. The difficulty arises in connection with Simmias' interpretation of the word *of*. He interprets this as indicating a substantial dependence. The non-living body is a separate substance, capable of being that which it is whether living or not. Life is an attribute, belonging exclusively to this substance, and arising exclusively from the arrangement of its material parts. It is not the form or harmony which dictates to the body, but rather the body which, arranging itself in a certain way, dictates to the harmony. This inversion of *order*, to which the thesis of epiphenomenalism must lead, encounters certain irreconcilable facts.

First of all we are reminded by Plato that among the various phenomena of life must be included the activities of recollection or knowing, which involve pure essences such as equality, justice, and the like. These structures cannot be identified with the various partial equalities, partial justices, and partial harmonies, belonging to the various bodies we perceive by the senses, without distorting them. Unless knowing, and therefore the human life to which it belongs, is somehow independent of the body, it would seem impossible to give any account of these pure essences which are recollected in the knowing process. This leads to a second argument based upon another wide range of phenomena equally difficult to reconcile with the inverted order of matter-form proposed by Simmias. These are the phenomena of human substantiality.

As we all know, the living individual is an independent being or substance, having certain properties like virtue and vice, as well as a host of other attributes and qualities like pale, thin, tall, etc. Thus we all attach substantive proper names and pronouns to such independent, living beings, recognizing that they are in some sense responsible agents, acting of themselves. We could not modify these modes of speech, which permeate all language, without losing our ability to speak intelligibly of ourselves and other men. As Plato points out, such a total break with these basic phenomena is involved in the inverted order of epiphenomenalism which would make the non-living body not only the condition but also the cause of life. If this is true, then the living man must be regarded as a mere property or "attunement" (*harmonia*) *of* a non-living thing. There is no escape. We must say either that the living man *is* the harmony *of* a non-living body, or that the harmony *of* a non-living body *is* the living man. In either case we shall find ourselves expressing absurdities which cannot be made to agree with the phenomena.

Let us consider the first alternative.[18] If the living man, X or Y, *is* merely a complex set of attributes or the harmony *of* something else which really dominates him, we should never be able to say truly that this is unqualifiedly a man, but only that this is a man more or less, or that this is a man to a certain degree. The whole would be rather a body than a man; so we should have to say that it was man only to a certain degree, as various qualities, like pale and thin, which do not dominate the whole structure, are always present only in a qualified manner, to a certain degree. Needless to say, this is not the case. When we see a man, we recognize the general form or pattern of humanity as *dominating* the whole being. Hence we say in unqualified terms this is a man, not this is a man to a certain degree.[19]

Furthermore, we know that this single being may perfect itself by various attributes to a greater or lesser degree and, therefore, may become virtuous or vicious in various degrees, though always remaining equally a man. But if the ruling form is itself dominated by another ruling form (the body) *of* which it (the man) is only a perfection to a greater or less degree, how can we correctly speak of *him* as dominating the rest, and hence as *having* virtue or vice? The same thing cannot be both dominated and dominating. If man is merely the virtue of something else which brings him into being, *he* cannot have virtue. It is silly to speak of the harmony of what is itself a harmony.[20] So

18 Cf. *Phaedo*, 93 A–D.

19 Cf. Aristotle, *Categories*, 3 B 36 ff.   In general, the ruling or substantial form of a thing does not admit of variation of degree, though this entity may be *perfected* to a greater or less degree and hence admit of variations of *virtue*.

20 *Phaedo*, 93 C 5.

this alternative must be abandoned. The *ruling* form of a living body, the man himself, cannot be the harmony, or attribute, or any complex set of attributes in, or dominated by, something else. Otherwise it would not be that ruling, substantial nature which the thing cannot lose without ceasing to be what it is, and which, therefore, maintains its ruling *position* even when more or less failing to rule through vice and distortion.

The point becomes even clearer if we turn the first alternative around into the second, and think of the subordinate harmony as though this were the ruling form.[21] If so, this harmony must maintain itself through distortion and disharmony, for the *ruling* form of a thing remains in its ruling position as long as the thing endures, even though in an evil state. Hence if the harmony brought forth by something else were literally the essential nature of man, all men would always remain equally harmonized, and we could attach no intelligible significance to disharmony or vice. But this is contrary to the facts. While we recognize that there is a ruling form in man that maintains its ruling position throughout all change as long as the man endures, we also recognize that the degree to which this form succeeds in dominating or harmonizing the other elements of human nature varies, so that one man may be more virtuous or perfect or harmonized than another. Hence we must conclude that epiphenomenalism involves a false inversion of the real hierarchical order between the living body and the life which animates it.

The non-living body by itself cannot *cause* the pattern or harmony of life, any more than the wood and the strings of a lyre by themselves can cause the harmony of music. It is rather the essential pattern of human life which dominates the body and causes it to move in an animate, human manner, as the pattern of song moves the hand of the skillful musician, thus dominating the lyre, and causing its strings to vibrate in a musical manner. This true hierarchical order is next illustrated [22] by familiar instances of that control which a living man is always capable of exercising over his body.

We may accept these phenomena, however, like Cebes, who agrees that the form of life dominates the body, and yet still refuse to agree that it *really* dominates it. There is the possible alternative of interactionism, which is so indigenous to the materialistic temper of modern thought since Descartes that it has often been attributed by

[21] *Phaedo*, 93 D ff.   [22] *Phaedo*, 94 B 7 ff.

modern commentators to Plato himself. The answer to Cebes, which occupies the whole latter portion of the *Phaedo*, and which involves the whole nature of coming into being and passing away, is the best possible answer not only to these interpreters but also to all those who have followed Descartes in seeking a "dualistic" solution to the so-called problem of mind and body. It brings clearly into the light that artificial separation of the two structural phases of cause and condition (Plato), form and matter (Aristotle), into two substances, lying side by side, which breeds confusion and ultimately materialism. We shall be able to trace only the general course of the argument without pausing for digressions and details.

Cebes is no epiphenomenalist. He is willing to admit that the soul or principle of life is independent of the body. He is even willing to admit that it may dominate the body, or even a number of bodies, as the weaver dominates and outlives successive coats. Nevertheless, there are a host of phenomena which seem to indicate that the body also influences the soul. The most evident of these are physical concussions and disturbances which certainly affect the mind or soul. Hence Cebes is a dualist. He believes that while the soul largely dominates the body, yet the body also in certain ways, at certain times, dominates it, thus exercising a wearing effect. Thus what we call life — the union of soul and body — may be the subjection of the soul to external and abnormal influences from the body, comparable to disease, a view which, largely on evidence supposedly provided by the *Phaedo*, has been widely attributed to Plato himself.

A blind reliance on Plato's many references to the body as a "prison," to the "chains" of sense, and, in general, a too literal interpretation of the famous σῶμα-σῆμα theme has been primarily responsible for this unfortunate tendency to interpret the *Phaedo* as a Manichaean tract. If the soul were naturally buried in the tomb of the body, the *Phaedo*, which incites men to free themselves from their *self-imposed* bonds, would never have been written. The imprisonment of the soul in the body, *unlike* ordinary imprisonment, is a self-imprisonment, which is brought about through desire (δι' ἐπιθυμίας), and the soul *herself* is the hidden accomplice who chains *herself* to the body.[23] The argument of the *Phaedo* as a whole does not condemn the things of the body as such, but rather the interest of the soul in such things "so

[23] αὐτὸς ὁ δεδεμένος συλλήπτωρ εἴη τοῦ δεδέσθαι: *Phaedo*, 82 E 6–83 A 1.

far as there is no *necessity* to make use of them." [24] To hold that the body as such is capable of confining the soul or wearing her down is precisely the non-Platonic view of Cebes.

As Socrates points out, Cebes is raising an issue of the most universal scope, involving the whole nature of coming into being and passing away.[25] The so-called mind-body problem will never be solved by those who restrict themselves to the phenomena of psychology and physiology. This problem confronts us not only in the case of the living individual but also in the whole realm of nature, wherever any cause acts on certain conditions to bring forth any discernible result. There is no such change which cannot be plausibly regarded in the dualistic manner as an *interaction* of cause and conditions. The heating of a brick by the sun may be dualistically regarded as an interaction between the waves or energy of light and the atoms or electrons of the brick. The growth of a plant out of the soil may be regarded as an interaction between the plant and its material environment. The building of a building may be similarly regarded as the "result" of an interaction between the builders and the bricks. Similarly, as Socrates remarks of his own case, here he is sitting in the jail at Athens waiting to be put to death by the Athenians. The incipient materialists or dualists might inform him, in a most learned understatement, that his waiting is the "result" of an interaction between himself and his bones, his muscles, his joints, etc., without which he would certainly be unable to sit down in the jail awaiting death. This is so obviously true that the cosmic fallacy involved shines forth at once from the background of a self-concealing irony.

But Socrates does not stop with this poignant and compelling illustration of the inversion. He goes on to explain it in exact and technical terms. "That without which the cause cannot be a cause," the material condition, is not to be confused with "the real cause." [26] Dualism, or interactionism, ignores this crucial hierarchical distinction between matter and form. The sun cannot heat the brick *without* a brick which is able to be heated. But the sun is *the cause* (*aition*). The plant cannot grow *without* soil, atmosphere, and light, which are capable of supporting plant life. But the plant is *the cause* of the growth. The build-

---

[24] ὅσον μὴ ἀνάγκη αὐτοῖς χρῆσθαι: *Phaedo*, 83 A 6–7.

[25] ὅλως γὰρ δεῖ περὶ γενέσεως καὶ φθορᾶς τὴν αἰτίαν διαπραγματεύσασθαι: *Phaedo*, 95 E 9.

[26] *Phaedo*, 99 B 3: τὸ αἴτιον τῷ ὄντι.

ing cannot be built *without* bricks and wood and other materials which are capable of being formed. But the builders are *the cause* of the building.

To regard the process as the "result" of various factors all *on the same level* is to ignore this essential distinction. It is to regard the cause as though it were a mere condition, and the condition as though it were a real cause, thus preparing the way for the complete inversion of materialism, according to which, instead of form determining matter, we find matter supposedly determining form, as in the "mechanistic" account of Socrates' refusal to escape from jail. He is sitting there because of (διά) his bones, his muscles, and his joints. We recognize the falsity of such an account, no matter how technically elaborate it may be in this case, because we are men ourselves and at least vaguely aware of the causal structure of human life. But even though we are not so clearly aware of it, such an account is equally absurd in every other instance of concrete change. In every such change, as Aristotle shows,[27] there are *necessary* material conditions *without which* the change cannot occur, but also the true cause *because of which* the change occurs.

These causes do not stand alone in nature. Each of them is sustained by some still higher cause, which is sustained by one still higher, and so on, until a highest self-sustaining cause is reached. All men are dimly aware of such a self-sustaining cause, which is the ultimate reason *because of which* everything is what it is. The ideal method of explanation would be to begin with this, as certain philosophers, including Anaxagoras, have claimed to do, and to show why this requires certain patterns and structures, which in turn require others, until at last we can see the reason why the concrete things confronting us are as they are.[28]

But the perfect nature of this first cause is beyond us and our weak faculties. Those, like Anaxagoras, who have attempted to begin with this, have been blinded by its light to such a degree that they have been unable to understand even what can be understood, lapsing into a mere account of the material conditions of things. We must, therefore take "the second best course,"[29] starting with the material conditions we may perceive by our senses and then moving *up* instead of down, forming various "hypotheses" concerning what is the real cause determining these conditions, what then in turn sustains this, and so on,

[27] *Physics*, II, chap. 9.   [28] *Phaedo*, 97 C ff.   [29] *Phaedo*, 99 C 9.

choosing in each case the stronger hypothesis.[30] In the case of the soul, we may thus come to see that life is not the condition for the living body, but that the living body is the condition for that of which life itself is the true cause. Thus we shall not become confused "as mere disputers, concerning the source and the things which flow from the source." [31] In other words, we shall not *invert* the true *order* of cause and condition at any level, and, therefore, we shall avoid both interactionism and epiphenomenalism.

The adjectival structure of language, which speaks of a beautiful picture, a just state, a living body, easily misleads us into the belief that the quality is not only possessed but also caused by the substantial picture, state, or body which *has* it. Nevertheless this is not the case. Beautiful things are beautiful not because of themselves but because of beauty,[32] with which they have some sort of communion or in which they somehow participate.[33] This is the safest answer to give,[34] though it is not illuminating, unless we are able to give some intelligible account of the nature of this universal form and its causal connection (*parousia*) with other forms. Each form, though connected with others, is nevertheless *distinct* from them and changeless. It has no opposition in itself [35] and does not take its origin from any other form.[36] The concrete things which somehow are acted on by them, or participate in them, are also capable of not participating in them. One such opposite thing emerges out of another opposite thing,[37] out of participation into non-participation, and out of non-participation into participation. The picture may lose or regain its *derived* beauty, the state lose its justice, and the bones and muscles of Socrates, following their material drift, may carry him away from the prison to Megara or Boeotia.

In such a case, it would *seem* as though the *conditions* took things into their own hands, completely freeing themselves from the influence of any higher cause. This certainly does happen in what we call the destruction of an ordinary thing like a picture. The color and pattern may *completely* fade, so that nothing but the canvas, or the elements of the canvas, is left. The snow may *completely* lose its form or pattern and dissolve into something else, water. The burning wood may be

[30] *Phaedo*, 100 A 4.
[31] *Phaedo*, 101 E 2.
[32] *Phaedo*, 100 D 7: τῷ καλῷ πάντα τὰ καλὰ καλά.
[33] *Phaedo*, 100 D 5–6.
[34] *Phaedo*, 100 D 8.
[35] *Phaedo*, 103 B 4.
[36] *Phaedo*, 103 C 1.
[37] *Phaedo*, 103 B 2.

dissolved into smoke and ashes. Even a given social community may *completely* lose its ruling form and dissolve into something else. The state is certainly not deathless. This is because the *ultimate* cause of its inherent pattern does not lie within itself. The snow does not of itself cause cold; the wood does not burn of itself; the state does not make itself just. The snow is maintained by the coolness of the winter air, the fire is maintained by the fuel and ventilation of the heating system, the state by the wisdom of the individual legislator. Each of these things is brought into being and sustained by something outside itself. Hence when its sustaining cause ceases to operate, perhaps through the failure of some higher cause, it is reduced to the opposite state of its conditions and is, as we say, destroyed.

Is this true of individual life? As we have seen, it is *conditioned* by the living body with its various urges and tendencies. It is *caused*, however, by a certain sort of motion, which "governs" the elements of the body, "opposing" them and "mastering" them.[38] "Life (*psyche*) is self-originating motion."[39] This vital motion has many forms, indicated by such English words as desiring, seeking, striving, struggling, yearning, willing, growing, tending, etc. Our word "life" has now become so far inverted as to mean rather the externally dependent processes which *condition* this self-originating motion, than the thing itself. Recurrent aspiration of some sort always moves the living human body. Even yielding to terror and running away is a kind of aspiration, the seeking for safety. We cannot seek *without* a body with which to seek. But the body does not determine the seeking. It is the seeking which determines the body to move as it does. It is *aspiration*, therefore, which rules the body and constitutes the form of life itself. Only a body which is governed by such a self-moving principle may be called humanly alive. May we then say that life consists of the motions of a living body, conditioned by the body, and caused by human aspiration?

When the body becomes unable to respond to desire, it sickens and dies. When it responds more readily to the seeking principle, it is healthy and lives. This is true. The body may be more or less dominated by its governing aspiration, and hence more or less well harmonized or healthy. But this is not the whole structure. The aspiration is itself dominated by a still higher principle. We cannot seek

---

[38] *Phaedo*, 94 C 9.
[39] Cf. *Def.*, 411 C 7: ψυχὴ τὸ αὐτὸ κινοῦν; and *Phaedrus*, 245 C 5 ff.

without seeking something, which directs the seeking. Aspiration, which governs the moving body, is in turn governed by some form of apprehension, which it must bring with it into the body to make it alive. We have thus discovered a twofold hierarchy of causes — aspiration which causes bodily motion, and apprehension which causes seeking. This hierarchy belongs to the essential structure of life.

As Plato takes great pains in pointing out,[40] such hierarchies are easy to discover in nature, which, indeed, is itself a vast system of hierarchies. The fever which enters into an organism, causing it to become disordered and inflamed, is itself determined by the pattern of a certain disease, which causes it to act in a certain way, and by which it may be dominated in a more or less virulent form. The fire, actively entering into the wood, carries with it the structure of heat, which it transfers to a greater or lesser degree into the wood, heating it more or less. The demands and aspirations of the community are directed by ideas or apprehensions preserved by law and education though ultimately emanating from the individual intellect. What, then, are we to say of that aspiration which causes individual life? Is it determined also by an apprehension impressed upon it from some external source? If so it must be contingent or corruptible, and pass away, when this external source fails to sustain it, as the fever passes when the bacterial complex bringing it about is no longer sustained, as the fire is quenched when its heat is no longer causally maintained, and as the state collapses into disorder and tyranny when rational guidance is no longer supplied by the individual intellect. This, however, is not the case.

The unitary aspiration of the living individual, unlike the compound aspiration of the state, is not dependent upon any external apprehension. It is determined ultimately by an apprehension wholly intrinsic to it and realized by itself alone, the apprehension of the pure *eidos*, or form. The forms in their totality, as they are accessible to individual insight, are not determined by anything beyond them. They are themselves the ultimate determining causes. Hence the individual person, so far as he actually apprehends them, and allows himself to be ruled and directed by them, is self-determining or free. Since these forms are also changeless or incorruptible, that which unites with them through rational aspiration and apprehension is, to that degree,

[40] *Phaedo*, 103 C 10–105 C 8.

also changeless and incorruptible. Aspiration, the breath of life (*psyche*) is not itself life as fire is not heat. But it bears life with it and introduces it into the body it enters, as fire bears heat with it and introduces it into the wood it enters.[41] The life of this life-bearing aspiration is the deathless structure of reason. As fire is inseparably connected with heat, so is aspiration inseparably connected with the deathless forms directing it always to some degree. Hence the breath of life (*psyche*) itself is to some degree and in some manner deathless.

This is the Platonic "argument" for immortality which is briefly epitomized at the end (105 C–107), but which really rests, as its classical interpreters have clearly seen,[42] upon the intricate phenomenology of life and knowledge developed in the earlier portions of the dialogue. This is the nerve of the argument. If the order of life is inverted, and we regard it as a process in which physical change (the condition) determines desire and reflection (the cause), then of course "immortality" is a fantastic delusion. But this inverted order cannot be made to accord with the facts. These facts indicate that the opposite order is primary. Individual life is a threefold hierarchy: first, a living body able to be controlled by aspiration; second, this governing aspiration, entering into the body bearing life or reason with it; [43] third, the *ultimate* cause, insight itself, which guides the governing aspiration.

To the degree in which the body is properly harmonized for desire it is healthy and alive. To the degree in which desire is properly harmonized by rational direction it is virtuous or really alive. The body is that *without which* no seeking can really seek. The seeking is that without which no reason can really direct. But the *cause* of the life in the living body is aspiration, and the *cause* of the actual aspiration is the direction of reason. All three factors are necessary to constitute a living, or self-moving being. Life as a whole cannot be lived without the body. It cannot be lived without aspiration. But as we have already been forced to notice, the cause is more essential than

[41] Cf. *Phaedo*, 105 C ff.
[42] Cf. Aristotle, *De Anima*, Bk. III, ch. 4–6; *Summa Theol.*, Part I, qu. 75, art. 6.
[43] ψυχή . . . ἀεὶ ἥκει ἐπ' ἐκεῖνο φέρουσα ζωήν: *Phaedo*, 105 D 3. The living body bears aspiration, and aspiration (ψυχή) bears life (ζωή). Cf. *Crat.*, 400 A 5 where ψυχή is said to hold (ἔχειν) and to carry (ὀχεῖν) the nature (τὴν φύσιν) of the whole body, and this "directing nature" of all other things is then identified with insight (νοῦς), following Anaxagoras. ψυχή is thus derived from φυσέχειν — that which *holds* or *carries* insight.

the condition. Hence aspiration is more essential to life than the body, and reason more essential to life than aspiration.

Whether life may ever grow into such a perfect union with its changeless source as to outgrow the need for its less important bodily condition, as Plato believed, we need not discuss here. In any case, we have arrived at a non-inverted definition of individual life, avoiding the fallacies of dualism and interactionism. Guided by the general pattern of such a real definition, we may now turn to the examination of the subordinate elements of this pattern in greater detail, in the hope of gaining a more adequate grasp of the complete structure of individual life.

3. The Structure of Individual Life

Since individual life, like social life, is a self-originating process or motion of a most peculiar and complex kind, we need first of all an image, like that of "the ship of state," before we may hope successfully to analyze it into its structural elements. Such a moving image, while necessarily confused and even distorted, will enable us, if it is not too carelessly constructed, to glimpse the process of life as a whole *in motion*, with each of its elements dynamically acting on the rest. Without such an image, our analysis is apt to lose sight of essential factors in the elaboration of detail and to end with a lifeless set of elements merely lying side by side. We can hardly hope to improve on the famous image of the chariot which Plato has constructed for this very purpose in the *Phaedrus*.[44]

"Let the life of the individual (*psyche*) be likened to the indwelling mobile power (*dynamis*) of a winged yoke of horses and a charioteer."[45] Our attention is called at once to the *wings*, which have no analogue in the myth of the ship of state, and which in fact dominate this figurative portion of the second speech of Socrates, the whole of which is devoted to the topic of aspiration (*eros*). We are left in no doubt as to what they represent. The dominant role of the wings, the most divine of all those "things which are in any way connected with the body,"[46] in raising the chariot to the supercelestial region where the divine spectacle becomes visible to the charioteer, corresponds to the dominant role played by aspiration in raising the living soul to the

[44] *Phaedrus*, 246 A 6–257.
[45] ἐοικέτω δὴ συμφύτῳ δυνάμει ὑποπτέρου ζεύγους τε καὶ ἡνιόχου: *Phaedrus*, 246 A 6.
[46] τῶν περὶ τὸ σῶμα: *Phaedrus*, 246 D 8.

level of peace and harmony where the broad structure of being becomes discernible to reason.

We are told that the wings are attached to the horses and possibly to the charioteer himself,[47] but they are not mentioned in the separate description of the two steeds.[48] Hence we are led to infer that they belong rather to the united power of the whole vehicle, as the living being aspires or loves with the whole of his being (*psyche*), rather than with any particular part. Nevertheless they are more closely associated with the charioteer than with any of the other parts. We are specifically told that it is due to the unskilful driving of the charioteer that the wings are smashed, while, under more skilful guidance, the wings are more properly nourished, the whole chariot is able to soar, and the driver's head is lifted into the upper region, where he may glimpse the beatific vision.[49] Thus driver and wings are dependent upon each other. Aspiration is the efficient cause of insight, while insight is the formal and final cause of aspiration. When reason ceases, aspiration fails, and when aspiration fails, the heavy weight of the vehicle drags it down to the earth. Without the guiding activity of reason and aspiration, the lower "parts" of life fall into confusion, and yield to the ever-present drift of physical impulse. But what are these other parts?

They are represented in the analogy by the two steeds which, by themselves, are able to pull the chariot around and around on a level, but cannot raise it up. Without adequate guidance, the finer and more powerful horse takes control, racing round the level course in conflict with others for "the first place," which is of no real advantage unless the wings are sufficiently developed to lift the vehicle into higher regions. The other and meaner animal is constantly getting out of control, taking the bit into his own teeth to follow his own interest, oblivious to the race as well as to the upper regions. By this constant interference, the motion of the whole vehicle is impeded, both animals are trampled by others eagerly pressing forward, the wings are crushed, and the chariot itself dragged down towards the earth by its own inherent weight. Such a fall, however, may be counteracted by skill on the part of the driver. If the meaner animal is first beaten into submission,[50] he will follow the nobler steed to positions free of the hurly-burly, where ascent is possible, and where the head of the char-

[47] *Phaedrus*, 246 A 7.
[49] *Phaedrus*, 248 A 1–C 2.
[48] *Phaedrus*, 253 E 7–255.
[50] *Phaedrus*, 254 E–255.

ioteer may be momentarily lifted into the clearer spaces. There he glimpses the goal, and is encouraged to greater exertion. Each horse, therefore, has an independent power of his own. Apart from the weight, which drags the chariot to the earth, its indwelling power has three more or less independent sources. First, there is the power of the meaner horse, who has eyes and ears of his own, to rush headlong at what is immediately before him. Second, there is the greater power of the nobler horse to exercise a restraining influence over his companion and to carry the chariot not up but ahead in the race towards a more distant goal. Finally, there is the lifting power of the wings, the greatest power of all, which can carry the charioteer to higher objects of contemplation. The meaner horse sees only what lies before him.[51] To him the aim of aspiration is invisible, though he may be trained to stand still in fear [52] before it. The better steed, though limited by what lies within the perspective of his longer view, does not disobey the driver, and hence becomes responsive to what he cannot see, feeling shame and astonishment.[53] The driver himself, though also seeing what the horses see, is reminded of something else invisible above. So he falls on his back to gaze at it and adore.[54]

Keeping all of these dynamic forces in mind, let us now turn to Book IV of the *Republic* where, as is commonly recognized, the myth is interpreted for us.

There are different principles which move the soul in different ways, as is evidenced by the fact that there is something capable of checking or restraining unqualified appetite.[55] Can we discern in the individual the same "structural phases and active dispositions" which we observed in the state? [56] An affirmative answer is given. Corresponding to the rulers (ἄρχοντες), the auxiliaries (ἐπίκουροι), and the workers (δημιουργοί), we find in the individual three sources of action, the planning faculty (τὸ λογιστικόν), the struggling faculty (τὸ θυμο-ειδές),[57] and the appetitive faculty (τὸ ἐπιθυμητικόν), which corre-

---

[51] *Phaedrus*, 254 B 3 ff.   [52] *Phaedrus*, 254 E 5 ff.
[53] *Phaedrus*, 254 C 4.   [54] *Phaedrus*, 254 B 5 ff.
[55] Plato, *Rep.*, IV, 436 B ff.   [56] *Rep.*, 435 D 26 ff.
[57] The usual translations of this word are, I believe, inadequate. "Anger" is too narrow, for θυμός certainly includes other passions, such as shame (αἰσχύνη). "Spirit" convoys something far too esoteric to the modern reader. In the *Cratylus*, 419 E, Plato derives θυμός from "the rushing and boiling" of that self-originating motion which is life — τῆς θύσεως καὶ ζέσεως τῆς ψυχῆς. It is a more intense and lasting form of vital aspiration. Ἐπιθυμία is less intense and lasting, being derived from τῇ γὰρ

spond to the three "appetitive powers" of the later Aristotelian tradition, will, irascible appetite, and concupiscent appetite.[58] Though we are specifically warned that this threefold division is inexact, and that a "longer way," later to be followed in Books VI and VII of the *Republic*, is necessary for an adequate understanding of the complex structure,[59] many commentators have either taken this tripartite psychology with such a stubborn literalness as to ignore all further complexity, or have been forced to discard it as an "early" and inadequate view. Neither of these alternatives is necessary. This will be evident if we take note of a cardinal Platonic principle to which modern thought has unfortunately become almost wholly blind — the intentional structure of psychic action.

Plato points again and again to the descriptive evidence on which this principle is based,[60] but it is stated with peculiar clarity and with special reference to aspiration in the *Symposium*.[61] All appetite (ἐπιθυμία) or voluntary aspiration (ἔρως) is *of* something, or in Aristotelian language is a mover which is of itself moved.[62] That of which the appetite is the appetite, or to which the aspiration aspires, must be first supplied by some mode of apprehension inseparably united with, but still distinguishable from, the mode of action it directs. So closely is the efficient cause psychologically united to the final cause determining it that Plato sometimes refers to the combined structure by the formal name, sometimes by the active name, never, however, implying that the one exists in *separation* from the other. Hence, in the passage before us,[63] the two lower faculties, which are

---

ἐπὶ τὸν θυμὸν ἰούσῃ δυνάμει, the power of going into θυμός (419 D 8). That we are not going astray in emphasizing the conative character of θυμός is indicated by *Def.*, 415 E 6, which defines θυμός as: ὁρμὴ βίαιος ἄνευ λογισμοῦ, violent impulse without calculation. The translation of θυμός by such terms as "striving" or "struggling" seems, therefore, to accord with the descriptive intention.

[58] Cf. *Summa Theol.*, Part I, qu. 81 and 82. For Aristotle θυμός, which is able to "draw us" into dangers, is the natural mode of conative passion with which, as in Plato, courage is concerned. Cf. *Nic. Eth.*, 1117 A 2 ff. As with Plato, anger, fear, and daring are all associated with this power: 1105 B 21, 22. St. Thomas, in exact agreement with Plato, lists hope, fear (including shame), daring and anger as passions of the *vis irascibilis* (θυμός): *Summa Theol.*, Prima Secundae, qu. XL–XLVIII.

[59] *Rep.*, 435 D.

[60] Cf. *Rep.*, 477 C–478 C; *Phil.*, 37 ff.; and *Soph.*, 262 E.

[61] *Symposium*, 200 ff.

[62] Cf. *De An.*, III, 433 B 17 and B 28 ff., where it is asserted that appetite is impossible without imaginative apprehension. Cf. *Summa Theol.*, Part I, qu. 81, art. 1: "Motus autem sensualis est appetitus apprehensionem sensitivam consequens."

[63] *Rep.*, 435–445.

primarily active, are actively named the appetitive and the striving faculty; while the higher faculty, which is primarily apprehensive, is apprehensively named the reasoning faculty.

We are certainly not to understand, however, on the one hand that appetite and striving occur with no apprehension *of* that which they seek, or on the other that reasoning has no efficient cause. On the contrary, we are informed that reason actively rules [64] the other faculties, and that within this small part there is one distinguishable phase which rules or apprehends, and "another to which the ruling part announces what it discovers, so that it also ($a\mathring{v}$ $\kappa a\acute{\iota}$) has within itself the stable understanding ($\grave{\epsilon}\pi\iota\sigma\tau\acute{\eta}\mu\eta$) of what is advantageous both to the part and to the whole." [65] That which is in a mean between ignorance and knowledge, and aspires after wisdom, as we are clearly informed in the *Symposium*,[66] is voluntary aspiration or *eros*. Thus the tripartite psychology of Book IV really contains within it a sixfold psychology. The ruling or planning faculty ($\tau\grave{o}$ $\lambda o\gamma\iota\sigma\tau\iota\kappa\acute{o}\nu$) involves both rational apprehension ($\nu\acute{o}\eta\sigma\iota\varsigma$) and rational aspiration ($\check{\epsilon}\rho\omega\varsigma$) or, as they were later called, theoretical and practical reason,[67] and we must suppose that both the seeking faculty and the appetitive faculty also involve two distinct modes of apprehension, if they are themselves really distinct.

We have not time at this point to take the longer and more arduous way [68] which is alone capable of arriving at an adequate classification of the various apprehending or knowing faculties. For this we must, with Plato, refer the reader to Books VI and VII of the *Republic*, and to a later portion of our discussion. In order not to mislead the modern reader, however, who approaches the subject with an exaggerated tendency to separate *reason* from *will*, and in general to separate the faculties of apprehension from the seeking faculties, we

---

[64] *Rep.*, 441 E 3.

[65] This sentence has caused considerable difficulty to commentators. See Adam's note *ad loc.* I suggest that the $a\mathring{v}$ $\kappa a\acute{\iota}$ refers neither to the $\theta\upsilon\mu o\epsilon\iota\delta\acute{\epsilon}\varsigma$, which has just been considered, nor to the rulers in the state, who are irrelevant here, but to the active phase of the whole rational element, which also ($a\mathring{v}$ $\kappa a\acute{\iota}$), like its ruling, apprehensive phase, possesses knowledge.

[66] *Symposium*, 202 ff.

[67] Cf. Aristotle, *De An.*, 433 A 14–15.

[68] *Rep.*, 435 C; cf. 504 A–D where the $\mu a\kappa\rho o\tau\acute{\epsilon}\rho a$ $\pi\epsilon\rho\acute{\iota}o\delta o\varsigma$ begins with an analysis of the higher *and lower* apprehensive faculties (505–511 E). This analysis of the different modes of knowing is what is omitted in the shorter description of the virtues in Book IV.

must at least briefly indicate the nature of this longer way. A brief section of the *Philebus*,[69] in which hope is distinguished from expectation, will provide us with the means of distinguishing between the mode of apprehension which guides desire (*epithymia*) and that which guides seeking (*thymos*). We shall then be in a better position to appreciate Plato's threefold, or rather sixfold, psychology.

First of all, there are two kinds of pleasure, that which is common to both soul and body, being simply perceived, and that which belongs to the soul alone,[70] being preserved by memory. This is the object of appetite (*epithymia*), a psychic faculty. This may be clearly seen from the fact that it runs counter to the bodily condition. When the body is empty, hunger desires food. When the body is parched and dry, thirst desires drink. When the body is too cool, we desire heat. When it is too hot, we desire coolness.[71] When *physically* in some form of pain, the soul *psychically* desires some opposite pleasure. Since this pleasure is always opposite to the "actual" physical state, it is not directly perceived, but is rather conjured up by the imagination on the basis of past perceptions stored in memory. Certain appearances have in the past been associated with certain pleasures. When stored up in memory, they guide desire as a system of expectations (προσδοκίαι).[72] Perceived food will be expected to satisfy the pain of hunger; perceived drink to satisfy the pain of thirst, and so on. This system of expectation, based upon *past* perceptions and their chance association with pain and pleasure, is the least adequate type of opinion (δόξα), which immediately directs appetite (ἐπιθυμία), the least stable type of aspiration. These pleasures, which are opposite to perceived pains and thus determined by them,[73] are unreliable, and the expectations, which they influence, are untrustworthy.

Mere relief from some acute pain will be conjured up by the fevered imagination as bliss itself, much more than it really is,[74] whereas some pure pleasure, which is not the opposite of any perceived state, will be neglected as no pleasure at all, much less than it is. Furthermore, since the expectations are based merely upon the purely accidental

[69] 34–41 B.
[70] ἡ ψυχῆς ἡδονὴ χωρὶς σώματος: 34 C 6.
[71] *Phil.*, 34 E ff.
[72] *Phil.*, 36 C 11; cf. p. 32 C 4: διὰ προσδοκίας; and *Rep.* (Adam), 584 C 19, ἐκ προσδοκίας.
[73] *Rep.* (Adam), 584 C 18 ff.
[74] Cf. *Phil.*, 43 C ff.

or perceived qualities of things, they are often false. That which looks like food and hence gives rise to anticipated pleasure may really be poison. In this case, the expected pleasure in this object will itself be false, and its subordinate appetite misguided. [75]

What we mean by appetite is a form of aspiration (ψυχή), directed by a form of opinion, which is in turn determined almost wholly by the accidents of past perception (αἴσθησις). [76]

This opinion, to be sure, runs ahead of the bodily state as it is now perceived. It enables us "to-be-pleased-before" (προχαίρειν) and "to-be-pained-before" (προλυπεῖσθαι). [77] What we expect or anticipate is not perceived. It is constructed by the soul alone, apart from the present bodily state, as an opinion or a belief. But it is nevertheless *determined* by past perceptions which happen to have become associated, rather than by the stable nature of things, and by a present, perceived pain, of which it conjures up the opposite, rather than by the intrinsically pleasant itself. This is that form of opinion (δόξα) which lies closest to perception, and which Plato called conjecture (εἰκασία). What it apprehends is not wholly false, but it embodies the very minimum of truth, as may be seen from its constantly shifting response both to different accidental associations and different experienced pains. While we cannot wholly avoid such subjective images, we are not wholly convinced of them, and never place our whole trust or hope in them. Since they do not endure through a long period of time but are constantly shifting and being modified by new associations and pains, we regard them as more or less likely (εἰκός). Hence this type of opinion is appropriately called likelihood (εἰκασία).

As Plato's analysis clearly indicates, [78] this system of expectation, preserved in memory, must be sharply distinguished from another more stable variety which is never wholly absent from human life. We may best become aware of its existence by referring to a certain familiar type of pleasure, which must be distinguished both from that which is "actually" perceived in common with the body, as well as from that which is more or less accurately conjured up by the imagination with the aid of memory and opposite pains. This is rejoicing (τὸ χαίρειν).

[75] *Phil.*, 37 A ff.
[76] Cf. *Phil.*, 38 B 12–39 C 5.
[77] *Phil.*, 39 D 4.
[78] Especially, *Phil.*, 35 E 1–36 C and 39 C 7–41.

Suppose we are striving for an anticipated pleasure at which we have not yet arrived. What sort of a state are we then in? [79] Protarchus suggests that it must be a sort of double pain, for there is not only the physical pain we are now "actually" experiencing, but also the pain which separates us from the purely anticipated pleasure.[80] This is clearly *not* true as long as we strive in hope.[81] The double pain occurs only when we fall into hopelessness.[82] Then we experience not only the present pain but also the psychic despair of permanent separation from the hoped-for goal. But as long as we strive for the goal with hope, we may rejoice in spite of the present pain.[83] This rejoicing is neither the present experienced pain nor the anticipation of the pleasure, but is rather in the middle, between the experiences.[84] It is no longer desiring, but striving, and is no longer guided by mere anticipation but rather by hope.

This structure is far more stable and far-reaching than the shifting expectations which guide our momentary appetites. "Through the whole of life we are full of hopes" [85] which guide our more permanent striving or struggling for "arduous" objects, as they were later called.[86] These hopes are not merely anticipations, for they are far less dependent upon the accidents of past perception. We may hope for that which we have never perceived at all, but which lies only in the distant future.[87] We may hope in spite of our expectations. We may go on striving in spite of frustrated appetite. We may rejoice in spite of past and expected pain. It is true that our hope must be grounded, but it is grounded rather in the broad, stable structure of things than in any association of particular experiences. Each hope is founded on a *logos* or structure,[88] involving a complex hierarchy of means and ends, which may persist through a long sequence of disappointed experiences and expectations. Each individual is guided from far

[79] *Phil.*, 35 E 9.
[80] *Phil.*, 36 A 4.
[81] ἐν ἐλπίδι: *Phil.*, 36 A 8.
[82] ἀνελπίστως: *Phil.*, B 11.
[83] λυπεῖταί τε ἅμα καὶ χαίρει: *Phil.*, B 8.
[84] ἐν μέσῳ τῶν παθημάτων: *Phil.*, 36 A 1. This condition, therefore, resembles the stable ἕξις which is neither upset nor restored again, which lacks both perceptual pain and perceptual pleasure, and which "is the most divine of all lives" — πάντων τῶν βίων ἐστὶ θειότατος: 33 B 7.
[85] *Phil.*, 39 E 5.
[86] Cf. *Summa Theol.*, Part I, qu. 81, art. 2, *Resp.*
[87] *Phil.*, 39 D–E.
[88] Λόγοι μήν εἰσιν ἐν ἑκάστοις ἡμῶν, ἃς ἐλπίδας ὀνομάζομεν. *Phil.*, 40 A 6.

ahead of himself by some such structure of hope, which he is able in some degree to formulate in a meaningful logos.

In addition to this, there is a painter in the soul of each of us,[89] the imagination, which paints pictures and images of those hopes which guide the more stable purpose of our lives. Since they are not so dependent upon accidental association and subjective circumstance, they are wider in horizon and hence more permanent than the corresponding pictures and images of expectation which guide our momentary appetites. Nevertheless, they also may be false.[90] That in which we put our lasting faith and hope may really be hopeless. In this case those things we finally fear, as, for example, the separation of life from the body, will not be really fearful, and those we finally strive for, as, for example, power and possessions, will not be worthy of the struggle. Nevertheless, this structure of hope, in which he who is "friendly to God" [91] finally puts his trust, and which either guides or misguides his permanent endeavors, is a more adequate and stable guide than the flux of conjecture. This is shown by the fact that the man himself is more convinced of it and stakes his life upon it. Hence it is the higher mode of opinion and is appropriately distinguished from mere conjecture (εἰκασία) by the name of faith or trust (πίστις).

We are now in a position to understand more fully the threefold psychology of Book IV of the *Republic*, and the theory of the virtues which is based upon it. The life of the individual, living body has three distinct though inseparable faculties: that of rational planning (τὸ λογιστικόν), subdivided into rational apprehension (νόησις) and rational aspiration (ἔρως) or will as it came to be later called; second, that of long-range endeavor or seeking (τὸ θυμοειδές), the *vis irascibilis* of the later Aristotelian tradition, subdivided into trustworthy opinion or conviction (πίστις) and the arduous [92] striving which it guides (θυμός), and finally third, that of short-range appetite (τὸ ἐπιθυμητικόν), the *vis concupiscibilis* of the later tradition, subdivided into the system of conjecture (εἰκασία) and momentary appetite (ἐπιθυμία). The actual living of life is achieved only by the hierarchical determination of the lower faculty by the higher. The anticipations and conjectures, arising out of past perception, must be guided by the structure of hope, arising out of some insight into the structure of life as a whole, including past, present, and future. This structure, in turn, must be guided,

---

[89] *Phil.*, 39 B.　　　　[90] *Phil.*, 40 B–C.　　　　[91] *Phil.*, 39 E 10–11.
[92] περὶ φόβων τε καὶ θυμῶν καὶ πάντων τῶν τοιούτων. Cf. *Phil.*, 40 E 2.

so far as possible, by that pure insight into the permanent structure of the world as a whole which is achieved by reason alone. So far as the apprehending faculties really function in this way, appetite will be restrained and guarded by hopeful endeavor, which, in turn, will be ruled by rational aspiration. The so-called virtues are simply four distinguishable aspects of this hierarchical order.

Justice, which runs through the whole and is not especially restricted to one part, is simply the order itself, viewed from the higher down to the lower, each part *determining* what lies beneath it, or "managing its own affairs." [93] Temperance, which also runs through the whole, is the hierarchy viewed from the lower up to the higher, each part *being determined by* what lies above it or being properly harmonized.[94] Wisdom, the most essential and ruling virtue, belongs especially to the highest rational part. This part must both apprehend pure structure and apply this apprehension in the direction of life.[95] Courage belongs especially to the endeavoring part. This part must stick firmly "through both pains and pleasures" [96] to that which is hopeful [97] and avoid those things that are truly fearful.[98] It must both receive the apprehension of these things and guard this apprehension internally against the surge of appetite by shame,[99] and externally against alien influences by anger.[100]

The actual carrying out of any act, or of life itself, demands first of all wisdom, which sees that it is well planned, justice, which allots to each subordinate phase of the act its due, courage, which clings to the plan persistently and carries it out through the changes of time, and finally temperance, by which each subordinate phase is harmonized to the plan. No one of these can be lacking without disrupting the act. Hence, as St. Thomas points out,[101] these four Platonic "cardinal

---

[93] τὰ αὐτοῦ πράττων, *Rep.* (Adam), 441 E 2.

[94] Justice is active and causal. Temperance is passive and consequential, as may be seen from the long sentence, *Rep.* (Adam), 443 C 19–444 A 2. Justice comes first — μὴ ἐάσαντα, εὖ θέμενον, ἄρξαντα. Temperance follows as a result (Cf. *Rep.* (Adam), 443 D 25–26), "being harmonized" — ἡρμοσμένον. Justice is *natura humana naturans;* temperance is *natura humana naturata.*

[95] *Rep.* (Adam), 441 E 31.

[96] διά τε λυπῶν καὶ ἡδονῶν: *Rep.* (Adam), 442 C 16.

[97] τὸ μὴ δεινόν.

[98] τὸ δεινόν.

[99] *Rep.* (Adam), 442 A 3–B 10.

[100] *Rep.* (Adam), 442 B 10–14.

[101] In *X Libras Ethicorum Ad Nicomachum,* Liber II, Lectio VIII. It is pointed out here that Plato is also correct in asserting that one of these phases of virtue cannot

virtues" are all included in Aristotle's definition of virtue as "a habit concerned with choice, lying in a mean . . ., this determined by a rational principle, . . . in both actions and passions." [102] Virtue itself is rooted in reason (wisdom), as governing action (justice), and passion; either by strengthening certain passions until they reach the rational mean (courage) or by restraining others until they reach the rational mean (temperance).

Without temperance, the act will fail because of insubordination. Without courage it will falter and never be carried through. Without justice it will be incomplete. Without wisdom, if the act is carried out, it will be useless and mistaken, and hence much better left undone. One phase of "virtue" cannot be present without the others. True wisdom will see that it is applied justly. True justice will persist through time. Courageous persistence must both guard against external dangers and restrain the internal passions. As in the case of social life, individual life must be carried on as a whole, all at once or not at all. It cannot happen part by part. The individual is distinguished from the state by the higher ranges of insight to which he alone has access. Wisdom itself in its purest form (νόησις) is unattainable by the state, which at best is guided by a derivative tradition or structure of conviction (πίστις).

4. THE INVERSION OF INDIVIDUAL LIFE

Individual life can be actually lived only under the guidance of rational insight into the permanent structure of the world, and of life in the world. Only such insight may provide the imaginative pictures of hope with a sound and enduring basis. Only such sound and rationally qualified hope may integrate the confusion of empirical anticipations into a trustworthy system of expectation. When expectation is directed by hope, and hope by reason, momentary appetite will be directed by long-range endeavor, and long-range endeavor by aspiration for what is truly lasting. Rational aspiration, governing hopeful endeavor, governing anticipatory appetite — this is the broad structure of the true or virtuous life. Such life is accessible to the

---

actually exist without the rest. The *specifically different* virtues must be defined in terms of their divergent *objects*. In the *practical order* (always Plato's point of view) even one of *these* cannot be possessed without prudence, and, therefore, without the rest. Cf. Liber VI, Lectio XI.

[102] *Nic. Eth.*, Book II, 1106 B 36 ff.

individual alone, for the state can only strive and desire. Unless its long-range endeavors or policies are guided by stable knowledge, they will be misguided by false hopes, and finally collapse into a blind opportunism guided merely by the fluctuating anticipations of public opinion. The social order can be saved from the tyranny which is its inverted destination only by individual aspiration, and the stable source of truth which is its destination. Before the just society must come the just individual. In other words, inversion, which is an ever-present danger, must be avoided. Since, as we have seen, the hierarchical structure of individual life is even more complex than that of the state, it is even more possible for subordinate elements to get out of control, and thus to "invert the whole of life." [103] We must now turn to this inversion or materialization of individual life.

Here the relation between individual and society is a different one. Social forces may actively aid in the preparation for personal life by hygienic and educational precautions. But the life itself must be lived by the individual. No one can seek after the ultimate truth and apprehend it for another. Hence Plato maintains that in the upward ascent of life, the individual must lead, society must follow.[104] In the downward path, however, this is not the case. Social consummation can only prepare the way for individual virtue. But social corruption can actively pervert the individual. This structural fact emerges clearly from Plato's description of the inversion of life in Book VIII of the *Republic*, where, in each instance, social decay precedes individual decay as actively accelerating individual degeneration. Let us now look more carefully at the ideal stages of such a degeneration.

We have yet to examine the many purely intellectual perils and difficulties which beset the individual pursuit of truth. But we have already become familiar with the reasons why even the inauguration of such an arduous pursuit is impossible for society as a whole, and why, without the most skillful and vigilant guidance, the state must fall prey to the sophistry of public opinion. Once this has occurred, we have a sufficient explanation for the derationalizing of individual life, apart from the intrinsic difficulties of philosophy itself, which following Plato, we must reserve for a later discussion. We need

---

[103] *Rep.* (Adam), 442 B 10: ξύμπαντα τὸν βίον πάντων ἀνατρέψῃ.

[104] *Rep.* (Adam), 497 C 20, and Aristotle holds that "a genuine statesman must be a wise and virtuous individual man": τὸν δὲ πολιτικὸν ἀναγκαῖον εἶναι φρόνιμον. *Pol.*, III, 1277 A 15.

only recognize that such a pursuit involves the constant exercise of humility before the truth, and a persistent detachment from both the more immediate as well as the more lasting concerns of social life. The real nature of things remains what it is, independent of the rise and fall of empires, even of the most persistent hopes and fears which guide social endeavor. Hence, the pursuit of philosophy cannot long be maintained "in an ill-governed city" [105] which is becoming more and more subjectively preoccupied with its own concerns.

It may fitfully start up here and there in some faithful soul occupying a protected niche, [106] but eventually, *in the next generation*, to employ the continued figure of Plato's exposition in Book VIII, it must yield to external pressure. The realm of reliable truth is accessible to private aspiration alone. It is a "kingdom within." [107] To explore it in any adequate manner, the philosopher must remain detached from the concerns of every day. Amidst the "battling and railing in the law-courts or assembly," he "takes whatever happens to him quietly," his thoughts "being centered within himself." [108] In "an ill-governed city" this detachment, which is in fact the greatest possible attachment, will be interpreted either as a weakness or as selfish indifference by friends and associates. [109]

Such tension cannot long be maintained. In the long run, in the next generation, social pressure must win. The young son "gives up the kingdom which is within him" to the middle principle of striving [110] and victory loving [111] and becomes "proud and ambitious." [112] Only truth is capable of keeping men humble before something not themselves. Only continuous devotion to such a reality, completely independent of human desires and endeavors, can save a man from worldly ambition. Without philosophical humility and detachment, human nature must at best come to identify its goal with the triumph of some long-range social endeavor (pride), and to pursue it through a long period of time without qualification (ambition). This is the first step in the subjective derationalizing of life — in Plato's terms, the honor-loving man. [113]

[105] *Rep.* (Adam), 549 C 2.   [106] *Rep.* (Adam), 496 B ff.
[107] ἡ ἐν ἑαυτῷ ἀρχή: 550 B 11.
[108] ἑαυτῷ μὲν τὸν νοῦν προσέχοντα ἀεί: *Rep.* (Adam), 549 D 24.
[109] *Rep.* (Adam), 449 D ff.
[110] θυμοειδεῖ.   [111] φιλονίκῳ.
[112] ὑψηλόφρων τε καὶ φιλότιμος ἀνήρ: 550 B 11.
[113] ὁ φιλότιμος ἀνήρ.

Such a man will be *friendly* to true culture without being really guided by it.[114] He will be a good listener to argument without fully understanding.[115] He is really governed by the opinions and images about the world which are embodied in the living tradition of his society, determining its long-range hopes and fears. He represents that universal quality which the ancients later came to call *pietas*, and which, though it is surprisingly absent from Marxian and other modern social psychologies, is never wholly absent from actual human life. The honor-lover respects the hopes and fears of his ancestors. He realizes that unless they had been influenced by such hopes and fears his own life would not have been possible. He entertains similar hopes and fears for those who will come after him, and realizes that these arduous long-range endeavors must not be sacrificed to more immediate demands. Law and custom, which outlive the generations, are, therefore, his guide.

He completely understands the loyalty expressed by Socrates in the *Crito* to the laws and traditions of the state which existed long before he was born, and which brought him into being and nurtured him.[116] But he fails to understand how this loyalty can be qualified by any higher devotion to a higher law, and is, therefore, utterly at a loss to understand how Socrates could ever have placed himself at variance with the laws in the first place. He mistakes the state, which is only his stepfather, for his true father,[117] and the humanly formulated laws for "their heavenly brothers." [118] Having little coherent understanding of the real structure of society, which alone can justify and guide the constant formulation and reformulation of tradition, he confuses some particular version of the law with the law itself, and develops an inordinate veneration for those particular institutions and agencies which in the past have reflected this law, so far as the limitations of public opinion and action have allowed. Hence he is "remarkably obedient to human authority," [119] guiding his life by the dictates of its code.

Since no such code is able to cover the infinite concourse of circumstance, large areas of life will be left uncharted. In these areas

---

[114] *Rep.* (Adam), 448 E 29.
[115] *Rep.* (Adam), 448 E 29.
[116] *Crito*, 50 C 4 ff.
[117] Cf. *Rep.* (Adam), VII, 537 E 32 ff.
[118] *Crito*, 54 C 6–7.
[119] ἀρχόντων δὲ σφόδρα ὑπήκοος: *Rep.* (Adam), 549 A 3.

he will first follow a policy of repression, ruthlessly subordinating both his own interests and those of his dependents to the supposed requirements of victory in the end. Obedience, thus pursued without adequate guidance, must lead to the suppression of much that is really legitimate. At many points, the rule of authority will become indistinguishable from the rule of force. Thus he will fall into conflict with himself, for necessary desires and habits of life cannot be long disregarded. Forced out of their legitimate place, they fight back to regain their lost power and weaken even more the ruling authority.[120] How can victory in the end be won if no care is taken for momentary survival? Why strive for such victory without the material means which condition it? Reinforced by social pressure, these arguments gradually weaken the authority of tradition within the man himself. Inevitably, he comes to confuse victory itself with the material power to achieve the victory. Desire for victory merges with desire for power,[121] and ambition is tinged with avarice. We have what Plato calls the money-loving man (ὁ φιλοχρήματος). "Of all changes . . . there is none so speedy or so sure as the conversion of the ambitious honor-lover into an avaricious money-lover." [122]

Rational insight, which is alone capable of apprehending the true richness and complexity of the world, can provide a framework of understanding broad enough to include each important phase of human nature. Even the guiding faith of a lasting tradition is able to reflect much of this, through its opinions and the concrete images in which they are clothed. Necessary expectations and desires, together with their necessary satisfaction, hopes and endeavors together with the joy of struggling persistently for lasting victory, even rational aspiration together with the pure joy of understanding,[123] all find some scope for unhampered development.

In the money-loving or oligarchic man, however, this is no longer true. Both aspiration and striving are now dominated by appetite. Reason is distorted into a mere instrument for devising means of satisfying as many desires as possible, while the spirited element is distorted into mere admiration and striving for gain.[124] Not only is the development of these natural phases of human nature narrowly distorted and suppressed but also the very structure of appetite falls

120 *Rep.* (Adam), 553 A 5 ff.   121 *Rep.* (Adam),553 D 25.
122 *Rep.* (Adam), 553 D 26.   123 *Rep.* (Adam), 583 B ff.
124 *Rep.* (Adam), 553 D ff.

into conflict with itself. Within the framework of a broader and more lasting purpose, both the labor and regimen demanded by expectation and the satisfaction of appetite, which this makes possible, can find a legitimate place. On the one hand, work must be done. On the other, "necessary desires" [125] must be satisfied. Without this, life cannot even survive. Both find their subordinate but legitimate place within life as a whole.

But when expectation comes to dominate both knowledge and permanent conviction, the mere accumulation of material power becomes the ultimate end — to which all else must be sacrifiecd, even the fulfilment or satisfaction of the appetites themselves, which has to be regarded as a waste of time and energy.[126] Expectation and work are for the sake of satisfying the appetites. Power is no good unless it is spent. But spending wastes the power. Hence the oligarchic life falls into bitter conflict between the rigid regimen demanded by expectation for the building up of power and the hoard of "drone-like desires" eagerly waiting to be feasted on the honey. Like the oligarchic state, such a man "will be at war with himself; he will be two men, and not one." [127] One man within him will be worried and expectant of the future, niggardly, miserly, and hesitant about expense. The other, though at first repressed, will be constantly rebelling at this repression, and waiting its chance to burst forth in an orgy of expenditure. Thus the oligarchic life wavers between a narrow repressive discipline and brief periods of wasteful escape and "relaxation," each becoming more and more antagonistic to the other.

For a time, the niggardly, saving discipline will succeed in jealously guarding itself against the ever-threatening inroads of spending and play. But the enforced discipline or virtue of such a man will be a pale and distorted image of true discipline. He acts justly or honestly not because reason demands it, but because it is the best policy. He restrains his growing spendthrift passions and desires not because of some great and overarching purpose which is more important than they, but simply because of the spendthrift passions. He is shrewd enough to see that he cannot spend without saving. So he saves for the sake of spending. He is temperate because he is ruled

---

[125] ἀναγκαῖαι ἐπιθυμίαι, 558 D ff.
[126] Rep. (Adam), 554 A 2–6.
[127] Οὐκ ἄρ᾽ ἂν εἴη ἀστασίαστος ὁ τοιοῦτος ἐν ἑαυτῷ, οὐδὲ εἶς ἀλλὰ διπλοῦς τις. Rep. (Adam), 554 D 26. Cf. 557 A and 551 D.

by intemperance.[128] He is just, as Glaucon suggests most men are just,[129] for the sake of injustice. He is able to stick to his purpose, even to take risks in a way which resembles courage, but it is only because he is so afraid of losing his money. He even plans his conduct over long periods of time, wisely subordinating all that he does to a seemingly overarching purpose, but this purpose is merely to acquire the material means of satisfying temporary appetites. So his wisdom is garbled by the madness of the miser.

In any long-range endeavor, really worth attaining and therefore requiring persistent hope and striving, he will be so afraid of awakening his expensive appetites that he will be unable to spend himself or his money, except in very small part. Like the oligarchic state,[130] he will be more afraid of internal revolution than of external conquest, and will draw back from any major effort. Consequently he will end by saving his money and losing the real prize.[131] Lacking practical understanding and thus being unable to tame the host of passions, which cannot be fitted into his scrimping regimen by rational persuasion, he can only suppress them more and more violently by force. As their rebellious power is increased by stimulation from those kindred agencies which always abound in a decaying social order,[132] his "more or less virtuous self-constraint" [133] yields increasingly to the demands of amusement and relaxation. At last, all discipline breaks down. The only end of blind production is blind consumption; so production must eventually come to its end. Production itself is regarded as a kind of consumption, having value only in so far as it immediately satisfies some appetite for work or expression. The necessary desires are not distinguished from the unnecessary ones, all appetite being regarded as on the same level. This anarchy of consumption, hailed by modern "ethical" theory as the normal state, is Plato's "democratic man."

The system of expectation which governs the oligarchic life is now decomposed into a succession of momentary conjectures and antici-pations responsive to appetite. Each transitory anticipation asserts itself against the legitimate claims of rational insight into broad structure, as well as against the demands of any overarching purpose for life as a whole. Wisdom, which also disagrees with prevailing

[128] Cf. *Phaedo*, 68 E ff.   [129] *Rep.* (Adam), 360 C.
[130] *Rep.* (Adam), 551 D 26.   [131] *Rep.* (Adam), 555 A.
[132] *Rep.* (Adam), 559 E.   [133] *Rep.* (Adam), 554 C 21.

opinion and demands complete submission, is easily confused with its opposite. Hence this insolent assertiveness of transitory conjecture (ὕβρις) is hymned as "true culture" (εὐπαιδευσία). Thus the democratic man loses all continuity of life. "He passes through the day, indulging each chance appetite." [134] As a result of this, there is an enormous growth of parasitic habits and interests, those "unnecessary appetites" with their "unnecessary pleasures" which have been fostered under an oligarchic regime. [135]

Justice, which renders to each thing its due, ignoring no necessary or important element, is also easily confused with its opposite — treating everything alike. [136] Hence this chaotic anarchy is hymned as liberty (ἐλευθερία). Temperance, which allows only necessary appetites and pleasures and prunes away all those that can be dispensed with, is easily confused with its opposite. This allows all chance appetites and pleasures as equally necessary, and prunes away restraint. This intemperate waste [137] is hymned as magnificence. [138] Courage, the maintenance of humility before the dictates of reason in accordance with what is to be hoped for and what is to be dared, is easily confused with its opposite, the complete absence of all humility in the impudent pursuit of appetite, whether it be necessary or unnecessary. This impudent persistence of all past pleasure which has been preserved in memory [139] is accordingly hymned as courage. The inversion of the virtues may proceed until finally hardly any element of discipline remains. [140]

Thus, individual life may be gradually inverted or turned upside down. The determination of conduct by systematic anticipation of the future is swept aside and yields to determination from behind. Only past pleasures which happen to have been preserved in memory, and thus stimulate appetite, are capable of conjuring up particular expectations which motivate action. The only elements of discipline are those necessary appetitive habits which past discipline has thoroughly traced in the soul and which are still capable of being painted in the imagination with alluring color. [141] Since these involve difficulty and concentration, they stand in the way of unbridled self-expression and are attacked by the agencies of anarchy which run rampant in a

134 *Rep.* (Adam), 561 C 18.   135 *Rep.* (Adam), 359 D.
136 *Rep.* (Adam), 358 C 3.   137 ἀσωτία.
138 μεγαλοπρέπεια.   139 ἀναίδεια.
140 *Rep.* (Adam), 560 D 27–561 A 6.   141 *Rep.* (Adam), 561 B.

society given over to "liberty." Since every organizing principle has been abandoned, the only way to break down these last traces of order is by cultivating some single master passion or lust in the soul of the victim to act as the "champion" [142] of all the unnecessary, drone-like appetites and pleasures, as the political tyrant emerges as the "champion" of the proletariat. [143] When his imagination is completely dominated by the lurid anticipation of some blissful relief from the perpetual anguish of craving which gnaws at him, he may be drawn away from every orderly desire, to fall completely under the sway of a superfluous but monstrously swollen appetite to which everything else is subordinated. Anarchy will thus inevitably lead to tyranny.

Even in this completely inverted mode of life which verges upon insanity and bestiality there is a certain analogue to virtue. The whole course of action is guided by an imaginative picture of *apparent* ecstasy. Everything else is subordinated to this single *idée fixe*, and allotted its seemingly correct or just position. Whatever interferes with the attainment of this goal is ruthlessly eliminated or suppressed by an inverted "temperance." The whole structure must be persistently maintained through the flux of circumstance. Threatening dangers must be anticipated and warded off by something easily mistaken for courage. But while such a life is *generically* human, it lies at the pole which is opposite to humanity.

The guiding image is a fantastic compound of past experiences of relief from intense pain, [144] disguised as the most enthralling bliss. This image constructed by a small part of the soul carries with it the maximum of illusion and the bare minimum of truth. [145] The democratic man subordinates reality to his desires and expectations and thus achieves subjectivism. But "the tyrannized life" [146] is subordinated as a whole to a single fixed idea, and thus goes one step farther. It achieves the solipsism of a single master appetite. Under its dominion the tyrant can allot no stable position to anything else. Hence the greater part of himself is never satisfied, and, pursuing his apparent goal, he never accomplishes what he really plans (to act justly in such a way as to achieve his whole purpose). Instead of

[142] προστάτης: *Rep.* (Adam), 572 A 1.
[143] Cf. *Rep.* (Adam), 564 D, 565 C ff. and Adam, note on 572 E 35.
[144] *Rep.* (Adam), 586 A–D.
[145] *Rep.* (Adam), 577 D 25–26.
[146] ἡ τυραννουμένη ψυχή: *Rep.* (Adam), 577 E 30.

achieving a just order of life, therefore, he is full of "tumult and remorse." [147] Appetitive pleasure can never remain. By its nature, it must be ever moving into its opposite, pain. It is only the order or structure of appetite (temperance) that can be maintained. But, having removed all temperance and restraint from himself, he can now maintain nothing, being "always needy and insatiable." [148] His phantasy-fed appetite can never be satisfied, but is ceaselessly stinging him internally to fresh convulsions.

Guarding his course by a seeming courage against all that threatens it, he becomes afraid of everything, since everything threatens it.[149] Not only is he unable to share his monstrous phantasies with other men, but also he is even unable to share them with the greater part of himself. Hence his "courage" leads him to fear not only the desires of others but also his own. He must be a "flatterer" [150] and "fawn on" even the worst of these, in order to maintain the shaky despotism of his obsession. More and more he must lock himself up in the narrow prison cell constructed for him by his phantasy and lust. If his passion is largely thwarted by the limitations of private circumstance, he may remain in this miserable and enslaved condition. But if, through the decay of society, he is able to gain more power for his mad pursuit, he becomes even more miserable.[151] In addition to the hopeless task of inflicting his disease on the whole of himself, he must now fight ceaselessly in the attempt to inflict it also upon others. Hence he must be more jealous, more treacherous, more unjust, more friendless and impious than at first. It is better to stand still than to go rapidly in the wrong direction,[152] better to be impeded in an unjust course than to have the "power" of carrying it out.[153] The public tyrant, therefore, with a whole city or state at his disposal, is the most inverted and miserable of men.

But black as we may paint this enslaved and inverted life, and Plato cannot be accused of any understatement in this regard, we must not forget that it remains human life. The tyrannized man still remains a man, as is shown by the very agony and remorse he continues to

[147] *Rep.* (Adam), 577 E 31–32.
[148] *Rep.* (Adam), 578 A 1.
[149] *Rep.* (Adam), 578 A–2.
[150] κόλαξ: *Rep.* (Adam), 577 E 29. Cf. the analogous phenomenon in τέχνη, pp. 56–57.
[151] *Rep.* (Adam), 580 ff.
[152] Cf. *Rep.*, 519 A.
[153] *Gorgias*, 479 A.

suffer. As we have seen, he cannot entirely suppress all traces of reason from his fantastic opinions, nor all traces of hopeful endeavor from his master passion. This confusion and disorder, which is the peculiar evil of life, cannot completely disorder it. The overarching structures of reason and hope fade into dimness, but they remain, nevertheless, breaking through the smoke of passion now and again, to cause repeated qualms and torments of remorse. Plato never allows us to forget this truly amazing fact and, indeed, offers it as an argument for the enduring toughness of the principle of human life.[154]

That the order of life should be preserved in spite of bodily sickness and decay is not so remarkable, for the body is distinct from the life which animates it. That a high order of individual life should be possible in the midst of a decadent society is certainly remarkable enough.[155] But that life should still be capable of persisting in spite of the vice that corrupts it at its very individual source is the most truly amazing fact. The most striking evidence for the "deathlessness" [156] of the vital principle of life is within the reach of all. It is simply to behold a really evil man. Such a man is a living argument for the deathlessness of life. In spite of the awful burden of disorder and corruption which weighs him down, he yet remains a man. Beneath the wreckage and confusion there remains a certain spark of essential humanity. No one can say that it can never be rekindled. There are too many astonishing cases of revitalization to indicate the contrary. But even if such regeneration is impossible, as may well be, the continued pangs of agony and remorse show that a spark at least remains. As Plato says, it seems that "the peculiar evil and inherent vice of individual life is insufficient to destroy it." [157] It is the confusion of something that cannot be *completely* confused, the inversion of something that cannot be *completely* inverted.

We have now ended our study of this process of inversion, as it gradually reverses the direction of individual life. Instead of being determined by what is beyond or ahead of itself, the inverted life more and more comes to be determined from behind. At its most vital pitch, it is directed by respect for that actual order of being which is entirely independent of human interest, and is accessible to rational contemplation alone. Insight into this independent order (σοφία) alone can provide the stable foundation for hope which is independent of

---

[154] *Rep.*, 608 C ff.   [155] *Rep.*, 496 B–497 A.
[156] ἀθανασία.   [157] *Rep.*, 610 E 31.

social and individual catastrophe. Only such hope can give sound and lasting guidance with respect to what is to be dared and what is to be feared.[158] Courageous persistence (ἀνδρεία) in the aspiration for such a goal (ἔρως) yields "true and pure joys," [159] which are independent of failure and pain. The actual daring of those things which are to be dared in their proper order and the actual avoidance of those that are to be feared (δικαιοσύνη) involve a restriction of appetites and pleasures to those which are strictly necessary (σωφροσύνη).

The first step in the inversion of life is the loss of respect for what transcends the human horizon, and the consequent subjectivism of pride. The hope for human victory (φιλονεικία) replaces reason as the ultimate guide. Hence persistent zeal replaces courage, and the ambitious pursuit of long-range endeavor replaces aspiration for stable ends, independent of the shifting human scene. Such endeavor (θυμός) is still able to provide rejoicing which persists through the immediate pleasures and pains of appetite. Since the goal is no longer one which can be adequately justified by reason, however, tradition (νόμος) replaces justice as the rule of positive conduct, and authority replaces temperance as the restraining power. The effect of this element of arbitrariness in restraint is to strengthen the push of pleasure and appetite from behind.

This opposition to arbitrary and hence weakening restraint is further strengthened by the infiltration of unnecessary habits and their pleasures which now merge with the necessary ones. These pleasures determine a system of expectation (προσδοκία), which now governs a new mode of conative clinging to past satisfaction, or avarice. Greed, the tenacious persistence of avarice, now replaces courage and determines from behind what is to be dared and what is to be feared. Whatever does not interfere with greedy expectation is to be dared. Whatever does interfere is to be ruthlessly repressed. But, as a matter of fact, almost everything interferes with this narrow system of expectation, except the anticipations of productive habit and appetite. Hence this productive order is nervously reinforced by expectation. But such appetite naturally demands satisfaction, so that the pressure of unproductive consumption is also increased, and we have the vicious circle of the oligarchic soul. Consumption works against production, and production against consumption. Yet each

---

[158] Cf. *Prot.*, 359 C 2.
[159] ἡδονὰς ἀληθεῖς καὶ καθαρὰς κ.τ.λ. *Phil.*, 63 E 3–7.

necessarily demands the other. Life is split in two, with the inevitable weakening of the productive principle.

In the next stage, all but a slight, remaining trace of determination from ahead is lost. The system of expectation, guiding avarice, is now disintegrated into a set of separate expectations, each guided from behind by a remembered pleasure. This past memory determines an appetite which is unchecked by any trace of humility before the future or what lies beyond it, and which is maintained against all such restraint by a wild disregard for even consequences (ὕβρις). Justice is replaced by its opposite, anarchy (ἀναρχία), and temperance by its opposite, waste (ἀσωτία).

The final stage of the turning around of life [160] is what Plato calls *tyranny*. Here determination is exclusively from behind. Remembered relief, exaggerated by phantasy, determines an insatiable craving, which leads to persistent obsession by an *idée fixe*. Nothing else is to be dared. Everything else is to be feared. A private subjective construction becomes the sole guide of life, and we have the ultimate extreme in solipsism. Still, in spite of inversion, the horizons of conjecture, conviction, and reason remain. The guiding phantasy has to be brought before the mind as an idea, held before long-range endeavor as a persistent hope, and placed at least vaguely within the over-arching framework of things as they really are. Regeneration is thus *possible*.

Human life is ever moving between these two extremes, the free life and the tyrannized or enslaved life.[161] It can move, however, either in the one direction towards organized expectation, organized by hope, finally justified by contemplation, or in the other towards the self-assertiveness of pride, greed, excess, and finally complete possession from behind by the fantastically reconstructed past. No life can achieve perfect justice and temperance. No life can achieve perfect liberty and waste. Each life, however, while it is living, must move in the direction towards greater life, or it must drift back in the opposite direction towards mere repetition of a distorted past which is the deprivation of life. In fact the opposed motions we have been studying, as Plato points out in the *Phaedo*,[162] are the two opposites life and death, the privation of life. Two opposites always come out of

---

[160] Cf. *Rep.*, 518 C 9, D 4, E 4.
[161] δούλην ἢ ἐλευθέραν τὴν . . . ψυχήν: *Rep.*, 577 D 27.
[162] *Phaedo*, p. 64 A 4–69 E 5.

INDIVIDUAL LIFE AND ITS DEFORMATION

one another.[163] One opposite is the possession, the other the privation of the very same thing. That which moves always lies between
the opposites. Hence it may move positively towards the thing, or
in the opposite direction, privatively, away from it.[164]

Clearly, as we are informed in the *Phaedo*, life and death are such
opposites. Only the dead can be brought back to life again, and
surely only the living can die.[165] That which lives (ἡ ψυχή) is between
these two opposites. Hence it can move, while still "alive," either
in the positive direction towards the actual possession of life itself,
or away from this in the inverted or privative direction, towards the
lack of life, or towards death, just as a sleepy man may move towards
the waking state by *re*awakening (ἀνεγείρεσθαι) as we say, or in the
privative direction and go to sleep.[166] Living and dying are the two
opposed directions in which the living being may move, either towards
virtue and wisdom, the essence of life, or away from these things,
in the blind drift of passion from behind.

We do not notice this, because we fail to grasp the peculiar nature
of human life as a rational, hierarchical structure, and think of it in
terms of those generic traits which human life has in common with
the other animals. Thus we may think of it as the mere animation of
a body, irrespective of the specific direction in which the life is moving, that is irrespective of whether it is really moving towards life or
towards death — i.e. whether it is living or dying. But if human life
is thus identified with one of its conditions, the mere animation of
a human body, death also should then be identified with the lack of
this condition, the mere absence of such animation, and we should
speak of inanimate objects as dead. But we do not speak in this
manner. A stone or a river is certainly non-living, or inanimate. We
do not, therefore, regard it as dead. Only that which is capable of life
can die. Only that which is *humanly* alive can die a human death.
The human body, as we have seen, is the condition, not the cause,

---

[163] οὐκ ἄλλοθεν ἢ ἐκ τῶν ἐναντίων τὰ ἐναντία: *Rep.*, 70 E 1.

[164] *Rep.*, 71 A 12 ff.

[165] *Phaedo*, 71 D 5 ff.

[166] *Phaedo*, 72 B 7. Throughout the argument the positive direction is indicated by
the prefix ἀνα: cf. ἀναβιώσκεσθαι (71 E 14); ἀνεγείρεσθαι (72 B 9); and ἀνάμνησις,
(72 E 5), *et passim*. We also speak of *re*generation, *re*awakening, and *re*membering,
not of being destroyed *again*, or *returning to* sleep (cf. returning to consciousness),
or *re*forgetting a thing. We indicate the privative direction by: he *failed* to live; he
fell asleep; and he *failed* to remember. We do not naturally say: he failed to be destroyed, he *fell* awake, or failed to forget.

of such life and death. Once the human body is humanly animated, then it may move either in the direction of genuine life or away from it. In other words, it may either live or die. Such death is not the mere cessation of animation (the loss of the condition). A man would first have to lose his humanity, and become an animal, before this could happen. It is not the loss of mere being. He would have to lose the generic properties of life, before this could happen. It is the inverted passage of a living man in the direction away from his essential humanity.

This is brought about primarily by precisely that sort of confusion we have just been considering. If we confuse life with certain of its material conditions, we inevitably come to confuse life as it really is with its opposite, both having the same conditions, or being included in the same genus. To think of ourselves as alive, when, as a matter of fact, we have only the conditions for life, is already beginning to die, for the whole process of inversion which we have traced has its roots in a failure of understanding. When understanding fades away, it must be replaced by conviction, and finally by conjecture and constructive phantasy. This turning around of the soul is really what we mean by human death, though most men confuse this sinking into sensory determination and appetite with life. As a matter of fact, it is the opposite — death. Can it be that we are actually unclear as to the nature of what we mean by the hidden structure of life, and that we are most of us so hopelessly confused as to scorn as death what is in reality life, and to eulogize as life what is in reality living death — the only death that *a man* can die? Such indeed is the daring suggestion of the *Phaedo*.[167] In fact, the bold confidence of most men, who would scorn such a suggestion as absurd, should not increase our trust in their opinion.

We must now turn to the study of that intellectual sophistry which lies at the root of such self-confident confusion. Thinking we know what we do not really know, we sink all the more hopelessly into the absolute darkness of an involuntary error concerning which we have not even the slightest inkling of awareness. Why do we think that we know what it is to live, what it is to die? Why do we pretend to know what we do not really know? The ultimate answer to these questions is certainly hidden in mystery. Nevertheless, we can become aware of certain tendencies closely associated with this progressive

[167] Especially 64 B 7–C 2; and 68 B 8–69 E 5.

failure of understanding, which Plato calls maleducation (ἀπαιδευσία). We can then gain further light by contrasting it with that opposite movement of the soul in gaining understanding which Plato calls education (παιδεία).

No procedure is more likely to help us in grasping this contrast than to study the two modes of vital motion so vividly portrayed for us in the famous analogy of the Cave in Book VII of Plato's *Republic*.

CHAPTER V

THE IMAGE OF THE CAVE

W E HAVE now traced the cultural inversion of the arts to its source in the inversion of communal life. We have traced this in turn to an inversion of individual life, and this to an inversion of education and the individual understanding. The *final* source of human evil lies in the disordering of human knowledge. Its correction lies in the achievement of knowledge in the individual soul. This achievement, together with its inversion, is a process in which both being and the individual faculties apprehending it are *together* involved, the process of human education, a natural aspect of the life of man, distinguished from the techniques and institutions of therapeutic education, devised to facilitate it. The techniques and institutions may wax, or wane, or be wholly absent, but, with or without them, the education of the human soul must proceed in a true or in an inverted form. When the soul finally leaves the body, it leaves all else behind, taking with it only what it has learned, its education ($\pi\alpha\iota\delta\epsilon\iota\alpha$), for a single lifetime is insufficient for the cultivation of a man.[1]

This education is a revolution or process of turning,[2] quite distinct from the forms and patterns which constitute its goal. Something other than formal analysis, therefore, is required if this historicity is to be suggested. It may be suggested by the device of the myth or image. There is a painter in the soul of each of us, which, if properly guided by the stable results of knowledge, may provide us with pictures which, like the images of Daedalus,[3] though incapable of representing its stable structure, are capable of suggesting *motion*, and thus of eliciting in us some apprehension of this historic revolution of the soul concerning which we should otherwise be at the mercy of any chance image or opinion. Of course, we might try to devise one of our own. But we should hardly be likely to succeed in hitting upon

[1] Cf. *Phaedo*, 107 D 2.
[2] *Rep.*, 518 D 4 and E 4 — $\pi\epsilon\rho\iota\alpha\gamma\omega\gamma\dot{\eta}$.
[3] Cf. *Euth.*, 11 C 7 ff.; 15, B 7 ff., and *Meno.*, 97 D 6.

a better one than that of the famous analogy of the Cave at the beginning of Book VII of the *Republic*. This is preceded by two preliminary analogies, some acquaintance with which is necessary for any serious interpretation of the Cave.

1. THE ANALOGY OF THE SUN

In our discussion of the structure of individual life, wisdom was formally recognized as the guiding principle and source of virtue. But at that time no effort was made to analyze the knowing faculty into its various divisions, or to determine its various objects. We are now in a position to follow Plato as he takes this "longer way" towards the end of the sixth book of the *Republic*.[4] As the false life is misguided by the results of an inverted process of education, so the true life of the human guardian must be guided by the results of a true process of education. What, then, is this process? The succeeding discussion, which persists until the end of the seventh book, is inaugurated by a fundamental question: what is the "greatest of all things to be learned"?[5]

It will be that without an understanding of which nothing else will be of value, and with an understanding of which all else will be understood in its proper position. This "greatest of all things to be learned" is the good. What is the good of knowing all things if one does not know the good, or of possessing all things if one does not possess the good? This good, which all men seek, must be real, for while many men come to possess only apparent goods, no man is satisfied with such goods. Each man at least thinks that the good he is seeking to possess, or has partially achieved, is real and not merely apparent. Hence all men, even those who have reflected carefully upon the matter, think they know what it is, and take for granted that other men also know. If this basic phase of the structure of human life should be false, human life itself would be false and not to be lived. In its very essence it involves some knowledge of the good. What, then, is the good, and how are we to learn of it?

Socrates says that the good in itself is beyond his capacity, but he is able to give an analogy, the analogy of the sun.[6] The lower senses, like hearing, are in a certain sense self-sufficient. If sound, which is capable of being heard, and the faculty, which is capable of

---

[4] *Rep.*, VI, 504 B 2.   [5] μέγιστον μάθημα; *Rep.*, 505 A.
[6] *Rep.*, 506 D 6 ff.

hearing, are both present with a connecting medium, hearing will occur. But sight is nobler than these other senses precisely because of its dependence upon a third thing higher than itself, which it is not able to see directly. Colour may be present in an external thing, and the ability to see may be present in a living eye — nevertheless, actual seeing will not occur unless the sun bestows its light. To the degree in which this light is absent, vision will be imperfectly or distortedly present, as at night.

There is, therefore, a remarkable analogy between sight which guides the body and understanding which guides the soul.[7] Reason, like sight, is actualized by a source higher than itself, and is, there-fore, not self-sufficient. There may be an intelligible structure, and an intelligence to grasp it — nevertheless actual understanding will not occur unless the ultimate source of being bestows being on what is known, and leads the understanding to actualize further its capacity. To the degree in which being is absent knowledge will be imperfect or distorted. Not only may the same essence be known in distinct modes of existence, but within each level it is known more or less distinctly in so far as its connections with other more luminous essences are also more or less distinctly grasped. Just as the faculty of sight is causally sensitive to the source of brightness, and passes up from dimmer objects to brighter ones until it reaches this source, so the faculty of knowing is causally sensitive to the source of being, and passes up from less intelligible objects to their more intelligible causes until it reaches the ultimate source of being and intelligibility.

2. THE DIVIDED LINE

The stable essences which are the objects of knowledge are divided "according to their clarity and lack of clarity"[8] as two unequal portions of a single line. The pure invisible essences, freed from all extraneous admixture with what is non-essential, are as much clearer than the visible essences as the upper division of the line is longer than the lower. In general, it is the pure structures which constitute the archetypes or causes of the sensible essences modelled after them, or structuralized according to them. It is the formal essence which *makes* each sensible thing *what it is.* The effect can be understood only in terms of its cause, the image only in terms of its archetype,

[7] Cf. Aristotle: ὡς γὰρ ἐν σώματι ὄψις, ἐν ψυχῇ νοῦς. *Nic. Eth.*, 1096 B 28.
[8] *Rep.*, 509 D 9.

the visible only in terms of its intelligible form or structure. But each portion of the line is divided, in turn, according to the same ratio. Sensible things are divided into those which actually become all together in nature, and the fragmentary figments and images of certain of these which are produced in human sensation, the supreme mimetic medium of nature,[9] cast as shadows,[10] or reflected on water [11] or glass in an inverted form.[12] The real things of nature, freed from all distortion introduced by a reflecting medium such as the human senses, are as much clearer and more stable than their re- $\rceil$ A flected images, as the upper part of this division of the line is longer than the lower. Here also the subjective image is an effect of the real thing in nature, which is its archetype.

Finally, the upper portion of the line is also divided according to the same ratio. Intelligible essences are divided into those which exist altogether in that which $\rceil$ B is the source of being as well as of understanding, and the *fragmentary* groups of these which are reflected in the scientific understanding.[13] Here also the essences all to- $\rceil$ C gether in their totality are as much clearer and more stable than the reflected essences derived from them as the upper portion of this upper division of the line is $\rceil$ D longer than the lower. Hence we have the proportion: as AC : CE/AB : BC/CD : DE. The very same *structures* $\rceil$ E exist in a certain mode at each of the four levels: (1) as they actually

---

[9] *Rep.*, 509 E 1: τὰς εἰκόνας πρῶτον. Unless the senses were able by their very nature to construct images, colours, shapes, sounds, etc., we should be unable to perceive the other natural images such as shadows and reflections. Sensations and imaginary fantasies are natural replicas of certain qualities of changing things. Cf. *Soph.*, 266 B 9, which mentions τά τε ἐν τοῖς ὕπνοις καὶ ὅσα μεθ' ἡμέραν φαντάσματα αὐτοφυῆ λέγεται as θείας ἔργα ποιήσεως — works of the God who moulded nature. Adam does not see that for Plato sensation is a natural εἰκών. Cf. his note to 511 E and to 517 A.

[10] *Rep.*, 509 E 1: τὰς σκιάς. Just as things in the outside world cast shadowy phantasms of themselves on our senses, so do they cast ordinary shadows of themselves on other media.| Hence the shadows on the wall are a most appropriate symbol in the Myth of the Cave for human sensations.|

[11] τὰ ἐν τοῖς ὕδασι φαντάσματα. The word φάντασμα is used also for "the shadowlike replicas" of impure souls which may be seen about burial places (*Phaedo*, 81 D 1), and generally for sensuous appearances, *Theaet.*, 155 A 2.

[12] *Soph.*, 266 C 3. Mirror images are a striking example of the inversion of order so apt to distort the seeming replicas of things. Cf. *Tim.*, 46 A.

[13] At *Rep.*, 598 B 7, Plato notes how a bad image, εἴδωλον, oversimplifies, grasping only a small phase of its archetype: σμικρόν τι ἑκάστου ἐφάπτεται.

are in relation to their source; (2) as they are scientifically or discursively understood; (3) as they *become*, in the material flux of nature; and (4) as this becoming is disjointedly reflected in sense and imagination. A thing at one level is different from anything at another, but between these levels there is an analogy of proportionality: AC : CE/AB : BC/CD : DE. The whole visible world of becoming, with its archetypes and images, is an image of the intelligible world with its archetypes and reflections.

The intelligible world is known by rational insight (νόησις) without the aid of sense. The structure of the visible world is judged by opinion (δόξα) which is unable to grasp things as they are in themselves but is forced to follow the relative appearances of sense.[14] But opinion is divided into two types: (1) that which judges according to the subjective appearance of the physical thing (εἰκασία); and (2) that which tends to correct such plausible conjecture by further experience of the physical thing itself which appears, and is the source of the appearance (πίστις). Rational insight is divided into two types: (1) that which lays bare the structure of some limited area of reality, which it simply takes for granted as an hypothesis without attempting to discover anything about its further connections or ultimate source (διάνοια); and (2) that which tends to correct such rational assumptions by direct contact with *the whole* realm of essence as it is in its source (νοῦς).

Each higher level is the formal cause and archetype for what lies below it. Sensory appearances are derivations and limitations of natural things. These are derivations and "embodiments" of their forms and essences. Finally, these essences are derivations and replicas of their archetypes as they exist in the ultimate single source of all being. We begin with an implicit confidence in the truth and

[14] Cf. *Soph.*, 264 A 4: τί δ' ὅταν μὴ καθ' αὑτὸ ἀλλὰ δι' αἰσθήσεως παρῇ τινι, τὸ τοιοῦτον αὖ πάθος. We then judge the thing (δόξα) not as it is but as it appears (αἴσθησις). This "mixture of δόξα and αἴσθησις" (B 2) is indicated when we say "it seems" or "it appears." Plato sometimes, as in the passage before us, refers to this as φαντασία, a view criticized by Aristotle in *De An.*, III, ch. 3. At other times he refers to it as δόξα or through some form of the verb δοκέω. Cf. Cornford, *Plato's Theory of Knowledge* (New York: Harcourt Brace, 1935), pp. 32, 62, 71 n. 1, and 109–110. This view is not contrary to Aristotle, who admits that, while φαντασία does not involve δόξα, the latter *does* involve the former. Cf. *De An.*, 434 A 10. Opinion is a mode of thought which is forced to fall back on sense and imagination at crucial points due to lack of insight. It is doubtful that Plato's many formulae (*Phil.*, 39 B, and *Tim.*, 52 A 7: δόξῃ μετ' αἰσθήσεως) mean any more than this.

reality of relative subjective images, but experience gradually teaches us to take these appearances lightly and to use them only as conjectural means of gaining more adequate knowledge of the real nature of the changing things which are their archetypes. Then, as the scientific understanding of the *pure structure* of such things begins to dawn upon us, we learn to take even these things more lightly, using them, as the mathematician uses intuitive diagrams, only as indications or effects of the pure patterns largely concealed within them.[15] Finally, we learn to be distrustful even of the limited, reflective conclusions of art and science, treating their first principles only as assumptions which we use as steppingstones, to carry us on to some philosophical insight into the structure of being itself, their *ultimate* source. Thus, in the order of knowing, each level becomes a steppingstone towards the next.

Finally, as our knowledge nears its completion, we are able to come down from this ultimate source as well as to stumble up towards it by faltering steps, explaining the isolated structures of science by an understanding of the whole pattern of things as derived from their first source, explaining individual natural changes by the pure patterns and laws of science, and finally the fluctuating appearances of sense and imagination by their natural causes. Both the way down and the way up have their own difficulties and confusions.[16] Neither way is easy. The sophist confuses the two. For him, the way up seems to be going down to lesser reality, and the way down to be clinging more firmly to what is true and clear. Hence he resists and obstructs the process of education at every point, clinging to becoming as though it were being, to science as though it were philosophy, and to the object of subjective conjecture as though it were the natural being of things. Sophistry is no isolated theory or doctrine but a transcendental confusion of direction in the individual understanding, which reverses the whole educational process, and thus inverts the very life of man. The historic nature of this transcendental inversion as it actually occurs in the concrete flux of history is poignantly suggested to us in the great image of the Cave.

[15] Cf. J. L. Stocks, "The Divided Line of *Plato Republic VI*," *Classical Quarterly*, vol. 5 (1911), pp. 73 ff.

[16] *Rep.*, 518 A–B.

3. The Image of the Cave

Although it is commonly agreed that Plato has constructed this image to aid us in grasping the import of philosophy for the crucible of human life into which we are all plunged, the confused variety of modern interpretations would seem to belie its helpful power. Perhaps the chief reason for this confusion is too great a tendency to dwell upon the details of the analogy apart from what they indicate, and a consequent inversion of direction, in which we tend to interpret Plato's philosophy in terms of the myth, rather than the myth in terms of Plato's philosophy.[17]

As we have already seen, a good image, or *eikon*, must be skillfully constructed so as to be readily assimilable by our sensitive faculties. But this is not the primary requirement. Starting here, it must then lead us on to a firmer and clearer apprehension of invisible truths. Hence the good image is self-effacing, eliminating itself, so to speak, in its pointing function. If it fails to lead us on to what is more important than itself, and still persists, either it or we have failed. Let us then see if we cannot make the *eikon* disappear by carefully studying it, in the light of those structures which should be now at least vaguely in mind, first of all confining ourselves strictly to the image, and then strictly to its invisible meaning (section 4, pp. 188 ff), never confusing the two, but using the former as a pathway to the latter.

The whole image, as Plato also informs us,[18] is a representation of education (παιδεία) and its opposite or inverted form (ἀπαιδευσία). Education is a revolution of the individual soul. Its inversion is being turned around in the opposite way, and moving in the opposite direction. True education is an ascent from the Cave, *and* a descent. False education is a confusion of the two. The famous analogy is a pictorial representation of the distinction between what is in reality more intelligible, and what happens to be more intelligible to us.

---

[17] One prominent example of this is Jowett's translation of εἰκασία as "perception of shadows." See *The Dialoguos of Plato* (3rd ed.; London: Oxford University Press, 1924), III, 213. Cf. Cornford, *The Republic of Plato* (London: Oxford University Press, 1941), p. 221, where it is translated as "imagining." As we have pointed out, note 14 above, Plato refers to that defective mode of thought, which, in lieu of definitions and demonstrations, merely points, at sensory examples sometimes as phantasy, φαντασία, in its lower phases, and sometimes as opinion, δόξα, in its higher phases.

[18] *Rep.*, 514 A 2.

Aristotle later stated exactly the key principle on which the whole Cave picture is based when he said: "Learning in all of us proceeds from what is less intelligible in nature (but known to us) to what is more intelligible (but at first less known to us)." [19] Plato himself tells us that we must refer the whole image to the four divisions of the divided line, and it is not difficult to identify these four divisions in the four stages of the ascent from the Cave. [20] Each level represents a stage in the noetic being of man, a state of his guiding faculty reason. As such, as we have already been told in the analogy of the Sun, it must involve four things: (1) the object apprehended (as visible colours in the case of sight); (2) the faculty of apprehension (as the faculty of sight); (3) the source of the apprehension (as the Sun); and (4) the result of the apprehension (as the actual seeing of colours in sunlight). Let us then proceed to examine these four structural aspects of each of the four succeeding levels, restricting ourselves first of all *only* to the image, and then *afterwards* (in section 4, pp. 188 ff.) turning to the interpretation, in which the image must eventually lose itself, if we conscientiously succeed in performing the former task.

Level I. The Perception of Shadows

Men are like prisoners in an underground cavern, chained so that they can only gaze ahead at a sequence of shadows, passing across the back-wall of the Cave. Professor Cornford has aptly compared the setting to that of a modern underground cinema. [21] The shadows are *of* certain images, made of stone and wood, carried above a raised platform in the Cave. These shadows are cast by a fire on the other side of the platform, but still in the Cave. The prisoners see only the shadows of these images, and the shadows of themselves. The voices of the people carrying the images are attributed by them to the shadows.

a. The object apprehended. The prisoners see only shadows, and various degrees of light or the absence of shadow. They are insensi-

[19] *Meta.*, 1029 B 4 ff. Aristotle constantly refers to this Platonic conception. Cf. *Phys.*, 184 A 16, 188 B 32, *De An.*, 413 A 12, and *Meta.*, 1095 B 2.

[20] Professor Richard Robinson has questioned this identification. *Plato's Earlier Dialectic* (Ithaca, N. Y.: Cornell University Press, 1941), pp. 192 ff. For a criticism of his argument cf. author's review, *Phil. and Phenomenological Research*, II, no. 4 (June 1942), 546 ff.

[21] Cornford, *Republic of Plato*, p. 223.

tive to differences in colour. A colourless image casts as much of a shadow as a brilliantly tinted one. They are also insensitive to differences in solidity. A thin, unsubstantial image casts just as much of a shadow as a thick, substantial one. They are sensitive to differences in shape and size, but in a distorted manner depending upon their position with respect to the image, the fire, and the wall. A square image easily casts a rectangular shadow, and a circular image an elliptical shadow. A small image, if it happens to be held closer to the fire, easily casts a larger shadow than a much larger image held farther from the fire. The prisoners are utterly unaware of the real causes which are actually holding and moving the archetypal images while they are being moved. They see only the sequence of shadows of images succeeding one another on the screen. The fire itself, which casts the shadows, will be represented only by brightness, or absence of shadow on the screen. Hence they must remain oblivious to it as a positive entity.

— b. *The faculty of apprehension.* The visual faculty by which they see the shadows is unable to see the solidity, the colour, the true shape and size which it is by nature able to see. This is due to the unnatural restriction imposed by the chains which prevent the prisoners from moving their necks. These chains are common and bind the whole society to the same restricted shadow perspective. If a *single* prisoner — should free himself and turn around to the images, he would be puzzled and confused, and turn back to the shadows which he would be better able to see.

c. *The source of apprehension.* The fire, which actually casts the shadow, and its direct light are not perceived by the prisoner. He sees only the shadows which force their way into his warped perspective. Bright spots caused by leaping flames of the fire will hurt his eyes; likewise any influence turning him towards the fire. It in general *is* perceived only as the *absence of shadow*, i.e. nothing at all.

d. *Result.* As a result of this unnaturally restricted apprehension, the prisoners together achieve not a wholly false but an altogether — inverted view of their environment. The dark fleeting shadows are more visible to them than the coloured, stable sources of shadow. Images of very different colour and solidity cast very similar shadows. On the other hand, similar or related images, owing to their relative differences in position, cast very different shadows. The shadows of the prisoners will loom very large on the screen, and blot out much that they might otherwise see. Unless an image comes between them and the fire, they will not see it at all. Even the motions of those images which fall within this range will be distorted. Perceiving nothing of the true motions or their real causes, the prisoners are left only with the accidental temporal sequence of the shadows as they pass.

Level II. The Perception of the Coloured Objects Casting the Shadows

To achieve this a single prisoner must not only escape from his chains, and turn around in the opposite direction, but also persist in spite of the dazzling and pain in his eyes. The prisoner described at 515 C 6–E 4 is freed from his chains, and made to look around "all of a sudden." [22] But he cannot stand the pain in his eyes and does not persist in his resolution. [23] Hence he does not really escape, but ends by "turning back to those things (the shadows) which he is able to see, and by regarding them as in reality more clear than what he has been shown (the solid objects casting the shadows)." [24] If he is able to endure this, he will become aware of his environment as a whole, and completely reverse his perspective. He now sees the light rather than the dark, and thus correctly interprets dark as the absence of light, rather than light as the absence of dark. He at once becomes sensitive to differences in colour, as well as solidity, now distinguishing what he had been unable to distinguish. His judgments of size and shape are corrected. He is able to see that brightness emanated from the fire, since things become brighter as they approach it, even though he may still be unable to look at it directly. If he persists in his resolution, and climbs over the platform, he will be surprised to see people actually carrying the images, and thus causing the movements of the images as they are moved. If he walks beyond the flickering light of the fire, and begins the arduous ascent up the steep incline, he may become aware of a steady point of light far beyond him at the opening of the cavern. As he ascends, this light will become stronger, and illuminate the shadowy walls of the cavern. He will then begin to realize that he has not been in the real world at all, but only in a subterranean vault.

[22] *Rep.*, 515 C 6.   [23] *Rep.*, 515 E 2.
[24] *Rep.*, 515 E 2–4. This unsustained escape is often confused with the *genuine* escape described from 515 E 6–517 A 6. Cf. Robinson, *Plato's Earlier Dialectic*, p. 195.

a. The object apprehended. At this stage, the escaping prisoner is able to see the solid, coloured images of animals and plants and other things, made out of alien wood and stone, which cast the shadows on the wall. By moving or changing his perspective, he can see them as they are in the colours which distinguish them, and more or less in their true size and shape. By shifting his position, and taking it lightly as a steppingstone, he will no longer see each new appearance as a separate thing, but will see the *whole thing*, as it moves from one position to another or maintains itself through some qualitative change. He will see not merely accidental qualities but the moving qualitatively changing *thing* as well.

b. The faculty of apprehension. The faculty by which he now sees these objects is no longer chained to a single perspective, but is able to move from one perspective to another, and hence to focus on the object of the perspectives. He can return to the restricted shadow perspective if he wishes, but since he is also able to correct it by what he is able to see in the unreflected light of the fire, he will hold it more lightly. His sight has passed through the initial pain and glitter of turning to the light, and is strengthened for further progress.

c. The source of apprehension. The fire, which he now sees to be the source of light and warmth, is the very same source as that which enabled him as a prisoner to see the shadows. But even though unable to look directly at the fire, he is no longer governed by the crude distinction between the two opposites, dark and light, confusing brighter light with the privation of darkness. He begins to see a vast hierarchy of degrees of light fading off into shadow, which he sees to be dependent on light, and finally into ultimate unrelieved darkness. The fire shifts and casts an unsteady light. His sight must be maintained by effort or all will grow dark, and neither images nor shadows will be seen.

d. Result. As a result of this ascent, he will see not so much what results from a certain restricted perspective, as that which is the cause of various perspectives. He will see those archetypal *objects* of which the shadows were only two-dimensional silhouettes. He will see animals, plants, and all manner of things not as they really *are*, of course, but imaged in the alien stuff of wood or stone, with shapes resembling the true shapes, and colours resembling the true colours. If he climbs over the wall, he will see the real, contemporaneous causes of the movement of the shadows — the living people back of the wall. But he will not yet see the archetypal causes of the images, the *real* plants, animals, etc. of the outer world. To see these, he must make a further advance up the steep slope towards the pin point of real light at the opening of the cavern.

Level III. The Emergence into the Upper World

His fellow prisoners will do everything to keep him back. They will tell him he is mad and only ruining his eyes. If possible, they will restrain him by force. Should he persist in his attempt, they will abandon him and go on with those competitive games in which they vie with one another in attempting to associate the different silhouettes with one another, in order to predict which will follow after which, knowing nothing of the real motions of the images nor of their real, contemporary causes.[25] If the prisoner allows himself to be dragged up the steep ascent, he may at last emerge into the upper world, and may discover that what he thought was the whole world was only a very minor, subterranean portion, existing under peculiar and disturbing conditions, but bearing a certain *analogy* to the world as it really is, *not* as derivatively reflected in some alien medium, but as it is *in itself*.

a. The objects apprehended. At first he will be capable only of looking at shadows or reflections in pools of water, the inverted images of things as they are reflected from an alien medium. These images will be partial, wobbly, and broken by ripples, and distorted by the angle of his perspective. Nevertheless he will see something like the real colour, and something like the real shape, though the order of one thing to another is apt to be strangely inverted, up being often reflected as down. Then, as his vision is strengthened, he will be able to see not mere reflections or shadows, but things in themselves, not things in relation to images, but images now in relation to things. Here and there, patches of things will become visible as they really are, though their relations to other patches and the visible world as a whole are plunged in gloom. While his vision is very weak, he may make the mistake of confusing the real light, in which he cannot see, with the absence of darkness. But, as his vision improves, he will become aware of the planetary sources and causes of light, and will come to realize that there is one *ultimate* source of this light.

[25] *Rep.*, 516 C 8–D 2.

b. The faculty of apprehension. His faculty will be capable of seeing only in light which is reflected from some shadowy screen or mirror. The real light is too bright. Hence his vision will be confined to some artificial perspective which cannot be varied. Hence he will confuse the peculiarities of this artificial perspective with genuine, existent qualities of the object, ripplings in the watery image, for instance, with real changes in the thing. It is only gradually that his visual faculty will become capable of varying the perspective, taking each single one lightly, and using them only as steppingstones to the apprehension of the thing. Even then, it will be capable of seeing only isolated shady patches, one by one, and will be forced to interpret the brighter areas in terms of the less bright.

c. The source of apprehension. The source of actual apprehension will be the real sun, though in the shadowy perspectives to which he is first confined it will appear merely as the absence of what he can see, and thus as nothing. As the individual visual faculty is sharpened, however, he will be able to see it at least as it is reflected in some alien seat, recognizing some such spot as the brightest of all the things he can see. Then gradually he will be able to see that they are only derivative reflections, and that other real things are brighter than they.

d. Result. The result will be a dim and hazy sight of things in the real world. What is really brighter and more visible will be dismissed as less bright and less visible, and brightness itself confused with the absence of darkness. The general order of things will be confused or inverted, though here and there isolated patches, accessible to some chance perspective, will be clearly seen in great detail. Even such visions, however, will be mixed with accidental features, derived from the peculiarities of the perspective from which the thing is seen, rather than from peculiarities of the thing itself. What lies between such lustrous patches will be hazy, and the whole order of visual things will be upside down, the brighter and more visible being confused constantly with the less bright, and really less visible, though apparently more.

Level IV. Real Vision of the Upper World

Unless he makes a constant effort to piece his separate visions together, and to gaze upon wider and wider perspectives in clearer light, withstanding the constant pain and glitter arising from such effort, he must remain limited to a distorted patchwork view of the whole. But if he persists, he may become capable of gaining an accurate, panoramic view of all these things together as they are in the light of the sun. He will then see that shadows and images are — derived from the things, not the things from the images. He will also see that bright light is no privation of darkness, but that darkness is — the privation of light. Gradually, from seeing which are the brighter objects, he will be able to discern the approximate position of the sun, then to gaze upon it, at least through darkened glasses or some medium of this sort, and possibly at last to look upon it "not in some alien medium but as it is in its own seat on high." [26]

  a. The objects apprehended. At this final stage, the real things are seen all together with one another, not isolated by intermediate patches of darkness. The images and shadows are also seen, but as images and shadows, not confused with their archetypal causes. These are now seen in their true solidity, in their full array of coloured qualities, and in their true size and shape. Most of all, even if the detail is blurred, they are seen in their true order, up being up, and down, down. The observer can even descend into the Cave again, and after a brief adjustment come to see "a thousand times better than the Cave-dwellers," [27] for he will see the shadows as what they really are, shadows cast by solid images of the *real* things of the real world. But he will be utterly unable to convince the prisoners of these things. They will laugh at the obvious confusion into which he falls when first returning from the realm of light, and condemn him as an impractical visionary, incapable of understanding the "real" problems of "real" life. [28]

  b. The apprehending faculty. The individual apprehending faculty is now free from any accidental restriction to a certain perspective, but may move lightly and easily from one to another, using them all in correcting one another to penetrate to the nature of each real thing. Thus all peculiarities arising from the particular position of a single perspective may be eliminated. Once being able to see by the light of the day, he will also be able to see in twilight, and at night. He will even be able to descend once again into the Cave, and, after initial blindness, "accommodate" his vision to the obscurity.

  c. The source of apprehension. The source of his apprehension will be the very same sun which enabled him before to see shadows, images, and murky night vistas. Now, however, he will not suppose

[26] *Rep.*, 516 B 4–7.   [27] *Rep.*, 520 C 2.   [28] *Rep.*, 516 E 8–517 A 4.

that day is the confused and dazzling absence of night, nor will he identify the ultimate source of the brightness of things with some brilliant spot in a pool of water, nor with the lustrous body of the moon. He will neither subordinate the object to his faculty nor the whole object to a part, but will be able to apprehend the true order of brightness as things are nearer or farther from the sun. He may even be able to gaze upon the real sun momentarily, when partially eclipsed. He will now see that just as the fire of the Cave is responsible both for the visibility of the coloured images and that of their shadows, so the sun is responsible both for the visibility of the real coloured things, their images, and their shadows. The fire is not the sun; the image in stone is not the archetypal real thing; the shadow is not a reflection in a pool. But when grasped all at once, he can see a proportional similarity between the Cave and the World: fire/image/shadow = sun/real thing/reflection.[29]

d. Result. The result will be an apprehension of real things, not as they are in some alien medium, or in some derivative effect, but as they are in themselves, not in some accidentally selected portion, but all together at once. He may be even less capable than before of tracing out the detailed pattern of some watery reflection or some dusky night vista. But he will no longer attempt to use such murky patterns as means of apprehending the actual trees and the sky which cast the reflection. He will no longer confuse effect with cause, partial image with complete archetype. He will apprehend something of the true hierarchical order of light and shade as it proceeds from its ultimate source, the sun, to real things as seen all together in the light of day, to shadows and reflections of these, to images of these real things made out of alien stuff, and finally to the shadows of these images. Such is the image of the Cave, apart from what it signifies.

4. THE INTERPRETATION OF THE MYTH

As we have already noted, Plato himself refers us back to the analogy of the sun, and that of the divided line for guidance in interpreting the image of the Cave, thus underlining the integral unity of all three.[30] As a matter of fact, the sun and the line provide us with the key to

---

[29] This is what Aristotle also later terms ἀναλογία; Meta., V, 1016 B 34–35, and Nic. Eth., 1096 B 28–30; and what was later called analogia proportionalitatis. Cf. Aquinas, De Veritate, qu. II, art. 11.

[30] Rep., 517 A 8 ff.

interpreting the Cave. In the analogy of the sun we are clearly informed that sight is to be interpreted as knowledge. *Seeing*, in the Cave, therefore, is always to be interpreted as *knowing*, the object *seen* as the object *known*, the faculty of sight as the faculty of knowledge, the source of sight, the sun, as the source of being and therefore of knowledge, the good. Hence in our interpretation of the myth we must never lapse into the language of sight and perception. To do so is to confuse the image with the archetype. The language of seeing is at every point to be translated into the language of knowing. The thing seen as it really is in itself is the essence, the what-it-is in itself as it may be known. Its colours are the qualities of the thing, its size and shape the quantitative properties.

In the analogy of the line, we are clearly informed that there are two major types of knowing, rational insight and opinion, each of which is subdivided into two: rational insight into scientific understanding (διάνοια) and dialectical knowledge or philosophy (νόησις); opinion into likelihood (εἰκασία) and conviction (πίστις). The *objects* of opinion are called "visible," [31] and are signified by the underground cinema.[32] This, however, does not mean that certain objects of *knowledge* (of a certain kind) are merely *perceived*, and that we should identify the seeing of shadows with perception. Even the lowest sort of opinion is not sensation or perception, as modern interpreters have maintained.[33] It is inconceivable that Plato at any stage of his "development" could have confused opinion with sensation.[34] Even in the earliest dialogues, the changing, individual object of perception, which can only be pointed at, is contrasted with the stable essence, the "what it is," which is the object of our most feeble and fallible opinions. By classifying the objects of opinion as "visible," therefore, Plato is not identifying opinion with sensation. The object of opinion is universal structure, not the universal structure as it is in itself, but the universal structure as it is mixed with the accidental accretia of sensation.[35] Opinion itself is, therefore, a kind of knowledge, that

[31] ὁρατά not αἰσθητά. *Rep.*, 509 D 3. Cf. 517 B 1–2.

[32] *Rep.*, 517 B 2–3.

[33] Cf. Jowett, *Dialogues*, III, xcv, and Raphael Demos, *The Philosophy of Plato* (New York: Charles Scribner's Sons, 1939), who says that the change from εἰκασία to πίστις is "one from sensation to perception," p. 273.

[34] Opinion is true or false, whereas sensation is infallible (ἀψευδές). Cf. *Theaet.*, 153 C 5, and Cornford, *Plato's Theory of Knowledge, ad loc.*

[35] Cf. the ὁρώμενα εἴδη of *Rep.*, 510 D 5, and *Tim.*, 51 E 6 ff., where the object of pure insight and opinion are contrasted in the following terms: "Concerning these

kind which allows itself to be governed and guided by the data of sense, or which judges reality according to the manner in which it appears.

The objects of opinion are not sensibles but knowables,[36] so far as they may begin to appear in the derived structure of sensibles. We may say that the *object* of opinion is closer to the *object* of sense than to the *object* of knowledge. Hence the *object* of opinion is called visible.[37] But the apprehending *faculty* is closer to the *faculty* of reason than to that of sense. The *visible* intelligible is a species of the intelligible, not a species of the visible. Hence we must be especially on our guard against confusing even the lowest stages of knowledge with sense experience. Every level of ascent out of the cave is a level of education (παιδεία) and hence of knowing, represented analogously by a level of sensory seeing. To grasp the meaning of the analogy we must completely translate the visual language at every point into the noetic language. If we do so, we shall not be confused, but greatly aided in apprehending the structure of the process of education and its opposite.

Level I. Likelihood (εἰκασία)

The noetic faculty of man has the capacity of constructing an indefinite variety of opinions both true and false about all conceivable objects, whether sensible or not. At first, however, it is unable to apprehend its own objects (the forms), but only those which are confusedly manifested through sense (the visible forms).[38] At this stage of *opinion*, the mind is forced to use some sensible appearance in lieu of the intelligible definition which it is really seeking. Instead of *defining*, it merely points at examples. Instead of *explaining*, it

two objects it must be agreed that one always maintains the same structure, ungenerated and indestructible, never admitting anything alien into itself, nor itself passing into anything alien, being invisible and altogether imperceptible, which it has fallen to the lot of reason (νόησις) to apprehend, while the other has the same name and is similar to the first, being perceptible, generable and ever-moving, coming into one place and then passing elsewhere, being apprehended by opinion (δόξῃ) together with sensation (μετ' αἰσθήσεως)."

[36] Cf. *Rep.*, 477 C 6–E, where sight and hearing are clearly distinguished as faculties from the faculties of ἐπιστήμη and δόξα. Opinion is also distinguished from sensation in other lists of faculties such as *Parm.*, 142 A 3 ff.: οὐδέ τις ἐπιστήμη οὐδὲ αἴσθησις οὐδὲ δόξα. Opinion combines intellectual apprehension with sensation, so it is stated last, though it is closer to ἐπιστήμη than to αἴσθησις.

[37] ὁρατόν. *Rep.*, 509 D 4.　　　　　　[38] *Rep.*, 510 D 5.

tells a string of sensible episodes. *Esse* is identified with *percipi*, and what cannot be sensed is dismissed as unreal. This inverted subordination of the higher faculty to the lower is what is meant by *being in the cave*.[39]

But as we have already observed, the structure of sensation is twofold. Like that of the other psychic faculties, it involves an object apprehended and the apprehension of this object, or the physical thing on the one hand, and on the other some more or less distorted phantasm or replica (εἰκών) of the thing in the organ of sense. At first it is not easy to distinguish these, and we readily confuse the thing perceived (as the real sun or the real stick) with its appearance to sense (as the small disc up in the sky or the bent stick *as they seem*). Instead of subordinating the relative appearance to the thing as it really is in itself, we subordinate the thing to the relative appearance. Thus we confuse the continuous motion of a ball with the succession of sensations we have of the ball at different positions, the good thing with the pleasure it gives to us, and ourselves with the various feelings and sensations we *have* of ourselves. This lowest level of opinion which is not sensation, since it employs universal concepts and is directed to reality as it is, but which confuses this reality with a sensible *appearance* or subjective image (εἴδωλον), is what Plato means by conjecture (εἰκασία). These *likely* opinions about things are first induced in us as children by those surrounding us. The first subjectivism to which we are *chained* is a social subjectivism, conjectures verified only by social agreement as to the likelihood of certain sensory experiences. The escape from such subjectivism can be achieved by the individual intellect alone (the prisoners cannot escape in a body but one by one).

a. The objects apprehended. The prisoners will know only what has appeared to them in the mode of sense experience. What is not sensed will be dismissed as unreal. They will be noetically oblivious to important qualitative distinctions in the objects of their sensations. A pleasure of low quality, for example, will *appear* just as violently, or even more, than one of higher quality. Hence they will judge the object of the former to be as good as the latter, or even better. They will be equally oblivious to the distinction between what is essential and what is only accidental, since sensory appearance is insensitive to this distinction. Fluency of speech makes just as much or even more

[39] *Rep.*, 517 B 1–2.

of an impression on sense than genuine understanding. Hence they will judge the one to be as likely as the other. Even in the case of quantitative structures, such as size, shape, and mobile pattern, where sensory appearance is less distorted, they will go astray, judging the motions of the heavenly bodies, for example, according to their appearances to us rather than the latter in terms of the former. The prisoners will be ignorant of the real, continuous motion of things and their contemporaneous causes, judging the motion to be only the succession of different appearances and thus confusing the cause with some appearance *preceding* the supposed effect.[40] The good itself, which is invisible, and the better things, like courage, justice, and virtue itself, which are also invisible, either will be confused with the production of pleasure and the avoidance of pain, or will be judged by them to be non-existent, since they make no impression on sense.

b. The faculty of conjectural opinion. The conjectural opinion, to which they are confined, is unnaturally restricted by a common obsession with the pleasures which accompany sensuous appetites, and lead the soul to seek only those sensible objects which are capable of satisfying them.[41] Such a soul confuses a good thing, such as food, with the pleasure of eating, i.e. the subjective likeness or appearance of the good. This prevents the prisoners from seeking after any other goal than the pleasant appearance of social wisdom, the pleasant appearance of social stability, health, etc., which are confused with the goods themselves. If a single prisoner should begin to wonder about what wisdom or stability really was, and thus begin to form different opinions from the accepted ones, he would soon become puzzled and confused, and turn back with relief to the accepted conjectures about these things, based upon past appearances of social success and failure, and the correlated experiences of pleasure and pain.

c. The source of apprehension. The actual good, which he and his fellows are really seeking, would not be judged to exist, since it is not represented in his fixed, distorted perspective. He will regard as real only those appearances which manage to force their way into this accidental framework, the warped structure of which he will take to be the inmost nature of being. Realities of which he is unable to take any account, because of the limitations of his point of view,

40 *Rep.*, 516 C 8–D 2.   41 *Rep.*, 519 A 8.

when they obtrude, will disturb him, and be judged as evil; likewise any influence tending to make him aware of these realities. On the other hand, anything which agrees with his habits and prejudices, and thus yields him pleasure, will be judged as good. He will use the appearance as a criterion of reality, admitting as goods only those things which provide him with pleasure, and because they do so.

d. Result. As a result of this restriction of their opinion-forming faculties, the prisoners will achieve not a wholly false but an altogether inverted understanding of their environment. The subjective and transitory appearances will be judged as more real than the real things which appear. Things of very different quality and importance will seem alike to sense, and hence will be judged to be the same, as, for instance, an act of courageous daring and an act of cowardly tyranny. On the other hand, things which are similar or related will seem and hence be judged to be separate, as, for instance, an act of courage and another of temperate self-restraint. Since the prisoners will always feel themselves and their own motions, they will judge themselves to be something of the greatest importance in the world. Purely intelligible structure and pattern they will not apprehend at all. Even the structure of changing things will be distorted, for they will judge according to the sensory appearance of these. Since the true motions and their contemporaneous conditions and causes do not appear as such, they will judge reality to be the accidental sequence of subjective appearances and images as they pass.

Level II. Conviction (πίστις)

As Adam clearly pointed out,[42] conviction is the belief in "visible, palpable things," but in these as opposed to their subjective appearances, which Adam did not point out. To achieve this, a single prisoner must think for himself, gaining the ability to question those opinions which have been forced upon him by the social pursuit of material pleasures. Even if his conversion is only "mental," he will suffer intellectual confusion and maladjustment. His conversion will become actual, however, only if he really acts on the basis of some opinion he has himself formed as a consequence of his own reflection without group support. An opinion which is thus capable of convincing a man to the point where he will take risks in pursuing it, apart from all

[42] Note to *Rep.*, 511 E.

artificial restraint, is no mere conjecture (εἰκασία), but conviction (πίστις).[43] Such opinion is fallible. Hence it must not be confused with science or philosophy. Yet it is the indispensable condition without which science and philosophy are humanly impossible.

If a man persists in forming his own opinions and suffers the dismal consequences of actually pursuing them, he will be forced to come up against the changing actualities of nature from different points of view. He will be forced to recognize that there is a reality independent of the appearance, and that many things exist which do not appear at all. If he persists, he will come to understand that the world is far more rich and complex than he had supposed, and will reverse his previous conjectural view of the nature of being. Instead of emphasizing the unstable appearance and discounting the reality, he will now distrust appearance, and seek beneath this for the more stable thing which appears.[44] He will become capable of distinguishing between the actual qualities of things, even though they seem the same, between the essence or "nub" of a matter and mere accidental detail. He will no longer judge the size, shape, and the mobile pattern of things to be as they appear to be, even though he has no scientific knowledge of what they really are. He will be able to understand that pleasures and pains are only the by-products of certain things which are really good and really bad, and that some of the good things are really more lasting and better than others.

If he persists in maintaining the flexibility of his faculties, he will also become cognizant of the real motions of things, and the real influences causing these motions. He will see that some of these causes are more powerful and stable than others, and will undoubtedly identify the basic source of things with the most powerful and stable

---

[43] This must not be taken as implying that the victims of εἰκασία do not have any faith in their subjective opinions. The prisoners have complete faith in the sensory shadows, since it is all that they can see. They act in accordance with their prejudices, and are even ready to kill anyone who questions them. (*Rep.*, 517 A 6). So Plato would not deny Aristotle's point (*De An.*, 428 A 20 ff.) that "every opinion (δόξα) is accompanied by belief" (πίστις). But there is a difference between a more or less automatic belief in appearances, and a belief which is able to sustain itself *in spite of appearances*. This is *rather* belief than appearance. So Plato calls it πίστις as opposed to εἰκασία, which is *rather* appearance than belief.

[44] As A. S. Ferguson has pointed out, "Plato's Simile of Light," *Classical Quarterly*, vols. 15–16 (1921–22), vol. 15, p. 131, Plato in the *Cratylus* derives πιστόν and ἐπιστήμη from ἰστᾶν and ἵστημι, — to stop or to stand. The thing which appears, once we grasp it, by πίστις, is more stable than its shifting appearances.

thing that he can see — the sun.[45] When he begins to realize that this is an unstable and impermanent thing, and that the changing existence it calls forth is not true existence, his mind will be led altogether beyond the things which appear, and he will begin to speculate about their causes and origins. As he begins here and there to grasp the intelligible patterns of this or that process, he will begin to realize that material, changing existence is not the whole of being, but only a particular, subordinate level.

a. The object apprehended. At this stage, the escaping prisoner will be able to discern structure as it is embodied in what we call "real" or material, changing things. He will be capable of forming opinions about these changing things themselves, not merely their relative appearances. He will distinguish in them what is truly essential, and what is only accidental or apparent, varying as he shifts his view. By taking this viewpoint lightly and making it flexible, he will be able to discern which qualities and patterns are really in the thing, and which are only relative to him. At every point, he will distinguish the actual thing, as it continuously changes or moves, from the succession of appearances. His convictions will no longer concern these appearances but the moving, qualitatively changing, material world which causes them, as it is in itself, as moved by active agencies.[46]

b. The faculty of apprehension. The faculty of conviction is no longer chained to a single framework of opinion, accidentally determined by the particular history and situation of a particular people. This faculty has become free and flexible, moving from one conjecture to another, and thus capable of eliminating what is artificial and subjective, in convincing itself of the sensible facts. Since "the facts" at this level are shifting and particular, the convictions themselves will be shifting and particular. But they will not so much determine the object as allow themselves, through their flexibility, to be determined

[45] Adam, note to 517 A, points out that fire = sun, but neglects to distinguish between the sun simply as perceived, and as perceived + *judged* as the source of all visible existence. Hence his view is subject to the criticism of Ferguson in "Plato's Simile of Light," *Classical Quarterly*, 15–16, 1921–22, pp. 131 ff.

[46] Plato believed that a multitide of "divine" or superhuman agencies ultimately controlled the motions of the material universe. Cf. *Tim.*, 41 D and 42 E. Hence Campbell (*The Sophistes and Politicus of Plato*, Oxford: Clarendon Press, 1867) is no doubt right in interpreting *the men* who cast no shadow and control the puppet show as δαίμονες (cf. Adam, note to 514 B 12). Thus in the *Laws* (804 B) men are compared to puppets (θαύματα) *for the most part* under the control of invisible, superhuman agencies.

by the object. They will not be hardened in pure subjectivity, but movable and yielding to what lies beyond themselves. The man with convictions, dictated by actually trying something, may agree with someone whose conjectural opinions have been accidentally governed by "hearsay" plus imagination, but he will hold his opinions in a different mode. The faculty of the former is determined by its independent object, while that of the latter is determined by some extraneous accidental source, such as a socially accepted image.

c. The source of apprehension. The man of conviction is seeking the very same good as the man of conjecture. But the former no longer confuses the apparent good with its source. For example, he does not judge anything to be good because it is pleasant, but rather to be pleasant or apparently good, because of some real material good. He will dwell only lightly on the appearance in attempting to discover its actual cause. By trial and error, and by intruding his own body into the nexus of physical processes, he will gain some knowledge of the actual dependence of material things on one another. Thus he will be able to lay the empirical foundations for the arts and sciences.[47] In spite of the immediate appearances, he will come to judge the sun as the largest and most powerful physical being, on which all the rest depend. Like the ancients in general, he will believe in the sun, therefore, as a divine being, and the source of all actual goodness and perfection, though none of these qualities appear to sense.[48]

d. Result. As a result of this ascent, he will see not so much what results from the accidental peculiarities of a certain experiential perspective as the single object of various perspectives. He will form his opinions directly about the real, material things of which his various sensations and unguided imaginations are only the appearances. By taking these appearances lightly, he will come to apprehend something of the nature of animals, plants, and all manner of things, not as they are in themselves, but as they are incorporated in the changing matter of the sensible world, with quantitative structure resembling

---

[47] All the arts (πᾶσαι τέχναι) as opposed to pure science (ἐπιστήμη), since they involve individual operations on material objects, involve an element of opinion, and are hence developed in the Cave. Cf. Rep., 533 B 10 ff.

[48] Thus when Plato tells us (517 B 3) that the light of the fire is to be compared with the power of the sun, τῇ τοῦ ἡλίου δυνάμει, he means not merely the visible sun as Adam suggests (note to 517 A 7), but the visible sun as believed to be the ultimate divine source of material motion and life. After all, power δύναμις cannot be perceived. It is an object of opinion.

the true quantitative structure, and qualities resembling the true qualities. By actual practice and experimentation he will establish empirical science (ἐμπειρία). If he becomes sufficiently distrustful of his successive images and sensations, and uses his own body to influence other material things, he will become vaguely aware of other unperceived forces and influences governing their motions and changes as they move and change. Thus he will learn how to produce certain desirable results by changing things in certain ways (τέχνη). But he will not understand *why* the results are produced, nor the *pure* structure of any of these material things. To understand these, he must come to concentrate his attention more seriously upon the causal structure he is barely beginning to discern in the particular examples surrounding him. Pure science (ἐπιστήμη), as opposed to art (τέχνη), is independent of opinion, and is not developed in the Cave at all.[49]

Level III. The Emergence into Intelligible Structure (διάνοια)

The emergence out of the Cave, as Plato himself tells us,[50] is the freeing of the intellect from its subservience to particular sensory examples, so that it can at last apprehend its own proper object, the pure form or essence, freed from all mixture with alien matter. The individual prisoner must do this alone. His fellow prisoners will do everything to keep him back. They will tell him that by turning away from the sensory appearances of things he is mad, and ruining his understanding. They will urge him to concentrate upon the concrete actualities of daily life, and that which serves its practical purposes, never dreaming that these are not the ultimate actualities, but the effects of independent realities, themselves the effects of invisible causes and structures which govern them, and so thrice removed from reality. Their view of the practical is, therefore, only an inverted and truncated version of the truly useful. If possible, they will restrain him by force. If he persists with what they call his airy speculations, they will abandon him, and go on with their "empirical" attempts to discover stable associations of different appearances, in order to predict which will follow after which, knowing nothing of the real motions and changes of which they perceive only the relative appearances, nor of the real causes of these changes.

[49] *Rep.*, 533 B 10–534.   [50] *Rep.*, 517 B 4–5.

If the prisoner allows himself to be guided by others, who have managed to grasp the universal structure of some area of change, he may at last gain stable knowledge of the true nature of something, not of a particular transitory example, but of the universal structure itself, freed from all admixture with accidents irrelevant to it. He may then gain some insight into the orderly structure of the world as a whole, and will discover that this structure is present in changing things under peculiar and distorting conditions. As the realm of intelligible structure confronts him, his situation will be analogous to that which he faced at the beginning of his exploration of the cave. These structures are first viewed from distorting perspectives, and then in a piecemeal manner, before they may be understood all at once as they are.

a. The objects apprehended. At first he will be incapable of apprehending pure structure as it is. He will be capable only of recognizing its normative power over technical activity. The arts must develop before the sciences, mensuration before geometry, navigation before astronomy, and logic before ontology. By a process of trial and error, he has already run across certain rules leading to a successful result. These are not so much structural principles themselves as the "shadows" of such principles in the alien medium of action determined by them, and hence accidental to them. It is not accidental to mensuration that it should be determined by the principles of geometry, but it is altogether accidental to the principles of geometry that they should happen to govern the art of mensuration. Hence the knowledge of geometry, which can be attained by successfully measuring plots of ground, etc., is exceedingly inadequate. Sequences of procedure will be learned by rote in the Cave of sense without a clear understanding of *why* they work out as they do.

Hence such knowledge will be "shadowy" and uncertain beyond the limits of the particular task in hand which may be successfully repeated over and over. Important rules, really essential to the project, will be mixed up with other associated norms of very limited scope, or with a mere routine, only accidentally associated with the project. Finally such norms, even if boiled down to what is purely essential, are limited to a certain particular sphere of action on certain particular things. Hence their universality will be marred and distorted. The real thing does not always cast a shadow (or influence action as a "norm"). Nevertheless the intelligent artisan, by acting in ways which are governed by the actual structure of things will gain an understanding of something like the real structure, though, outside the special area to which his technique applies, his conception of the relative order of one thing to another is apt to be strangely inverted, the more important often being subordinate, in his opinion, to the less.

No doubt the first structures to be thus explored will be those of arithmetic and geometry.[51] These are not *pure* forms, since the different units of arithmetic are diversified by something unintelligible which prevents them from being purely one,[52] and the shapes and figures of geometry are composed of something unformed and continuous. Hence while mathematics does abstract from *sensible matter* as this was later called, it does not abstract from intelligible or mathematical matter.[53] Hence Plato places the realm of mathematics between the objects of sense and the pure forms, as Aristotle places the objects of mathematics between those of physics and those of metaphysics.[54] Before the mind can apprehend the latter, it must first learn to understand them so far as they can be quantitatively reflected in "pools," i.e. in the alien mathematical matter which is "itself apprehended without the senses by a sort of bastard reasoning, and is hardly an object of belief." [55] Then, as his noetic faculty is strengthened by mathematical study, he will be able to grasp not only the pragmatic norms or heuristic principles, but also the actual patterns and structures governing them, no longer seeing the structures merely in relation to what can be done by acting in accordance with them, but accounting for what can be done by an understanding of the structures. For a long time, he will confuse peculiar phases of the process of understanding with what is understood, like a man who constantly sees spots on his retina. Similarly the mind is peculiarly apt to become unduly conscious of the logical machinery of its apprehension, confusing the accidents of logical syntax with the structure of being itself. This type of fixation may proceed to the point where the victim may despair of ever seeing anything but the spots upon his retina.

[51] Cf. *Rep.*, 524–528.
[52] Cf. *Rep.*, 525 A, *Parm.*, 142 D–144 A, and Cornford's commentary in *Plato and Parmenides*, pp. 137–145.
[53] ὕλη . . . ἡ δὲ νοητή. Aristotle, *Meta.*, ch. 10, book VII, 1036 A 9. Cf. Aquinas' commentary *ad loc.*
[54] Cf. *Meta.*, 1026 A.
[55] *Tim.*, 52 B.

If this danger is avoided, if logic is subordinated to ontology rather than ontology to logic, here and there patches of structure, first of all the quantitative structures of mathematics, will be understood as they really are, even though their relation to other patches and the intelligible order as a whole are quite obscure. While his insight is still weak, he may continue to regard the ultimate causes and sources, which he cannot yet clearly understand, as in themselves unreal and unintelligible, through his inability to understand them. But, as his insight is sharpened, he will become at least vaguely aware of the more intelligible principles of things, and will come to realize that there is an ultimate source of being and truth.

b. *The faculty of apprehension.* The faculty of scientific understanding will at first be capable of apprehending structure only so far as it dictates action on certain material things. In geometry, for instance, it will be constantly in need of sensible examples and diagrams. By making use of such artificial constructions, it may achieve a dim sense of the structure, but insight is not clear enough to dispense with them. Hence, when plunged into an entirely different material situation, the technician is apt to be at a loss, even though the structural situation is really the same. The mathematician can proceed with his proof only if a certain construction is employed, the navigator is utterly at a loss without a given instrument, the doctor recognizes only certain symptoms, not other symptoms, of the same disease.

He has confused certain particular accidents with the universal pattern of the disease, which he has not yet come to understand as it is in itself apart from all such accidental admixture. It is only gradually that his faculties will become capable of grasping this in varying circumstances, taking the particular details of each such situation lightly, and using them only as stepping stones to the apprehension of the mathematical pattern itself. Even then, at the level of scientific insight (διάνοια), he will grasp only isolated concatenations of structure. Studying these in the greatest detail, one by one, he will have only a hazy conception of their mutual interrelations, and will be forced to interpret the more fundamental and all-embracing structures in terms of what he knows. Thus theology will be interpreted in terms of philosophy, philosophy in terms of science, and science will be operationally interpreted in terms of technical procedure.

c. *The source of apprehension.* Technical insight will be restricted by a common obsession with a plurality of goods or good things achieved by the various sciences and arts. The good itself will be apprehended only so far as these partial goods partake of it, and so far as they are necessarily ordered in some hierarchy to an end beyond. Technical insight, however, will be far more easily achieved with respect to lesser goods, such as the manufacture of useful articles, and health, than with respect to greater goods, such as the making of illuminating images and education. Hence the latter are apt to be subordinated to the former, on the ground that less is known about them, and their results are actually inferior, which is apt to be the case. So the better things, being far more difficult, will be subordinated to the lower things, being easier to achieve and to test. Scientific insight is even apt to doubt whether there is really any sovereign good, and therefore any actual hierarchy of goods at all.

To the individual, however, reflecting on the world as a whole and on human culture, it becomes evident that the unity of the world demands a single source, and the unity of culture a single aim. He may thus come to understand that if there is no universal order embracing all the objects of the sciences, there can be no order embracing each of the objects of the sciences. He will then seek after this first source of the order in things. At first he will continue to identify it with the loftiest sensible object, the sun, the cosmos as a whole, the vital force of nature, or the progressive aspiration of man, but gradually he may come to see that these are only derivative effects of an *ultimate* immaterial principle of order.

d. Result. The result will be a dim and hazy knowledge of the nature of the real world. What is more real and more intelligible will be dismissed as less real and less intelligible, and being itself will be confused with the absence of non-being. Structural effects will be understood more clearly than structural causes. The general order of things will be confused or inverted, though here and there selected patches of structure, accessible to some chance phase of human interest or action, will be clearly known in great detail. Even such insights, however, will be mixed with irrelevant features derived from peculiar sensory images and the rules or operations governing these, rather than from the peculiar structure of the thing itself. The border areas between the sciences, for example between physics and biology, biology and psychology, science and philosophy, will be hazy, and the whole order of things will be inverted, the higher and more intelligible structures, that of man, for example, being confused with the lower, animal, for example, concerning which more technical knowledge is available.

Level IV. Philosophic Insight (νόησις)

Unless the individual intellect is driven to piece its separate insights together, and to grasp wider and wider ranges of structure in a single order, under a single source, notwithstanding the constant mental fatigue and confusion arising from such effort, it must remain limited to a distorted, patchwork philosophy. But if the individual persists, he may become capable of gaining an accurate, philosophic understanding of all things as they are in relation to the source of being itself. He will then understand that the normative rules and concepts of the mind are derived from the actual structure of being, and that the inverse is not true. Gradually, from noting which are the more intelligible and universal causes, he will be able to discern something of the nature of the good, then to meditate upon it through the use of sensible images, or analogies, and possibly, at last, to contemplate it "not in some alien medium but as it is in its own seat on high."

a. The objects apprehended. At this final stage of earthly education the real order of things is apprehended together as one, not isolated by intermediate, border areas of vagueness and confusion. The norms and concepts of the mind are also understood, but as norms and concepts, not to be confused with the actual structures causing them. These structures are grasped in their true importance, in their full array of consequential properties, and in their actual quantitative structure. Most of all, even if the detail is blurred, the broad structure is grasped in its true order, cause being understood as cause, and effect as effect. Thus the mind can not only argue from effect to cause, the argument *quia*, as it was later called, from the remote effects up to the first principles, but can also now argue from cause to effect, the argument *propter quid*, as it was later called, from first principles down to the effects.[56]

b. The apprehending faculty. The individual philosophic faculty is now freed from restriction to any conditions of learning or to the limitations of a certain body of knowledge, but may move lightly from one to another, treating the basic, unquestioned assumptions

[56] These crucially important distinctions of Aristotelian philosophy are, therefore, developments of Plato's notions of the upward path (*quia*) and the downward path (*propter quid*). *Rep.*, 511 B 3–C 2.

of a science, as, for example, the matter, time, and change of physics, as "hypotheses" to be further examined in the light of the broad structure of things, until their real nature is not merely vaguely taken for granted, but clearly and sharply understood. Thus all accidental peculiarities, arising from the special character of the basic structure of a single art or science, such as physics or mathematics, may be eliminated. Once being able to grasp these basic structures as they really are, the individual will be able to give an intelligible account of them, as well as their subordinate patterns, without blindly assuming them as "absolutes," disconnected from everything else. He will even be able to judge the particular changing events of nature and human history, and the succession of human experience in which these events are distortedly reflected, in relation to their final source. After habituating himself to the fluid matter, in which structure is here embodied, he will be able to form opinions concerning the nature of what is occurring, which are far more trustworthy than those of his fellows, whose faculties have been unnaturally restricted to the data of what they call "experience," though he will be utterly unable to convince them of what he understands.

c. *The source of apprehension.* The source of his apprehension will now be the very same good which guided him in the establishment of technical procedures and sciences. Now, however, he will not invert the order of the importance of things, identifying the ultimate source of their being with some perceptible structure such as the visible cosmos, or the actual end of some cultural endeavor, such as health or education. He will neither judge the object in terms of the structure of his knowing faculty, nor the whole of being in terms of a part, but will be able to apprehend the true order of things as they more or less closely resemble their source. He may even be able to contemplate it intermittently under the guise of well-controlled images constructed by the imagination. He will now see that just as the apparent good, which governs the formation of human opinion, is responsible both for such order as may be discerned in the changing things of the material world, and for that of the sensory experiences which are their effects, so the actual good, being itself, is responsible both for the order of things as they are, and the images and concepts which are their effects

d. *Result.* The result will be an apprehension of real patterns, not as they appear in the subjective phantasms of sense and imagination, nor as they are embodied in the fluid matrix of matter, but as they are in themselves, not in some accidentally selected scientific area, as reflected by human logic, but all together at once, as they are in themselves. He may be even less capable than before of tracing out the detailed pattern of some technical construction, mixed with imaginary content, and artificial things of reason, or of some scientific theory. But he will no longer attempt to use such partially intelligible patterns as a means of apprehending the real structures of which these constructions are only models and images. He will no longer confuse effect with cause, reason with being. He will apprehend something of the true hierarchical order of things as they proceed from their ultimate source, being itself.

Such is the nature of education — the revolution of the soul away from the less intelligible things (subjective sense data in us) which happen to be better known *to us*, towards more intelligible things (existing in themselves) which are less well known to us. In this moving process the human soul passes from a social or individual subjectivism, in which man seems the measure of all things, to a realism, in which man, both social and individual, is allotted his proper subordinate station, and God, not man, is finally known as the measure of all things.[57]

[57] *Laws*, 716 D.

CHAPTER VI

BEING AND ITS INVERSION (*THE PARMENIDES*)

I N THE MYTH of the Cave, Plato has given a composite image
of the composite process of education and the inverted opposite
with which it is sophistically confused. Here we see the two phases
of being and rational apprehension as they exist together in the concrete moving life of humanity. As we have already had occasion to
point out, Plato's distinctive contribution to philosophy lies in these
composite images which are so poignantly portrayed as to incite
the mind to the further task of formal analysis, and so carefully constructed as to lead it from the very beginning along the proper lines.
Without such images, human reason has no malleable material with
which to work, and is apt to remain dormant in the face of the confused
and unassimilable array of sense experience in the raw. Hence the
earlier dialogues are filled with vivid pictures taken from the life of
Socrates, and other images, such as that of the chariot and the ship
of state, constructed with great skill to prepare the way for dialectical
analysis.

But the image is only a necessary but insufficient condition for
understanding. Unless it leads the individual reader to analyze the
picture into its universal structural elements, and to grasp the order
of this structure, it has not only failed to perform its protreptic function, but has even obstructed the process of understanding, as in the
case of those who become so fascinated with the rhetorical beauty of
Plato's style that they insist upon regarding the dialogues as though
they were purely literature or poetry, instead of literature and poetry
capable of leading the mind to genuine philosophy. Such a misinterpretation, characteristic of the post-Renaissance tradition of classical
scholarship, is most at home in the earlier dialogues, where the intro-
ductory, protreptic element of myth is at a maximum, and the culminating, dialectical element of analysis and definition is at a minimum.
It is least at home in the later dialogues, where the element of myth

is at a minimum, and the arduous task of dialectical analysis is undertaken with unremitting zeal.

Modern commentaries have dwelt upon the literary form and easy imagery of the early dialogues, and have slurred over the intricate philosophical discussions of the later dialogues, interpreting them as a "later development of Plato's views," or even completely discounting such difficult passages as the final portion of the *Parmenides* as a *jeu d'esprit.* As a matter of fact, however, it is only in the analytic conclusions of the later dialogues that we shall ever find a reliable key to the Platonic interpretation of the half-interpreted myths and images of the earlier works. As Plato reminds us,[1] it is well to begin with a carefully constructed image in which the outlines of rational structure are already partly visible. But, as he also constantly reminds us, it is fatal to end there without completing the process of abstraction. This is certainly true of the famous analogy of the Cave. It is the ideal beginning for an understanding of Plato's view of education. But this understanding can be completed only by an attempt to assimilate the results of the *Parmenides* and the *Theaetetus.* It is to this task that we must now turn.

We have seen in the previous chapter that the process of education involves two factors, being, which is the object of knowledge, and the human knowing faculty. The analogy of the Cave presents us with a most suggestive composite picture of these two factors as they merge with one another in the moving process of education (παιδεία) and its opposite (ἀπαιδευσία). But a genuine understanding of the composite demands a genuine understanding of the elements. We cannot hope to gain a clear understanding of the Cave until we have attempted to consider what being is in itself and for itself, and what knowledge is, in and for itself. These two questions are dialectically examined in the *Parmenides* and the *Theaetetus.* We shall start with the *Parmenides,* which deals with the prior question of being, and which was, in all probability, the prior dialogue, in the sense that it was intended to be read before.[2]

Modern thought has only recently been awakened to the importance of the problem of being. Hence, of all the dialogues, the *Parmenides* has offered the greatest difficulty to modern interpreters. Why this superlative concern for the meaning of those ubiquitous but obvious

[1] *Rep.,* 376 ff.
[2] Cf. Auguste Diès, *Parmenide* (1923), p. xii, in *Oeuvres Complètes* (Paris, 1920–26).

words being and one? While such concern may come as a surprise to the anti-metaphysical tradition of modern scholarship, it is certainly no surprise to the careful reader of the earlier dialogues of Plato himself, which constantly call our attention to the inescapable presence of the notion of being in all discourse, and to certain important distinctions in its meaning. In the *Phaedo*, for example,[3] we are left in no doubt as to the primary importance of a distinction between two kinds of things which are (τῶν ὄντων): that kind which is "invisible" holding itself ever the same, and that which is "visible," never holding itself the same. We have also noted the emphasis of the *Republic* upon the realm of becoming (γένεσις) which, contrary to the expectations of common-sense ontology, lies between (μεταξύ) that which really is and nothing at all.[4]

It is not surprising, therefore, to find that the first of the later dialectical dialogues, the *Parmenides*, is devoted to the task of distinguishing different senses of being and non-being, in conscious opposition to the *simple* ontology of Parmenides and his disciple Zeno. The inversion which results from the confusion of these different modes or levels of being with one another distorts every act of understanding, corrupting reason at its very source, since the concept of existence is involved in all other concepts. Hence we are here approaching the very root of sophistry, or philosophical misunderstanding, and the primal source of those subordinate distortions to which we have thus far been devoting our attention.

1. THE TREATISE OF ZENO

The whole dialogue is told by Cephalus of Clazomenae to an unspecified audience. It is what he heard from Antiphon, Plato's half-brother, who had memorized it as heard from Pythodorus, an Athenian general sent to Sicily in 427, who had entertained Parmenides and his favorite disciple, Zeno, at the time of the Panathenaic festival. According to his account, Socrates, at that time very young, had paid a visit

[3] *Phaedo*, 79 A 6 ff.
[4] *Rep.*, 477 A 4–5. Plato is clearly seeking concepts through which he can grasp the mysterious phenomena of change without destroying the phenomena or falling into contradiction. As Aristotle points out, however (*Phys.*, I, ch. 9), he has not yet succeeded. If change is viewed as a compound of being (form) and nothing (privation), this is certainly a contradiction. The third principle, matter or substratum, has not yet been focussed, but is still confused with its accidental privation (*Phys.*, 192 A 4 ff.)

to the two philosophers while they were staying at the house of
Pythodorus. Zeno had read his treatise to them, and was almost
finished when Parmenides and Pythodorus, who had been absent,
returned, together with Aristotle, later of the Thirty. After finishing
the last remaining portion of the treatise, the dialogue began. Socrates
asked to have the first hypothesis reread. According to this, if the
many *are*, they will be *unlike*, since *many*, as well as *like*, since they
all *are*. This being impossible, the hypothesis would seem to be false.

Socrates has correctly understood the purpose of the treatise as a
whole, which is to show the various, absurd consequences of supposing that the many *are*. Parmenides provided brief and effective evidence to show that all is one. Zeno provides a vast array of variegated
evidence to show that the many are not.[5] He is really saying the same
thing in a roundabout way. All his arguments are directed against
the being of the many. This is why he has attacked the concept of
change and motion, for motion is a kind of diversity or manyness.[6]
If the space to be traversed is all one, there is no *different* space for
motion to be moved into, and hence no motion. But if the space
to be traversed is really a many, more disastrous consequences follow,
for each one of the many is divisible into a further many. Hence an
infinite number of spaces would have to be traversed to arrive at any
given space, and no motion could ever get started. Even if it did,
it could never reach any distant point, for an infinite many would
first have to be traversed. If the many positions of the arrow in its
so-called flight really *are*, each must be what it is, and the same with
itself. Hence, in each successive position the arrow will be at rest.
If the many *are*, then they are all alike in *being*, but *unlike* in their being
many. But likeness is simply what it is — likeness, and unlikeness
is what it is — unlikeness. Hence the one cannot be the other. If
the word *is* always carries the same univocal meaning, these conclusions cannot be avoided.

Socrates at once suggests a possible distinction in the meaning
of being as the way of avoiding the paradox.[7] Are there not different
levels or modes of being? On the one hand, there is the being (εἶναι)
of the pure form by itself (αὐτὸ καθ' αὐτὸ εἶδος), for example, unlikeness as it is. On the other hand, there is the becoming [8] of those

---

[5] *Parmenides*, 128 A–B.   [6] Cf. *Parmenides*, p. 145 E–146 A.
[7] *Parmenides*, 128 E 6 ff.   [8] Cf. *Parmenides*, 129 A 4: γίγνεσθαι.

things which only come to partake of the former. Bearing this distinction in mind, we may avoid all of Zeno's difficulties. The space to be traversed may contain something indefinite, subject to unlimited divisibility, and yet not be wholly lacking in participated, finite definiteness, and thus be traversable. The moving arrow need not *be* at each point in its flight. It may rather *become*, or move through them, in coming to be. Finally, a concrete, changing thing, which only partakes of a form without completely being it, may also, without any contradiction, *partake of* another opposite form. Hence it is not surprising to discover that the many things about us, including ourselves, *become* both one and many, both hot and cold, both like and unlike, and so forth, without really *being* any of them. It is not logic which causes these sophistic difficulties, but rather an over simple ontology which confuses pure being with the participated being of material things.

The dialogue as a whole is a perfectly consistent development of this original suggestion. It represents an attempt to work out an ontology adequate to deal with the various fundamental facts of the world of becoming. But before this attempt is made, certain preliminary objections to the whole enterprise as such must be considered. It is fitting that these basic objections should be made through the person of the great Parmenides himself, whose followers have clung so doggedly to certain phases of his doctrine as to argue eristically with their opponents, instead of dwelling on the thought of their master, and thus of deepening that understanding of being itself which is the primary aim of philosophy. Let him then make those objections for which he himself has been only indirectly responsible, and which have brought philosophy into confusion and disrepute.[9] This is perhaps appropriate. But what is really appropriate is to allow the great master then to *answer* these objections, in a genuine dialectical display, showing how his original doctrine may be purified and enriched by going further and deeper in such a way as to preserve the truth which it originally contained. First of all, what are the major objections to such an ontological distinction as Socrates has suggested, not only here but in many of the earlier dialogues as well, particularly in the *Phaedo*?

[9] Cf. Francis H. Bradley, *Appearance and Reality* (New York: Macmillan, 1902), ch. v, for a modern version of these objections to motion and change.

2. THE OBJECTIONS TO ONTOLOGY

The easiest way of interpreting a distinction between x and y is to think of them as two separate existing things. Hence we are readily led into thinking of the concrete, changing things and the forms as two realms of being, each existing apart from the other. We regard a difference between two levels of existence just as we regard two different *things*, both of which fall within the level of existence commonly confronting us. This tendency is reinforced by our ability to conjure up abstract, imaginative pictures of those quantitative and moral forms with which we are most constantly concerned in daily life.

We are all forced to consider the quantitative structure which belongs to all material things. In doing so, we can easily make pictures or diagrams either in something outside us or in our phantasy to aid us in grasping the form itself. In such pictures we easily disregard everything but that aspect in which we are interested. They thus become hypostatized formal entities, "things *as* purely and simply alike," [10] "things *as* purely and simply equal," [11] *as* purely and simply one, or *as* purely and simply many, and so on, readily confused with the forms themselves (αὐτὰ καθ' αὑτὰ τὰ εἴδη); [12] which are not things at all.

The same is true of important phases of our own nature, such as courage, justice, temperance, and so forth, which we apprehend as clearly belonging to us, but which we also know we are constantly failing to realize. There is a painful chasm (χωρισμός) between the ideal pictures of our imagination and the stark reality, also between the ideal equality of mathematical imagination and the vague and approximate equality of things we sense. Hence we are confirmed in our tendency to separate what is really only distinct, and to think of the inadequate, changing things on the one hand, and the ideal normative things on the other, with a chasm between. Nothing ever *is* as it *ought* to be, and the *ought* or norm never *is*. Facts on the one side, values on the other, with a gulf between. Plato's early dialogues clearly reveal this tendency first to abstract quantitative and moral forms. As soon as the intellect is capable of becoming exact, it fixes

---

[10] αὐτὰ τὰ ὅμοια; *Parm.*, 129 B 1.

[11] αὐτὰ τὰ ἴσα; *Phaedo*, 74 C.

[12] Cf. Cornford, *Plato and Parmenides* (New York: Harcourt Brace, 1939), pp. 70–71, for a good discussion of this distinction.

quantitative and moral exactitude, becoming clearly aware of accidents before substances.

Nevertheless the intellect cannot long remain unaware that formal structure is not restricted to accidents of quantity and moral quality. Substantial things such as fire, earth, mud, etc., which *have* number and extension, are themselves not wholly without structure. Also we ourselves, who are the subjects of virtue, have a substantial nature of our own. But here we fall into great difficulty, for *we* are changing, material beings, and it is hence impossible to conjure up any sort of abstract picture of ourselves, either in our imagination or elsewhere, which would not embody something in it besides mere form. This is equally true of fire or mud. In *these* cases, the form cannot be separated from the matter. No matter how far we try to idealize it, ideal mud remains mud. This does not mean that mud has no universal, definable nature. Plato defines it in the *Theaetetus* as "moistened earth." [13] This is a universal nature common to all instances of mud. But, unlike the nature of such an accident as quantity, it is a *substantial* nature, which cannot even be imagined apart from some individual earth of determinate dimensions existing at a particular time and place. It is the same with ourselves. We also have a common, human nature. But in distinction from its moral accidents, we cannot separate this nature, even in imagination, from an individual matter possessing other traits and accidents. We cannot imagine man, simply so far as man. [14] The forms of material substances cannot be abstractly separated as the forms of accidents.

This, as Socrates admits, constitutes a grave objection to the doctrine of forms as we are at first inclined to imagine it. Moral norms or ideals and quantitative accidents are not the only forms. If they were, we might persist without a qualm in maintaining two separate realms, each existing apart from the other. But there is a form of every identifiable quality or thing. In the case of such substances as mud and fire we cannot imagine the form as existing without the matter. Only two alternatives seem possible.

In the first place, we may regard the united forms as normal, in which case we must explain the separation of certain of these forms through the intervention of some agency such as the intellect, other than the normal existence of the thing. Or, in the second place, we

[13] *Theaetetus*, 147.
[14] αὐτό τι εἶδος ἀνθρώπου: *Parm.*, 130 C 2.

may regard the separation of things and forms as normal, each existing in the same mode, trusting with Socrates that somehow or other we may be able to explain how the forms became united with matter, some of them inextricably so. It is so easy for us to imagine the mathematical and moral forms as separate existences, each existing in the normal, material way, that we are tempted with the very young Socrates to embrace this course rather than to introduce another agency with another mode of existence. Nevertheless the argument proceeds to show further and even more serious difficulties confronting this tempting view.[15]

If the forms exist in themselves as separate *things*, the concrete things can come to partake of them only by including the whole or the part of a form. But if a thing absorbs into itself the whole of the form, there will be nothing left over of the form as thus imagined, for any other concrete thing. Hence no two things will ever truly be said to have the same form. Furthermore, if the whole form can enter a thing, it will seem necessary to speak of the thing as wholly what it is, and the separation of formal existence from concrete existence will have to be abandoned. The only other alternative is to think of participation as only *part* of the form entering into the thing. In this case, we may never speak of a thing becoming *really* beautiful, or *really* white. We shall have to alter radically our whole mode of speech, and refer to a thing as really being partly-beautiful, or really being partly-white.

The absurdity of this is made abundantly clear in the case of the quantitative accidents. If largeness is itself a quantitative thing, and being large means to partake of only a small part, then a concrete thing will become large by reason of something small. In the case of equality, we shall be forced to say that a thing may become really equal by reason of something much less than equality. And finally in the case of smallness we shall have to make the ridiculous assertion that something becomes truly small by reason of something much smaller than absolute smallness itself. Surely we cannot accept these ridiculous consequences of tampering uncritically with our common speech, which clearly understands that the form itself, not merely a *part* of it, is somehow present in the thing. We must be far more careful than common speech, however, in distinguishing the mode of existence belonging to things which become, and that which belongs

15 *Parm.*, 130 A–134 E.

to the pure forms by themselves. Likeness is purely and simply what it is. A concrete thing is like, only in becoming more or less like. The imperfection, however, lies not in the participated form as such, but in the mode of being which it has in a concrete thing.

The next argument, that of the so-called third man, clearly reveals the insuperable difficulty of attributing concrete existence to the form. If we think of humanity, for example, as something *having* humanity, in addition to the humanity of individual men, then we shall have to postulate "a third man" in which these both participate. But this third man also, if he is imagined as something concretely existent, will only participate in humanity. Hence we will be led into an infinite regress. The form must not be confused with one of its instances, even though this instance be unspecified, as "some man" or "any man." This is not the form itself, but *the form as participated by an unspecified instance*. The usual way in which we arrive at the concept of a universal is by conjuring up various particular instances in our imagination, noticing that they are invariable in some respect, and thus coming to see that the universal holds of *any* instance, or of some particular, representative instance. But such an instance, as for example *a* geometrical construction, is still not the pure universal in itself. To confuse this pure structure with a representative image or diagram is to commit the fallacy of the third man, to regard the form as a thing.

If the form is regarded as such an unspecified *thing*, the soul is then forced to think of still another *thing* in which the first participates, and so on. But what if the form is this very thinking (νόημα) of the soul? As Socrates suggests,[16] this would seem to offer us a way of escape from the infinite regress of the third man, for we should then have to assume only the many individual things participating in the form, and the psychic act of thinking or conceiving. Thinking is not something that materially participates in the form. Thinking simply thinks the universal. Why then may we not follow the conceptualists of all ages in identifying the form with our thinking of the form? Parmenides offers two basic criticisms of this view.

In the first place, it entirely ignores the evident structural differentiation between the thought of *x* and the *x* which is thought of. It is true that this intentional structure of thought and the object of thought must not be confused with the hylomorphic structure of

16 *Parm.*, 132 B 2 ff.

the individual material thing, which Plato called participation.[17] Nevertheless any careful examination of the rational process will reavel a structural differentiation of act of thought vs. object of thought, which stands in the way of any conceptualistic identification of the two. Hence, as Plato, through Parmenides, remarks, each psychic thought is *of something*,[18] and *of something* in some mode of existence,[19] and hence one. This intentionality of thought is factually incompatible with the oversimplified thesis of conceptualism, which would identify that *of* which we are thinking solely with our thinking of it.

In the second place, as Parmenides goes on to show, conceptualism must lead to some type of idealism. All material things somehow partake of forms, as has been agreed. But if the forms are to be identified with psychic acts, then all things will be made up of thoughts. This will mean either that all things are constantly thinking,[20] or that there are unconscious or non-thinking thoughts.[21] Modern idealists have not hesitated to embrace one, or the other, or both of these consequences. The ancients were too clearly aware of the distinction between the living and the non-living to entertain panpsychism as a serious possibility.[22] Hence Socrates sees at once that it is a *reductio ad absurdum* of conceptualism. There are at least three distinguishable elements in the knowing process which it is disastrous to confuse with one another: (1) the hylomorphic individual things; [23] (2) the psychic acts of thinking or intending either such a thing, or a pure form; [24] (3) and finally the pure forms themselves,[25] which may be sometimes intended by an intentional act. The pure form (3) cannot be unqualifiedly identified with either the hylomorphic thing (1) or the psychic act (2). This is the upshot of the discussion so far.

But the original question still remains as to how we are to understand participation or the relation between 1 and 3. Socrates now abandons the difficult notion of participation altogether and embarks upon a new and even more dangerous course. The forms are models or archetypes (παραδείγματα) which exist somewhere in nature by

---

[17] μέθεξις.   [18] τινός.   [19] ὄντος.
[20] πάντα νοεῖν: *Parm.*, 132 C 11.
[21] νοήματα ὄντα ἀνόητα εἶναι.
[22] Cf. *De An.*, 411 A 8.
[23] ἐμὲ καὶ σὲ καὶ τἆλλα ἃ δὴ πολλὰ καλοῦμεν: *Parm.*, 129 A 3.
[24] νόημα.
[25] αὐτὰ τὰ εἴδη: *Parm.*, 131 C 5.

themselves. The hylomorphic things do not *partake* of them, but have a completely independent existence of their own, being images or likenesses of the forms. Thus the picture of a man exists entirely apart from the man, having nothing of the real man in it, being a likeness of the man. But this view only intensifies all the difficulties of the chasm, and we are back again at the beginning.

The previous views assumed two existing things, one of which was supposed to share in the other. Now we are confronted by two existing things so independent that the one cannot even do this, but can only be *like* the other. What then can this likeness mean? For one thing, it is clear that likeness is a symmetrical relation, and thus different from participation. If A is like B, then B is like A. But if A *participates* in B, B does not participate in A. Hence if the individual thing is like the archetype, then the archetype will, in this respect, be like the individual thing. How else can we account for this, except by supposing that in this respect they both *partake* of the same form? Hence likeness presupposes some sort of non-symmetrical participation which is precisely the conception we have been trying to avoid. Far from being a new, independent relation, likeness is only a special sort of participation, i.e. participation in a certain respect. If the picture of a man does not in some respect at least, partake of some form, say the shape of the features, in which the man himself also partakes, then the picture cannot be said to be like the man. Hence likeness is itself a *certain sort of* participation, and is not an independent notion. We are caught once more in the old difficulty. Either there is no participation, in which case the hylomorphic world becomes unintelligible, or we must give some satisfactory explanation of participation, which we have as yet altogether failed to do.[26]

---

[26] Professor Cornford points out that Plato continues to speak of the forms as archetypes in the *Timaeus* and elsewhere, as well as of individual things as likenesses. Hence he tries to detect a fallacy in the preceding argument of Parmenides (*Plato and Parmenides*, p. 94). The archetypal form may partake of another form (likeness) in which the thing partakes. Hence the thing may be said to be a likeness of the first archetypal form. But this is beside the point. Plato is speaking of that form (the second form) in which the thing must at some point partake. The thing is not a likeness of this form which is somehow in it, nor is this form the archetype of itself. Participation, as Professor Cornford admits, is not the same as likeness, but is its basis. Hence the argument is altogether sound. This does not mean, however, that changing things, existing imperfectly, may not appropriately be termed the likenesses of that single archetypal form which does not embody the other forms, but lifts them

It is now pointed out that there is an insuperable difficulty in the way of such an explanation, if we think of the forms as existing apart by themselves, in the same way that we think of ordinary, individual objects of knowledge as existing apart from one another. Even though we may somehow imagine the forms as existing separately from ordinary things, we cannot think of the forms themselves without thinking of them in relation to one another. The ideal circle can be made intelligible only in relation to its ideal center and ideal radii. An ideal accident, such as justice, is just as unintelligible an abstraction as a concrete justice wandering about in the world without belonging to anyone. If the ideal justice exists apart from all concrete men in the world, it will require an ideal substantial man to which it is attached. The accidental form of mastership will require an ideal master, and since he will exist altogether apart from this world, he will require an ideal slave *of whom* he will be the master.

If we think of the ideal, mathematical entities and moral norms, which we first find it easy to abstract, as existing apart in a separate "realm" of subsistence, we must also drag their substances, and everything else, with which they are substantially related, after them. We cannot really stop until we have formed some sort of a complete duplicate of the concrete world imagined in an "idealized" form. Plato does not dwell upon the many difficulties and absurdities, later carefully analyzed by Aristotle, which follow upon any attempt to make such a twin-world intelligible. He is content to call attention to a single most crucial difficulty — the position of human knowledge, which is the key to the resolution of the difficulty.

The realm of forms cannot exist apart by itself until it becomes a complete and substantial duplicate of our world. Hence we shall have two complete and independent, substantially existent worlds, one concrete and material, the other abstract and unchanging. Now the question is, to which world does human knowledge belong? Authentic knowledge is clearly of the changeless form, but *we* are obviously in the material world. Surely if anyone is to have knowledge of the pure forms, it will be some divine being dwelling in the perfect world. But in this case, *we* shall be utterly deprived of genuine knowledge, and cease to be men. But if we *do* have it, we shall be gods, and

to the level of pure being. Here we are thinking not of the relation between the thing and the form *as such* (participation), but between the thing and the form as *existing* at a higher level of being (likeness), later developed into the theory of analogy.

cease to be men. The chasm or χωρισμός between concrete things and forms, which is involved in the present-day picture of Platonism, is, according to Plato himself, incompatible with the actual existence of human knowledge.[27] It is inconceivable to me that the very man who saw and who stated these objections so clearly could have gone on holding the very misconception he has so destructively criticized. What then is the alternative view? It is suggested by the concluding remarks of Parmenides,[28] and developed with great detail in the culminating dialectical portion of the dialogue.

3. THE DIALECTICAL EXERCISE

There are many more dangers and pitfalls facing anyone who, like Plato's own disciple Aristotle, attempts to maintain the existence of forms in the face of such criticism. Many subtle distinctions and refinements must be made, and the difficult terrain of ontology must

[27] Like other commentators, Professor Cornford seeks to defend the view attacked by Parmenides in this section (133 C–134 E) rather than to refine it — surely Plato's purpose. He accuses Parmenides of confusing the pure form αὐτὴ δεσποτεία with its perfect instance, αὐτὸς δεσπότης (*Plato and Parmenides*, pp. 98–99). Mastership is a separate form, but *that which exists apart by itself is substantial.* Hence mastership must be substantialized into *the perfect master*, which further demands *the perfect slave.* This is merely the fantastic, hypostatized other world of later Platonism. On the other hand, if we try to think of the perfect master as an inhabitant of *this* world we are confronted with all the difficulties of participation. Surely the form itself cannot be its own instance, as Professor Cornford would seem to suggest. What then is meant by instance?

As Plato suggests, it is really knowledge which makes the χωρισμός impossible. If we possess genuine knowledge as distinct from opinion, then we know the forms here in this world. If we do not know them, then there is no refuge from scepticism. All is flux and knowledge is impossible. We fall into a similar difficulty if we place knowledge in the realm beyond, for *this* knowledge will then be separated from us and our world. Perfect knowledge will then be incapable of knowing something which exists. This is surely a contradiction. It is the nature of knowledge to be capable of knowing anything, and thus to transcend all chasms, as the familiar discussions of Spinoza's doctrine of attributes have clearly shown.

Professor Cornford would seem to admit this in maintaining that the human soul "partakes" of the pure forms and in agreeing with Wilamowitz that it is intermediate between these and the material things. But then the χωρισμός is really transcended, and the two-world view unnecessary. We shall require only *one* world containing understanding which contains the forms. This does not mean, of course, that the forms have no substantial archetype or first cause. But the χωρισμός is overcome by knowledge.

If the only answer to Parmenides' objection is to abandon the theory he is objecting to here (the χωρισμός), it is hard to see any justification for Professor Cornford's reference to it as "grossly fallacious," p. 98.

[28] *Parm.*, 134 E–135 C.

be thoroughly explored. But the task must be performed. The forms do in some sense exist, perhaps in several senses. Otherwise it will be impossible to determine the intelligible nature of each one thing, the intellect will have nothing fixed to fasten upon, and thus the whole capacity of reflection will be completely undermined. Where then are the forms, if they are not things existing apart? Where can they be if not in the intellect itself — though not as the purely psychic acts by which the intellect understands what it understands?

These forms exist imperfectly in individual changing things.[29] They exist even less perfectly in the imaginal content of our phantasy and sense-experience.[30] They exist purely and insubstantially as the objects of understanding.[31] Finally they have their source in the unique unity of being itself.[32] Being has at least these four distinct meanings. We say that our dreams, hallucinations and feelings *are*, though they do not exist in the same way as the changing material things from which they are derived. These material things also *are*. They come into being and pass away, though they do not exist in the same way as their universalized structure, apprehended by the intellect. The essence of human nature *is*, and has properties, though not in the same sense as being itself.

Needless to say, these four levels of being correspond to the four parts of the divided line in Book VI of the *Republic*, which are apprehended by conjecture, conviction, scientific understanding, and rational insight respectively. The process of education involves a turning, first of all, away from the partial and distorted images of experience to the complete pattern of the material world from which they were derived. It involves, in the second place, a turning away from the partial and distorted patterns of this world, as apprehended by the separate sciences, to the complete pattern itself as derived from its first principle or source. The danger of confusing these levels with one another is clearly suggested to us in the analogy of the Cave. Each level is in a sense complete. The real things can be perceived as watery reflections of becoming, or thought as immaterial reflections of being. Any one of these things can be embodied in a stone image, and taken down into the Cave. The prisoners can then apprehend the shadow of any of these by sense. To them, such an experience is the whole of reality, and the shadows more real than their brighter

---

[29] Hypotheses II and III.   [30] Hyp. VII.
[31] Hyp. V.   [32] Hyp. I.

source. They are blinded, when turned around, and cannot see in the light. Like the Heracliteans, they cannot see what is more stable, more intelligible, and more real than the passing flux.

This is a common and pitiable type of ontological confusion.[33] But as Plato remarks,[34] there is also the opposite type of confusion. The man who has learned to see in a bright light, when he returns to the Cave, is apt to become confused, and to identify what is less real with nothing at all. Like Parmenides, he dismisses what is not perfectly real as mere delusion. This confusion, however, is the indication of a happy state, and may be more easily rectified. No doubt this is the reason why Parmenides himself is allowed to correct and purify his own ontology, and to lead the way in making those further distinctions without which it cannot be defended. The famous dialectical portion of the *Parmenides* is simply the great master himself — learning to see in the dark. This is a matter of practice and exercise.

To the many, who think that they know already what being is, such ontological exercises seem mere useless hairsplitting,[35] but they stand at the very gateway of philosophy, for without them we must inevitably fall into a simple view of being, thus failing to distinguish things which are very far apart, and separating things which are really on the same plane. From whom would we be more likely to learn some of these basic distinctions than from Parmenides himself, who, in spite of many crudities and distortions, did actually glimpse the ultimate source of all intelligibility, being itself, in its unique and changeless existence? It is fitting, therefore, that the whole ontological investigation should begin with a purification of his ontology. Parmenides, however, suggests two important modifications of the traditional Eleatic procedure.

Instead of taking such an entity as the one, and trying to see what must follow if it is, as though the word *is* were unambiguous, he is also going to attempt to see what follows if the one is not. Of course, if *is not* means utterly nothing, nothing will follow. But there may be other beings *between* perfect being and absolute non-being. Parmenides is sensitive now to the possibility of these intermediate modes of being which may not absolutely be, but still may not be nothing. In the second place, he will not ignore the connexity of entities, as those naive proponents of the forms, who try to establish what a single form such as mastership is, apart from all relations to

---

[33] *Rep.*, 518 B 3.   [34] *Rep.*, 518 A 6–7.   [35] ἀδολεσχία: *Parm.*, 135 D 5.

what is other than itself. If there are different levels of being, they may each reveal a different mode of unity or connexity. To lay bare, so far as possible, such diverse levels of being and connexity is thus suggested from the start as the primary purpose of the exercise. Let us now attempt to interpret it, at least in part, without further preliminaries. We shall not, of course, be able to follow it through in every detail, but must be content with the attempt to grasp its major import, and what would seem to be the more important of its culminating insights.[36]

4. THE FIRST HYPOTHESIS

If there is a perfect coincidence between being and one — if One itself *is* (εἰ ἕν ἐστιν)[37] — we have Parmenides' Way of Truth or, as he says in his Poem, "the only way left to be spoken," namely that Being is. Of course this phrase is ambiguous. It *may be interpreted* as meaning "a certain being is one,"[38] or "a certain being is only one" (Hyp. IV).[39] The following exercise is an attempt to purify Parmenides' real meaning from these confusions. It is, as the Neo-Platonists rightly supposed, a purified Eleatic theology. What can we say of that one being which simply is, or in later language, whose essence is its existence?[40]

The one whose unity is existence, and whose existence is unity itself, can have no parts. It does not *have* its being, but rather *is* its being. Neither does it *have* its unity, but rather *is* its unity. Parmen-

---

[36] We shall refer throughout the text to the recent translation and commentary of Prof. F. M. Cornford, *Plato and Parmenides*. For a critique of Cornford's interpretation see my review, in *Phil. and Phen. Research*, I, no. 2 (December 1940), 233 ff. For an illuminating philosophical commentary see Andreas Speiser, *Ein Parmenideskommentar* (Leipzig, 1937).

[37] Grammar is here inconclusive. The phrase may be translated "if there is a one" (Cornford, p. 116) but the one here discussed is surely not one among many ones, *a* one. This is the *meaning* of the formula in Hypothesis II where Cornford translates "if a one is" (p. 136). But surely there is a difference of *meaning* in the formulae of I and II. The notion of Hypothesis I cannot be accurately conveyed by any linguistic formula since it is really ineffable. It is that of a One and a being which are simply one.

[38] ἕν εἰ ἐστιν: Hyp. II, which Cornford translates "if a One is" (p. 136), and Taylor, *The Parmenides of Plato* (Oxford, 1934), more accurately renders "if there is one" (p. 73).

[39] Which Cornford renders "if there is a one" (p. 214).

[40] Cornford's attack on the Neo-Platonic interpretation of this first hypothesis (pp. 131–134) succeeds only in reducing it to 0, and thus of identifying it with Hypothesis IV. But if the original suppositions of I and IV are one and the same, why two hypotheses?

ides and other absolutists have tried to think of such being as an absolute whole made up of all existent parts. Since this whole is one, and all of its parts are also one, it is ever the same, and identical with itself. But existent unity has no parts. Hence it is not a whole or absolute. Nor can this being be identified with the oneness of any existent thing, which is distinct from the thing which has it. Even though we abstract this oneness from all such things, and think of it alone as the number one, that which might be this one, or that one, or any other one, but by itself is only one, we have not grasped the "being-one," for nothing other than itself can have this. Hence it is not "like" anything, as the number one is like all material things, namely in so far as they possess any quantitative oneness. The existent one *has* no otherness in it whatsoever. So it cannot be other than anything, nor properly referred to as *this*, or as *that*, or as *a* one among others. All such ones, including the number one, have some otherness in themselves besides their being-one. The number one, for example, is a number, in itself different from two and three, etc. But the unique one-existent *has* no difference in itself at all. It is neither the same as nor different from itself, nor is it the same as or different from anything else.

A being, whose existence unifies itself, *has* no limit, for in any *such kind* of being it would be possible to distinguish between the limited *kind* or *essence*, which would be able to exist, and the existence given to this essence. Such entities would thus consist of at least two parts, their essence and their existence. A material entity, like a tree or a river, must have, in addition to its kind of unity or determinate nature, some matter of determinate dimensions, able to receive this nature. As Plato points out, any limit imposed on such matter must itself have a spatial beginning,[41] middle,[42] and end.[43] Any such material entity, as the famous sphere of Parmenides, is very far from the simple unity he supposed it to be. It must consist of at least the following parts: matter able to assume this form, the form of sphericity, the existence of the whole. Needless to say, such complexity is far from the unique simplicity of being itself.

Being one, it cannot be *in* anything, either as the various parts which are *in* itself, as the various parts of a sum are *in* the whole sum, or *in* another, as all the parts of oxygen and hydrogen are *in* the whole of water. Certainly the One cannot be any such spatial whole as that

[41] ἀρχήν.   [42] μέσον.   [43] τελευτήν.

imagined by Parmenides, for this would have to be either all of space, in which case it would be in itself as a collective whole, or some part of space, in which case it would be in another space surrounding it, and in contact with it at *many* points. In neither case would the one be one.

The one has no otherness or diversity in itself. Hence it cannot change or alter, for this necessarily involves diversity. It cannot spatially revolve about itself, for in this case it would have to have a center and other parts. Neither can it move in a straight line from one place into another, for in doing so it would have to be neither wholly in the one nor wholly in the other, but partly in one and partly in the other. But, having no parts, the one cannot be *partly* anywhere. So it cannot change in any manner, and cannot be of the same age as, or older, or younger than, anything. Temporal equality is a sort of equality, and as we have seen, the one cannot be quantitatively equal to anything for it is neither commensurable nor incommensurable with any parts. Since it does not become at all, it cannot, like all temporal things, become older or younger than itself or any other thing. It does not occupy time at all, but simply is.

Since all the things we know directly are spread out in time, either as having become, will be becoming, or as becoming, it is impossible for us to imagine any being which does not partake of being in one of these temporal modes. Hence, *if* we follow imagination rather than pure reflection, we shall conclude that "there is, accordingly, no way in which the One *has* being," and that "the One itself in no sense *is*." [44] In this case, coinciding with utter nothingness rather than with utter being, the one could have no quality or relation. It could not be expressed in language, nor could there be any knowledge, or perception, or opinion of it. [45]

---

[44] *Parm.*, 141 E 9–10. Doubt, however, is at once cast on this conclusion at E 12: εἰ δεῖ τῷ τοιῷδε λόγῳ πιστεύειν, since the one itself does not, of course, *have* or *partake of* being for a certain time only, but is its being necessarily or non-temporally.

[45] Following the discussion of the *Theaetetus*, we may briefly characterize the faculties here enumerated as follows. Discourse (λόγος) is the flowing out of knowledge or opinion into words. Perception, or feeling (αἴσθησις), is the infallible apprehension of something flowing in relation to some sensitive faculty. Opinion (δόξα) is the fallible apprehension of pure structure in the flux. Knowledge (ἐπιστήμη) is the infallible apprehension of this pure structure independent of the flux.

5. Hypotheses II and III. Material Being

We are now introduced to *a* one which exists in a different manner. Hypothesis I concerned *the* one whose essence is its existence.[46] Now we are to consider not a one which *is* existence, but a one which *has* existence. The "is" and the "one" now "stand for different things."[47] This is the mode of existence which belongs to the "ordinary," changing things surrounding us, from which is derived the "standard" sense of the word "to be." Hypothesis II describes the composite structure of *the one* which exists in this way, Hypothesis III that of *the others* which similarly exist. But since the one is now other than its existence, and has otherness in it, while the otherness itself must nevertheless be one, the two overlap and may be considered together. There is no material one without others, no material others which are not one. Let us now examine the composite structure of material existence so far as it is sharply distinct from the simple structure of pure existence (Hyp. I), and then pause to examine a few important phases of this composite structure where sophistic confusion especially occurs.

Since the unity and the existence of such a thing are distinct, it will be a whole made up of at least two parts, unity and existence. No whole is purely and simply one. It is at best a more or less unified manifold. Even the simplest of such wholes, the number one, is made up of three distinguishable phases: (1) unity; (2) existence; and (3) the difference between them. Hence it involves the indefinite plurality of what we call the number series, which may be derived from the notion of unity and the quantitative matter, with which it is unified in the number one, by addition and multiplication. These "operations" are simply ways of unifying mathematical matter. When we say "two *times* one," we mean two material instances of unification, not diverse in their unity, but in their existence, which materially spreads them out, and numerically diversifies them. Whatever is

---

[46] Professor Cornford's note, *Plato and Parmenides*, p. 136, interprets Hyp. I as the barren tautology one-one, which ignores the ἔστι in the original formula, the many references to *being* throughout the first hypothesis, and the whole intention of the exercise (*Parm.*, 136 A–B) to examine what follows if the one *is* and if the one *is not*. The phrase ἕν ἕν at 142 C 2 is not "a more accurate expression than εἰ ἕν ἔστιν for what *was* our supposition in Hyp. I." If so, it would have been utilized there. If one *is* being, then either term, taken singly, may be expanded into the other, ἕν τε εἶναι, therefore, being equivalent to καὶ "ν ἕν (142 C 2).

[47] *Parm.*, 142 C 5.

only numerically one, even the pure number one, is only *an* entity (not being itself), which has such distinct, diversified existence bestowed in some way upon it. Furthermore, every such entity is only unified in a certain way, not really one. Thus both being and unity are never given in their entirety to the standard entities surrounding us, but only divided and distributed among them.[48] Each entity will be divided into at least two parts (being and unity), and will be further divisible, since each part must also be and be one.

As a whole of parts, the material entity will have beginning, middle, and end. Whatever lacks any one of these cannot be a whole. Such a quantitative entity may be extended, with a spatial middle, and spatial extremities.[49] Zeno and the sophists had maintained that it is "contradictory for a thing both to be in itself and in another."[50] Not only is this not a "contradiction": it is an essential aspect of the composite structure of any limited magnitude, or whole of parts. As *all* the parts, it lies within its limits, and is *in* itself. But as *the whole*, it includes its limits, and is in another.

Zeno and the sophists argue that rest is contradictory to motion, and that a thing cannot at once be susceptible to both. Thus the flying arrow, being at each instant *in* itself, or *in* a place coinciding with its own limits,[51] is at rest, and thus not susceptible to motion. In the sense in which a magnitude is *always* contained within its limits it is indeed always "at rest." But this is not what "rest" means. In the sense in which the limits are always contained *in another*, a magnitude is never at rest, or "in the same." Physical rest means that the limits remain in *the same other*, physical motion that they are in *another other*. Hence rest and motion are not contradictory, but contrary phases of the same structure "being in another."[52]

Since material existence distributes the one into an indefinite multiplicity, an entity cannot be absolutely enclosed within itself as what is really one, but must *possess* relations to itself as well as to other entities. Being unified or one (within its limits), it is the same as itself, but being a whole (including its limits), as well as all the parts (within the limits), it is different from itself. Furthermore each one, as one, is the same as another one, and yet the other is of course dif-

48 *Parm.*, 144 A–B.   49 *Parm.*, 145 A–B.
50 Cf. Cornford, *Plato and Parmenides*, pp. 148–150.
51 ἀεί . . . κατὰ τὸ ἴσον: Arist., *Phys.*, 239 B 5.
52 *Parm.*, 145 E–146 A.

ferent. We are apt to think of this material or numerical difference as a purely *formal* trait, and Plato takes great pains in suggesting this confusion. Thus if difference were a *formal* property, contrary to sameness,[53] it could not exist in sameness without contradiction, and we could never refer meaningfully to two entities. We must realize that there is a mode of difference far more basic than any formal property *later* attaching to an already existent thing, and making it different in some formal respect. This basic difference arises from the material being of the thing, which is already numerically different from all other things, no matter what their properties must be.[54]

So far as the one is in some respect the same as the others, it is like them, but so far as it is already numerically distinct, it may be given the formal character of difference in this respect. Hence, in this respect, it is unlike. Great confusion, however, arises when we mix this universal, conceptual property which we conceive with the particular, numerical diversity in the thing, on which this property is founded. When this happens, as in Hegel,[55] the conceptual property of difference, abstracted from its material foundation, is seen to attach to both things *alike*. A is different from B, and B from A, by the very same formal difference. Hence we may sophistically argue that so far as they are unlike they are like (i.e. by the same formal concept), and hence, so far as they are alike, they are unlike. We have confused the relation with its foundation in the thing, and have forgotten the basic, material diversity which already constitutes one entity, in its very existence, as diverse from another. The root of such Zenonian sophistry is the neglect of *matter*.

This neglect leads to a further nest of misapprehensions concerning quantitative continuity and contact, which can be corrected only by a recognition of the important distinctions between continuity (ἐν ἑαυτῷ), contact (ἄψις), and succession (ἐφεξῆς), suggested in the next portion of the argument, and further clarified by Aristotle.[56] A line, for example, involves not only indivisible termini, which give it unity and distinctness, but also an indistinct and divisible matter between.

[53] *Parm.*, 146 D 1.
[54] Cf. especially Cornford's discussion, pp. 160–161, and his references to corresponding passages in Aristotle.
[55] Cf. *Hegel's Science of Logic*, trans. by W. H. Johnston and L. G. Struthers (New York: Macmillan, 1929), p. 48.
[56] *Parm.*, 148 D–149 D. Cf. Aristotle's definitions of continuity, contact, and succession in *Phys.*, V, 3 and VI, 1.

But the sophistic mentality, seeking a spurious "clarity" and "exactitude" rather than truth, still tends to follow Zeno in attempting to eliminate this embarrassingly unintelligible factor by reducing it to points, or indivisible spatial units. Hence Zeno insisted that the finite racecourse must be dissolved into an "infinite" number of points, and modern philosophers insist that a "dense" series is to be defined simply as one such that between any two points there is another *point*. But the word "infinite" really conceals a basic distortion of the facts. No matter how *many* points we conceive, we cannot get a line, for points, by their very nature, are discontinuous. An indivisible one, as Plato points out, cannot be in contact with another.[57] Aristotle reproduces this same argument [58] in showing that the continuous cannot be reduced to indivisibles, as a line to points. Two points *in contact* would simply be one and the same point. Hence the neglect of the divisible matter between the points inevitably breeds paradox. To this extent, Zeno was right, though he failed to recognize the source of the difficulty.

Zeno and his followers throughout the ages have committed a similar fallacy with respect to time, as Plato clearly points out in the important corollary to Hypothesis II.[59] The continuous flight of the arrow, for example, is imagined as a series of indivisible instants, at which the arrow is at rest. But to be at rest requires at least *two* such instants with something divisible between. "At an instant," a body can *neither* be moving *nor* at rest. The instant ($\tau\grave{o}$ $\dot{\epsilon}\xi\alpha\acute{\iota}\phi\nu\eta s$) is not an "infinitesimal" piece of time, both indivisible and divisible at once, but "it occupies no time at all." [60] Change takes place not *at the instant*, but "to and from the instant." [61] Finite entities are made up neither of their indivisible limits alone nor of these limits combined with infinitesimal amounts of matter. They are the indistinct matter (Plato's dyad of the great and small) *limited* by indivisible form (the one). But neither the one nor the other can exist in separation. Points must have something else between, and spatial or temporal stretches must have limits. Spatial matter is incapable of "contact," except in the sense that it comes up to its limits.[62] Thus Aristotle defines the continuous as that which is contained within the same limits.[63]

---

[57] *Parm.*, 149 C 4.
[59] *Parm.*, 155 E–157 B.
[61] *Parm.*, 156 E 1.
[63] *Phys.*, V, ch. 3.

[58] *Phys.*, 236 A 21 ff.
[60] *Parm.*, 156 D.
[62] *Parm.*, 148 D–E.

At least two units are required for contact,[64] when their extremities coincide. Two such units must be next to one another, or in succession, i.e. with nothing of the same kind between them.[65] Points or instants may be "next to" or succeeding one another. They cannot, by their very nature, be either continuous or in contact with one another. These hylomorphic distinctions, when clearly held in mind, are sufficient to "answer" the first three of the four paradoxes of Zeno.

The continuity of matter involves its infinite divisibility. This breeds a further nest of paradoxes.[66] Thus Zeno, and probably Gorgias, argued that the parts of a quantitative whole must be a certain definite number, just as many as they are. But there are always more parts between these many parts. So their number is infinite. But the container is greater than the contained. Hence the finite whole will be greater than the infinite parts. The fallacy, of course, lies in our neglect of the distinction between potentiality and actuality. Bearing this distinction in mind, we may, without any contradiction, safely assert the following apparent "paradoxes."

1. Greatness and smallness are not inherent properties in a magnitude; they are relative to other terms in the material dyad of the great and small; [67] no magnitude is in itself absolutely great or absolutely small, as Plato himself had supposed in the *Phaedo:* [68] each magnitude is thus relative, referring to such other members of the quantitative series. 2. Since it is not *in itself* either great or small, each magnitude may be correctly said to be equal to itself, i.e. neither exceeding nor being exceeded by itself. 3. But this magnitude is not a purely existent indivisible one; it is both a certain indivisible limit, and the continuous matter lying within this limit and only coming up to it; hence, as a whole, *including* the limit, the unit magnitude is greater than itself, but as all its parts, *excluding* the indivisible limit, it is less than itself. 4. Any magnitude will lie next to lesser magnitudes and be succeeded by greater magnitudes, thus being "in the others"; but since its own matter is infinitely *divisible*, all the others, no matter how great or how small, will lie within it. The dyad of the great and small, material quantity, lies within any definite magnitude. 5. In spite of this potential, material content, any magni-

[64] *Parm.*, 149 A–B.
[65] *Phys.*, 231 B 7.
[66] *Parm.*, 149 D–151 E.
[67] Aristotle developed this late Platonic insight at *Cat.*, 5 B 14–30 and elsewhere.
[68] Cf. Cornford's illuminating discussion, pp. 174 ff.

tude, if actual, is also actually measured by certain actual parts constituting its definite quantity or number, and as such is equal to them.

The pure, existent one, being indivisible, cannot exist in time. But units, which consist of material parts, come into existence and pass away. Such a temporal unit, as it becomes, grows older than the self it was, and younger than the self it is coming to be.[69] Nevertheless this continuous advance of time is infinitely divisible into indivisible "nows." Time, as we say, is "datable." *At* such an instant, as we have seen, a thing is not becoming, but *is* younger than what it is coming to be, or *is* older than what it was a moment before. And yet the temporal thing is both the continuous becoming as well as the timeless limits of this process. As such, at a given date, it is always of the same age as itself.

The one, as the indivisible limit, or form of itself, must first come into being, for all its other parts are the parts of *it*. *Causally*, therefore, the form, or the indivisible unity of a thing, must precede its generation. But since the thing is not only indivisible form, but also the whole of its continuous matter, "it" does not reach material existence until the last of its material parts. *Genetically*, therefore, the one is younger than its material parts (the others) and succeeds them in time. But as a concrete whole of form and matter, coming into existence together with its parts, the one will be neither older nor younger than its parts. The causal and the genetic order are two distinct phases of one and the same process.

The time relations between different processes are another fertile source of paradox.[70] Thus if one person (x) was born four years before another (y), x permanently remains four years older than y; and does not become either older or younger, from this standpoint of their fixed dates of birth. But from the standpoint of the material process, the *proportional difference* in age is constantly diminishing. When x is 5, he is five times as old as y; when x is 6, three times; when x is 8, only twice as old; when x is 12 only $\frac{3}{2}$ as old; when 16 only $\frac{4}{3}$, and so on. The older thus becomes less *older-than*, and the younger less *younger-than*. Time, while it cannot eliminate fixed differences, nevertheless eats into them, constantly diminishing them.

Finally, while such an entity cannot be said to *be* its existence all at once, it nevertheless *has* an existence spread out piecemeal in time. It *has* a past, a present, and a future,[71] and *having* this defective mode of existence, which is nevertheless real, it may be perceived as temporally unfolding into what it is, believed as an essential nature suggested by this perceived process of unfolding, or essentially known as what it really is. Hence, while Parmenides was no doubt correct in asserting in his poem that self-existent Being could only be thought, not perceived or opined, we need not agree with his assertions that belief and perception are objectless and illusory. As Aristotle constantly remarks, "being is said in many senses" (τὸ ὂν πολλαχῶς λέγεται). The participated being of finite, material entities is not being itself.

6. HYPOTHESES I–IV. THE TRANSCENDENTAL CONFUSION OF BEING AND COMING TO BE

Even such a brief survey as this is capable of revealing certain basic structural differences between that pure being which *is* one and that partial being which is distinct from its unity, belonging to all the finite or determinate entities of which we have direct perceptual awareness. Since being and one attach to all entities whatsoever, we may follow later usage in referring to them as *transcendental terms*, and to the confusion of two distinct modes of being as a transcendental confusion. It is now clear, especially from Professor Cornford's illuminating commentary,[72] that one primary purpose of Hypotheses I–IV is to call attention to such a transcendental confusion lying at the root of human sophistry.

Thus many of the negative assertions of Hypothesis I are certainly directed against the historical Parmenides, who, while he was correct in asserting that being itself, one itself, and knowledge itself must coincide, and in denying all non-existence and temporality to what is in this sense, was certainly incorrect in thinking of it as an integral whole, or as a spatial sphere, and thereby guilty of a transcendental confusion of being itself with *qualified* being. The sophistic tendency to perpetuate and to elaborate this confusion has continued throughout the history of thought to our own day, and is correctly termed pantheism. Hypothesis I may be adequately summarized as a purified Eleatic theology, warning against pantheism, or any admixture of finite structure with the simple structure of being itself. All that we may strictly assert of such being is that it is, and it is one. All other attributes must be denied except in an analogical sense. Indeed

---

[72] See especially 119–120, 138–139, 151–153, 168, 193.

all *attributes* must be denied, for the one does not *have* attributes; it is. It does not *have* unity as an attribute, but *is* one. *In* it, the many aspects and parts, through which we gain only an inadequate apprehension of it, really coincide. It is neither the whole cosmos, nor the absolute whole, nor any sort of whole, for a whole requires diverse parts. The One simply is.

To distort being by mixing it with the composite structure of finite being is a disastrous root of human confusion, but to distort finite being by mixing it with the simple structure of being is an equally disastrous root of sophistry. Thus many of the positive assertions of Hypothesis II are certainly directed against Zeno and his followers, who, throughout the ages, have tried to apply the simple notion of being to material existence, thus blinding themselves to its materiality, and landing in scepticism and paradox. Thus the sophist applies the notion of pure simplicity to a material whole, and finds that *in this sense* it is not one at all. Using the pure concept of difference (*in itself* the same) he blinds himself to the fact of material, numerical difference. Insisting that what is vague and contrary is really a contradiction, he thinks of change as a mere succession of definite, fixed "stages," and tries to reduce a continuous line to a series of discrete points. This phase of the transcendental confusion, when developed and elaborated, is correctly termed *intellectualism*. When compared with the simplicity of pure being, the material reality about us seems to have no structure, and no stable existence at all. By mixing God with the world, we only betray our inability to grasp Him, and by mixing the world with God, we only betray our incapacity to grasp the world. Pantheism is the beginning of atheism, and intellectualism is the beginning of nihilism. By either path we eventually land in scepticism.

Thus, after all composite structure has been denied of that one which coincides with existence, at the very end of Hypothesis I, it is pointed out that "there is accordingly no way in which the One *has* being." [73] This is because it *is* its being. However, our familiarity with the changing things, which only *have* being in the present, past, or future, leads us to ignore being as such, and, together with many commentators, including Professor Cornford, we fall into the trap. Since pure being does not *have* any being, either present, past, or future, "therefore it in no sense is." [74] The one which is purely one, with no admix-

[73] *Parm.*, 141 E 10.   [74] *Parm.*, 141 E.

ture of anything alien, cannot be *mixed* with being. Such a one, "if we can trust such an argument as this," [75] can neither be nor be one. Hence it can be the object of no cognitive faculty whatsoever. Atheism is thus a final natural consequence of the simple sophistic view of being. One itself does not exist as ordinary things which have existence. Therefore it is sundered from existence itself, and, as the barren form of abstract unity, does not exist at all.

This abstract one, divorced from all existence, the ghost of God, looms on the horizon at various points of the argument of Hypothesis II. [76] But in Hypothesis IV, it once again becomes the center of attention, in connection with what we may call the obverse fallacy of acosmism. In the immediately preceding discussion of Hypothesis III, we have just learned that a unity which is not pure, but only distributed "in part" to *a* unit, may also be similarly distributed to others, which, apart from the unity they come to acquire, must possess "some nature other than the form." [77] This material nature is referred to as a sort of multitude, [78] though this is really an inaccuracy, since any multitude is a multitude of ones. What altogether lacks unity can neither be one nor many. Hypothesis IV goes on to examine more carefully what such complete non-unity may be. If the one is "separate" from the others, then it cannot be distributed to them *in any way*. The others can be neither unified wholes of material parts, nor a multitude of ones, nor can they possess any single character, nor a multitude of characters. It is clear that "they" cannot be at all. The complete separation of God from the world thus leads either to atheism, if our attention is centered upon the world, or to extreme acosmism, if our attention is centered upon what we call God, just as Parmenides and other "absolutists" have "denied" the reality of finite things.

So far, then, two legitimate levels of actual being have been described, and four transcendental confusions suggested. There is that which simply *is* being on the one hand, and that which merely *has* being on the other. The four confusions arise from the illegitimate combination or separation of these two modes of being. If we think of God as possessing only finite existence, thus confusing Him with the world, we have pantheism. If we think of the world as possessing unrestricted existence, thus confusing the world with God, we have

[75] *Parm.*, 141 E.
[77] *Parm.*, 158 C.

[76] *Parm.*, 147 A–B and 149 C.
[78] πλῆθος.

absolutism. If we separate the two and attribute existence to the world we have atheism. If we separate the two and attribute existence to God we have acosmism. These confusions lie at the very source of our understanding, and hence confuse everything that follows upon them. They lie at the root of false philosophies which have misled men and cultures throughout the course of human history. If men are mistaken about being itself, how can they fail to be mistaken about anything whatsoever, for all things must be. Such transcendental mistakes are the ultimate root of human sophistry. We must now pass on to consider further confusions of the same transcendental type which are suggested in the succeeding Hypotheses V–VIII.

7. HYPOTHESIS V. THE NON-EXISTENT BEING OF THE INTELLECT

In addition to unqualified existence and the distributed existence of changing things, there are further entities which do not exist in either of these senses. Thus we may *mean* some entity without asserting its existence. But when we say x *does not exist* we do not mean by x sheer non-entity.[79] We are speaking "in the first place of something knowable,[80] and in the second of something distinct from other things."[81] Hypothesis V is a brief account of the structure of such meanings, essences, or forms,[82] with special reference to the arguments of Gorgias and others that a thing cannot be and also not be. As a matter of fact, whenever we *mean* something, we are involved with a mode of being which is not material, but which nevertheless is not non-existence.

We cannot mean without meaning *something*. Ordinarily, in what was later called an act of first intention, we mean a materially existent thing. But by an act of second intention we may also grasp the meaning *by which* we mean the thing. Plato called these objects of second intentional acts forms or essences. They are knowable and different from other things. They thus have unity, and various relations to other

---

[79] μὴ ἔν.   [80] γνωστόν.

[81] ἕτερον τῶν ἄλλων: *Parm.*, 160 C 8.

[82] It should be compared to *Sophist*, 263 B–D, where error is shown to involve a reference to non-existent beings, τὰ μὴ ὄντα, i.e., the forms, as Professor Cornford points out in his commentary, *Plato's Theory of Knowledge*, pp. 311 ff. His unfortunate tendency to identify being as such with the material being of Hypotheses II and III has prevented him from identifying the being of Hyp. V with the being of the forms, and thus of working out his own interpretation to its requisite conclusion. Cf. *Plato and Parmenides*, pp. 218–219, and my review of this work, *Phil. and Phen. Research*, I, no. 2 (December 1940), 233 ff.

entities, whether or not they themselves are materially existent. Two *material* things may be exactly alike, and yet numerically different and unlike. But two essences, if exactly alike, are one. Hence each essence is unlike all the rest, and always like itself.[83] Among essences, numerical distinctness [84] coincides with formal distinctness.[85] A quantitative essence, such as the number two, has inequality to the others, and relations of greatness, smallness, and equality.

Furthermore, essences in some sense *do* possess being, though they are not materially existent. Hence they both are and are not without any contradiction, so long as the two senses of existence are distinguished. An essence cannot change or move in any way, but it can pass from material existence to essential existence, as when a thing comes to be understood or meant, or from essential existence to material existence, as when a technical concept is realized as we say through art.[86] The very same essences may change their modes of existence. They cannot change in any other way. So much for the non-existent being of forms or essences. Here again, following Plato, we may note four transcendental confusions, as this distinct mode of existence is either falsely mixed with or falsely separated from the ordinary changing existence of material entities.

8. HYPOTHESIS VI. THE TRANSCENDENTAL CONFUSION OF ESSENTIAL AND MATERIAL EXISTENCE

If we think of the forms as having substantial, material existence, reifying them into "things," we are guilty of that transcendental confusion which has come to be known as "extreme realism." Plato does not offer any detailed criticism of this tendency at this point, because just such a criticism has already been offered by Parmenides in opposing the "extreme realistic" views of the youthful Socrates.[87] If we think of the forms in this way as material substances, we are faced with all the difficulties of the gulf or χωρισμός, and participation becomes an insoluble mystery. We are forced into the infinite regress of "the third man," and cannot account for the evident phenomena of human knowledge and discourse.[88] Plato's answer to these difficulties, the only answer in fact, is in terms of ontology. There is no use of asking what sort of *material* existence such things as the

---

[83] *Parm.*, 161 A–C.
[85] ἑτεροῖα.
[87] *Parm.*, 130 E–134 E.

[84] ἕτερα.
[86] *Parm.*, 162 B–163 B.
[88] *Parm.*, 135 B–C.

forms may have, or *where* materially they have it. They do not have such existence, nor do they have it *anywhere*. The forms are not different from the things, existing in the same mode, somewhere else, in a different, physical place. They are formally the same as the things, but existing in a different mode of existence, in a non-physical place. The epistemological difficulties raised by Parmenides can be answered only by actually performing the wearisome, hairsplitting exercises of ontology, with Plato and that "scholastic" philosophy which is the genuine continuation of the *dialectic* of the later dialogues. This is the meaning of the dialogue as a whole.

To confuse the forms with material things generates the sophistries of "extreme realism." To confuse material things with forms generates the sophistries of "intellectualism" and "idealism," which are presented with pointed exaggeration in the *Euthydemus*. The forms are purely knowable. Hence the idealist denies matter, which is unintelligible. Each form "is like itself and unlike all the rest." Hence the sophist embraces the principle of the identity of indiscernibles, and denies material or numerical difference. The forms do not change or move. Hence the idealist, like Bradley, insists that change and motion are contradictory, as they certainly would be in the case of formal existence. But, as is clearly suggested in Hypothesis VI, the separation of these two modes of existence leads to equally dangerous confusions.

If we follow the natural tendency to identify that material mode of existence, which is most familiar to us, with existence as such, then the forms which do not exist *in this sense of existence* do not exist at all, and they are confused with non-entities.[89] This, of course, breeds what we now know as "nominalism." Unless "thought" can be reduced to some kind of material change, it does not exist at all. We may also note the contrary extreme, which identifies being with ideal being, and hence denies all existence whatsoever to the material world. These tendencies may be observed in various degrees of intensity, and in various combinations in the history of human sophistry.

9. HYPOTHESIS VII. THE NON-EXISTENT BEING OF IMAGINATION

So far, we have been constrained both by the text of Plato and by the facts themselves to recognize three distinct senses of the verb

[89] *Parm.*, 164 A–B.

to be. First, there is being itself, which simply *is*. Second, there is the being of essences or meanings, as when we say that "the definition of man *is* rational animal." Here we are asserting no material fact, but an essential structure, which has essential existence. Third, there is the material being of changing things, as when I say that "the pencil *is* now on the table." But there is still a fourth sense of the word *to be* which occurs in our common speech. This is the sense of seeming or appearing.[90] We may say that the sun *seems to be* only two feet in diameter, or that such and such an apparition appeared in a dream. All material things may be "given" in this minimal mode of existence and unity. Hypothesis VII offers a brief account of its essential structure, so far as it differs from the other modes.

Essences are distinguished from ordinary things by their peculiar mode of existence. In comparison with such things we say they are not. According to Plato, dreams, hallucinations, and appearances of all sorts are distinguished from ordinary things rather by their lack of unity. In comparison with such "things" they are indistinct or relative to one another.[91] Failing to discern any distinct character in the thing itself, we are forced to visualize them over against each other. No one is anything in itself, but in relation to another it may be greater or smaller, hotter or cooler, and so forth. What seems to be the very same, but is really only an apparent "mass," [92] is subject to sudden shifts and transformations as its relations change. "If you take what seems to be a minimum, suddenly, as might happen in a dream, what you took to be one (with the unaided eye) appears many, and what seemed to be least (with the unaided eye) appears enormous (under a microscope)." [93] Thus the appearances alter with "the point of view."

As with "shadow-silhouettes," [94] to the distant spectator all will appear as one thing, and seem to have the same character, and so to be alike; but if you approach nearer, they seem many and different, and this semblance of difference will make them seem different in character, and unlike one another.[95] The various traits are so vaguely visualized that they are constantly shifting into one another "in every sort of motion and rest; both coming to be, and ceasing to be, and

---

[90] *Parm.*, 164 B–165 E.
[91] ἄλλα ἀλλήλων: *Parm.*, 164 C.
[92] ὄγκος.
[93] *Parm.*, 164 D.
[94] ἐσκιαγραφημένα: *Parm.*, 165 C 7.
[95] *Parm.*, 165 C–D.

doing neither." [96] A dream is not an ordinary existence of a certain sort. Ordinary things do not lose their self-distinctness, and fade into relative appearance. This shows that we are dealing with an ontological or transcendental distinction which applies to all entities. Appearance is that relational mode of being which lacks independence and lasting power. Appearances are not "other entities," but entities of an entirely different mode. Failing to see this, we fall into further transcendental confusions.

10. Hypothesis VIII. The Transcendental Confusions of Pan-Realism and Relativism

In the first place, thinking of apparitions as a peculiar type of entity, existing as other ordinary things, we confuse them with "realities" of the ordinary mode, and try to discover where in the world they really are. When we find that they are really nowhere in this world, we must conjure up special "realms" within the world for them to inhabit. In these special realms they are as real as anything else. Confusing appearance with reality in this way, we suddenly lose the distinction altogether, and are confronted with the so-called problem of "error." The illusion, which is there momentarily before me, is as much there as an ordinary existent. This confusion easily turns into its opposite — the confusion of reality with appearance. If illusions are just as real as appearances, then why are realities any more real than appearances? After all, everything is subjective and relative. Hence it is easy for Protagoras and his followers to dissolve the world into appearance. The illicit combining of these two distinct ontological levels thus breeds two types of sophistic misapprehension, pan-realism (the confusion of appearance with reality) and subjectivism or relativism (the confusion of reality with appearance), which are closely associated with two further fallacies of illicit separation.

The distinction between different levels of being is not a sharp distinction between essences with no common ground between. It is more like a distinction of degree. To say that x *is not a triangle* is to say that it is not a triangle at all. But to say that x *is not real* is not to say that it is not real at all. Nevertheless we are apt to separate appearance from reality in this way, as Hypothesis VIII suggests. Discovering that apparitions and illusions have no stable unity, we infer that they have no unity at all, and dismiss them as non-entities.

[96] *Parm.*, 165 D.

But that which has no distinct character of any sort cannot even be imagined or perceived in any way.[97] Appearances still obstinately continue to appear. Having once consigned them to oblivion, the only recourse of the sophist is to confuse them with reality. Hence he arrives at extreme panrealism by the way of separation or abstraction. The opposite may also occur. Identifying being as such with that momentary minimal "givenness" which is presented even by an illusion, he may consign all higher modes of being to oblivion. Consequently, such stable entities must be reduced to appearance, and he arrives at extreme panrelativism by way of separation or abstraction.

11. CONCLUSION

Such is the conclusion, I believe, in outline to which we are led by the illuminating investigations of Diès, Cornford, and others who have approached the *Parmenides* with minds unbiased by modern predilections. This interpretation is quite opposed to that of Hegel, who read his own dialectic into the ontological exercises of the dialogue, seeing in Plato's dialectic an anticipation of his own attempt to make thought "move" by self-contradiction. But any attempt to play fast and loose with the fundamental ontological principle of contradiction or to confuse contraries with contradictories is thoroughly un-Platonic. What is perhaps the first clear statement of the law of contradiction is to be found in the *Republic*.[98] In the *Euthydemus*[99] Plato exposes the sophistic argument that a real contradiction is impossible and hence meaningless. When carefully read, there is no single portion of the *Parmenides* which reveals any attempt to make one category "grow" out of another, or breed its opposite. The notion that Hypothesis IIa is somehow a synthesis of I (non-being) and II (being), while not suggested in so many words by Hegel himself, has been suggested by certain Hegelian interpreters.[100] It is in itself fantastic in the light of the text, and even if accepted, fails utterly to account for the later hypotheses. This idealistic mode of interpretation, we may now safely say, is thoroughly discredited.[101] The exercises reveal no transcendental movement in which being somehow contradicts itself. They reveal precisely those distinct senses of existence, based

[97] *Parm.*, 166 A–B.   [98] *Rep.*, IV, 436 B 4 ff.   [99] *Euth.*, 286.
[100] Cf. Leon Robin, *Platon* (Paris: F. Alcan, 1935), p. 131.
[101] Cf. Cornford's discussion, *Plato and Parmenides*, pp. 202–203.

upon cognizable facts, the clear recognition of which will enable us to avoid such contradictions. As Aristotle later remarked, "being is said in several senses," and his own ontological discoveries probably owe much to these preliminary academic investigations.[102]

It is the confusion of these different senses, and especially the notion that this transcendental term has only one simple and unambiguous meaning, which lies close to the root of the sophistry of all ages.

Thus Parmenides, in denying all being to whatever cannot measure up to unqualified being, and in maintaining that "it must be altogether or not at all," [103] committed acosmism. In asserting that it is whole and all-inclusive, he committed absolutism, while in identifying it with a well-rounded sphere "everywhere equally poised from he midst," [104] he certainly committed pantheism. But, since God is invisible, this leads easily to the denial of God. Hence it is only a step from the pantheism of Parmenides to the atheism of the later sophists.

The misapprehension of that intellectual mode of being which belongs to forms or essences breeds four similar confusions. The idealists, mentioned in the *Sophist*, who separated the ideas from generation, and refused to grant genuine existence to the mere flux of becoming, may have been younger students of the Academy.[105] In any case, they have been followed by numerous disciples in modern times, who have ignored matter, the blind spot of the "intellectualist," and have tried to treat material things as though they were pure forms. But the confusion of things with forms leads easily to the confusion of forms with things. Hence "intellectualism" leads easily to that "realism" which we have seen Plato in the person of Parmenides so sharply criticizing in the youthful Socrates, possibly his own youthful self. To trace the many elaborations of this sophistic tendency, from the days of Plato's own followers to the "neo-realists" of our own day, with their special "realms" of subsistent, universal entities, would require a volume of many pages.

But if the forms themselves are materialized into things, supposed to exist in some undiscoverable kingdom of their own, separated by

102 Cf. Cornford, *Plato and Parmenides*, pp. 110–111.
103 *Frag.*, 8, 10. Diels, *Die Fragmente der Vorsokratiker*, 3 vols. (5th ed.; Berlin: Weidmann, 1934–38), I, 155.
104 *Frag.*, 8, 43–44. Diels, *Fragmente*, I, 158.
105 Cf. *Sophist*, 248 A 4 ff.

an unbridgeable chasm from this world, it is easy to conclude that there is in reality nothing but particular, individual things, and to lapse into that "nominalism" which, as Plato points out, must "destroy all meaningful discourse." [106] The atheist denies being itself. The nominalist denies the forms. Both denials are combined together in the panrealism of those materialists who "maintain stoutly that that alone exists which can be touched and handled; for they define existence and body (σῶμα) as identical." [107] But there is a still less stable mode of existence than that of body — seeming or appearance. Starting out by confusing the fleeting images of sense and hallucination with substantial change, the subjectivist ends by confusing substantial change with relative appearance, and thus lands in the relativism of Protagoras, for whom being and seeming are one and the same.[108] That minimal mode of being which has the least distinctness and lasting power is identified with being as such. Sophistry can go no further. Protagoras has been rightly identified as the original sophist par excellence.

These confusions may be revealed, so far as they may be revealed at all, only by suggesting the different senses of the transcendental term being. According to the framework of the *Parmenides*, these are at least four in number, differing from one another not in their formal nature, but in their mode of being and unity. One and the same formal nature may be represented in relation to sense as an appearance, materialized as a substantial thing, understood in relation to the intellect as a pure form, or embraced in the simple being of being itself. When the unity is least distinct and least independent we have the level of appearance, which cannot exist of itself at all. Material being is independent, but in itself composite (Hyp. II), and thus imperfectly unified. The pure form is just what it is, and distinct from all other forms, but in reason, and not able to exist of itself. Being itself, which is one, is perfectly one in itself and perfectly independent. Everything whatsoever, existing at any level, has existence and unity, but it may "have" them in four diverse degrees of distinctness, constituting the four major levels of being described in Hypotheses I, II–III, V, and VII of the *Parmenides*.

All men are at least vaguely aware of these four levels of being, no matter how sophisticated their official philosophy may be. The process of education, as we have seen in the analogy of the Cave,

[106] *Parm.*, 135 C 2.   [107] *Soph.*, 246 B.   [108] *Theaet.*, 152 A 6.

is always a kind of ascent from a lower level to a higher. The individual child must first learn to become sceptical of the private images in terms of which he pictures himself and his surroundings. By actual experience, which brings him up against the less hazy and less unstable material facts, he learns to discount these early impressions as subjective fantasies. This first step of understanding is to some degree achieved by all men. The distinction between subjective appearance and objective, independent fact cannot be completely blurred without imperilling life itself. But if life is to be lived well, further steps must be taken also along this upward path. Upon closer study, what at first seemed clear and stable proves to contain a vague and unstable factor, and unless the permanent form, law, or structure of such material facts is clearly abstracted from its material base, by scientific analysis, a relapse into relativism cannot be avoided. In comparison with the intermittent, intermixed, and oscillating, particular facts, these pure, formal structures of science are integrated and enduring. But the intellect cannot find real permanence and stability until it has taken a further step, and gained some insight into the perfect unity which is the source of all such structure. To find this is the ultimate aim of understanding.

Sophistry is not restricted to any one level of being, or to any particular realm of knowledge. In all realms, and at all levels, it works against the upward course, at every stage becoming sceptical of the higher rather than of the lower, and thus reversing the process, reducing unity to multiplicity, and being to non-being. Instead of explaining what is less real in terms of what is more real, it attempts to explain what is more real in terms of what is less real. Thus, as Plato says, the philosopher and the sophist are most hard to distinguish. Each is concerned with the very same things, but in opposite ways, the philosopher being concerned with being, the sophist with non-being.[109] There is a philosopher as well as a sophist in every one of us. The philosopher is sceptical of the less real, struggling towards being; the sophist is sceptical of being, struggling towards non-being. The one moves up, the other down. As Aristotle points out,[110] each is concerned with the very same things — namely everything, but the one is the opposite of the other, and it is, therefore, without philosophy, almost impossible to distinguish them.

109 *Soph.*, 254 A.
110 *Meta.*, IV, 1004 B 17–27.

Unless they can be distinguished, and philosophy of the upward ascent can be established in the individual intellect, human life, both in its individual and social phases, must be inverted, and the whole cultural hierarchy overturned. Such cultural anatropism has its ultimate root in the ontological inversions so clearly indicated in the exercises of the *Parmenides*. To misunderstand being is to misunderstand everything. There are no more fundamental misunderstandings than these. This inversion of being, however, is associated with an allied inversion of the apprehensive faculties. Being not only *is*. It is also *known*. Hence these ontological inversions are allied with certain inversions of the apprehensive faculties, which always attend them in the complex human phenomenon of sophistry. It is to a brief study of these, as portrayed in the succeeding dialogue, the *Theaetetus*, that we must now turn.

CHAPTER VII

THE INVERSION OF THE APPREHENSIVE FACULTIES
(THE *THEAETETUS*)

THE UNIQUE COHERENCE of agent and patient, action and passion is carefully noted and described in many passages of the Platonic dialogues. Thus in the *Gorgias* [1] it is shown that every mode of action is correlated with a mode of passion in its object, and that the object or patient suffers *just as* the agent acts. Knowing is a mode of action which, therefore, requires an object on which it may act. There is no knowing which is not the knowing *of something*,[2] the faculty and the object of the faculty being interdependent. If the faculty truly knows, the object must be truly known. If the faculty is distorted, the object is distorted as well. Hence the inversion of noetic *objects* we have traced in the preceding chapter involves a corresponding inversion of the noetic *faculties*. But since the formal structure of things and the source of this structure are both apprehended by the same faculty of rational apprehension (νόησις), we have to deal only with three major faculties not four: sensation (αἴσθησις), the object of which is the seeming thing; opinion (δόξα), the object of which is the changing, material thing; and knowledge (ἐπιστήμη), the object of which is being, and its stable formal structure. What is the general nature of these faculties? How are they distinguished? How are they apt to be confused? To anyone seeking an answer to these questions the *Theaetetus* is full of fertile hints and suggestions, later clarified and developed by Aristotle and his successors. Let us turn to them for further light.

The dialogue purports to be a record of a conversation between Socrates, Theodorus the mathematician, and Theaetetus, later a promising student of the Academy, but at the time of the dialogue, "a little before" Socrates' death, "a mere boy." [3] Eucleides of Megara, who

---

[1] *Gorgias*, 476 B 3–D 4.
[2] Cf. *Rep.*, 477 C–478 C; *Phil.*, 35 B; and *Soph.*, 262 E.
[3] *Theaet.*, 142 C 6.

was present at Socrates' death, made an exact record of the conversation, and it is read to his friend Terpsion (also present at Socrates' death) [4] at Megara soon after the battle at Corinth,[5] at which Theaetetus was fatally wounded. It has been legitimately inferred that the dialogue was actually written by Plato after 369 B.C. when about sixty years of age, perhaps on the eve of his departure for Syracuse. From internal evidence it is now clear that it is meant to be read *after* the ontological discussions of the *Parmenides*. The serious student of Plato is *first* directed to being, and then to the nature of knowledge. But before the student can be expected to make any headway in epistemology, his mind must be delivered of certain false images and misconceptions, not easy to distinguish from the truth.[6]

If these misconceptions are not soon discerned and "thrown away," students will make very little headway. They may "associate profitably" with Prodicus[7] and other learned professors, but they cannot hope for progress in the truth. The *Theaetetus*, therefore, is a warning, testing exercise, from which all direct statement of the truth, and consequently all mention of "the forms" is carefully avoided.[8] The order of knowing is not the same as the order of being, and in the teaching of philosophy the "shorter" way is often that which seems to be roundabout, indirectly suggesting the truth by a criticism of widespread confusions and inversions. That the mind is susceptible to these inversions, through its very structure, is evidenced by the persistent vitality of the dialogue up to the very present time. The major inversion of *sensationalism*, to which more than half the dialogue is devoted, is certainly as prevalent now as it was in Plato's day.

1. SENSATIONALISM AND ITS ROOTS

All men possess the apprehensive faculty of sensation, which provides them with a constant stream of odours, colours, sounds, and other images. These are apprehended "before" anything else is apprehended. Hence to the youthful Theaetetus, as to the "empiricist" of all ages, it seems unnecessary to seek for any further noetic faculty. Knowledge is simply sensation. To be is to be perceived. This is the view of the wise Protagoras, who denied all complexity

[4] Cf. *Phaedo*, 59 C 2.　　　　　[5] 369 B.C.
[6] *Theaet.*, 148 C–152.　　　　　[7] 151 B 5.
[8] Cf. Cornford, *Plato's Theory of Knowledge* (New York: Harcourt Brace, 1935), pp. 28 and 106.

in the notion of being, and hence in the notion of knowing. Things either are, or they are not,[9] and each individual is the infallible judge of his own sensations, which are either there or not there. To be infallibly certain of something is to know.[10] I am infallibly certain of those sensations I actually have. Hence in *having* them I know.

Of course this means that knowledge is "relative," for my sensations are not those of another man. The breeze which appears cool to me may appear warm to another. This consequence is to be frankly accepted. No matter how wrong or distorted a sensation may be, if it is actually there, it *is*, and must be accepted. All else is mere hypothesis, which may be questioned. I can be infallibly certain only of those sensory appearances which actually appear to me. Protagoras' written statements go no further in explaining this "to me." Relativism is usually accepted by the "relativist" as a sufficiently obvious fact. My sensations are clearly not those of another. But how do I know this? Is this also a sensation? Why should two men differently perceive what is the same? Until we can give some intelligible account of what is meant by "relativity" we cannot hope to understand the doctrine.

That which does not change is not relative. It is simply as it is. Only changing things are relative. The hidden source of the doctrine of relativism, the "secret teaching of Protagoras," is to be found in the Heraclitean doctrine of the flux.[11] A thing can *exist* in itself. It cannot *change* of itself. Something else must intervene to act upon it, or the change would be an unintelligible contradiction. But all men know that change is everywhere proceeding. This is the common theme of the poets and teachers of all ages. All things are in flux. This evident fact has moulded our primary intuitions and the very structure of our speech.[12] To be, to live, is to be in change and movement. To cease to be, to die, is to lapse into changelessness and rest. But if all things are thus in flux, all things are interacting with one another and mutually interdependent. Nothing really exists

---

[9] Commentators have not sufficiently noted the fact that these are the *only* ontological possibilities visualized in Protagoras' famous formula of "relativism" (152 A 2–4). This "simple" conception of being would be at once focussed by an academic reader of the *Parmenides*. See Wild, "Husserl's Critique of Psychologism," *Philosophical Essays in Memory of Edmund Husserl*, ed. by Marvin Farber (Cambridge: Harvard University Press, 1940).

[10] *Theaet.*, 152 C 5.

[11] *Theaet.*, 152 C 10.

[12] *Cratylus*, 401 D–404 B.

alone by itself.[13] Protagoras, and his "empiricist" followers, whether they knew it or not, were all disciples of Heraclitus. His doctrine of universal flux is the "secret" root of relativism, which is only an attempt to interpret knowledge in the light of the universal fact of change. But is this Heraclitean offspring really legitimate? What kind of change is sensation? Can this change be identified with knowledge?

Plato's intricate analysis of sensation,[14] further developed and clarified by Aristotle in Book II of the *De Anima*, may be summarized as follows. Sensation is a kind of change. As such, it involves always not one thing but *two;* for example, whiteness in some external thing, and the general faculty of sight. The actual process of sensation cannot occur until the two are brought together, and the external thing acts physically upon the sense organ by "rapid," physical locomotions from one place to the other.[15] As this physical action takes place, the general faculty of sight undergoes a "slow motion" or qualitative change, becoming not merely "sight" in general [16] "but a seeing eye," [17] and the object is correspondingly altered, becoming not "whiteness" in general but a particular "white." [18] All these factors, physical motion between the thing and the organ, qualitative alteration in the thing, and corresponding qualitative alteration in the sense, are involved in the complex structure of a single sensation.

This sensation is, in each case, a single complex of locomotion and qualitative change.[19] It depends primarily upon two factors, the external agency and the relatively passive organ. The sensation must vary as these vary. The same sensation cannot be derived from another object, nor from a different condition of the sense faculty (as from Socrates drunk or Socrates healthy). In the process itself the agent and the patient "come together." [20] Hence the process as a whole,

---

[13] μηδὲν αὐτὸ καθ' αὐτὸ ἕν ὄν. *Theaet.*, 153 E 4.

[14] 153 E 4–160 D.

[15] Cf. Cornford, *Plato's Theory of Knowledge*, p. 50, and *De An.*, 417 A 7–10.

[16] οὔ τι ὄψις. *Theaet.*, 156 E 3.

[17] ἀλλ' ὀφθαλμὸς ὁρῶν. *Theaet.*, 156 E 4.

[18] οὐ λευκότης αὖ ἀλλὰ λευκόν: *Theaet.*, 156 E 5.

[19] Cf. *De An.*, 418 A 4.

[20] συνέλθῃ: *Theaet.*, 157 A 5–6. Cf. *Soph.*, 247 D 8–248 C 10. In these passages Plato clearly recognizes the efficient cause, and is recasting his earlier theory of participation in a markedly Aristotelian direction. Agent and patient coalesce in one single process, or motion, which is both the suffering of the patient and the action of the agent. Cf. Aristotle, *Phys.*, III, ch. 3.

the sensation, is neither "something separate in itself outside the eyes" as the "realists" of our day suppose, nor "something in the eyes" as the "idealists" suppose.[21] It is not *in* any stable "place" at all, but is rather "in becoming" between the two.[22] All this hidden structure is facilely concealed under the term "relation," which can be safely employed only if we bear in mind this whole complex foundation. Thus it is incorrect and deceptive to say that the sensation white is actually present *in* me, for the actual sensation is not "in" me, but rather between me and the object, and it is not fully and actually anywhere, but rather in becoming.

Plato refers us to the analogous "relations" which arise from comparing one number with different numbers.[23] For instance, we say that 6 *is* half again as large as 4, but *is* only half as many as 12. But how can 6, which remains just what it is, *be* at once two contrary things, both greater and less? In the *Phaedo*, Plato was clearly puzzled by such paradoxes.[24] Now he has come to see that the solution lies in an ontological distinction. Being is said in different senses. Being-related is not the same as being-in-itself.[25] The "relation" of "greater than 4" does not actually inhere in the 6 alone. It is "in" neither the one nor the other, but obtains between the two. We cannot appropriately say that 6 alone by itself *is* this, but rather that it becomes this when brought by the mind into juxtaposition with something else.

What a thing really is in itself must be distinguished from what it "is" or rather becomes accidentally in relation to other things. Analogously the sensation does not inhere "in" the mind or the thing. It is between the two, or "relative." Furthermore, strictly speaking, "it" is not, but rather becomes. With these essential reservations, we may certainly agree with Protagoras and the "empiricists" that the process of sensation is infallibly proceeding as it proceeds, though denying that it "is" in itself infallibly. Sensation proceeds rather than is. Hence it is "relative" rather than "in itself." As such a relative process, it is, indeed, infallibly apprehensive.

21 *Theaet.*, 153 D 8–E 2.
22 ἐν γενέσει γίγνοιτο: *Theaet.*, 153 E 2.
23 *Theaet.*, 154 C 1–155 D 7.
24 *Phaedo*, 100 E 5 ff.
25 Cf. Cornford's illuminating commentary, *Plato's Theory of Knowledge*, pp. 43 ff. and Aristotle, *Cat.*, ch. 7.

2. THE CONFUSION OF SENSATION WITH OPINION

When sensation is thus correctly understood, the assertion of sensory infallibility is a harmless truth. But when sensation is confused with "judgment" or "opinion," a radically different faculty, the assertion of "sensory" infallibility breeds those sensational paradoxes which have made Protagoras and many of his empiricist followers famous. Those which are in most evident conflict with "common sense" are stated by Socrates in the succeeding section.[26]

First of all, opinion is fallible. But if it is confused with infallible sensation, it will be impossible for any opinion to be "false," and all men, and even animals, will be unrestrictedly infallible. How then can one man, with no more sensations than another, be said to know more? What, indeed, can be meant by teaching and learning? In the second place, the object of opinion always embraces more than the stream of sensations now proceeding in relation to my sense organs and their objects. My opinion is about the thing as it really is in itself, and consequently may be held in mind or remembered, even when I am not sensing the object. Hence common sense distinguishes between hearing the sounds of a foreign language and judging the remembered meaning of the sounds.[27] In the third place, opinion also differs from sensation in its independence of any single organ of sense. Thus in closing one eye and opening the other, we both see and do not see all at once, but we do not both know and not know all at once. We cannot localize any single organ with which we opine or know.[28] Finally, the opining faculty does not vary with the physical oscillations of sensory interaction. The hearing of a sound may be "sharp or dull," sight may be "close at hand" or "at a distance," and all sensing is either "intense" or "mild." But thinking is not so characterized.[29]

These phenomenological observations certainly point to a basic difference between sensory and rational apprehension. But the sensationalist will dismiss them as purely verbal entanglements.[30] The plausibility of his "answer"[31] only shows the dangerous extent to which common sense itself is apt to confuse seeming with being,

[26] *Theaet.*, 161 C 1–164 C 1.
[27] *Theaet.*, 163 B.
[28] Cf. Aristotle, *De An.*, 429 A 24.
[29] *Theaet.*, 165 D. Cf. *De An.*, 429 B 1–5.
[30] *Theaet.*, 168 C.   [31] *Theaet.*, 166–168 C 5.

and the faculty of sense, which is capable of apprehending the former, with the faculty of opinion which is *capable* of apprehending the latter. Do we not commonly refer to both faculties by the ambiguous term "seeming"? "It seems to me" and "it appears to me" are synonyms both for "I think" and "I perceive." Words like "theory," "insight," "point of view," and "looking into" show how natural it is to regard reason in terms derived from sense. Similarly the Greek verb δοκεῖν ambiguously refers to the having of a sensation or the holding of an opinion based upon such a sensation.[32]

In his reply to the second of the "eristic" objections raised by Socrates, Protagoras takes full advantage of this ambiguity. He ignores the possible, intentional reference of an opinion to a past or future or timeless object, regarding such an intention subjectively, simply as a new sensation, now actually occurring, and, therefore, different from any opinion or sensation in the past. Subjectively, of course, this is true. But the structure of opinion is twofold or intentional in character. My having had an opinion is different from my now having it. But the *object* of the two acts may be the same. This is never true of sensations which are neither subjectively nor objectively repeatable. Utterly disregarding this intentional structure, the sensationalist merely asks if each new opinion, or sensation, is not individual, and hence, like sensation, different from every other?[33] He passes over the third and fourth objections, seeing no difficulty in connecting opinions with the various sense organs on which they materially depend. Thus the last three objections are side-stepped or avoided.

The first is more obviously at variance with common sense, and is, therefore, singled out for special comment.[34] Here again the *object* of the opinion is ignored, and the opinion is regarded simply as an occurrence in the mind. I either "have" the opinion, or I do not have it, as I either "have" a bitter taste or do not have it. The confusion is complete. This "having" or feeling of the opinion is certainly infallible. The "seeming" or "being" (what is the difference?) of another individual may be distorted, or diseased, or "evil." But if he *has* it, whatever it is, I have no right to discard it as "false," for the being

---

[32] Cf. *Theaet.*, 162 D, and Cornford's note *ad loc.*, *Plato's Theory of Knowledge*, p. 61; also p. 73 and p. 116.

[33] *Theaet.*, 166 B 1–4.

[34] *Theaet.*, 166 C 6 ff.

of what is not is a contradiction, and "to think what is not (falsity) is impossible." [35] The teacher is not different from a gardener, who simply intervenes externally to weed out certain noxious realities and to substitute others of a more helpful kind. Seeming is certainly not nothing at all. Hence it "is." Having an opinion is, like sensation, the infallible having of something. Hence seeming to be is to be, and sensing or feeling something is the same as thinking of something. Sensation is knowledge, and the confusion is complete and perfect, as in present-day positivism, where a similarly complete confusion or inversion of the two distinct faculties is performed.

3. The Confusion of Sensation with Knowledge

The confusion of the faculty of sensation with the faculty of opinion or thought is fraught with serious consequences. On the one hand, since opinion is certainly fallible, it may lead us to the erroneous conclusion that certain sensations are somehow false, though sensations are incapable of being either true or false except by accident. They provide us with a flux of appearance which simply seems as it seems. The appearance may be changed by altering the thing or the organ, but it does not lie within our power to feel differently than we feel. Right or wrong, for better or for worse, the sensations are "given" as they are "given." If the wind feels cold to me, it makes no difference that its "actual" temperature is very high, and I am in a fever. The feeling infallibly feels as I feel it. A doctor may change my condition and restore me to normal. But, as Protagoras says, this does not make my "abnormal" feelings any the less infallible. He has merely substituted one set of infallible feelings for another. Hence this may lead to the erroneous conclusion that the *judgments* I make on the basis of my sensations are equally infallible, that they also are not within my power to alter, except by the external substitution of one set of opinions for another.

This Protagorean conclusion is certainly false. The faculty of opinion is within our rational power. As we have seen, the very structure of human speech reveals the tendency of human opinion to adjust itself to the seeming data of sense. But this adjustment does not necessarily occur as the result of some external agent. No matter

---

[35] οὔτε γὰρ τὰ μὴ ὄντα δυνατὸν δοξάσαι. *Theaet.*, 167 A 7–8. This conclusion, of course, follows directly from Protagoras' "simple" view of being, according to which a thing must either be or not be.

how cool the wind may seem, it is within my power to judge it as actually warm, or indeed any other temperature, though any such judgment may of course be false. My judgments aim to be true, though they often miss their aim. If they achieve it, they constitute knowledge, which, like feeling, is incapable of falsity, or infallible.[36] The "free" faculty of opinion thus lies between two infallibilities, that of sense and that of knowledge. Each is attended by subjective certainty. Perhaps then the "empiricist" is right, and we should think of the two as one. Why not define infallible knowledge as infallible sensation, and truth simply as that set of opinions which accord with the given data of sense?

This confusion is far more dangerous than the preliminary confusion of sense with opinion, which merely prepares the way. After all, the faculty of opinion, which is capable of truth or falsity, is distinct from the faculty of sense, which is incapable of either truth or falsity, and no amount of opinion will make them the same. But the faculty of opinion is not automatic. It lies within our power to direct it towards its actual goal of knowledge, or to direct it in the opposite direction, on the mistaken opinion that this is the true course. The empiricist confusion of sense with knowledge, the *terminus a quo* of opinion with its *terminus ad quem*, achieves precisely such an inversion of direction. Instead of directing opinion to its proper goal, it directs it *along the same road* in the *opposite direction*, away from knowledge rather than towards it. That is why Plato's attention is primarily concerned with laying bare this confusion. To do this, he must suggest three things to the serious reader: first, that the infallibility of sense is distinct from the infallibility of knowledge; second, that the flux of seeming is not as such the object of knowledge; and finally, in the third place, he must offer some positive hints as to what this object really is. These three tasks are fulfilled in the heart of the dialogue which lies in the succeeding section.

I. The Infallibility of Sense vs. the Infallibility of Knowledge

If we possessed no faculty distinct from sense, the phenomenon of mutual discussion and disagreement would be impossible. At

[36] Αἴσθησις ἄρα τοῦ ὄντος ἀεί ἐστιν καὶ ἀψευδὲς ὡς ἐπιστήμη οὖσα: *Theaet.*, 152 C 5. As Professor Cornford points out, Plato denies that sensation is τοῦ ὄντος but he never disputes that it is infallible or ἀψευδές. This is, in fact, the basic ground for the confusion of αἴσθησις with ἐπιστήμη. *Plato's Theory of Knowledge*, pp. 52 ff.

any given moment, one man simply has the feelings he has, and another the feelings he has. Since each is aesthetically infallible, no argument concerning these matters is conceivable.[37] It is impossible that either party to such a discussion could be wrong. But discussion and disagreement do occur. Hence the faculty of opinion, by which we disagree, is not the infallible faculty of sense. It is a faculty which is capable of reaching beyond the present appearance, and intending something which may also be intended by another. Plato uses the famous argument of "turning the tables" to bring these familiar facts into a sharper light.[38]

An opinion is not merely "had" as a feeling. It is "maintained" against other possibilities. This is even true of Protagoras' own sub-jective relativism, which he does not simply "have" infallibly, but which he puts forth in the mode of an opinion. Like Protagoras, we are very apt to confuse our theory concerning the true nature of experience with the infallible experience which is neither true nor false. Hence it is the distinct product of a distinct faculty. Let us take Protagoras' relativism as an example.

It is not an experience but a theory, since others may disagree with it, and in fact do disagree with it. This is shown most clearly in times of danger and crisis, when our insight is forced to emerge from the fog of speculation which usually beclouds it, and to distinguish between the easy opinion of the amateur and the tested opinion of the man who knows. Even when deceived, we shall seek at such moments of peril to follow the expert opinion of the shipmaster, the skilled physician, or the trained soldier. Most men, therefore, actually disagree with the opinion of Protagoras. They hold that all men in their opinions are not equally infallible. They hold that some opinions are true, and others false. So must Protagoras hold this, for on his theory all opinions are true for those who hold them, even those of the many. But their opinion is that he is unqualifiedly wrong. He also must concede this. If he goes on maintaining his theory as an opinion, he is thus in contradiction with himself, maintaining all at once that his theory is both true and false. Either this, or he must abandon his theory.

[37] As Aristotle later pointed out, this applies only to the qualities peculiar to each sense, as colour to sight, and sound to hearing. It does not apply to the common sensibles, such as motion, size, etc., and to what is perceived by accident — that which *has* these qualities. Cf. *De An.*, 428 B 17 ff.

[38] *Theaet.*, 170–171 C 7, repeated by Aristotle in the *Meta.*, Book IV, 1012 B 13–18.

Sometimes a theory may be *known* to be true. Such noetic certainty is, indeed, the aim of all opinion. But this noetic infallibility must not be confused with the solipsistic infallibility of sensation, though, as Aristotle pointed out, there is an analogy between the two.[39] Plato suggests two differentiating marks. The first, which emerges from the "turning of the tables," is what we may call the *horizontal spread* of such knowledge, which is not confined to a single experiencer, but is communicable from one subject to another. The second, which emerges from the next argument,[40] is what we may call the vertical or temporal spread of such knowledge, which is not confined to the relative process of sensing as it is proceeding, but concerns the nature of the thing in itself, and is, therefore, capable of maintaining itself in the future. In contrast to sensory certainty, which is confined to one experiencer, and which is constantly shifting into another certainty, noetic infallibility is communicable and endurable. These two infallibilities mark two distinct faculties.

It is easy to note their difference in the case of objects such as future events which are not sensed at all. It is more difficult in the case of sense experience itself, where the sense "object" is materially the same as the object of opinion. Hence there arises a strong tendency to transfer the infallibility attending the experience to some opinion concerning its actual nature. Such an opinion can never be justified by falling back on empirical data as such, though without empirical data no opinion can ever be justified. I am *sensuously* certain of a jumbled stream of appearances, mixed and confused together as they flow. But this does not mean that I am *rationally* certain that "I am seeing the colour yellow." No amount of visual "seeing" will verify this proposition. To verify it, I must not only see in this sensuous sense, but also rationally "see" into the *essential nature* of sensory seeing, the *essential nature* of colour, and the *essential nature* of yellow, clearly distinguishing these from the many "accidents" of relative motion, position, intensity, etc., with which they are materially confused in the sensuous process. As Aristotle points out, it is by reason, not by sense, that we distinguish the essential character from its accidents.[41]

This is the achievement of another faculty (reason, νοῦς), which works on the confused mixture of sense appearance, and which is

---

[39] Cf. *De An.*, 430 B 27–31.
[40] *Theaet.*, 171 C 3–172 C; resumed at 177 C 6.   [41] *De An.*, 429 B 13 ff.

capable of providing the communicable, lasting certainty of truth. "Empiricism" offers us a most alluring short cut, which saves us the trouble of exercising our reason.[42] To be sure, it provides us with infallibility, the ephemeral, solipsistic infallibility of sense, which is always open to any man or animal by lifting the lid or turning the head. To hold with modern "pragmatism" and "empiricism" that such "experience" is capable of verifying the judgments of reason is to turn the faculties upside down, to move backwards rather than forward, an anatropism of the mind. Sense cannot clarify and verify reason. It is reason alone that can clarify and verify the vague and fleeting data of sense.[43]

Protagoras himself is inconsistent. While maintaining that whatever seems just and honourable to a state is infallibly true for that state, as long as the seeming endures, he nevertheless is forced to admit that certain enactments are "more advantageous" than others in the long run. Only thus can he justify his own life, and the teaching profession in general, and account for scientific control over nature.[44] But he will be followed by others who will soon remove this inconsistent lip-service to "reason."[45] They will ask, what does the advantageous mean? If each man and each state are the measure, then each man and each state will be the measure of the advantageous, and what infallibly *seems good* to opinion, allowing itself to be misguided by sensory appearance, will infallibly *be good*.

Thus, instead of trying to correct their opinions, in the light of what is *really* advantageous by the further exercise of reason, "those who do not in every way assert the doctrine of Protagoras"[46] (eliminating the inconsistency) will try to correct their opinions, in the dim darkness of what seems advantageous, by adjusting them con-

[42] Cf. Wild, "The Concept of the Given in Contemporary Philosophy," *Phil. and Phen. Research*, I, no. 1 (70 ff.).
[43] The modern philosophy of empiricism is, of course, based upon this ancient anatropism. As two peculiarly flagrant examples of this tendency, we may mention the contemporary "critical-realist" doctrine that sense perceives "essences." Cf. *Essays in Critical Realism*, by Durant Drake, Arthur O. Lovejoy, and others (London: Macmillan, 1920), p. 168, note (Santayana), and pp. 228 ff. (Strong), and Mr. G. E. Moore's many attempts to prove certain epistemological and even ethical doctrines by falling back on sensory infallibility. The word "intuition" is now peculiarly apt to mask a confusion of rational and sensory apprehension.
[44] *Theaet.*, 172 A.
[45] *Theaet.*, 172 B.
[46] *Theaet.*, 172 B 6–7; i.e. Hippias and the *later* Sophists who maintained that human law and justice had no basis whatsoever in nature — φύσει.

sciously to the deceptive feelings of pleasure and pain, the infallible, subjective seeming of good. They will then be willing to say of the just, the holy, and other things of this sort, which cannot be apprehended by sense, that none of them "has by nature a being of its own." [47] They will thus complete the inversion inaugurated by Protagoras, confusing reason with sense, the infallibility of truth with the infallibility of seeming, nature with experience, and what is really good with the apparent good. [48]

Plato refers casually to the succeeding contrast between the seeker of wisdom and the seeker of apparent wisdom as a "digression." [49] It is, however, a change of style, not a changing of the subject. The famous passage provides us with vivid images of the vital consequences which flow from the seemingly slight difference between plausible opinion and rational opinion, seeming to be and being, the way of Protagoras and the way of Socrates. They are both, of course, proceeding on the very same way. There is no other way. But one is going up and the other down. The "liberal" humanism and idealism of Protagoras, which exalted the appearance of human culture, is naturally followed by the unmitigated naturalism of Hippias, Thrasymachus, and Callicles, who care nothing for even the appearance, as the liberal culture of Periclean Athens was actually replaced by the brutal tyranny of force.

But even those who give themselves over completely to the tyranny of sub-human nature still remain men and therefore thinkers. They *think* that their barbarous acts are marvellous and stupendous. [50] The root of their disease does not lie solely in the "will," in "instinct," or in their "animal nature." It also lies in reason, their ruling faculty, which has abdicated in favor of seeming. Hence they must be told the truth — "that precisely because they do not think so, they are all the more such as they do not think they are." [51] Idealism lies at the root of *Machtpolitik*, and humanism [52] is the next step to barbarism.

---

[47] *Theaet.*, 172 B 2–5.
[48] For Aristotle also this confusion of the real and the apparent end marks the lowest extreme of vice: ἡ μοχθηρία. *Nic. Eth.*, VI, 1144 A 34–36.
[49] *Theaet.*, 176 C 6.
[50] *Theaet.*, 176 D 3.
[51] *Theaet.*, 176 D 5–7.
[52] Which denies that there is any higher being than man.

II. *The Flux of Sense and the Object of Knowledge*

We have seen that the noetic apprehension of being and the sensory apprehension of seeming are distinguishable *subjectively* from the stand point of the faculty, where they are attended by two different modes of infallibility, the one capable of maintaining itself against opposed opinion and the future course of events, the other crumbling away before both. But all apprehension is *intentional*, or "of" something. We must, therefore, now turn to the objects of the two faculties. If they are not distinct, the faculties will not be distinct, and we may still have to admit that sensation is knowledge. What, after all, it may be asked, can we hope to know, other than the things that appear before us? Nothing else, as Plato clearly answers in the next section of the argument. And yet the *object* of sense is not the object of knowledge.[53]

Our attention is at once directed to the process of change between the external thing and the sense organ, "out of which sensations and the opinions according to these" emerge.[54]   If the followers of Heraclitus are right in asserting that all is in flux, then the shifting "object" of perception will necessarily coincide with the object of knowledge, and the two faculties, having the same object, will also be the same. So this Heraclitean doctrine must be examined. Is its major thesis correct? Can it give an adequate account of knowledge, or even of perception?

As Theodorus remarks, we are confronted with a peculiar difficulty. The ancient flux philosophers, like their modern Bergsonian disciples, express themselves in cryptic utterances and aphorisms. In accordance with their doctrine, their thoughts are in perpetual motion, and never come to rest in any stable conclusion. They despise all history and tradition, and "never become pupils of one another." Each one grows up by himself without bothering to learn anything, "getting his inspiration from any chance source," and "each believes that the

---

[53] They are *materially* the same but *formally* distinct. Cf. Aristotle, *Meta.*, V, 1015 B 16 ff.

[54] *Theaet.*, 179 C 2. For Plato, opinion is rational apprehension according to sensations: κατὰ ταύτας δόξαι. Cf. *Phil.*, 39 B 9–10, ἀπ' ὄψεως. He does not clearly distinguish *sense* from *imagination*. Hence, Aristotle's criticism at *De An.*, 428 A 28. But he never criticizes Plato's view that the construction of opinions in accordance with sensory appearance (as the *apparent* good) is an important source of error.

other knows nothing." [55] Beyond the general thesis that all things flow, it is as impossible to learn any intelligible doctrine from such men as it is for them to learn from others.

However, the general thesis that all things flow is based upon an ancient insight, governing the structure of speech, and darkly indicated by the poets who say that the flowing streams, Oceanus and Tethys, were the origin of all.[56] The modern followers of Heraclitus now assert this ancient wisdom openly as something new. Hence simple men, who first believe that some things flow and some stand still, are easily beguiled into this superior wisdom, or into that of its closely allied opposite extreme, the theory of Melissus and Parmenides that all is motionless. Socrates speaks of an earlier meeting with Parmenides, who impressed him by "a noble depth of mind," [57] and decides that this is not the place for a criticism of his doctrine of being.[58] We must now restrict ourselves to the opposite pole. Is it true, as it seems, that all things are in motion?

As we have seen, sensing or seeming is itself a mode of motion. Hence the natural alliance between sensationalism and Heracliteanism.[59] But, as rational beings, we are not only able to *feel* change, and "point" to it by gestures and aphorisms, but also to formulate opinions about it, and eventually perhaps to understand it. "What sort of thing" is motion? Such a question can never be answered by feeling alone. It demands another faculty, capable of laying bare the structure of the thing felt, not in relation to us, but as it is in itself.[60] Such eidetic structure may be discerned in motion itself, which possesses at least two distinct varieties, change of place,[61] and change of quality.[62] Such a distinction is only implicit in the appearances of sense. Hence the fluxist doctrine, which is based upon sensory "evidence," is stated in an unqualified form: all things

[55] *Theaet.*, 180 C 2–3. In striking contrast to the modern assumption of "progress," with its resulting scorn for past achievement, especially in philosophy, both Plato and Aristotle emphasized the need of historic continuity, and the need of *maintaining* insights once achieved.

[56] *Theaet.*, 180 D 2. Cf. *Crat.*, 402 A 4–D 2.

[57] *Theaet.*, 183 E 7 — a reference to the "prior" ontological discussion of the *Parmenides*.

[58] *Theaet.*, 184 A 1–5. This is a discussion of knowledge, *not* being. Plato is far from any idealistic identification of the two.

[59] Cf. pp. 244 ff.

[60] αὐτὸ καθ' αὑτό: *Theaet.*, 182 B 3–4.

[61] φορά: *Theaet.*, 182 C 6.

[62] ἀλλοίωσις: *Theaet.*, 182 C 7. Cf. Aristotle, *Physics*, V, 226 A 23 ff.

move in every conceivable manner of motion. But this extreme view fails to account even for what we have already seen to be the structure of sense, to say nothing of the structure of knowledge.

As we have already seen, sensation, as a mode of motion, involves both an active agent and a passive organ, able to be acted on. The organ by itself does not perceive, nor is the object by itself perceived. The process of perception arises "from the union of the two with one another." [63] As this motion takes place, the general *faculty* of perception becomes *actually* percipient,[64] and the general quality becomes perceived as something of a certain sort.[65] Two phases of this mobile structure are to be noted. First, since the perception and what is perceived merge with each other, the quality, as perceived, is not as it is independently, but rather "in relation to" the percipient. Second, the quality, as perceived, is not the *universal* "heat" ($\theta\epsilon\rho\mu\acute{o}\tau\eta s$) or "whiteness" ($\lambda\epsilon\upsilon\kappa\acute{o}\tau\eta s$), capable of being known as inhering in other things, but "a particular hot thing" ($\theta\epsilon\rho\mu\acute{o}\nu$) or "a particular white thing" ($\lambda\epsilon\upsilon\kappa\acute{o}\nu$).[66] What we perceive is thus "relative" to our percipient organs, and particularized.

Nevertheless the single quality, though relativized and mingled with all sorts of accidental accretions not itself in the process of perception, does emerge, in some defective degree of clarity and purity. Unless the original whiteness of the thing remained throughout the process, we should never perceive the thing as white rather than black. Without *some* structural stability in the thing, the motion of perception would be impossible. Furthermore, the different senses must possess some stable structure in their flux, or we should be unable to distinguish seeing from hearing, or, indeed, perceiving from non-perceiving. This stable structure, which can be clearly and distinctly apprehended only by *another faculty*, is implicit in the flux of sense, though partially concealed by the admixture of subjective and extraneous factors. Feeling is a constant flux, but without its implicit structure, this flux would be impossible.

This implicit structure of the flux is precisely the object of knowl-

---

[63] *Theaet.*, 182 B 4–5. Cf. *De An.*, 418 A 3 ff.

[64] *Ibid.*, 182 A 6–8. Before the actual particular sensation the faculty is only a general capacity to perceive. Cf. Aristotle's further determination of this capacity in *De An.*, III, ch. 5.

[65] Before it acts on a particular sense organ, the quality is a general, indeterminate capacity to act $\pi o\iota\acute{o}\tau\eta s$, not $\pi o\iota\acute{o}\nu$ $\tau\iota$, a particular, determined quality.

[66] *Theaet.*, 182 B 1.

edge. Both reason and sense apprehend the same material thing, but they apprehend it in different ways. Their objects are distinct, though not separate. Sense grasps the flux of the structure, reason the structure of the flux. Hence, if the Heraclitean view were correct, knowledge would be clearly impossible. If what we know changes as we know it, there is no stable "it" to know. "Every answer to every question whatsoever is equally correct"; a thing is no more thus than not-thus, and even the word "thus" is nonsense, since it is changing as we think it.[67] Such conclusions are too much at variance with well-known phenomena. The facts show that the rational faculty is able to play on the subjective appearances of sense, to grasp the structure of their motion, its general nature and kinds, and to understand the nature of both agent and patient in their universal nature, as they are in themselves, without extraneous admixture.

Sense apprehends this white thing, or this hot thing, as it seems to me in my particular situation. Reason apprehends whiteness itself as it really is, in relation only to those other essences with which it is naturally related. The theory of universal motion is irreconcilable with even the remotest approximation to such apprehension. Hence it is not only inconsistent with knowledge, but with sensation as well, upon which its claims are based. Not only is the faculty of sense subjectively distinct from the faculty of reason, but the objects of the two faculties are also distinct. What then, we may ask, is the object of reason? We may say stable structure, but what is this structure? The whole science of metaphysics would be required to provide an adequate answer to this question. Nevertheless Plato gives a few pregnant suggestions in the next and concluding section of the argument.

4. THE OBJECT OF KNOWLEDGE

However it may be in the animals, in *man* sensation almost never occurs without opinion and knowledge. When his sense organs are being changed by external events, his opinion-forming faculty is also functioning. He hardly ever suffers a sensation without at the same time having some idea as to *what* it is. Hence words like "sensing," "perceiving," "seeing," "hearing," etc. in ordinary discourse signify not only the flux of appearance *between* the external agent and the receptive organ, sensation in the strict sense, but also the

[67] *Theaet.*, 183 A.

rational judgment concerning its stable structure, *what it is*, the contribution of a different faculty. As Socrates suggests, this causes considerable confusion, and leads Theaetetus to say, for example, that he judges some fleeting appearance to be a colour "through his eyes," [68] as though these organs were capable of literally "seeing" such an essence as colour, and distinguishing it from other essences. This, in itself, is sensationalism, and is incorrect, for each sense, strictly speaking, perceives only what is appropriate to it, as colour to sight, sound to hearing, and so on. The ability to *compare* these different data together and to *distinguish* them belongs to another distinct faculty. [69]

Nevertheless, without the data provided by the senses, we should not be able to make any judgments about their objects. Hence, if we are to speak exactly, we must say that we "perceive" colour, sound, and any other stable structural elements characterizing the object of sensation, not strictly "through" the senses, but through the senses only as instruments. [70] Anything that can be intelligibly expressed about sensation itself, or about its object, comes from another faculty, which is tied down to no particular organ, since it is capable of comparing them all, and distinguishing them all in common. [71] No single sense is capable of going beyond its own province in this way, and grasping what is common to all. What are these universal, common structures, [72] which transcend the restricted relative data of the senses, and constitute the object of knowledge? The most common and most universal of them are the objects of knowledge par excellence. Plato concludes his discussion with a most suggestive list.

The most universal, transcendental term is being, [73] which must in some sense belong to any entity whatsoever about which any judgment is made. Next is the determinate unity of the thing, which makes it *like* certain things, and *unlike* certain others. No special sense organ apprehends these, for they characterize the objects of all such organs, as well as the organs themselves. Then there is the beautiful and the ugly, the good and the bad. These also characterize all things, as an aspect of their common structure. The apprehension of this transcendental structure can be achieved only by a long and laborious learning process. It does not simply occur, as sensation

[68] *Theaet.*, 184 C 8.
[70] ὀργάνων: *Theaet.*, 184 D 4.
[72] τὰ κοινά.
[69] *Theaet.*, 185 C.
[71] *Theaet.*, 185 C 4 ff.
[73] ἡ οὐσία: *Theaet.*, 186 A 2.

occurs, from the moment of birth in all men alike. Finally, there is truth, which also attaches to all being, so far as it is capable of being known.

These *transcendental* terms, as they were later called, characterize all being. They are exhaustive in scope. They are involved in any opinion about anything whatsoever. They define the object of knowledge — what *is*, what is *one*, what is *beautiful* or *ugly*, *good* or *bad*, and *true*.[74] These are not apprehended by any *special* sense, through the action of some external agency, "but the soul herself appears to me through herself to apprehend what is common to all things."[75] Sensation is infallible. But it is *of* appearance, not *of* the real. So sensation is not knowledge. But this, in itself, is not enough for a definition. A further confusion looms on the horizon.

5. THE CONFUSION OF KNOWLEDGE WITH OPINION

Opinion or judgment is certainly not sensation. It is about the real. Hence why should we not follow Theaetetus in his next suggestion that knowledge is opinion?[76] The beginning of an answer is to be found in the qualification which Theaetetus is at once forced to make. False opinion is not only possible but a well-known fact, while *false knowledge* is certainly a contradiction.[77] This indicates that there is a real distinction between the two. Nevertheless, without a clear understanding of the nature of this distinction, we are still apt to persist in the confusion, following Theaetetus in identifying knowledge with true opinion.

Both knowledge and true opinion may be expressed in the same words. Both have the same beneficent consequences, being borne out by future trains of sensed events. Both are also capable of persuading others.

There are many passages in Plato's dialogues, among which the *Meno* deserves special notice,[78] which emphasize the great importance of

---

[74] Aristotle lists being and one, *Meta.*, 1059 B 22 ff.; truth, 1051 A 34 ff.; and good, 1027 B 26; and *Nic. Eth.*, 1096 B 27, but omits beauty (τὸ καλόν). Plato's list is, therefore, more complete.

[75] αὐτὴ δι' αὐτῆς ἡ ψυχὴ τὰ κοινά μοι φαίνεται περὶ πάντων ἐπισκοπεῖν: *Theaet.*, 185 E 1. Cf. Aristotle, *Meta.*, 1004 B 20; and *De An.*, 429 A 18; in order to know *all* things, νοῦς must be ἀμιγής.

[76] *Theaet.*, 187 A ff.

[77] Cf. Arist., *Posterior Analytics*, I, ch. 33.

[78] *Meno*, 97 ff.

right opinion in the guidance of both social and individual life. The great personality is able to formulate correct judgments about his friends and acquaintances, and about the future course of events, and the great statesman is also able to persuade his fellow citizens in such matters, and thus to direct the course of the state successfully amidst the confused nexus of events. Why then should we think of knowledge as anything more than opinion which works out well?

In spite of the plausibility of this doctrine, which has attracted the allegiance of "pragmatists" throughout the ages, it represents an anatropic confusion of psychic faculties more difficult to unravel, and hence more dangerous even than that involved in sensationalism, to which it finally leads. The discourses of Socrates were directed towards showing his individual interlocutors in a thousand different connections that they did not really know what they thought they knew. A man believes that in general he is on the right track, that he knows the difference between good and evil, justice and injustice. In truth he does know something. Opinion is not utter ignorance. But does he *really* know? The confusion of opinion with knowledge breeds dogmatism and inflexibility of mind. The confusion of knowledge with opinion, on the other hand, breeds relativism and instability of mind. Hence the sophist, falling prey to both opposite tendencies in the wrong way, becomes sceptical of truth by clinging too ardently to opinion, and confuses this false or misdirected scepticism with humility. The philosopher, while he cannot live without opinions,[79] holds them lightly, clinging desperately to the truth he can attain, with an *intellectual* humility which it is all too easy to confuse with the pride of opinion.

One or the other dogmatism is inescapable. If we do not trust opinion, we must trust in truth. We become sceptical of truth only by falling back upon opinion. These opposed *directions* of thought closely resemble one another and are easily confused. Scepticism of opinion resembles scepticism of truth, because opinion resembles knowledge. Hence it is easy for the sophist to put himself forth as a humble seeker after truth, when, as a matter of fact, he is repudiating truth and moving in the opposite direction. The only means of laying bare such fatal confusions is to become clearly aware of that distinction between opinion and knowledge which is developed in the following analysis.[80] This distinction is twofold in character.

[79] Cf. *Phil.*, 62 B 8–9.   [80] *Theaet.*, 187 A–201 D.

Opinion is always combination or synthesis, and it is potential rather than actual knowledge.

I. Opinion as Knowledge Combined with Sense

Opinion can be false. Knowledge can only be true. But how is falsity to be explained? No apprehensive faculty can be mistaken in apprehending its *simple* object. As we have seen, sense is infallible in the apprehension of its simple, relative objects. Certainly this is also true of the *simple* objects of knowledge. We cannot confuse what is known with what is known, nor what is altogether unknown with what is unknown, nor what is known with what is entirely unknown.[81] The psychic faculties are intentional. We cannot perceive without perceiving something.[82] We cannot know without knowing something. Hence on the assumption that we either know or do not know a simple object,[83] we cannot opine without opining something that is, and is known. We cannot think that which is not at all. So falsity eludes us.

It must elude us until we question the assumption that the object of knowledge either is or is not, with no further complexity of structure. This assumption is first questioned at 191 C, and light at once begins to dawn. Let us suppose that the object is not simple but complex, and that the thing known is also the thing sensed. In this case, *two* faculties will be involved in the acquisition and maintenance of knowledge. Each faculty *in itself*, with respect to its *simple* objects, is infallible, but *between* the faculties confusion may arise. I cannot confuse what is sensed with what is sensed, nor what is known with what is known. But where *both* knowledge and perception are involved, there are certain cases where I may mistake one thing for another thing without committing the absurdity of apprehending what is not, fitting the wrong sensation together with the wrong knowledge, each in itself being infallible. As Aristotle points out, "where the alternative of true or false applies, there we always find a putting-together of objects of thought." [84]

In this way, false opinion will become intelligible. It involves *two* objects and *two* faculties, not one. Opinion is a *combination of* knowledge and sense, not the simple apprehension of a single object

[81] *Theaet.*, 190 C 5–D 8.   [82] *Theaet.*, 188 E 5–189 B 1.
[83] *Theaet.*, 188 A 7–8.   [84] *De An.*, 430 A 27–8.

THE INVERSION OF THE APPREHENSIVE FACULTIES 263

— this cannot be false — but the mental combination of what is not combined in reality.[85] In order to judge or opine, I must infallibly sense a stream of appearances. I must also infallibly know the nature of certain realities. But in applying the latter to the former, I may become confused, fitting the wrong nature on the wrong appearance and thus producing a false opinion. This will not be the thought of what is not at all, but the thought of one thing (an appearance) *as* something else (a structure or form) which does not belong to it.

Hence truth and falsity *presuppose* the infallible apprehension of simple objects. If I am mistaken in asserting that *this is a man*, the proposition presupposes that *this* is infallibly sensed as before me, and that I know infallibly what *a man* is. It is out of just such discussions as these that Aristotle must have developed his more precise doctrine concerning the infallible apprehension of simple essences, and the mental combinations of these which may be true or false.[86] But this does not explain falsity in general. I may also be mistaken with respect to purely structural matters such as numbers, which are not sensed at all. This leads to the second phase of the distinction between opinion and knowledge.

II. *Opinion as Imperfect or Potential Knowledge*

We must distinguish the possessing (κτῆσις) of knowledge from the having (ἕξις) of knowledge. The knowing faculty is compared to an aviary, well stocked with birds, some clustered together in large groups (genera), divided into smaller groups (species), and some single birds flying by themselves through all the rest (the basic forms or transcendentals).[87] All men "possess" these simple items of knowledge flying about. They know what being is, what difference is, what good and bad are, what certain generic terms such as animal and plant are, and how certain species of these differ. These unitary apprehensions are sound and changeless. But they are not "held" in any stable, complex configuration or pattern. In terms of the image, as Plato tells us, the birds are all of them flying about, constantly

---

[85] Opinion is thus not simply δόξα but ἑτεροδοξία, thinking not simply of *x* but of *x as y*, one thing *as* another. *Theaet.*, 193 D 2.

[86] See especially *Meta.*, 1059 A 32 ff., and *De An.*, III, ch. 6. Plato further clarifies this conception in his definitions of truth and falsity at *Soph.*, 263 A 8–D 8.

[87] As Professor Cornford points out, *Plato's Theory of Knowledge*, p. 132 n. *Soph.*, 252 ff. *certainly* suggests this interpretation.

combining and separating from one another to form new configurations of opinion. Men do not *have* the knowledge which they already
possess, until they may hold it in such a complex stable pattern,[88]
combining the units that are really combined, and separating those
that are really separated. As long as the simple meaning is stable,
but the compound judgment fluid, knowledge is still only potential.
As long as any birds are still left free to fly about at random, we have
not freed outselves from opinion and the possibility of error.

Theaetetus makes the mistake of regarding knowledge as a set
of isolated bits which are simply heaped together as we come to know
more and more. Hence we can only interpret error as an actual "bit"
of ignorance, a non-bird flying about in the aviary.[89] But this is
ridiculous, and plunges us into the old difficulty of thinking that
which is not. Complete knowledge does not consist only in the unitary
apprehensions, but in the ordering of these together in a judgment
which, in Aristotle's language, knows that they cannot be ordered
otherwise. Only so may we explain the difference between the correct
opinion of a judge who has merely been persuaded by plausible argument and the judge who knows *why* his opinion is true.[90] Without
the infallible apprehension of basic units of meaning, knowledge
would be impossible. But such apprehensions constitute only the
raw material for knowledge. They must be fitted into a stable order
with reference to one another before knowledge may be achieved.
Knowledge is not a thing, or a set of things, but an order. Hence
the next definition, which is really correct if correctly interpreted.[91]

6. The Attempt to Reduce Knowledge to Sensation

We have now arrived at a definition of knowledge which is verbally
correct. It is pointed out in the *Timaeus* [92] that the existence of formal
structure follows from the distinction between knowledge and true
opinion. If we not only hold the correct view but also know the correct
reasons for holding it, then we are said to know. Such knowledge
of the structural ground does not come from the outside by mere
persuasion, though it may be suggested, and elicited through skillful
questioning. Once arrived at, it is unshakable by persuasion and
permanently held in the understanding. But to hold this right *opinion*

[88] *Theaet.*, 198 D 1–9.   [89] *Theaet.*, 199 E 1 ff.
[90] *Theaet.*, 201 A–C 11.   [91] *Theaet.*, 201 C 8.
[92] *Timaeus*, 51 D.

concerning the nature of knowledge is not to know its nature.[93] What is meant by such terms as "ground," and "reason"? The inveterate tendency of opinion to fall back on sense rather than to pursue its own course leads us once again to the inversion of sensationalism.

In this final section of the dialogue,[94] Theaetetus, who has now been made to see the distinction between true opinion and knowledge, expresses those major misinterpretations of the distinction which, instead of revealing the peculiar nature of knowledge as it is, and leading opinion, the intermediate faculty, to its proper goal, only invert it once more to its material source. Theaetetus is relieved of these misconceptions by the midwifery of Socrates. In any case, he will be "milder and less harsh to his fellows," [95] since in these respects he will not longer think that he knows what he does not know. If he ever again tries to think of these matters, he will be in a position to conceive better thoughts "by reason of the present search." [96]

The readers of Plato must themselves take this protreptic exhortation to heart and try to clarify the many hints of a true solution which are contained in this concluding section of the dialogue. What do we mean by "explanation" (λόγος), the justification of a true opinion? The true answer is never explicitly stated in this critical dialogue but is certainly suggested in the elaborate criticism of the materialistic theory of "analysis" (to follow a current vocabulary), with which the discussion begins, as well as in the criticism of Theaetetus' misconception of the true definition of "explanation," with which it ends.

I. The Theory of "Analysis"

There is a certain theory of the nature of explanation which Socrates has heard "in a dream." [97] According to this theory, the primary "elements," of which all things are composed, are without any further parts. No predicate can be attached to them, not even existence,

[93] Aristotle also holds that the very same things may be known as incapable of being otherwise, and opined as capable of being otherwise. *Post. An.*, I, ch. 33.
[94] *Theaet.*, 201 C 9–end.
[95] *Theaet.*, 210 C 2–3.
[96] *Theaet.*, 210 B 11 ff.
[97] *Theaet.*, 201 D 8 ff. Antisthenes is probably meant. Cf. Guy C. Field, *Plato and His Contemporaries* (London: Methuen & Co., 1930), pp. 160 ff. Aristotle attributes just such a view as this to Antisthenes, and criticises it for similar reasons at *Meta.*, 1024 B 32. Cf. 1043 B 24.

because they are utterly indivisible.[98] Hence they cannot be known, but only had, or perceived and named. The combinations of these, however, may be expressed as the objects of opinion.[99] When analyzed, or cut up into their irreducible elements, *they* may be known, but not their simple elements. Hence this provides us with an "easy" and plausible account of the nature of explanation, and thus of the difference between true opinion and knowledge. To understand a thing, as the present-day positivistic "analyst" says, is simply to analyze it into its irreducible, sensory elements. What of this view?

First of all we may well ask with Socrates, how knowledge can be produced by unknowable principles. The data of sense, as they flow past, are not themselves the source of knowledge, but rather something to be known. By bringing us back to these data, as they are ineffably sensed, the analysts have receded only to the material starting point of knowledge, not its essential source. As we have seen, the explanation for this confusion lies in that infallibility which attaches to the simple elements both of sensation and knowledge. But sensory certainty is not to be confused with rational certainty. I may be certain that I am having the sensation I am having, say the colour yellow, but this, by itself, does not make me certain of *what* the colour yellow is. Nor is it true that such sensory "units" are unintelligible and "indefinable."

"The colour yellow" may be only a crude and incipient definition, but it is a definition in terms of universal essences which are never sensed as such, but only with the admixture of many extraneous elements such as supporting surface, intensity, distance, light and shade, etc. To determine the nature of a certain sense datum, even to cognize it as a sense-datum, to relate it together with other essences to which it is essentially related, is not achieved by sense but by another faculty, working in its own way on the data of sensation. Do we come to understand the nature of a house by tearing it up into wood and bricks? The analyst has confused the formal cause of knowledge with its material cause.

Socrates next confronts the analytic theory with an interesting dilemma. Let us take SO, the first syllable of Socrates' name. According to the analytic theory, the S and the O are irreducible, indefinable

---

[98] *Theaet.*, 201 E 3–4. Cf. the current "logical" doctrine that *x exists* is an "analytic" proposition.
[99] *Theaet.*, 202 B 6–7.

elements. But how about the "whole" syllable? It must be either: (1) a mere aggregate of the S and the O, or (2) a new "emergent," distinct from the mere combination of the S and the O. In either case, the result is embarrassing for the analytic theory. An aggregate or sum is no more than its quantitative parts. It is precisely "all" its quantitative parts, as a mile is simply 5280 feet, and 5280 feet are precisely a mile. Any such quantitative "whole" is reducible to its parts, and what is true of all the parts is true of it. But if the whole to be analyzed is no more than such an accidental aggregate, it will be as unknowable as the parts. The sum of two unknowables which are merely juxtaposed will also be unknowable, for juxtaposition *still* leaves the parts essentially as they were. So the analyst is forced to the second alternative.

Perhaps the syllable SO is a genuine or essential whole, in modern terminology a "new emergent," something *more* than the mere quantitative sum of the parts. This is, of course, true of any individual, material thing which is one whole *of* many parts.[100] But this is equally embarrassing for the analyst, since, by enumerating all the parts, he will not have enumerated the parts of this "new" whole, but merely the parts of an accidental sum or aggregate. The "whole," which is distinct from all the parts, will still confront him as *another*, unique, irreducible "element" besides the parts. On his own theory then, this new "emergent" will be as unknowable as the "single" elements, since it, like each of them, is "single" and irreducible. Hence, neither the irreducible elements nor the irreducible whole, which "mysteriously" emerges out of the material elements, will be knowable.[101]

There is no escape from this Socratic dilemma. If the syllable is a mere aggregate of the material letters, then it is as unknowable as they are. If it is a new emergent, it is itself an unknowable element. So in neither case is knowledge possible. Far from having given an account of knowledge, we have merely lapsed into the faculty of sensation and the noetic matter of its object. The modern theory of "logical-analysis" is simply materialism of the intellect.

Since this is a critical dialogue, which avoids all mention of formal structure, the solution of the *aporetic* is only hinted, never explicitly developed. One may find such a solution at the end of Book VII of Aristotle's *Metaphysics*, in a passage which uses the same example of

---

[100] μὴ τὰ στοιχεῖα ἀλλ' ἐξ ἐκείνων ἕν τι γεγονὸς εἶδος: *Theaet.*, 203 E 3.
[101] *Theaet.*, 205 E 2–4.

the letters and the syllable.[102] The syllable is no mere aggregate of material "parts" (σωρός) but "the form which makes it of a certain kind." [103] This form "emerges" out of the material facts, it is true, but as the effect of an external cause. The syllable itself also has "parts," but they are the formal constituents of the alphabet, *the* universal S and the universal O,[104] not the individual ink-marks on the paper. Knowing the syllable is not to sense the individual ink-marks, but rather to apprehend rationally the formal system of the alphabet as specified in the ideal syllable SO.

This is clearly suggested in the final argument adduced by Socrates against the analytic view. Here he appeals to the phenomenology of the learning process, and shows it to be quite opposite to what the analytic theory demands. Learning to read is clearly not a matter of reducing knowable compounds to unknowable letters, which are merely seen and heard. It is precisely the other way around. The individual compounds are at first unknown. We do not come to understand them by "analyzing" them into their *sensory* elements. We must *first* discover the *noetic* elements, the universal letters A B C, etc., and the universal system of the alphabet. It is precisely these universal elements which are intrinsically knowable, because they fit into an intelligible generic system. From an understanding of this system, we then gain the ability to understand the structure of any specific combination of individual sounds or marks.

II. The Threefold Meaning of Logos as the Expression of Genus and Difference

We are now presented with what is in substance a definition of explanation or *logos*. Socrates suggests that it is one of three things; [105] either the verbal expression of thought, or the enumeration of the elements, or finally the giving of a distinguishing mark. The upshot of the discussion is that no one of these is sufficient, but that all three are essential to constitute a true explanation or definition.

First of all, it is clear that the mere vocal expression of an opinion is not a definition or an explanation. The verbal expression of an opinion certainly does not transform it into knowledge. Nor is the

102 *Meta.*, 1041 B 11 ff.
103 *Meta.*, 1041 B 8.
104 Cf. *Meta.*, 1035 B 3 ff.
105 *Theaet.*, 206 C 7.

second *by itself* sufficient I may know the universal letters or elements which enter into the word Theaetetus, as they appear in this particular order, but I may not know them in the generic system of the alphabet, and hence may make a mistake when I try to spell some other word, like Theodorus. In this case, I have merely learned a particular phase of a more universal structure by rote and have not yet come to understand it. To know a thing always means to know some more general pattern than the pattern of the specific thing, or, in other words, to know the genus.[106] But this also is insufficient. If I know only what wheels are in general, I may not know what the wheels of a wagon are, for a chariot also has wheels. "So long as you cling to some common quality, your explanation will pertain to all those objects to which the common quality belongs."[107] An explanation which applies equally well to a chariot is certainly not the explanation of a wagon. Hence, in addition to the genus, we must give the difference, or the distinguishing mark of the thing which we are explaining.[108] We must grasp something of the generic structure, and then come down to the specific, differentiating pattern of the thing itself.

Theaetetus misinterprets this difference as some individual *sensory* mark, like the perceived brilliancy of the sun, and the concluding criticism warns us again against the persistent danger of lapsing into sensationalism. Each sensory perception is materially distinct from every other. Hence, if knowledge is right opinion of the generic traits plus *sensation* of the distinguishing mark, right opinion will already be knowledge, since it is always about some individual thing which is either perceived or remembered.[109] I need only open my eyes to grasp the distinguishing mark in *this* sense. What is required is knowledge of the *intelligible* difference, not sensation of the material difference, which is already presupposed by opinion. It is essential "to know and not to opine the difference."[110]

Any definition of knowledge which leaves opinion intact at any point is inadequate. The generic system must be known. The difference must be known. So far as we are still forced to fall back upon sensory indices or images, our knowledge is still incomplete. It is "simple-minded"[111] to say that knowledge is "right opinion together

[106] κοινοῦ τινος ἐφάπτῃ: *Theaet.*, 208 D 8.   [107] *Theaet.*, 208 D 7–9.
[108] τὴν διαφορὰν τῶν ἄλλων προσλάβῃ: *Theaet.*, 208 E 4.
[109] *Theaet.*, 209 C 4–9.
[110] *Theaet.*, 209 E 6 ff. Cf. Cornford, *Plato's Theory of Knowledge*, pp. 162–163.
[111] εὔηθες: *Theaet.*, 210 A 7.

with knowledge, whether of difference or of anything else whatsoever." Knowledge is not sensation, nor opinion of any sort, nor
anything but knowledge. The whole essential pattern of the thing itself,
its generic elements, together with the peculiar form of their combination, must be *rationally* apprehended. To say anything less is to
confuse the higher faculty with the lower.

7. CONCLUSION

Although the dialogue proceeds critically, and never explicitly
formulates "conclusions," it has clearly suggested the structural
order of three distinct but inseparably related apprehensive faculties,
sense (αἴσθησις), opinion (δόξα), and knowledge (ἐπιστήμη), the major
inversions of this order, and an explanation of these inversions. The
faculty of sense infallibly apprehends seeming, which *comes to be*
relative to the percipient, and is particularized. The faculty of reason
infallibly apprehends being universally as it *is* in itself. It is the infallibility attaching to each faculty which explains the inveterate tendency
to confuse them. But the infallibility of knowledge is communicable
and enduring, while that of sense is solipsistic and ephemeral. Correspondingly the object of knowledge is universal and stable, while
that of sense is individual and changing. Hence these two faculties,
being subjectively and objectively distinct, are themselves distinct.

Opinion lies between them, though closer to knowledge than to
sense. It is unlike either, because of its fallibility. It is like knowledge
subjectively, in that it is communicable, but also resembles sense subjectively, in that it is ephemeral. It resembles knowledge objectively,
in that its ultimate intentional object is the real as it is in itself. Since,
however, it is only incipient or potential knowledge, emerging out
of sense,[112] it is apt to confuse this object with that of sense, allowing
itself to judge according to appearance, rather than pursuing its
painful course, through constant dialectical correction and purification,
towards its goal. This inversion of direction, towards the beginning
rather than towards the end, is encouraged and even produced by
the sensationalist theories of Protagoras and his followers, which
are based upon the confusion of infallible knowledge with infallible
sensation.

---

[112] Cf. the formula of the *Republic* (Adam): ὅ τι οὐσία πρὸς γένεσιν, νόησιν πρὸς δόξαν,
534 A 3–4.

Such a confusion of the psychic faculties of apprehension, to which all men are prone, has a disastrous effect upon the opinion-forming process which constitutes the life of mind. Instead of making the arduous effort, which leads through self-criticism and self-correction to stable and communicable knowledge, men, beguiled by sensationalism, relax in their search and allow their opinions to be determined by any chance source. The mind of such a man is like an aviary, in which the units of knowledge never wholly absent are never firmly grasped and held in stable configurations, but are allowed to fly about in random response to ephemeral, external pressure. Instead of becoming more stable, coherent, and communicable, his opinions become ever more pliable, incoherent, and incommunicable, except to those responding similarly to the same external influences. Instead of judging sensation by opinion, and opinion by what he knows to be so, he allows what he knows to be judged by plausible opinion, and opinion to be governed by the random impacts of sense. This turning upside down of the psychic faculties is not something wholly subjective, involving himself alone, for his faculties are intentional in structure. They cannot be inverted without a corresponding ontological inversion of the realities they apprehend.[113] Not only is the individual mind upside down, but also the world itself, misapprehended by such a mind, is upside down. Being is confused with the flux of becoming, and becoming itself with the relative appearance or seeming of such becoming.

Both types of confusion are to be found in the inverted man, the sophist. Since his faculties are inverted, he is a sensationalist, confusing knowledge with opinion, and opinion with feeling. Hence he cannot fail to apprehend the world in an inverted or "materialistic" manner, confusing being with the shifting flux out of which things come to be. Finally, the very order of object and apprehensive faculty is inverted. Instead of allowing his faculties to be determined by their objects, so far as possible he reverses the order, allowing the object to be determined by the faculty. Hence his understanding becomes idealistic and subjectivistic, achieving no verisimilitude of reality but only some "novel" or "original" construction of his own, which, as Aristotle says, "appears to be philosophy but is not." [114] Since the ultimate source of such confusion, and hence of all the social

[113] Cf. the last chapter.
[114] *Meta.*, 1004 B 26–27.

and cultural inversions we have so far studied in this work, is to be found in the individual sophist himself, we must now try to analyze his composite nature, in the dialectical attempt to discover a sound definition. We shall be greatly aided in this task if we use Plato's dialogue, the *Sophist*, as our guide.

CHAPTER VIII

THE *SOPHIST*

THE MYTH of the Cave is not only the portrayal of different levels of being and knowledge. It is also the portrayal of two opposite motions or directions of life, the ascent into being [1] and the descent into non-being.[2] It is tempting to identify the ascent with philosophy, the descent with sophistry. Plato leaves us in no doubt as to the basic opposition, and, therefore, connection between the two, for immediately after the analogy, he plunges at once into a discussion of sophistry and sophistic education. It is impossible to understand sophistry without first understanding something of philosophy. Sophistry is no particular sect, or school, or set of opinions. It cannot be rectified by substituting one set of "exalted" opinions for another debased set, but only by substituting knowledge for opinion. As Aristotle says: "knowledge and opinion of the same thing can coexist in two different people." [3] One may opine all the opinions that Plato himself held, and still be a sophist.

Sophistry is not the inversion of this philosophy or that philosophy, but something far more fundamental, the inversion of philosophy itself. Now, having attempted to suggest the hierarchy of nature, art, social life, personal life, the moving image in which these levels are presented all together as stages in the ascent of the soul, and, in the last two chapters, the true order of being, and finally that of the apprehensive faculties, we are prepared to grasp the complex phenomenon of sophistry as a unitary inversion of order, a descent from understanding to opinion, from personal life to social life, from art to the accidental domination of nature. To ascend out of the Cave is to be a philosopher; to descend is to be a sophist. But, as Plato warns us in terms of the analogy itself, the matter is *not* so simple.

Every level in the hierarchy plays its necessary role, and there is no such thing as a permanent escape from one level to another. The philosopher is bound by the ties of nature to his fellow prisoners in

[1] *Rep.*, 519 C 8.   [2] *Rep.*, 519 D 4 ff.   [3] *Post. An.*, I, 89 B 1–2.

the Cave. He cannot avoid conjecture and opinion, even though here and there he may achieve stable knowledge. Hence, in terms of the analogy, he must move down as well as up. As he does so he experiences two types of confusion, that involved in passing from a lower to a higher level, and that involved in passing from a higher level to a lower level.[4] He is subject to both types of confusion, is ready to suffer them both, and is, in short, like Socrates himself, in a more or less constant state of confusion, moving in one direction or the other. However, since he is more at home in the higher level than the lower, the confusion involved in descending to a lower level will seem to him to be more natural, more worthy, and hence less ridiculous than the opposite and less natural confusion.[5]

The sophist, on the other hand, while he cannot altogether avoid all traces of knowledge, clings obstinately from the very first to the opinions induced in him and his fellows by the natural course of events. He confuses these with the very truth itself, up with down, and down with up. Though actually plunged in the deepest shadow, he thinks he is standing in the glaring light, with no need of moving at all. Hence he moves neither up nor down, suffers neither type of confusion, and is himself confused to the minimum degree. To him both types of confusion will seem unnatural and ridiculous, and he will laugh at both. To him, as he stands in the shadow, the confusion of one turning away towards the light will seem more natural and far less ridiculous than the confusion of one turning into the shadow, who cannot see in what he regards as the clearest conceivable light.

The sophist runs away into the darkness of non-being, feeling his way in it by practice, and is hard to discern on account of the darkness of the place. . . . But the philosopher, always devoting himself through reason to the idea of being, is also very difficult to see on account of the brilliant light of the place." [6]

The result is the truly transcendental anatropism we have noted. Dark is confused with light, and light with dark. Up is confused with down, and down with up. The sophist, remaining where he starts, does not move at all and suffers no real confusion. All confusion seems to him unnecessary and ridiculous, though that which is more worthy and excusable seems to him even more unworthy and more ridiculous than that which is truly less unworthy and less ridiculous.

---

[4] *Rep.*, 518 A.   [5] *Rep.*, 518 B 2–4.   [6] *Soph.*, 254 A 4.

In the discussion of sophistry which is so closely intertwined with the description of the true philosopher in Books VI and VII of the *Republic*,[7] two further aspects of its complex nature are made clear. First, the sophist is no particular man or group of men. All of us are sophists. Only so may we account for the success of those great sophistic teachers of all ages and all generations, among whom Pericles,[8] Protagoras, and the other leaders of the Periclean Age are, according to Plato, outstanding examples. Sophistry, the opposite of philosophy, and hence most closely allied with it, as its inversion or privation, represents a constant, tempting tendency in the very nature of man. Just as all men are philosophers, and Socrates is the typical man, so are all men also sophists, and thus susceptible to the lure of anatropism.

Second, the sophistic mode of education is contrasted with the philosophical mode, so far as the former proceeds by injecting something external and unnatural into the mind, whereas the latter merely removes such sophistic impediments as interfere with the natural functioning and apprehensions of the mind. The sophist is himself governed by artificial man-made ideas and opinions, which he then injects, so far as possible, into others, stunting and distorting their natural insights by external contrivances. He is in a real sense an artificial product, a humanly moulded or man-made man. How does this happen, we may well ask? How, and by what means, does the sophist contrive to mismake himself? What are the subjective opinions which hold sway over him, and which finally imprison both himself and others in shadowy constructions falsely confused with reality? In short, what is the sophist?

We have now acquainted ourselves with the complete upheaval of culture, of social and individual life, of the whole process of human education which is the essence of life itself, of the order of being, and finally of that inversion of the knowing faculties for which he is responsible. Surely it is time to attempt a closer examination of his nature. What is the definition of the sophist? For an answer we must turn to that dialogue which is, as its present title indicates, primarily concerned with this very question. In studying this dialogue, however, we must pass summarily over certain subsidiary matters examined there in great detail. What does this dialogue tell us about

[7] Cf. Book VI, 495 B 8–496 A 10 and Book VII, 518 B 6–521 C.
[8] Cf. *Gorgias*, 515 D–520.

the sophist? This is our question. The answer is there and if read carefully sheds an amazing light.

1. The More Apparent Properties of the Sophist (216–232)

The dialogue begins with an induction in which certain easily recognizable traits of prominent sophists are carefully noted and classified.[9] Such prominent traits usually result from the real nature of that which we are examining, for the essential nature itself is hidden and hard to discern.[10] But by carefully classifying such "obvious" traits we may be led to that which is responsible for them all.[11] What then are the more striking characteristics of those who are commonly agreed to be sophists? That which first impresses us is the acquisitive aspect of their art, the tremendous power exerted by the great teacher over his pupils, who fall unwittingly under his sway, and the vast wealth accumulated by men like Protagoras and Gorgias from their scholarly trade. This consists not only in acting as middlemen, transmitting the wisdom of others both in wholesale to those who are about to become themselves teachers and in retail to individual pupils, but also in selling original theories and manufactured wisdom of their own.

The sophist, therefore, is most strikingly evident: (1) as a hunter of young men, exerting a mysterious power over them, which they do not understand; (2) as a wholesale dealer in intellectual wares, travelling about from city to city, and from school to school, supplying the local masters with new information and new theories when their own stock runs low; (3) as a professor, or wise man, established in some particular place where he is able to maintain himself by a purely local trade in other men's wisdom; or (4) as a local dealer, original enough to manufacture his own intellectual wares. These acquisitive attributes, however, obviously do not penetrate to the nub of the matter. What is the source of this mysterious power? What are these articles which are sold for such incredible prices both wholesale and retail? The sophist is *the maker of something*. His acquisitive power results from some sort of production. What does he produce?

---

[9] Cf. Cornford, *Plato's Theory of Knowledge* (New York: Harcourt Brace, 1935), pp. 184–187 for an illuminating discussion of the Platonic and Aristotelian uses of the term ἐπαγωγή.

[10] *Sophist*, 218 D 2. Cf. 239 C 4–7, *et passim*.

[11] Thus Aristotle points out that it is often necessary to start with the properties in order to apprehend the essential nature. Cf. *De An.*, 402 B 21 ff.

It is this that constitutes him a sophist, whether he is lucky enough to find a market for his wares or not.

Another evident, acquisitive trait of the notorious sophists is their disputatiousness, their skill in debate, and their general cultivation of the art of logic, the ability to defend any statement or to attack any statement whether it be true or false.[12] Such skill in open debate has characterized the great teachers of the past. Without it, they would have been overcome by opponents, representing opposite points of view, and would never have been able to sell their wares in a competitive market, nor to achieve any permanent fame. Hence the sophist is an open controversialist. He must be able not merely to make long speeches in public, but to oppose the individual mind in private argument by asking and answering questions.[13] He must not merely be able to do this in a random manner, but must know something of the technical rules of logical procedure if he is to possess the maximum proficiency.[14] But no dispute is absolutely aimless. What then is the aim of this logical dexterity? What is the teacher trying to do to his pupil? Through his logical dexterity, he is attacking certain views and defending certain others. Hence we are led to the next obvious aspect of the great sophist or teacher of mankind.[15]

He is clearly trying to get rid of certain opinions and to substitute others in their place. As a "teacher" his aim is to make us "change our minds." Hence he is a "purifier" of the soul, proceeding by logical methods of question and answer to keep the soul in a healthy state by enabling it to correct its involuntary ignorance on fundamental matters.[16] This brings us closer to the essential nature of the sophist. He is certainly an educator or teacher of men. First in himself, and then in others, he carries out some sort of purification, eliminating one set of opinions and preserving another, "better" set. But this presupposes, of course, that he himself can adequately discriminate between the two. If so, then he is truly a philosopher, who achieves for himself and leads others to make for themselves the most perfect

---

[12] Thus Protagoras wrote a treatise on disputation, τέχνη ἐριστικῶν, and taught his pupils first to praise and then to blame the very same thing. Cf. Diels, *Fragmente der Vorsokratiker*, pp. 219 and 225.

[13] ἀντιλογικόν: *Sophist*, 225 B 10.

[14] *Sophist*, 225 C 7–9.

[15] *Sophist*, 226 B–231 B 8. We have already commented on this account of the purifying, therapeutic art of education, pp. 67 ff.

[16] *Sophist*, 230 A 5 ff.

and essential of all purifications,[17] that which cleanses us from involuntary ignorance about the most important matters.

This will be the case if by skilful question and answer he enables his pupil to see that his own subjective opinions really distort the truth, to rid himself of all "personal" ideals, and every trace of constructive interpretation, and thus to open his mind to the sheer and unadulterated truth. Of course the great teacher *seems* to do this. Does he do so, or only seem to do so? If he only seems to do so, he will be an exact opposite of the true philosopher [18] resembling him, as opposites always resemble, as the wolf, the wildest of animals, closely resembles its opposite, the tamest of animals, the dog.[19] We must be "especially on our guard about resemblances for they are very slippery things." [20] Beneath this external cloak of resemblance there may be concealed the most fundamental of all oppositions falling within the scope of human nature.

If the teacher is perhaps slightly confused in his original discriminations, then, of course, he will still *seem* to be purifying the mind of false impediments to knowledge and further establishing it in the truth. The only difficulty will be that what he thinks is false is really true, and that what he thinks is true is really false. In this case, he will proceed in exactly the same manner as the philosopher, purifying and establishing the soul, only he will purify it of all traces of truth, and establish it in the maximum of subjective construction. So this purifying aspect of the sophist is not final. It does not enable us to distinguish between the philosopher and the sophist, the dog and the wolf, the true and the false mode of purification. The fact that we have stumbled upon so many disparate phases of the sophistic art, lying side by side, shows that we have not as yet grasped that *essential* aspect involved in all the rest.[21] The various acquisitive and purifying phases of teaching have shown us only something relational and, therefore, derivative. We have seen the teacher as he is in relation to other men. What then, we now ask, is the teacher *in himself*? What is the essential nature of the wise man?

---

[17] *Sophist*, 230 D 6–7.

[18] *Sophist*, 231 A 4–B 1.

[19] Cf. *Rep.*, II, 375 D 10 ff., where the philosophical traits of the dog are called to our attention.

[20] *Sophist*, 231 A 7–8. Cf. *Phaedrus*, 261 ff.

[21] ἐκεῖνο αὐτῆς εἰς ὃ πάντα τὰ μαθήματα ταῦτα βλέπει: *Sophist*, 232 A 4–5.

2. The Essential Nature of the Sophist (232–236 D 9)

This vital discussion begins at 231 C. The whole argument up to this point is first recapitulated, and the six prominent, accidental phases of the great sophists which we have considered are briefly repeated. Surely there is some reason for calling the sophists by a single name. What is the one essential trait with reference to which we may see how these six otherwise disparate traits may be fitted into a single nature?

The fifth of the enumerated traits is the point of departure, for, as the stranger says, this is the one "which seemed to me to characterize him most plainly." [22] He is an arguer or disputer. He must know how to argue in private in a logical manner. If he does not know how to do this, he will be unable to devise convincing discourses or speeches, or to work on the minds of men either in private or in public. But, as we have seen, argument cannot be carried on unless it is *about* something. What is the subject matter of sophistic dispute? [23] *What* is it that the great teachers teach? This is the question which leads us to the essence of the sophistic nature — the universal sophistry inherent in the very nature of man.

Sophistry is not limited to any *special* subject matter or range of being. In its own way, it deals with divine things, earthly things, and the whole world of man.[24] Like philosophy, of which it is a privative mode, sophistry is unrestricted in scope. As Aristotle points out, the sophist, like the philosopher, speaks of all things.[25] The art of disputation, or "formal logic," as we now call it, "seems to be a power sufficient for arguing about all things," [26] and there is no combination of arts, or any single art, which is not subject to "logical" treatment. But how can one man be a master of all the arts, and thus be in a position to dispute with one who really knows? This is impossible.[27] It is difficult enough for a man in a single lifetime to become the master of a single art. Hence the knowledge of the sophist is "an opinionative knowledge." [28]

As Theaetetus points out, this is "the most accurate statement we have made about him so far." [29] What, then, is the difference between knowledge and opinionative knowledge? To know is neither

[22] *Sophist*, 232 B 3–4.
[23] περὶ τίνος: *Sophist*, 232 B 11.
[24] *Sophist*, 232 B 11–C 5.
[25] *Meta.*, Bk. IV, 1004 B 17–25.
[26] *Sophist*, 232 E 3.
[27] *Sophist*, 233 A 7.
[28] *Sophist*, 233 C 10.
[29] *Sophist*, 233 D 1–2.

to make nor to do. It is to discover the nature of something already in existence. Opinionative knowledge involves a constructive factor. When something is known only imperfectly we have to *construct* images, and pictures, and hypotheses in lieu of what we do not know. Such subjective knowledge is opinionative. Of course we are never entirely without knowledge, and the ability to distinguish between a subjective theory and the thing itself.

When we are placed at a maximum distance from things, however, and forced to view them from an unfavorable position, it is possible for us to confuse a theoretical construction with the thing of which it is a subjective construction. This is, in fact, the art of the sophist. It works especially well upon the young, who are lacking in experience, and hence "at a distance" from reality.[30] Having removed reality to as great a distance as possible, the sophist then begins to bewitch us by eristic and dispute, inducing in us that intellectual befuddlement which is least able to distinguish the various modes and levels and types of being from one another. In this state, he is able to make us think that his own creations are "true" and that he himself "is the wisest of all men in all things." [31]

In *essence*, then, the sophist is an "original" thinker, a constructor of subjective opinion, which only resembles the truth. He is not a knower at all, for the knower constructs nothing, but gives himself entirely to the task of hunting the thing as it already is.[32] The sophist, on the other hand, is the *maker* of something, namely a subjective imitation of being as it is. God himself is the maker both of independent things, such as animals, plants, and stars, and of the *natural images* of these, such as shadows, the reflections in water, and the similitudes of animal sensation.[33] So also man is the maker of certain independent, artificial things, such as shoes, houses, and machines, and of imitations, first in the imagination itself, then in colour, sound, etc., as well as other media.[34] The sophist thus practices the making art in its mimetic division.[35] In a word, he is a subjective or "creative" thinker.[36]

---

[30] *Sophist*, 233 B 1 and 234 B 8 — πόρρωθεν τὰ γεγραμμένα ἐπιδεικνύς.
[31] *Sophist*, 234 C 2–7.
[32] Cf. *Euthyd.*, 290 B 8 ff., where scientists are compared to hunters.
[33] *Soph.*, 266 B 8–C.
[34] *Soph.*, 266 C.   [35] *Soph.*, 235 A 1.
[36] Hence sophistry always tends to ignore the intentionality of thought, regarding reason not as the apprehension of an object, but rather as an isolated process of

The philosopher also is an imitator. God alone is the maker of the actual things. The philosopher can at best construct imitations in words and discourse of these things.[37] Nor is the sophist *completely* without knowledge of that concerning which he discourses. Every opinion, no matter how subjective or fantastic it may be, is *about* something, the nature of which is known to some degree.[38] So what then is the difference between the philosopher and the sophist? Each of them talks about all things, constructing in the soul verbal images of the actual realities. As Aristotle later remarked, "the sophists assume the same guise as the philosopher." [39] Each knows something of being. Each universally images this being in his soul. How then are we to distinguish them? The answer is to be found in the next division of the copy-making art, which we have already discussed so far as it bears upon the order of the arts,[40] but which is also of crucial importance in classifying the sophist.

It is tempting to think of the sophist as a *complete* subjectivist, living *wholly* in a world of his own opinions and constructions, and of the philosopher as a complete "realist," who has eliminated every subjective factor from his thought. But this is to regard the former as though he possessed a knowing faculty which could be exercised without knowing anything, and the latter as though he possessed the thing in itself without having to know it — precisely sophistry itself. No faculty can be exercised without an *object*.[41] In all cases of apprehension there is, on the one hand, that which is apprehended, and on the other, the faculty apprehending it. The distinction does not involve the simple presence or absence of a single factor, but an inversion of order or direction of the *two* factors, both of which must be present. *Every* imitator attempts to reproduce a similitude of the original thing as it is.[42] But he must also take account of the peculiar

making hypotheses or theories in the mind. This tendency to regard reason as though it had no *object* of its own is common to modern idealism and pragmatism.

[37] Nevertheless it must be remembered that there are two kinds of image, the divine and the human. The faculties of understanding and of discourse are the natural gifts of God to man. Hence the true likenesses in the soul, according to nature, may be said to be divine or natural images — φαντάσματα αὐτοφυῆ (266 B 9–10), in opposition to the opinions and constructions which are man-made (266 C 7–9). [38] Cf. *supra*, pp. 262–264.

[39] *Meta.*, Bk. IV, 1004 b 18. [40] Cf. *supra*, pp. 81 ff.

[41] Cf. *Rep.*, 477 C–478 C, *Phil.*, 35 B and 37, *et passim*, and Aristotle, *De An.*, 415 A 20, *et passim*.

[42] *Soph.*, 235 E 3. "Do not all imitators try to do this?"

situation and limitations of the apprehensive faculty. Which is to dominate over the other? This is the crucial decision he must make.

Is he going to allow the archetype to determine the true proportions of the image? Then he will reproduce an exact and accurate replica (εἰκών) of the thing, which, to those "unfavorably situated," [43] as men gazing up at a temple frieze from below, will doubtless be apprehended as a distortion. If so, he will have followed the natural order, and will have performed his proper function in reproducing a true image. The defect will arise not from his work but from the unfavorable point of view of the beholders. Should they be enabled to overcome this apprehensive limitation, they would find in the image an adequate representation of the original, and thus be led to the truth.

Or is he going to follow the inverted order, not allowing himself to be determined by the proportions of the original, but yielding here and there to the limitations of some accidental point of view from which his image is to be beheld? In the case of the frieze he will then make the upper parts larger and the lower parts smaller, thus achieving an illusion of verisimilitude for those restricted to an unfavorable position. Should the observer be freed from this limitation, however, and gain a more favorable viewpoint, he would behold a monstrosity, incapable of leading anyone to the truth. [44]

The situation confronting the philosopher is analogous. The rational apprehensive faculty, to which he must appeal, is unfavorably situated, far from the real natures of things, for it is accidentally attached to a particular, material body equipped with senses yielding only a biased awareness of certain superficial aspects of the world. What then is he to do? Is he to keep his eyes upon being itself, the original, and in his discourses and arguments follow exactly and accurately the proportions of this original? If so, he will reproduce an accurate replica (εἰκών) of the archetype, which, to those unfavorably situated, as in this case all men are situated, in the accidental perspectives of sense, will doubtless seem false and fantastic. Nevertheless he will have followed the natural order, and will have performed his proper function as a philosopher. The defect will not lie in his discourses and arguments, but rather in the biased, subjective point of view of his listeners. Should he and they be enabled to overcome this apprehensive limitation, perhaps through these very discourses,

[43] *Soph.*, 236 B 5.   [44] *Soph.*, 236 B 4–6.

they would then find in the image an adequate representation of the original, and thus be led to the truth.

Or is he going to follow the inverted order, not allowing himself to be strictly determined by the proportions of the original, but yielding here and there to the accidental limitations of the sensory perspective from which his discourses are to be first understood? In this case, he will then not reproduce, but rather *produce* an artificial construction (φάντασμα) of his own, achieving by some "original theory" an illusion of verisimilitude for those temporarily restricted to an unfavorable position. Should the listener ever be freed from this limitation, however, and gain a more favorable viewpoint, he would behold a monstrosity, incapable of leading anyone to the truth. Such is the analogy.

There is one essential point of difference between the two cases. Those who gaze up at the frieze, of course, are provided with *other means* of access to the original, say the human face. They can also study books of anatomy, etc. Hence in this case the sculptor's adjustment to an accidental limitation of perspective does no harm, and is a legitimate part of his art. But if the sculptor's frieze were the *only* means of purifying the dim conception of the human face which all men gain from the contacts of daily life, then his responsibility would be greater, and his pandering to a necessary limitation of perspective inexcusable, for it would mean obstructing the *only* path to a more adequate vision, riveting the prisoners to their chains.

This is the unique position of philosophical discourse. It is the *only* medium leading to a more correct insight into the nature of being, as it is the *only* means through which we may be freed from the relativistic limitations of sense. The sophist, who inverts the natural order, allowing his discourse to be determined not by the *exact* proportions as he actually understands them to be but rather by the subjective restrictions of some private sensuous perspective, filling the libraries with novel and original theories, constructed in such a way as to seem plausible to his contemporaries, is heaping obstacles in the only path to greater understanding, permanently barring the only road to truth. He *seems* just like a philosopher. He talks just like a philosopher. In fact we may say that he appears even more like a philosopher than the philosopher himself. There is only this slight difference between the two.

They are proceeding in *opposite* directions. The one is a reproducer, submitting to his archetype, the maker of a replica (εἰκών), careless of how it may *seem* from this or that restricted point of view. The other is a *producer*, an original fabricator, submitting to the subjective sensory bias of his audience, the maker of an idol (εἴδωλον), and careless of the truth. To his unfavorably situated audience, far distant from reality, his novel theories and original speculations seem marked with the very earmark of truth. They *seem* to be just what reality has seemed to them all along. Hence he is just their idea of a philosopher. In reality, his constructions are distorted monstrosities, and his art is a perversion (τέχνη φανταστική) of the true mimetic art (τέχνη εἰκαστική). [45]

3. THE DIFFICULTY — HOW CAN THAT WHICH IS NOT BE?
(236 D 9–242 B 10)

This definition of the sophist as a subjective deceiver, however, plunges us at once into serious difficulty. The deceptive constructions of the sophist only *seem* to be without really being. Hence we ourselves seem to be asserting the being of non-being, that very *logos* against which the great Parmenides was constantly warning us. Surely he was right concerning that which is not at all in any sense.[46] This cannot be applied to any existent entity nor to anything of any sort.[47] Furthermore, nothing whatsoever can be attributed to it, such as unity or plurality in number. Hence since "non-existence in itself"[48] is nothing of any determinate sort, and has no attributes, it is "unthinkable, inexpressible, ineffable, and without reason."[49] But let us glance back at what we have just said. We ourselves have asserted that this unthinkable, inexpressible, etc.: (1) *is;* (2) is something determinate — i.e. unthinkable, etc.; (3) is singular in number. We are, therefore, involved in a certain difficulty concerning non-being, the exploitation of which is the very fountainhead of sophistry.

We have defined the sophist as the maker of false, subjective idols. But being and truth are convertible. What is is true, and what is true is. Falsity is the opposite of truth. Hence the false is nonexistent. How then can we refer without contradiction to a "false idol," or to the sophist as a *real* falsifier? We cannot think without

45 *Soph.*, 236 C 7.
46 παντάπασι μηδέν: *Soph.*, 237 E 2.
47 *Soph.*, 237 C 10–D 4.
48 τὸ μὴ ὂν αὐτὸ καθ' αὑτό: *Soph.*, 238 C 9.
49 *Soph.*, 238 C 10.

thinking something. Surely thinking and discourse are a mode of being. But the sophist, thinking his false opinions, is thinking things that are not. Surely this is impossible. Non-being cannot be. To assert such a proposition is utterly absurd and impossible. This is no mere captious objection, nor is it a purely "logical" question to be answered by distinguishing different *logical* senses of "the logical copula" is.[50]

It involves the real sense of the word "is," being itself, which belongs to every thought, every essence, every particular, every entity of any type or mode whatsoever. Unless we can show clearly and intelligibly, first, that non-being can somehow be; and second, that non-being can somehow attach to discourse, we cannot maintain our definition of the sophist.[51] Thus we are plunged into a fundamental discussion of the transcendental term truth.[52] This discussion has two divisions. The first, or ontological division (A), summarizing the dialectic of the *Parmenides*, shows that a legitimate meaning can be given to "negation," or to non-being in things. The second, or logical division (B) shows, on the basis of this, that a legitimate meaning can be given to non-being in discourse (i.e. the assertion of what is other *as* the same, not the assertion of that which is not absolutely). Both together show that false opinion may be *asserted* to exist without involving a contradiction, when the complex relational structure of discourse is understood. Both together, therefore, enable us to defend our definition of the sophist as a subjectivist.

4. The Defense of the Definition (242 B 10–264 B 9)

A. ONTOLOGICAL NON-BEING (242 B 10–261 B 5)

I. *A Critique of Prevalent Ontological Views (242 B 10–253)*

Plato begins the discussion with a consideration of the prevailing views. These fall into two groups: (1) those which take the meaning of being for granted, devoting their attention primarily to the many beings — "how many and what sort they are"; [53] and (2) those which

---

[50] According to Professor A. E. Taylor, "the main interest of the *Sophistes* is logical," *Plato, The Man and His Work* (New York: Dial Press, 1927), p. 374, and "the main result of the whole dialogue" is "to distinguish the use of 'is' as the logical *copula*, or sign of assertion, from the existential sense of 'is' " (p. 392).

[51] Like the modern positivists we shall be forced to hold that truth is the same as necessary truth, and that falsity is the same as the contradictory, i.e., nothing at all.

[52] Hence this passage goes beyond the *Parmenides* which restricts itself to being.

[53] *Soph.*, 242 C 6. This proceeds to 245 E 6.

differ concerning the nature of being itself.[54] He finds that past philosophical thought has differed not so much with respect to being itself as to how many beings there are.

Thus, as in modern times, there is the clear-cut issue between the pluralists, who maintain that there are two, or three, or more principles,[55] and the Eleatic monists, who maintain that "all things are really one." [56] In addition, there are those who try to combine monism with pluralism, some, like Heraclitus, holding that "being is joined together in its very separation," [57] and others, like Empedocles, holding that it is sometimes one and friendly and sometimes, many and at variance with itself.[58] But since these last conceive of unity only as the result of many beings mingling with one another, they may be classed with the pluralists, and may be seen to fall under the same fundamental criticism.

a. *Critique of pluralism* (*243 D 6–244 B 6*). Let us then turn to the pluralists who say that all things are more than one,[59] choosing the simplest case of *two* as an example. All things, they will say, "are two." What then is this "are," which so strangely intrudes upon their argument? What is this being, which is apparently asserted of each, as well as of both? We must be exact. Does it coincide with both, or only with one? There are only three possibilities: (1) being is a *third* thing extraneous to the two, in which case we shall not only have difficulty in understanding their assertion that only two "are," instead of three, but in understanding how the two can be at all, since they themselves are distinct from being; or (2) being will coincide with only *one* of the two, in which case the other will not exist at all, and their dualism will be reduced to monism; or (3) being will coincide with both,[60] in which case the two will tend to disappear into the one being which they both *are*.[61]

---

[54] *Soph.*, 246 A 5. This proceeds to 251 A 3.
[55] *Soph.*, 242 C 8–D 4.
[56] *Soph.*, 242 D 4–6.
[57] *Soph.*, 242 E 2–3.
[58] *Soph.*, 242 E 4–7.
[59] *Soph.*, 243 D 6 ff.
[60] Professor Cornford, in his commentary *Plato's Theory of Knowledge* (pp. 219–220), omits alternative 1. Hence he has to interpret being as a third form, in which the two "partake." But then whatever *distinguished* the one from the other would not exist. Plato surely rules out this impossible view at *Soph.*, 243 E 2–3. Being is not a third entity over and above the two.
[61] *Soph.*, 244 A 1–2.

Thus the pluralistic way of thought, as soon as it tries to deal with being, is reduced necessarily to monism. Being either lies outside the many, and *they* will not exist at all, or being coincides with one of the many, and *the rest* will not exist at all, or being coincides with them all, and *they* are all absorbed into its unity. As Aristotle pointed out, these difficulties cannot be avoided if being is regarded merely as a *summum genus*.[62] In no one of these three possibilities can pluralism avoid monism, nor does there seem to be any other possibility for pluralism, which must think of being as one single thing or genus among many. Such pluralism leads to its contrary, monism. Let us then examine the monistic view.

b. Critique of monism (244 B 6–245 E 6). There are those who follow Parmenides in saying that "the one only is." But they also fall into insoluble difficulty as soon as they are questioned about the "is." As we have already noted, in that which is really one, the "one" and the "is" coincide.[63] "One" and "is" are then merely two names signifying the same.[64] But if nothing other than this two-named one exists, how are we to account for the *two* names? Furthermore even the existence of *one* name is inconsistent with monism. Here there are two possibilities: (1) the name is *other* than the thing, and we will then have two entities not one; or (2) the name is the same as the thing of which it is the name, and we are confronted with only two impossible alternatives: (a) the name is *of* nothing, in which case it will not be a name; or (b) the name is of something, namely itself, and "the one" will be both the name of one and the one *of* which this is the name, i.e. two.

The second set of difficulties is a development of the basic criticism of Parmenides, embodied in the first hypothesis of the dialogue of that name.[65] If the one alone exists, is it or is it not whole or complete? If we allow ourselves to use Parmenides' unfortunate analogy of the well-rounded sphere, we must suppose that the one is whole. But that which is whole has parts, and, therefore, is not strictly one.[66] One and whole are, therefore, opposed notions, and we must choose whether we are to think of being as a whole, and not one in the strict

---

[62] Cf. *Meta.*, 998 B 22 ff., and 1059 B 22 ff.
[63] Cf. *supra*, pp. 229–230.
[64] *Soph.*, 244 C 1–2. This is of course the existent-one described in Hyp. I of the *Parmenides*.
[65] Cf. *supra*, pp. 220–222.
[66] τὸ ἓν αὐτό: *Soph.*, 245 A 6.

sense, or as one in the strict sense, and not whole. But each alternative involves us in contradictions. The first is incompatible with monism. In this case, being will be a many, having unity only in some respect. The second makes being strictly one, and therefore not complete. Here two alternatives confront us.

Either (a) the *complete* whole exists or (b) it does not exist at all.[67] If the whole exists (a), then it will follow that being will lack something of itself, being will be non-being. Also the one, which alone is, will be more than one, since being and whole will each have received a different nature. If the whole does not exist at all (b), then the first consequence above will follow — that is, being will lack something of itself; and also being will never have come into existence, since whatever comes into existence becomes a whole. Also it will follow that being will then have no quantity, for any quantity, however small, is the whole of that quantity. Hence the monistic view that being is only one seems subject to objections as grave as those confronting the pluralistic view that being is two or more. Let us then turn to those "who speak otherwise," not merely taking being for granted as obvious, but really trying to define this fundamental concept.[68]

c. Criticism of materialism (245 E 6–248 A 4). Those who have attempted to define being fall into two groups who carry on a sort of battle of the giants with each other through the ages. The first group consists of those who judge by the sense of touch, and who maintain that "body and being are the same." [69] But they must admit that there is such a thing as a mortal animal, and that this is a living body. Hence they must admit the existence of soul or the source of life which makes a body live. Furthermore they, like the rest of us, say that one soul is just, another unjust, one wise, another foolish, and that the soul becomes just or unjust by the presence or absence of justice in it. But that which is capable of entering into a thing or departing from it exists. Now the critical question arises. Are these things which enter into the soul, and the soul into which they enter, visible and tangible?

The materialists may insist that the soul has a kind of body, but all except the violent extremists would agree that wisdom and the other qualities are neither visible nor tangible.[70] If such things exist,

[67] These are stated at *Soph.*, 245 C 2 (a) and 245 C 11 (b).
[68] *Soph.*, 245 E 8–246 A 5.
[69] *Soph.*, 246 A 1.   [70] *Soph.*, 247 B 7–C 2.

they will be forced to broaden their definition of being, and to seek "what that is which enters into the nature of the incorporeal as well as the corporeal, and with regard to which they say that both are." [71] They may then be led to see that while body has the capacity to be acted upon, the source of life has the capacity to act upon that body, as well as the capacity to be acted upon by justice, wisdom, etc., which act upon it. They may then understand that their original definition included only the lesser half of the truth, and that being involves not only body, that which has the capacity to be acted upon, but also that which has the capacity of acting. [72] But before we examine this more adequate definition of being to which the critique of materialism leads, we must turn to the idealists, who maintain the opposite view.

   d. Criticism of idealism (248 A 4–253). The idealists distinguish between being and becoming. [73] According to them, we partake of becoming by the body through perception, and we partake of being by the soul through thought. This is the language of the *Phaedo*, [74] and it is most reasonable to suppose that by the phrase, "friends of the forms," [75] Plato is referring to students in the Academy, who, even during his lifetime, pushed the opposition between being and generation to exaggerated extremes. [76] But let us ask them about this participation. [77] What is this? Here is a most critical question, since the idealist maintains not only that we partake of becoming by the body, and of being by the soul, but that the whole realm of becoming gains being only by somehow participating in stable form. What then is meant by participation? Plato now, in the person of the Eleatic stranger, clearly answers this question.

   It is precisely that causal interaction of which we were just speaking. [78] Participation is "an active or a passive condition arising from things coming together in relation to one another ultimately derived

---

[71] *Soph.*, 247 D 2–4.
[72] *Soph.*, 247 D 8–E 4.
[73] *Soph.*, 248 A 7–9.
[74] Cf. *Phaedo*, 79 a ff., for the contrast between the body, which is most like the mortal, the destructible, and what is never the same; and the soul, which is most like the immortal, the indestructible, and what is always the same. Also, 65 ff., for the word κοινωνεῖν. For οὐσία cf., 65 d 13.
[75] *Soph.*, 248 A 4.
[76] Cf. Cornford, *Plato's Theory of Knowledge*, pp. 242–245.
[77] τὸ κοινωνεῖν: *Soph.*, 248 B 2.
[78] *Soph.*, 248 B 3.

from a certain potency." [79] As we have been told in the *Theaetetus*,[80] the agent which is able to act and the patient which is able to be acted upon come together in a single motion *between* the two. What Plato tells us *now* is that this is what is really meant by participation. That which acts on another, gives to this other something of its being. Hence by being acted upon, this other comes to partake of being. Even the capacity to be acted upon to the slightest degree is to be in some manner. The ability to act on everything else would seem to be in the highest degree.

But the idealists will not agree to this. They wish to restrict action and passion to the realm of generation, excluding it altogether from being, which they hold to be fixed and immovable, though of course they admit that it can be known. But how can they admit this? Here is an inconsistency in their dualistic view, for surely knowing is some sort of action, and being known some sort of being acted upon. A fixed and immobile being which has no capacity either to act or to be acted upon in any way certainly cannot be known.[81] Furthermore can we suppose that "what exists completely in every way" [82] itself has no insight? In view of what the idealists themselves say about that which truly is, this would be a shocking admission. But if perfect being is to know, and therefore to act, it must also be living and possessed of a source of life. Plato now sees that in addition to a material cause and a formal cause, the structure of reality also demands action or what was later called an efficient cause. This greater emphasis on the moving cause distinguishes the "later" dialogues from the "earlier." [83] Hence we must dismiss the formalist view of being as

---

[79] πάθημα ἢ ποίημα ἐκ δυνάμεώς τινος ἀπο τῶν πρὸς ἄλληλα συνιόντων γιγνόμενον. *Soph.*, 248 B 5–6. Cf. *Theaet.*, 156 A 2–157 C 3. Since the *Phaedo*, Plato's theory of causation has been dynamized. Becoming and being are not two separate realms. Becoming is both the being acted on of matter (πάθημα) and the action of an efficient cause (ποίημα). Such action is now clearly seen to explain the phenomena of formal causation (κοινωνεῖν). It is out of such considerations as these that Aristotle's theory of the union of cause and effect in a single κίνησις must have been developed. Cf. *Phys.*, III, ch. 3. I have discussed the relation of this view to modern doctrines of causation in *Phil. Rev.* (January 1941).

[80] *Theaet.*, 157 A 5–6.

[81] Cf. the objection to the separated ideas in the *Parmenides*, 130 E–135: also the emphasis in Hyp. V that the non-existent forms are knowable. Cf. *supra*, p. 232.

[82] *Soph.*, 248 E 7–8.

[83] Cf. *Phaedrus*, 245 C 5 ff., where the soul is first clearly defined as that which moves itself, *Phil.*, 26 E ff., where in addition to form (πέρας) and matter (ἄπειρον) another universal cause of the mixture of the two is recognized, τὸ ποιοῦν (27 A 5°) and

static, lifeless form, together with the materialistic view that being is fluid or passive matter, and return to the less one-sided definition already suggested.

II. *The Definition of Being Arising from This Criticism*

Plato has a way of expressing his most fundamental insights as casual suggestions — no doubt because of the maieutic purpose of the dialogues. The definition which emerges from the preceding critique of ontological views is such an undeveloped suggestion. Nevertheless, since it is the only definition of this basic term to be found in the writings of Plato, we must try to reflect upon its meaning. Being, he says, is power or potency (δύναμις).[84] Let us see how this dynamic conception of being can meet the criticisms urged against the four other static views we have considered.

First, if being is power, it is not a number of separate, unrelated things.[85] If so, we cannot maintain that they all are. Power is common to the most disparate things, to that which is wholly unformed and possesses merely the capacity to be acted upon, as well as to that which is wholly active and possesses the power to act upon everything else. Second, being is not one thing nor a whole of many parts. If so, only one thing would be. But power is not one. The power to act involves the power to be acted on, which may be possessed in various degrees. Nor does being in the fullest sense, purely active power, have to be conceived as a whole of parts. It may have many effects, but may itself be purely one. Third, being is not exclusively vague and passive, like "body." If so, the forms, like life, which act upon body to determine it, and the further forms, like justice and wisdom, which act upon life and determine it, would not be. Fourth, being is not exclusively determinate and active. If so, there would be no motion and change, and the processes of life and of thought would not be.

Finally in the light of this conception, participation need not be viewed statically as a mixing of two disparate things with one another.

τὸ δημιουργοῦν (27 B 1), and *Tim.*, 28 C 2–3, where it is stated that "all that becomes must become by some cause" and where the efficient cause of the world of becoming is referred to as ὁ δημιουργός (28 A 6), ὁ ποιητής, and ὁ πατήρ (28 C 3). Cf. also *Laws*, X, where the existence of God is proved by showing the necessity of a first moving cause: ἀρχὴν ἄρα κινήσεων πασῶν καὶ πρώτην κ.τ.λ. (895 B 3).

[84] *Soph.*, 247 E 3–4.

[85] As Aristotle points out, δύναμις is always πρός τι: *Meta.*, 1021 A 26 ff.

It may be conceived dynamically as some active or passive result of the causal interaction of agent and patient. Each thing is the result of some power causally bestowed upon it by some active agency. Its own existence consists in the exercise of passive or active power. Thus this definition enables us to arrive at the conception of being as a hierarchy of causal entities, ranging between that which is wholly passive and responding to all the rest, to that which is wholly active and dominating all the rest.

While this conception certainly represents an advance over the static views of the past, including those defended in certain of Plato's earlier dialogues where, as Aristotle remarks,[86] the efficient cause is not adequately distinguished from the formal, it is nevertheless subject to at least two important defects, which emerge with greater clarity in the subsequent history of Platonism. In the first place, while action is certainly close to being, and follows upon being, there is a distinction between the two. This is indicated in Plato's own language, for he cannot avoid saying there is something which acts, or something to which the action belongs.[87] This is no doubt one of the reasons why Plato himself speaks very cautiously about his suggestion as a sort of stopgap until something better may be offered.[88] In his later followers, who were less cautious, it led to a certain voluntarism or emanationism which made the first link in the chain dependent upon the other links, and, in general, the cause dependent upon the effect.

In the second place, Plato thinks of active agency exclusively in terms of motion ($\kappa \acute{\iota} \nu \eta \sigma \iota s$),[89] speaking of life and even thought as motions. That which moves or influences another must thus itself be moving. This, of course, leads to the conception of a first cause such as soul or life which is self-*moving*, a contradictory notion which mars much of the Platonic psychology and metaphysics. These difficulties can be avoided only by the Aristotelian distinction between $\kappa \acute{\iota} \nu \eta \sigma \iota s$, the imperfect exercise of becoming actual, and $\acute{\epsilon} \nu \acute{\epsilon} \rho \gamma \epsilon \iota \alpha$, the pure exercise of actuality without change.[90] In spite of these fundamental defects, Plato's dynamic ontology is a brilliant and fertile suggestion, enabling him to reach many sound and important con-

[86] *Meta.*, I, 991 B 3.
[87] *Soph.*, 247 D 8.
[88] *Soph.*, 247 E. Cf. 249 E. Cf. Cornford, *Plato's Theory of Knowledge*, pp. 238–239.
[89] *Soph.*, 248 E 6. Cf. 249 B 5–6.
[90] Cf. *Meta.*, IX, 1048 B 18 ff., and *De An.*, I, ch. 3, for a critique of Plato.

clusions, as we shall see if we examine summarily the succeeding applications to current philosophy.

Neither materialism, which regards only that which is passive, indeterminate, and capable of being acted upon, nor formalism, which regards only that which is determinate and capable of acting, is able to arrive at the true notion of being, which is "a third something," embracing both motion and rest, itself neither resting nor moving.[91] But rest is rest and motion is motion. How then can one thing be two? If we look about us, we at least see in countless instances *that* this is true. Each actual thing is composite, not only man, for example, but also all the colours, shapes, sizes, vices, and virtues we attribute to him. Each single thing, which we regard as one, participates in many as a result of its acting and being acted upon. Logical "atomists," who insist that we cannot say that man is good, but only that man is man, and good is good, really eliminate all power (δύναμις) from the world, and at the same time make discourse impossible. All discourse consists in "calling something by the name of another, because of its participation in the effect of this other." [92] The logical atomists, therefore, like Antisthenes,[93] are refuted by their own discourse which attributes "being," "separation," and many other terms to whatever they may be talking about.

On the other hand, the partisans of the flux, who insist that all things have the power of participating in one another, also eliminate determinate power, and hence make discourse impossible. The various terms of discourse must be distinct. We cannot suppose, for example, that rest is wholly motion, and motion is wholly rest. Knowledge is impossible under either assumption. The only remaining possibility is that certain things act upon certain others, which come to participate in them in certain determinate ways. This is verified by a brief examination of the structure of the various arts. Each art concerns itself with a certain kind of thing, say letters or musical sounds. In each case, the practical scientist must know how the different elements interact with one another to cause certain results. Each art does this for a restricted subject matter. What science devotes itself to the world as a whole, attempting to determine, in the case of the supreme genera of things, which interacts with which, and which is separate from the rest? This is the greatest of all the sciences, which belongs

[91] *Soph.*, 250 B–C.   [92] *Soph.*, 252 B.
[93] Cf. Cornford, *Plato's Theory of Knowledge*, p. 254.

to free men, and in looking for the sophist, we have unwittingly stumbled upon the philosopher.[94]

The two are most closely allied, for the one is, indeed, an imitation of the other. We can now begin to see how this is so. All the things about us partake of existence, through having had *being* bestowed upon them. The philosopher, "always devoting himself to the concept of being by reason," [95] is constantly led upwards from that which is passive and indeterminate to that which is active and determinate, until he arrives at the ultimate cause or source. The sophist, on the other hand, moves in a contrary direction, "running away into the shadow of non-being" [96] — the passive and indeterminate, which is not itself stable and determinate, but only *able to be*. We ourselves, placed between the two, find it difficult to discern either the sophist or the philosopher, and are susceptible to the influence of both in both directions. But before we study further the nature of this inversion, we must follow Plato in his examination of the widest and most important kinds. If we can briefly note how some of them mingle, while others remain separate, we shall perhaps gain a clearer notion of that non-being which is the source of all falsity, deception, and sophistry itself.

III. The Mingling of the Genera and Dialectic (253–261 B 5)

The kinds of genera (γένη), which Plato here considers, are not "concepts" [97] but the forms of real things. Sensible things for example really move. The forms or structures of these do not move. Let us take these two forms of rest and motion, comprising the objects of knowledge and the objects of sense, and see how they are related. First of all, we can see that each has a nature of its own, which does not mingle with the other.[98] Rest cannot itself be motion, nor can motion itself be rest. Each is only what it is, through its own nature.

But in addition to the essential nature which each thing is, there

---

[94] *Soph.*, 253 C 8–9.
[95] *Soph.*, 254 A 8–9.
[96] *Soph.*, 254 A 4.
[97] Cf. N. Hartmann, *Platos Logik des Seins* (Giessen: A. Töpelmann, 1909), pp. 112 ff. This otherwise illuminating discussion is marred by his interpretation of γένος as *Grundbegriff*, pp. 125–126. The γένη are the forms of real things. If this is ignored, we miss the point of the transition to the logical point of view at *Soph.*, 259 E 4. *Here* we are still in the field of ontology.
[98] *Soph.*, 254 D 7–8.

are other "kinds," in which each thing participates. The most important feature of the passage before us [99] is its clear indication of these super-universal, or "transcendental" terms, as they were later called. Thus, though motion and rest are universal terms which may attach to an indefinite number of individual moving or resting things, they are mutually exclusive of one another. Motion cannot be rest, nor rest motion. Nevertheless, since both of them *are*,[100] they must both participate in being, which is, therefore, a third *transcendental* kind, more universal than any ordinary universal. If being were to be motion, then rest, which is opposed to motion, could not be. But since both rest and motion *are*, being is a third *transcendental* in which both participate as a result of some causal action. Are there any more such transcendental genera? Plato calls attention to two more, the same (ταὐτόν) and the other (ἕτερον).

Motion is certainly the same as itself. So is rest. But motion is not *essentially* sameness, for it is other than rest, and hence also partakes of otherness. Hence when we say "motion is the same" we mean only that it *partakes of* sameness, not that it is the same as the same. Motion must really partake of sameness in order to be at all.[101]

But while motion partakes of the same, it must also partake of the other in order to be what it is, for it cannot be, without being other than rest. So motion is other. Here again, however, we mean no mere identity. Motion is not the same as otherness, or it would be other than itself, which is impossible. Nevertheless motion is other, in the sense that it must *participate* in otherness in order to be.[102] The same is true of rest.

Thus in the case of the broadest universals, motion and rest, we have been able to see that they must participate in three modes of being which are broader still, which are so broad in fact that any existent entity whatsoever must participate in them. Any entity first of all must, like motion and rest, be a certain essential nature. But in addition, if it is to be, it must participate in being, in sameness with itself,[103] and in difference from other essential natures.[104] Furthermore these transcendental terms, while never separate from one another, are distinct in nature. *Being* does not coincide with *same*, for if this were so, we could not assert that being and rest are, without asserting that they are the same.[105] Furthermore, *being* does not coincide with *other than*, for *other than* is relative to some other. Being, however, is wholly in itself and not relative, for if we exclude being, the only "thing" to which it could be relative would be nothing. Since this "opposite" of being does not exist at all, being is not relative to anything, and hence is sharply distinct from otherness.[106]

IV. *Ontological Otherness (257 B 1–261 B 5)*

The chief defect of Plato's account lies in his unfortunate choice of the *logical* relations, *the same as*, and *other than*, rather than the transcendental "one" on which they are founded. It is true that any entity, *in relation to the mind*, is the same as itself, and other than others, but in itself it is one. This leads him in the two preceding arguments to speak as though being could be without being the same (which is true), without being other (which is true), and finally perhaps without being one, on which these two logical relations are founded (which is false). He also overly emphasizes the fact that otherness is a true transcendental term, dispersed through all, as though this were not true of the same.[107] But being no more excludes one (and therefore sameness in relation to the mind) than it excludes otherness. As Aristotle was later to point out, "in a sense unity means the same as being," [108] and *same* and *other* are derivative from one.[109] This confusion of logic with ontology is, however, overcome in the discussion of "otherness," where the dialogue reaches a pinnacle of perspicacity, and ontological insights of the greatest importance are developed with clarity and precision.

Since all entities whatsoever either are being or partake of it, and also partake of being other than the rest, all entities both are and are not. Each existent entity must be. Also, since being is broken up into many beings, each with a distinct essential nature, each entity must be other than the rest. Each is what it is, and each is not what the others are. Hence all things both are and are not.[110] This transcendental not-being, however, which permeates all being, is not absolute nothing at all, the contradictory of being. On the contrary, it is perfectly compatible with every finite being as well as with being itself.

---

105 *Soph.*, 255 B 8–C 3.   106 *Soph.*, 255 C 8–D 8.
107 *Soph.*, 255 E 3–4.   108 *Meta.*, 1054 A 13.
109 *Meta.*, 1054 B 21.   110 *Soph.*, 256 E 2–3.

Each finite entity, since it is only being of a certain, limited sort, is not being itself. Hence it is not (being). Also it is not something else, limited in some other way. Hence the essence of any finite thing demands that it not be. In the case of being itself, from which the being of finite things must be derived,[111] it is simply itself. Its very essence is to be. It has no otherness in its essence. Nevertheless, since the other finite beings are essentially not it, it is extraneously or accidentally not each of them nor all of them. We have thus passed beyond the prohibition of Parmenides, and have shown that not-beings *are*, in a perfectly legitimate and even necessary sense.

Sophistry takes its root in a neglect of these transcendental terms and distinctions. It is expressed both in those endless, eristic quibbles concerning the sameness of difference, the difference of what is the same, and the non-being of what is not, as well as in that metaphysical indifference, which casts the whole arduous work of ontology aside as verbal quibbling, though perhaps rather in the latter than in the former, when the former is carried on with any minimum of serious-ness. Both these attitudes have their root in a carelessness about the most general and fundamental aspects of reality which are expressed by those most ubiquitous and opaque words, such as "is," "not," "one," and "other," so deeply embedded in the very structure of all meaningful discourse. It is to discourse that we must now turn, discourse, that is, in the broad sense, including both thought and the verbal expression of thought, in order to examine the nature of that peculiar otherness of falsehood, which constitutes the essence of the sophist, or inverted man.

B. LOGICAL NON-BEING (261 B 5–264 B 9)

So far, the discussion has been restricted to being itself, apart from logical discourse. We have been forced to abandon the simple view of being as a single entity, which simply is, or as a set of such deter-minate entities incapable of acting upon one another. In its place, we have been led to substitute the dynamic conception of being as cause or power. Perfect being is not a static "sphere" as Parmenides imagined. It must rather be conceived as perfect power, capable of acting upon everything else. This action is, therefore, participated in by all those imperfect beings whose limited nature makes them other

---

[111] *Rep.*, 509 B 6.

than perfect action and restricts them to the passive capacity of being acted upon, or to act only in certain determinate ways.

These restricted beings are not only acted upon by being itself, and thus enabled to be in various limited ways, but they are also acted upon by one another, and thus participate in each other, depending not only upon being and other transcendental agencies, but also upon each other in various ways which it is the business of the practical arts and sciences to understand and to exploit. If all things were simply one, there would be no such causal dependence of one thing on another. We need only to open our eyes, however, to see that all things are many. While each thing shares in existence, each thing itself is other than existence. It is, and it is not. This not-being permeates all things and even attaches, at least in an accidental sense, to perfect being itself, which *is not* all the other imperfect beings.

But our task is not yet finished. We may have established the being of non-being, in the things of the world. But how about the world of discourse (λόγος)? We may probably grant that it is not nothing at all. Unless we are willing to identify thought with being itself, we will grant that it is one limited kind of thing among others in the world. If so, we will agree that, like other finite things, it is both other than being, and yet partakes of being. Is this enough to enable us to understand the difference between true and false discourse? Can we simply say that so far as it is, discourse is true, but that so far as it is limited and distinct from others, it is false?

We cannot say this, for if so, any existent thing, like a man or a tree, would be partly true and partly false, which is absurd. Furthermore, all discourse whatsoever, so far as it actually occurred, would be partly true and partly false, which would make it impossible to distinguish between discourse that is true, i.e. wholly true, and discourse that is false. It is evident, then, that we have not yet justified our definition of the sophist as a falsifier, for he may reply first that his discourse, while not perfectly existent, is perhaps as existent as any other finite mode of existence, and second that his discourse, while a mixture of being and non-being, of true and false, is, in this respect, no whit different from any other discourse. We must then examine the *peculiar* nature of discourse in order to see if we cannot find in it still a third sort of non-being, not that absolute nothing which does not even share in being, nor merely that non-being which partakes of being, but some mode of the latter which shares in a certain further privation which will enable us to grasp the falsity of the sophist.

I. *The Nature of Discourse* (*261 B 5–263 B 2*)

First of all, it is important to notice that discourse is not only a certain kind of being (an existent non-being), but also is *about* being. If it is not *about* something, it is impossible.[112] Plato calls this *relational* aspect of discourse, a quality.[113] Strictly speaking it is not a quality but a *relation*. Discourse is a peculiar sort of being *related to* the being we have so far described. Discourse is made up of names, and, as we have already seen, each name is the name *of* something.[114] Each existent entity, from the most perfect which is able to act upon everything down to the least perfect which is only able to be acted upon, may be relatively represented in discourse by a name or a definition.

But just as being as a whole is not made up of fixed entities standing alone in perfect independence, so discourse is not made up of separate names like "lion," "stag," or "horse" uttered in succession.[115] Real beings are dependent on one another, or participate in one another, because of their causal interaction. This causal interaction is represented in discourse by the active words, or verbs, such as "walks," "runs," "sleeps." These are either active or passive, and thus represent the action of one thing on another, or the being acted upon of one thing by another. Neither names alone nor verbs alone are sufficient to make up discourse, for being is power, and discourse represents being. But the combination ($\sigma\upsilon\mu\pi\lambda o\kappa\acute{\eta}$) of a noun and a verb is sufficient to provide an elementary unit of discourse such as "man learns," [116] since the being of things consists in their action or inaction with reference to one another.[117] Hence discourse is either a combining of what is really combined or a separating of what is really separate. When we say "man learns" we combine. When we negate the affirmation and say "man does not learn" we separate. All discourse is thus a mirroring of the action of things upon one another,

---

[112] λόγον ἀναγκαῖον, ὅτανπερ ᾖ, τινὸς εἶναι λόγον, μὴ δὲ τινὸς ἀδύνατον: *Soph.*, 262 E 5–6.

[113] *Soph.*, 262 E 8: ποιόν τινα αὐτὸν εἶναι δεῖ.

[114] *Soph.*, 244 D 3 ff.

[115] *Soph.*, 262 A 9 ff.

[116] *Soph.*, 262 C 9.

[117] *Soph.*, 262 C 3: πρᾶξις; ἀπραξία.

or the results of such action, in various complex combinations and divisions.[118]

II. The Meaning of Truth and Falsity (263 B 2–263 D 6)

All thought, whether true or false, is a certain kind of being, and, therefore, of action, distinct from what we may call *real* being. Hence it is not being itself, but a certain mode of being other than *real* being. It is that being which grasps or apprehends all being including itself. Unless what is represented by the so-called subject and predicate of discourse is really apprehended, there can be no discourse at all.[119] For instance, if I assert "Theaetetus flies," I must know who Theaetetus is, and what flying is. Otherwise I cannot even be mistaken. The elements of discourse (noun and verb) are neither true nor false. They are simply apprehended.[120] Truth and falsity belong not to these elements but rather to the combinations or separations of these elements which are the simplest units of discourse.[121] What then is false discourse?

Like all finite being it is a "mixture of being and non-being," far from nothing. *In the mind*, falsity is a real combination of noun and verb, in the simplest case. Furthermore there is something in reality corresponding to both noun and verb. There is such a thing as Theaetetus. There is such a thing as flying. What is missing in reality is the combination of the two. This is only in the mind.[122] But mind is essentially *of* something, a *relation to being*. Hence this combination is in the mind *as though* [123] it were in things. This is the essence of falsity, to combine two real concepts of two real things in the mind *as* being really combined, when this is not the case. True discourse is the opposite of this, to combine two real concepts of two real things in the mind *as* being really combined, when this is the case.[124]

If we grasp the whole of this complex structure, we can answer the ontological objections of the sophist. False discourse is not nothing.

---

[118] Plato mentions only *combination*. This, however, includes division, which is a kind of combination. Cf. *De An.*, 430 A 34.

[119] *Soph.*, 263 C 9–11.

[120] *Soph.*, 263 D 1–4. It is only the σύνθεσις ἔκ τε ῥημάτων γιγνομένη καὶ ὀνομάτων that becomes true or false λόγος. This synthetic view is already foreshadowed in the suggestion of the *Theaetetus* that falsity is ἑτεροδοξία. Cf. *supra*, pp. 262–263.

[121] *Soph.*, 262 C 5–7.

[122] *Soph.*, 263 D 8.

[123] ὡς ὄντα: *Soph.*, 263 B 9.

[124] *Soph.*, 263 B 4–5: ὡς ἔστιν περὶ σοῦ.

It is not *about* nothing. It is about *two* real things that exist. These two things are other than one another and possess relative power (δύναμις). Unless this were so, no one would ever make a false judgment. But the two things may be incapable of interacting, or even if capable, they may not actually do so. Under these conditions, if we combine them in thought as though they really participated, saying "things other as the same, not being (together) as being, such a synthesis made up of verbs and nouns really and truly becomes false discourse." [125] Aristotle also says "falsehood always involves a synthesis" and he gives precisely the same definitions of truth and falsity as Plato.[126]

In these dialectical discussions of the *Sophist*, Plato is thus laying the foundations for the epistemology of classical and medieval thought: (1) the intentionality of thought; (2) the infallible intentionality of the simple essences; and (3) the fallible intentionality of synthetic or discursive reflection.[127] These basic insights were maintained until the advent of modern idealism and conceptualism.

Falsity, therefore, is not "saying the things that are not," as the sophist argues. This is impossible. It is not merely saying what is other than being. All saying is this.[128] It is saying what is other than being *as* being. It is founded on ontological otherness or dynamism. Without this, it would be impossible. Things really act upon one another and participate in one another. It is itself a mode of apprehensive action, which grasps this dynamic synthetic being of things. False thought is a misapprehension, which truly apprehends the disparate natures of two things, but falsely apprehends them in *combination* when not combined, or in *separation* when not separated.[129]

III. The Modes of Discourse (263 D 6–264 B 9)

Having considered truth and falsity in relation to the composite structure of being, we must now consider them in relation to the various apprehensive faculties of the soul. First of all, as we have noted, all discourse is *about* something concerning the simple nature of which it is impossible to be mistaken. Unless we possess such a faculty of apprehending the nature of being as it is, reasoning and

[125] *Soph.*, 263 D 1–D 4.
[126] Cf. *Meta.*, 1051 B 32 ff.
[127] Cf. Aquinas, *De Veritate*, Qu. I, art. 1–3.
[128] For it is always of being — cf. *Soph.*, 263 A 4–5.
[129] Aristotle, *De An.*, 430 A 33.

discourse would be impossible. This is the faculty of rational insight. Since this faculty, so far as it is actualized, cannot be mistaken, it is not mentioned at this point where attention is focussed on falsity. But it is defined in the *Phaedo* [130] as "the immaterial apprehension of things as they are in themselves by the soul in herself." If being simply existed, perfect in itself and one, there would be no possibility of error. By insight [131] we should either apprehend it infallibly or not at all, for rational insight cannot be mistaken.

But as we have seen, the being surrounding us is mixed with imperfection. It is causally dependent and manifold. Hence we cannot grasp it by a single, indivisible apprehension, but only piecemeal by a composite process of reasoning which passes from effect to cause, or from cause to effect. The faculty by which we pass from one thing to another is reasoning (διάνοια). [132] This faculty is in an intermediate position. On the one hand, it may lead to rational insight into the cause of an effect. In this case, the passage from one to the other loses its arbitrariness, and is seen to be necessary. We not only understand that S is P but we also arrive at an understanding of the reason which links the two together in one. Thus the motion of reasoning comes to rest in a culminating opinion. [133] But this is very seldom the case. Our rational faculty is too weak. We usually have only a very vague and inadequate knowledge of the nature of S and the nature of P.

In this case, we passively accept the connection of the two *from sense* without knowing the reason why. [134] But sense alone is incapable of revealing the nature of things as they really are. It reveals neither the real cause nor the real effect, but only the transitory results as they manage to affect some particular sense organ. Confronted with this confused jumble, we may grasp through insight that this is S and that is P, but the understanding, in passing from one to the other, may succeed in apprehending no real causal link other than the sensory togetherness of the two. They *seem* to belong together. Whether they belong together in reality we do not know. Like Theaetetus and "flying," they may be separate. In this case, the understanding either oscillates between the two possibilities of combination or separation,

[130] *Phaedo*, 66 E 1: αὐτῇ τῇ ψυχῇ θεατέον αὐτὰ τὰ πράγματα.
[131] νόησις.
[132] ὁ μὲν ἐντὸς τῆς ψυχῆς πρὸς αὐτὴν διάλογος ἄνευ φωνῆς γιγνόμενος: *Soph.*, 263 E 3.
[133] δόξα: *Soph.*, 264 B 1.
[134] *Soph.*, 264 A 4–5.

or arbitrarily follows sense or imagination in asserting or denying [135] that S seems to be P or does not so seem.

No matter how dogmatically such opinions may be held, if the causal link, or reason cannot be given, they are not pure opinions but only a mixture of opinion with sense which is truly indicated by the expressions "seeming" or "it seems." [136] Such mixed opinions, of course, may combine or separate things which in reality are not combined or separated. Hence they may be true or false. Indeed, even the pure opinions, which terminate "the inner silent conversation of the soul with herself," [137] may be false, if she is not at every step guided by pure insight, and unwittingly falls back upon sense or memory to establish some connection, rather than a clear apprehension of the causal link.

The discursive flow of thought, ever seeking the cause, in passing from one imperfect thing to another, may either flow silently within the soul, or may flow through the mouth with vocal utterance, called logos or speech, which materially mirrors every phase of "thought," just as thought immaterially mirrors every phase of active and passive being. Thus there is a word which expresses the concept of that perfect being in which everything participates, a word which expresses the concept of that impossible nothingness which is the opposite of being, and a vast array of nouns expressing the concepts of those finite beings which are imperfect in nature and hence only partake of being as well as of one another. Finally there are the active and passive words which express our concepts of the ways in which these act upon one another and suffer from one another.

These are the *elements* of verbal discourse (λόγος) which combines these together and separates them from one another as the things they signify are really combined and separated through causal interaction. When discourse combines or separates them not as they are really combined and separated but only as they seem to be combined and separated in the inchoate flux of sense and imagination, there is false opinion and false discourse.

---

[135] It is unfortunate that Plato never sharply distinguished the faculty of imagination, φαντασία, from sense, αἴσθησις. For him, sensation also is a kind of seeming. Cf. *Theaet.*, 152 B 11. Indeed, in the concrete, we never actually have a sensation without some admixture of both imagination and opinion. Hence it was easy for him to slur over imagination, and to think of it as a mere σύμμειξις αἰσθήσεως καὶ δόξης, *Soph.*, 264 B 2. Cf. Aristotle's critique in *De An.*, III, 424 A 24 ff.

[136] Aristotle, *De An.*, 424 B 1–3.   [137] *Soph.*, 264 A 8–B 1.

5. THE COMPLETION OF THE DEFINITION OF THE SOPHIST

(264 B 9–end)

Having now answered the ontological objections of sophistic philosophy and thus having justified our partial definition of the sophist as essentially a subjectivist, or a maker of bad likenesses of reality, we must return to our original task, the complete definition of the sophist. We are first reminded of the acquisitive traits in which he first appeared to a superficial examination.[138] Now, however, in view of our defense of the notion of falsity, he is firmly enclosed in the mimetic art which is a species of the making art — the making of imitations.[139] As we have already seen,[140] he is not, like God, the maker of *natural* likenesses such as shadows, dreams, and perceptions, but of artificial human likenesses — man-made dreams,[141] not in color, like the human painter, nor in bronze, like the sculptor, but also in discourse, the most plastic medium of all.[142]

Furthermore, according to our last division, he belongs in the phantom-making species of the copy-making art.[143] He is the maker of bad images which are not true likenesses but only seem alike to one unfavorably situated. We can now defend this definition of the sophist so far. But we shall not have *completed* it until we have "stripped him of all common qualities, and left him only his peculiar nature." [144] After all, there are many varieties of subjectivism or bad image making. To which type does the sophist belong?

He is what we should now call an "idealist" or subjectivist thinker, having his own *original* ideas of things. But we have not yet adequately distinguished him. After all, there are constructive thinkers in various fields who "have their own ideas" about *lesser* matters with which all men are not themselves necessarily concerned. These are matters which can be dealt with by some instrument other than the man himself. A false theory about the object of some such instrumental procedure will, of course, lead the whole procedure astray, but it need not affect the very substance of the man himself. There are other *more important* matters, however, such as good and evil, justice and injustice, which cannot be dealt with by any instrument,

---

138 *Soph.*, 265 A 7–8.
140 Cf. *supra*, pp. 279 ff.
142 Cf. *Soph.*, 234 B 5–C 2.
143 τὸ φανταστικόν: *Soph.*, 266 D 8–E; cf. *Soph.*, 236 C 7.
144 *Soph.*, 264 D 10 ff.

139 *Soph.*, 265 A 10–B 2.
141 *Soph.*, 266 D 7–9.

but which must be dealt with by the man.[145] For example, all men seek the good. All men are trying to possess it, or to produce the best possible imitation of it in their lives. There is no set of techniques or instruments to which we can safely assign the task of making human happiness. Each man must do something himself about making himself happy. It is clearly to this province that the sophist belongs. He is the subjective fabricator of theories about the most general and the most important things, which he himself and other men must imitate. He is *himself* the victim of his fabrications.

But here a new distinction arises. Those who seek after something and try to imitate it in their lives either really know what it is they are imitating, or they have only a vague sort of opinion about it. For instance, there are those who have no knowledge of justice or of virtue in general, but only a hazy opinion, and yet who try with the utmost eagerness in thought as well as in deed to make this seeming seem to exist in them.[146] We may distinguish this opinion-imitation [147] from that genuine variety which knows what it is trying to imitate.[148] Clearly it is the former spurious variety to which the sophist belongs. But does he really think that he knows, or does he suspect that he does not know? Here we face a further division.

Plato's answer seems at first surprising. As we have already been informed, the most abysmal and hopeless ignorance is the involuntary ignorance of him who does not know but thinks he knows.[149] Of all the modes of ignorance surely that of the sophist is the most formidable. Hence we should expect Plato to place him in this class. But such is not the case. If we bear in mind the essential dynamism which belongs to the process of reflection, as to every other phase of human life, we shall see that there is a type of ignorance which is even more destructive and terrible than this. Only those who have never really been subjected to the purifying process of refutation and who have never felt the slipperiness and instability of arguments can cling to their subjective opinions without a qualm. But the sophist is anything but simple-minded.[150] Through his experience in "the rough and tumble of debate he strongly suspects and fears that he does not know those things which before others he pretends to know." [151]

---

[145] *Soph.*, 267 A.
[147] δοξομιμητική.
[149] ἀμαθία: *Soph.*, 229 C 1–10.
[151] *Soph.*, 268 A 2–4.

[146] *Soph.*, 267 C 2–6.
[148] ἱστορική.
[150] εὐήθης.

Hence his ignorance is not merely a *passive state* into which he happens to have fallen, and from which he may be awakened by a purifying refutation. It is an *active tendency* moving towards that ignorance of which it is already dimly aware.

This deepest of all inversions, therefore, is not wholly involuntary, and Plato has come to see that the greatest evil is done ignorantly (ἀγνοῶν) *not* because of an excusable ignorance (δι' ἄγνοιαν).[152] Sophistic ignorance is an ignorance for which the sophist is himself responsible. Hence it can be corrected only by a complete "wheeling around of the whole soul," to make it move in the opposite direction.[153] This, of course, is far more difficult than merely to arouse a soul from its dogmatic slumber and set it in motion. The sophistic soul, like the philosophic soul, which it exactly resembles in every respect, is already in motion, but instead of moving away from opinion to a truth which it strongly suspects, it is moving away from the truth towards an ignorance which it strongly suspects. Thus the sophist is far more dangerous than the simple-minded imitator who has complete confidence in his subjective point of view. The sophist is not a "simple-minded imitator," rather "a dissembling or ironic imitator." [154]

It is of course not accidental that this essential trait of the Socratic spirit is introduced at this crucial point in the definition of the sophist, who is an inverted Socrates, no more no less, bearing within himself an inverted replica of every philosophic trait, including even irony. Thus Socrates is sceptical of all subjective opinion and humble before the truth. The sophist is sceptical of all truth, even of the possibility of achieving it, and humble before opinion, confusing this with genuine humility. The Socratic dialectic is a purifying process, leading us away from opinion towards reality and truth. The sophistic dialectic is also a purifying process, leading us away from reality and truth towards opinion.

Both Socrates and the sophist are in an intermediate position between knowledge and ignorance, but they are *moving* in opposite directions. Each knows something of the goal towards which he is leading himself and others. Socrates knows something of the truth. At least he knows that he does not know, and embraces this learned ignorance, devoting himself to its further exploration. So does the

---

[152] Aristotle, *Nic. Eth.*, III, ch. 7, 1113 B 3 ff.
[153] *Rep.*, 518 C 7–8.   [154] *Soph.*, 268 A 6–7.

sophist know something of the truth. He strongly suspects that he does not know, but instead of embracing this knowledge in the attempt to develop it, he runs away from it towards the opinions he actually knows to be only opinions.

Socrates, in order to keep this precious spark of knowledge alive within himself and to arouse it in others, pretends to be more ignorant than he is. This is his irony. The sophist, in order to kill this precious spark of knowledge within himself and to quench it in others, pretends to know more than he does. This is his inverted irony, which leads us on towards ignorance. He is a dissembling or pretending imitator, leading both himself and others voluntarily towards an ignorance which he himself strongly suspects. Instead of bravely nourishing these doubts, he uses all his skill to quench them, until he finally succeeds in producing that death-like state of thinking we know, from which every sceptical suspicion has been removed. The sophist, therefore, is not only deceived but self-deceiving, not only ignorant but an active producer of ignorance. There is still, however, a further division before us.[155]

We can distinguish clearly between two types of such ironic imitation. There is first of all the more obvious variety consisting of those who pretend to know without really knowing before great crowds and public audiences, in long discourses prepared beforehand. But the popular orator could never succeed in the relatively easy task of betraying great multitudes into embracing false opinions, unless he himself had already been betrayed as an individual either by himself or by someone else capable of facing individual questions and objections. A man does not convince himself or quiet his own doubts by making long speeches to himself. This technique will not work on the individual intellect. In order to soothe and paralyze it another art is necessary, an art which is the exact counterpart of the Socratic questioning process, which betrays a man into the truth. In order to deal with his own reason, or that of another individual whom he confronts face to face, the sophist must possess the ability, by means of short speeches, to make his individual opponent contradict himself, thus betraying him into opinion. Here we have arrived at the last peculiar difference of the sophist.

As Campbell correctly translates: "The artist of the contradiction-causing, conscious section of unknowing mimicry, who has taken

[155] *Soph.*, 268 B 1–C 4.

for his own the word-juggling portion of human, not divine creation, in the phantastic species of likeness-making, such undeniably is the lineage of the true Sophist." [156] Proceeding the *other* way, from the higher genus down to the last difference, we may say that the sophist is essentially the maker or constructor of something; of something human not merely natural; of a replica whose very nature is to represent something else; of distorted replicas adjusted to some subjective point of view rather than to the thing itself of which it is a replica; of such replicas in words (theories and systems); which cannot be constructed or imitated by any subordinate instruments, but by the man himself; which imitate what is only vaguely opined rather than clearly known; which imitate ironically, that is pretending to know what is strongly suspected to be not known; which are capable of convincing the individual questioning mind.

6. The Complete Nature of the Sophist

We are now able to see that the sophist is *essentially* a maker or fabricator of ideal replicas, though he is also, as a result of this, a persuader of the young, a wholesale or retail dealer in intellectual wares, a retail maker of goods for retail sale, a false purifier, and a practitioner of the art of eristical dispute. These last two general properties, however, are much closer to his essential nature, and hence fall within his definition. Nevertheless once in possession of this *essential* definition, and having defended it against attack, we may see how these general accidental traits are derived from his essential nature. We can, indeed, do this.

The sophist must *essentially* possess the art of contradiction, or else he would not be able to oppose within himself those strong suspicions of the truth without which he would not be a man.[157] But since he does not live alone, he cannot practice this art of "saying the opposite" invisibly within himself without also manifestly practicing it upon other individuals. Hence open disputatiousness will be the first, more obvious, accidental trait of the sophist.[158] In the second place, through this art he invisibly purifies himself of truth, removing this so far as possible, and substituting opinion for it.

---

[156] Lewis Campbell, *The Sophistes and Politicus of Plato* (Oxford: Clarendon Press, 1867), p. 192 note. Jowett's translation (IV, 407) is definitely misleading.

[157] Aristotle, *Nic. Eth.*, 1114 A 10.

[158] *Soph.*, 225 A 2–226 A 4.

But since he does not live alone, he cannot do this within himself without manifestly leading others in the same direction, mildly purifying them by question and answer of the vague suspicions of truth they bear within them. Hence this practice of logical purification will be the second, more obvious, accidental trait of the sophist.[159]

Since he is able to attack individual adversaries by eristic disputation, he is by nature favorably disposed to the easier method of display and lure. Thus in the third place, since the goods whose replicas he is by nature capable of defending openly by eristic disputation are in great demand (all men seek virtue and truth), he easily develops the further subsidiary art of displaying his constructions in public,[160] luring on his victims by rhetoric and persuasion, and thus avoiding the hazards of open conflict. Thus he wins an *easy* victory over them, taking advantage of their natural love of the truth, hunting them down one by one or in great groups as a seeming educator and benefactor of mankind.[161]

Once he has developed this art of display with its secret power over the soul of men, it is only a short step to the fourth obvious trait of the sophist, the traffic in theoretical goods. He is by nature the fabricator of original ideas and conceptions of the things all men desire to possess. He is by nature capable of defending them in open disputation, and of displaying them as genuine by rhetoric. Hence he soon finds himself in a position to sell his theories and systems for money, in a process of exchange which is technically "voluntary," though the buyers are involuntarily deceived. Thus the sophist is obviously and almost universally a retail salesman of fabricated, original doctrines and theories at least in his own city.[162]

In the fifth place, if he is sufficiently expert in the subordinate arts of argument and display, he may become a wholesale dealer in ideas, selling new theories and systems and doctrines to the different retailers in some great market, who then retail these original masterpieces at home.[163] Or finally, in the sixth place, the individual sophist may

---

[159] *Soph.*, 226 B 4–231 B 8.

[160] The art of display is clearly subordinate to the art of manufacturing what is displayed. Hence, in the *Gorgias*, false rhetoric is subordinated to sophistry as true rhetoric is subordinated to philosophy. Cf. *Gorg.*, 520 B 2 ff.

[161] *Soph.*, 222 A 5–223 B 7.

[162] *Soph.*, 223 C 6–D 7.

[163] *Soph.*, 223 D 9–224 D 2. Cf. *Prot.*, 312 B 7–314 C 2, where the analogy between goods of the body and goods of the soul is further elaborated.

not only sell his manufactured philosophy retail or wholesale but may also make it up himself as he goes along, though such goods wear out quickly and it is far easier to pick them up from some other wholesale source.[104]

Thus all seven definitions of the sophist fall into place. As Professor Cornford has pointed out,[165] the first six represent obvious "superficial" traits of the great teachers and professors, gained by a sort of preliminary, inductive survey, though the last two of the order in the dialogue, eristic disputation and educational purification, are closer to the essential nature than all the rest. This essential nature is given only in the seventh and last definition of the dialogue, which requires an elaborate defence. As a result of this dialectical discussion, which takes up by far the greater portion of the dialogue, we finally see that the sophist is essentially a fabricator of subjectively distorted theories of being. From this subjectivism or "idealism" we may then easily explain the two characters of eristic skill, and inverse purification, which lie closest to the essence, and the remaining four traits which, though almost universally found in the sophists, are only accidental consequences of the sophistic nature.

We have then completed our discussion of the process of inversion, and have traced it to its basic root, a fabricative tendency in man which leads him to confuse his own constructions with real being, the fabrication of God. All men, including the sophists, have certain strong suspicions of this. They know it, at least vaguely, and they seek to know more. When those who have sought it for its own sake alone find out something more about it, they do not try to tell others about this, as though it were original with them. If they are wise, they do not try to deck it out as something either very new or very fascinating. The truth which men have discovered is bound to seem like an old story, relatively dull and commonplace.

And in a sense, this is always true of what is true. Men are not apt to be charmed and fascinated by that which in a sense they all know already, nor are they apt to pay money for it. An original theory, however, a new system, a new science, a new technique — this is another story. With a little argumentative skill and persuasive capacity, this can easily be made out to look at least as good as the truth, if not a great deal better. This respect for the novel and the original,

[164] Soph., 224 D 4–E 4.
[165] Cornford, Plato's Theory of Knowledge, p. 173.

for our own subjective acts rather than for the objects of these acts, is the root of sophistry, and there is a sophist in every man. His great sin is not merely that he takes money for that which is incommensurable with money in its absolute preciousness. His sin is that he substitutes for this precious, ancient, prosaic truth the sort of substitute that thoughtless men are willing to pay money for.

We have now completed our task in tracing back the many manifestations of moral inversion which we have studied to their ultimate source in that deceptively masked human subjectivism which Plato called sophistry but which is perhaps less obscurely suggested to modern minds by the term *idealism*. Is it not true that this word suggests that refusal to respect what is greater than man, that confusion of human experience and theory with being itself, of man with the creator, that thinking it knows what it does not know, and that choosing to do what it cannot do, which is precisely what Plato, in the deepest opposition to modern thought, has analyzed as the first root of moral and social disorder? Spreading out from this hidden root of subjective pride the disease of sophistry or idealism first inverts the understanding of being, then substituting higher faculties for lower, and lower for higher, turns education into its opposite, until individual life is turned upside down, social life collapses into tyranny, and the whole vast cultural structure of the arts is overturned.

INDEX

Where several page references occur in this index, the more important are in ordinary type; the less important in italic.